A Little Knowledge is a Dangerous Thing:
A Life in Football

BY JOHN SIT TON

First published in Great Britain in 2016
Copyright © John Sitton
Published by Victor Publishing - victorpublishing.co.uk

John Sitton has asserted his right under the Copyright, Designs and Patents Act 1988 to be identified as the author of this work.

All rights reserved. No part of this publication may be reproduced, distributed, or transmitted in any form or by any means, including photocopying, recording, or other electronic or mechanical methods, without the prior written permission of the author.

ISBN: 9798635186091

DEDICATIONS

To my dead twin, I guess it set a precedent. I survived. To Grandad from your "Sonny boy."

The greatest man I ever knew.

You taught me to build, to provide and to try to plan ahead. I'm sorry for two things: Firstly, shame on everyone involved, family or otherwise that all your genius, hard work and initiative was wasted. If I'd been of age I'd have done something about it. Secondly I never had you for long enough.

To Mum for your patience, tolerance, support, understanding and unconditional love. Same as Grandad, your Dad, it's only when I look back I see that your generosity, love and decency was abused and taken for granted by some. Also, like Grandad, I never had you for long enough and I think of you both every day.

To mine and my wife Loiza's children.

To the three we lost, I think of you every day To the three we had, Lucy, Georgina and Jack I love you more than my own life.

To my childhood sweetheart, wife, lover, confidant and best friend Loiza who is also a fantastic mother to our three children. Patient, calm, serene, understanding, loving, affectionate, dignified, classy and unsurpassed powers of forgiveness. Only me and you know that you've saved me from myself more than once.

To my father, father-in-law and all my Uncles. As I observed your selfish lifestyles and self-indulgences, you taught me by your sheer excess how not to behave as a man and to put family before anything else. Especially before a visit to the bookmakers. A perverse and profound thank you.

To everyone I've met at school, in football and socially, only with experiencing your conduct have I come to realise it's part of life's rich tapestry. I hope that's the last cliché but thanks to you all for making me the person I am, whether real or perceived.

To the reader and my followers on social media, thank you for your support. It seems there is a great nostalgia for a world that has now gone. For the first time in my life, ever, I'm about to let you in.

FOREWORD

Who the fuck's going to write one?

INTRODUCTION
OYE MI CANTO (Hear My Voice)

I don't have eighty England caps. If I've learned one thing from my experiences in the fickle, shallow world of football it's all about credibility. Too many people assume that lower division players, coaches and managers don't have the same deep understanding and profound knowledge of what is fundamentally the same game. I earned the majority of my meagre living from football in the lower divisions after mending some of my wild and carefree ways at Chelsea Football Club. Without being a household name there's no need or inclination for any journalists to collect, dissect, agree or disagree and write my opinions on football or my inner thoughts as a human being or former professional athlete and football coach so I have done it myself in the hope I can redress the balance on my perceived poor conduct caught on camera over twenty years ago. One thing I have learned the hard way is, a career in football after your playing days seems to be about either being high profile or being able to sidle up to someone higher profile than yourself and play clever politics that ensures you a living out of the game. But I'm a leader not a follower. Slightly contradictory to the Channel Four documentary that sealed my fate, I feel I've always been able to articulate the game of football. In my case even though I knew the game, could coach it, had a strategy and was decisive, it sometimes boils down to the people around you being incapable. I have stared in disbelief at the goings on in the game since. In fact I even had one journalist insult me saying in a blasé, matter of fact way "you had your chance and you weren't good enough." It was in the press room at Arsenal and it broke my heart but I never had long enough to give him the reasons and answers why. Another one with a high opinion of himself and I suggest a low opinion of me, no more than a supporter with a pen who forms an opinion without knowing the facts.

I couldn't even turn to any of my former managers, who with one or two exceptions, with the benefit of experience and hindsight and no small amount of realisation, I hold in the same utter contempt they must have had for me. I only arrive at this conclusion due to how my complete love for football was exploited come contract renewal time.

At this juncture, I look back and a lot has happened. Some good, some not so good, some bad.

When you've had to scrap, battle, kick bollock and bite just to get by and survive you just hope to have more good memories than bad ones. Unfortunately it's part of our make up as human beings that the not so good memories get highlighted. All my good work that at the time was over a period of twenty two years was washed away in a fifty three minute documentary. I've even said it to my wife it's ironic, if that's the right word, that the thousand times I may have been polite, courteous, cooperative, funny and good company gets washed away by a rant or me complaining or standing my ground. I suppose even if the things you say have substance, it's down to how you word things, but I believe political correctness is just another way to keep you down.

Not self-pity, just a fact. By and large it's a fact I can just about live with.

The way I see it if you can't go through life as a man and be yourself, what's the point?

It seems to be only the privileged or the chosen few who get to skip down the street. It's only my opinion but as a player I think all you can ask and should ask of a coach or manager is can he coach and is he honest? Maybe that's over simplistic but your only concern as a coach or manager should be strategy and improving players. I've never understood the complications of what the media call "managing egos." For me as a player it was about turning up and doing your best every day. My ego was suitably serviced at the end of ninety minutes after a good performance and a win.

As a thirty-four-year-old rookie manager I was not only too honest but brutally so.

I think I ticked some boxes easily but because I couldn't tick some of the others, in my opinion less important ones, I was outcast, ostracised and paid the price in full where any sort of future career in football was concerned. But I am compensated by the fact that even some of the privileged few fuck it up. It's only my opinion but vast fortunes have been squandered, great working conditions abused and supporters money taken for granted. Unfortunately when I look back at family, maybe I should have been more devil may care wisecracking my way through life. Instead I took to being over protective and got no thanks for it. Ever. In actual fact with experience and maturity a lot of what I did for everyone was taken for granted. I can't believe now I assumed responsibility, particularly when I shouldn't have, but I did. What is it they say? "Never volunteer for anything." That's just me and the way I am. Or the way I used to be.

You live, you learn.

As you'll read I learned the hard way, but everything in this book happened and it's written candidly, honestly and from memory with no research. Knowing that it all happened, if one or two incidents I mention are not accurate date wise, I apologise but the accuracy of the events are undeniable and unquestionable. I was there.

The famous Manchester United and England full back Gary Neville once wrote that his England career was a "waste of time." Along with everyone else I know what he means. He's disappointed not to have won anything with England. It's a good job I have been physically strong enough and mentally tough enough to get qualified in and turn up to do a shift in my Black Cab every day for the last fourteen years. What someone like Gary Neville should realise is, with millions in the bank and medals coming out of his arse, imagine after you've read this how I feel.

CHAPTER ONE
No More Mr Nice Guy

Well? Do you miss it? The question I have been asked the most over the last twenty one years that I have been out of football. I wish I had a ten pound note for every time I'd been asked that question then I might have every Monday off from driving my cab. The short, simple answer, which is probably the same given by ninety nine per cent of all ex-players, coaches and managers is yes of course I do. A deeper more reflective answer would be yes there are bits of it I miss, but the vast majority of what I went through in particular, I don't. No way. "Football reflects life," a phrase I heard from Bill Songhurst Leyton Orient physiotherapist in 1985. Bill said where I'm concerned on a football field I made my presence felt, was resourceful, resilient and read things well. For me not just football reflects life, but also one of my other great loves music, which is why I have named each chapter after a song that I like and goes a long way to explaining how I feel or felt at the time. May I suggest you listen to each song to get a feel for my emotions. Then and now. I hope you get it. Nothing is ever plain sailing and there tends to be ups and downs for everyone. I'm not saying for one minute I should have been exempt from the madness. My problem has always been my reaction, which is where the truculence comes in. I may have appeared defiant on that now infamous channel four documentary. The problem is I might have to appear defiant again in defending myself and redressing the balance.

It's too late for me now. I won't change my mind just because I am fifty-seven this year. I've always thought a coach's optimum period as a proactive, get around the field teacher is thirty-five to fifty-five years old. Mind you managers now have a staff as big as a UN delegation. When it was my turn, if you can call it that, me and Chris Turner had to do it all between us. After some rather unpleasant experiences in non-league football as well, you sometimes through experience learn to take a hint. I dealt only in reality. Not fantasy. I once saw Brian McDermott, ex Reading and Leeds manager say in an interview that football coaches and managers don't fail, they give up. I would gladly contest that theory as living proof that despite my best intentions and attention to detail, I failed to not only get back in football at the level I'd known for twenty-five years, but I never even got an interview. I applied for every job going for nearly eighteen months after I got the sack and I never even got the courtesy of a reply, never mind an interview as my reputation was cast in stone on that Channel Four documentary.

These days of course certain managers have enough profile and money in the bank as a consequence of their numerous job opportunities and their reward for failure compensation packages. Although it has to be said only Premier League managers get fully compensated on their contract if terminated and lower down you get only a proportion. In my case nothing at all. So it was never a case of me "giving up." It was a case of feeding a seven-year- old, a four-year-old and a three-year-old with no tangible means of income and putting aside my own ambition in a profession I'd been in and around for twenty-five years, take a reality check, be pragmatic and reinvent myself.

After spending five and a half years studying the topographical "Knowledge of London" and going through a five stage examination process and being vetted by the Criminal Records Bureau in Liverpool and Scotland Yard in London I have been a Licensed London Taxi Driver for nearly fourteen years. Now I only have to please the person in the back of my taxi who has been discerning enough to hire a Black Cab. Can you believe even that has been ridiculed? A smart arse on social media said: " what a come down, from being a player, then a manager, to cab driver." So someone's even had a pop at the fact that I turn up and do an honest days work, and a fifty to sixty hour week. This after showing the fortitude, dedication and cerebral ability to complete a five stage exam, absorbing and retaining six thousand four hundred major routes, one hundred and forty four cross sections (posh name for short cut,) sixty six suburbs (twenty of which start from Heathrow Airport,) thirty five routes between all the football stadiums in London and incorporated within all of that approximately six and a half thousand points of reference. Thick as shit me. And along with my cab driving brothers and sisters an honourable knight of the road. But I still know football like the back of my hand and once it's in your blood, it's in your blood. More importantly I know down to the last detail what happened to me twenty one years ago and the circumstances surrounding me at the time.

The options that were available to me at the time when I was manager, first team coach, reserve team coach (shared), youth team coach (shared), scout, and in the end commercial manager were give up, suffer the same apathy as everyone else, resign, or just stay in situ laughing, relaxed and philosophical about it all. I chose to fight. I chose not to surrender. Maybe I chose wrongly considering how it damaged my career. If any coach or manager has suffered the same sort of circumstances I endured, my heart goes out to you. If you have taken over at any level a similar situation I hope you learn from my mistakes and approach it differently. The only two guarantees are, there are no guarantees and you are bound to meet cheats, duckers and divers. People have since had a career based on "the gift of the gab." Now managers seem more like politicians who have the ability to fade into the background, talk and remain grey and if the circumstances dictate are able to keep their heads below the parapet. They survive, stumbling from one failure to the next, riding the football gravy train for years. Hardly, sometimes never, contributing to the improvement of players, the greater good of the game. For me the hierarchy in football is similar to the hierarchy of the country. You can either be self serving or be part of the improvement of a bigger thing. I think that's reflected in our lack of achievement on the International stage. Philosophically I've reconciled myself by saying "so be it, for me it wasn't to be, because if I've ever gone after something I've never given up in my life." I defy any manager to have succeeded under the conditions you'll read about, that I had to try and negotiate and contend with.

Those of you and I profoundly thank you, who have been interested enough in me following the totally unbalanced Channel 4 documentary first aired in late 1995, will I hope now be able to get a true reflection of what actually went on and the circumstances behind my three or four now infamous rants in the dressing room as co-manager and first team coach at Leyton Orient Football Club as I lay out before you the true facts of what went on behind the scenes at that time. I look back and I confess I am embarrassed by them because I know that I am better than that. The bottom line is not only did I struggle to accept defeat but I struggled even more with an act that for me is unforgivable in football and committed by some people I came across at Leyton Orient, namely surrender. I will leave it to you to decide on whether I overreacted, wasn't up to it and knowledgeable or professional enough. All criticisms that at one time or another have been levelled at me by unknowing, ignorant, judgemental morons who could never be bothered with the facts.

The syndicated rights have since been sold and sold, and then sold again. I've not only never profited, but in the end paid the price in full by being excluded from the only thing I ever knew.

They can be seen at the click of a button on YouTube. Even though, as "friends" in football have told me, it happened thousands of times before and thousands of times since, it was a mistake I never recovered from.

When I look back as a coach I wasn't found wanting. Working daily, along with going to upgrade qualifications, attending workshops, and making full use of the plagiarism in the game, I'd have only got better. As a manager I worked too far above and beyond my remit to help a club survive, my clarity of thought was affected, leading to my conduct being perceived as poor. If I'm wrong, I'll hold my hands up and accept my guilt. What I will then do is what's been done to me, divert your attention to what's happened since in the game, point the finger and say, "look at this carry on." The difference between me and most of the so called football family is I live and let live and I tried not to judge and highlight other people's faults and weaknesses to enhance my reputation or personal ego and momentary feel good factor. Not anymore. No more Mr Nice Guy. It's time to defend myself. From a gift that keeps on giving I now believe it is my turn to redress the balance and make you aware, if you wasn't aware before, that my crimes of momentary foul tempered lunacy pale into insignificance. I find the hypocrisy in football and even life, astounding.

Corruption at the highest levels of the game involving the world ruling body, bung scandals,(I can give you a list of ex managers as long as your arm involved in nothing more than pure greed), drugs, alcoholism, gambling, (some addicted to all three), violence, prison sentences, lots of unsavoury incidents involving women, racism, kerb crawling, fighting, under age sex, and yet if a face fits, he's forgiven and it's still the beautiful game. People have even been rehabilitated back into football after taking a life, heinously killing somebody through drink driving. So I sat back and long ago said fuck it, it wasn't meant to be and took a different turn. The only thing I will concede is that I am arrogant enough and had enough belief in my ability to think if it wasn't football's loss, it was one team's or one player's loss who I might have helped. Because that's the job in my opinion. Improving the greater good, and the individual. As for the "Football Family" I can only assume that when that phrase was thought of the person saying it must have been thinking of a Mafia family. You see in football I witnessed back stabbing, duplicity, hypocrisy, attempts at mini empire building and through it all, the overriding need for survival. Sounds like a Mafia family to me.

I've been an overwhelming giver. To football and to those I've had around me over the years. Am I angry and bitter? Absolutely!! Do I have regrets? Ditto. Introduce me to someone who says they have no regrets and I'll show you either a liar or someone who doesn't have human emotions and just doesn't give a fuck.

My trouble was I did and I controlled very poorly how it manifested itself because I cared. As I look back at me as a player I went from being expressive, confident and almost cavalier and audacious at Chelsea as a young man, to being ultra conservative, cautious and playing the percentages for the next ten seasons at three clubs. That's because you get to a stage where it's possible that you fear failure and fear not being offered a new contract. I had made football my living and a way of life and on more than one occasion I paid for it.

In a world and an industry where I've been called mad, what's your definition of mad? Especially when you see what's gone on and continues to go on in my old profession. The list of misdemeanours is endless and some of them I'll mention, if only to compare me in a world and an industry where I've been labelled untouchable and high maintenance. It's all about perception. The list of misdemeanours I give you are not to make myself feel better, but to allow you to draw comparisons with what my perceived shortcomings were. It ran and ran and ran. Even when Pat Holland got me some work as a scout on behalf of Manchester City and I had games allocated to me by Jimmy Frizzell it wasn't a really pleasurable experience until I was in my seat, pen and paper at the ready. I would walk into hospitality lounges and get the vibe that I was received like the mad person on the bus or the tube. Looking back I felt I'd have been better off killing someone in my Range Rover. At least someone might have said "it's nice to see you out (of prison) put it behind you." For the record I recommended three yound players to Jimmy Frizzell and Manchester City, a centre half called Arjan de Zeuw, and two young midfielders, Tim Cahill and a seventeen year old called Frank Lampard. Also for the record, I lost my job when a new manager called Joe Royle came in and got rid of everybody including Jimmy.

Some people in the game have got off lightly compared to me. I have to laugh.

To give you various examples of not being held to account I could cite my own inside knowledge of various goings on in the game whilst I played and coached. For instance, one manager who took his team on a pre-season tour (I won't divulge the club or destination) cruised a red light district in his hire car with all the money meant for players to have as living expenses whilst on tour and having picked up two prostitutes was relieved of all the funds by their pimps on arrival at the place where he had other nocturnal activities in mind. It was put down as a "mugging" which I suppose it was, but the details of him procuring prostitutes was left out when he contacted his club to replenish the lost funds.

At a club I played for, in the hotel the night before the game, I heard a member of the management team knocking on doors because he was locked out of his room, wandering the corridors with a sheet round him, hastily waking another member of staff to fetch the night porter with a master key after his fraternisation with a female salesperson in the hotel on business. You'd be naive to think it doesn't go on.

Another club I played for had leisure facilities and I walked in hoping for a game of snooker to find a player with a female in a compromising position. Giving a whole new meaning to in off the red and potting the pink.

I also had to cover for a member of staff who after an all-night drinking and shagging session I saw put the female in question in a cab by the door to the breakfast room in the hotel we were staying at.

There was a player who told his wife that every Friday the team stayed in a hotel enabling him to entertain a female without arousing curiosity. The only problem was I knew every detail and I kept it to myself. Another well-known face, high profile, used his scouting missions off the beaten track as an opportunity for him and his trusty lieutenant to take a detour to a club that I was playing for and have a time of it with some of the female staff. How do I know? I walked in on them as one of the females was about to perform a sex act.

Lastly, well I've got to stop somewhere as the list is endless, a manager I played for used his club expenses to go scouting for two days and one night on a regular basis to a county where there's only one football team to meet up with a long term mistress and have his rest and relaxation. But don't worry. Their secret lifestyle is safe with me. Why? Because it's none of my business, I smiled and got on with what I've always done, which is live and let live. If only it could have been reciprocated.

In football like life, people love to gossip and revel in the fact that it gives them a perverse power or upper hand. One manager's greed was the thing that surprised me the most from what is a bottomless pit of stories. At the time he was manager of one of the biggest football clubs in the world. My team mate was due a testimonial and enquired as to whether he could provide the opposition with this massive club. He had to have a rethink when this very well-known person wanted five grand cash in an envelope and a woman for the night. I thought this mutt was seedy and had no class.

Another manager of a club I played for used to charge non league clubs for pre-season friendlies and would only accept the money in cash in an envelope which paid for his family holiday at the end of the year. It's strange I think, people's opinion on what's classy and dignified and what's classed as unacceptable behaviour. Particularly in football, a profession, industry, or business, call it what you will that is remarkable I think, in its duplicity and hypocrisy. It seems to me if your face fits or you can call in some favours you can be forgiven and your misdemeanours almost forgotten and in light of more recent events you have the added piss take to supporters of someone receiving an obscene amount of money as a pay off even though they were in breach of contract!

On a personal level when I played, I just kept myself to myself in terms of training, resting and playing. I wasn't really interested in gossip and extracurricular activities. Although at one stage I did become slightly paranoid because at one club I played for so many players were fraternising with some of the staff, which is the politest way I can find of wording it, I started to think I was the only one who never had it written into my contract. I don't say any of this in defence or to condone what I did or didn't do. But I suppose when liked, you're a geezer, a cheeky chappie, one for the ladies, a bit of a lad, if like me you may have upset a few, any gossip is an ideal opportunity for hypocritical, duplicitous, back stabbing dogs to try and put another bullet in the gun for further character assassination. I was just frustrated and angry at the state of pure apathy that existed and had done for a good few years at Orient whilst I was trying not to lose my job and the foothold in the game I'd worked so hard for. I knew that I was now past the point of no return and was hanging by the skin of my scrotum to any job of any description enabling me to coach. I'd ignored advice from Bernie Dixson and some absurd, questionable ideas from Bill Songhurst, as you will read, to find myself faced with a nightmare dilemma. I didn't want to be seen as not good enough because believe me I was, I didn't want to be seen as a coward and I didn't want to be seen as giving up. With more hindsight and experience now and me in a right mind I wouldn't have gone near the job. I was doomed to failure. Not because of incompetence believe me. There's a difference between perceived incompetence and inexperience. Even an experienced manager would have struggled to cope with the constant stream of bullshit, incompetence and the diabolical state of finances. But the thing is, in football there's always someone ready and willing to walk in a dead man's shoes.

At thirty four my life had taken this trajectory. I fought tooth and nail to get back in after being let go as a player at thirty-one and when I look back and see that in a lot of cases I wanted success more than some players, I knew I was in trouble. Maybe the desperation was transmitted quite openly. I'll leave you to determine that. In Songy's case, the suggestion of quitting and going back to the youth team to me seemed like an act of capitulation. To reward myself a new two-year playing contract, Bill's other suggestion, would have been fraudulent. I wanted to forge on, earn my stripes and be seen for what I was. Determined, passionate about the cause, knowledgeable on the subject matter, able to coach and organise and as much as anything, decisive. Able to decide on all things relative to running a football club. Again it's only my opinion, but I honestly believe running a football club is massively oversold. Once you have proper people above you, giving you support and an agreed strategy forward and proper people on your staff and decent players who are decent people, it should be the easiest most enjoyable job in the world. If you can, compare what you are about to read with how the game is now. I think perceived hardships articulated by players, coaches, managers and even supporters on phone-ins might compare quite favourably with some of the nonsense I experienced. I can only repeat some of what I heard as a kid in reference to people's experiences in the second world war "they don't know they're born."

Nothing should be too much trouble. No problem is insurmountable. Allowing for blips and overcoming disappointments to me it would never have seemed like work. It was for me a partial continuum of playing. The time of your life. Now it's the same but with massive compensation packages if some of the above doesn't quite work out. I mean how bad can it be? You are about to find out.

CHAPTER TWO
House of The Rising Sun

I've been told, that every story has a beginning, a middle and an end. So, let's start at the beginning. I was born on "Murder Mile" in Hackney. The Salvation Army Mother's Hospital, 153 Lower Clapton Road. It wasn't called Murder Mile at the time though. It was an affluent area full of middle class people mainly made up from the Jewish community. The hospital itself was staffed by nuns. My Mum told me a few days after I was born I pissed on a nun's sleeve as she checked me over. Mum said it was to confirm I'd arrived and everything was working properly. I loved my Mum. The majority of the time she spoiled me. I don't care who knows it I was a complete Mummy's boy. I would have done anything for her and this led to my first confrontation at a very early age. I remember it well. I suppose the defiance inside of me started at a very young age. Mum decided she needed some cigarettes and took me with her to the shop so that I could get some sweets. As we returned home there was a blind spot as we turned into our road caused by a hedge or what they used to call a "privet". Anyway as we turned the corner, a kid coming the other way ran into us on his bike. All my Mum said was "oops! be careful pet" and the kid replied: " You be fucking careful you fat old bag..." He was about nine years old, I was about seven, and everyone in the neighbourhood knew his family. I let go of my Mum's hand and said: "what did you call my Mum?" Bang, I hit him. As soon as he saw a drop of claret he started crying. My Mum said "you mustn't..." It gave me an early insight into false bravado and people being out of their comfort zone when they're not in a gang.

There was a follow up to this as I was approached by two of his brother's within earshot of my Aunt Nell. They had come for their revenge. My Aunt said "he'll take you on one at a time. If the other one jumps in I'll jump in." She then turned to me and said "if you don't stand your ground and take your own part I'll give you a good hiding when you get home". Needless to say they refused the invitation, probably because of my Aunt's reputation rather than me. Funnily enough it was something I repeated when I was shopping with my son many years later and he was confronted by local scum who had been bullying him at secondary school. One versus one in an old school "straightener," they didn't fancy it either. Years later, probably when she thought I was old enough to handle it, my Mum told me something. I was one of twins. My twin was born dead.

I was also told by my mother I was a breach birth pulled to life by forceps using my ears, which probably explains a lot. It started on 21st October, 1959 and that was given as my date of birth. Although with all the complications, it ran well into 22nd October. My Mum said I was a troublemaker even then, but to her it was worth it. Apart from my wife and children my Mum couldn't have been more loving, giving and protective, I felt truly loved. Something I've tried to repeat with my own children.

It was explained to me as I was growing up that for the first two years of my life I lived with my Mum and Dad in a flat above a shop in Walthamstow. Then my Grandad pulled some strings, bunged someone a few quid to get our hands on a rent book and brought me, Mum and Dad and my new born little brother Chris to a house a few doors away from my grandparents and my Uncle Alf (Mum's brother). This now meant two things. We had the dubious pleasure of a two up two down with a scullery and a coal bunker in the back garden and the other being the family that I knew and grew up with all lived within a stone's throw of each other. There was my Mum Daisy, Dad Reg, Grandad Alf, Nan Helen, Uncle Alf (Mum's brother,) Aunt Nell (Helen my Mum's Sister,) her Husband Uncle Albert and their daughter my Cousin Sandra. My Mum didn't really want us to have too much to do with my Dad's side as there seemed to be a constant stream of trouble. Mainly with the law. Just as well it would have been hard work at Christmas because my Dad had five brothers and three sisters! My Grandad on my Dad's side was also called Alfred and my Nan's name was Louise. That was us.

The main man was my Mum's Dad, Grandad. The only one I had and really knew. His full name was Alpha Edwin Emigara Wackett. He was a businessman who was revered and respected. He always had and earned money. He was into just about anything and everything. Shops, stalls, lorries, used cars, second hand timbers, fireplaces, slates and bricks before the word "recycling" was thought of. We also owned twenty-two acres of land in our area of North London. It was called Provident Park and its relevance was to have a profound effect on the family. I have I think, been affected by it for the whole of my life. But more on that in due course. Back then I was introduced as Alf Wackett's grandson and even among so called "friends" I was seen as the kid from the rough family and it led for a long time to me being socially awkward. All I'm left with are the memories of insults, sometimes from people I never expected it from.

There's a saying "give me a child until he is seven and I will show you the man." It probably explains a few things where I'm concerned. By and large my childhood was ok. Like a lot of people it was ok. Not perfect, not super, but there were more good memories than bad ones. What hit home to me was it seemed to go quickly. Even at aged five I remember my Grandad's death, funeral and the earthquake it felt like it had on the family. Neighbours lined the street in the old neighbourhood of Brettenham Road East. Women he'd helped cried, men doffed their caps and my Mum let me see the coffin then ushered me inside. I wasn't allowed at the crematorium. Then the house filled up again as they returned for tea, cake, sandwiches and in a few cases a stiff drink. For a kid, big changes were on the horizon.

Life felt different. I was at school, Grandad died, then we were moved to a new house in Brookfield Road. All this seemed to happen at once but it was spread over a couple of years. The row of old houses where we lived made way for maisonettes and two tower blocks with a block of garages for each. Obviously building outwards had turned to building upwards and on the other side of all this was Craig Park. I was equidistant between two parks which for football with your mates was superb and over the coming years we made absolutely full use of both of them.

In the aftermath of Grandad's death stuff started to come out. Even as a kid I was a watcher, a listener, always around on the periphery of adult conversations. Maybe I'd have been better off not seeing or hearing some of it.

A lot of things came to light when it came to the family businesses. We'd lost the shop to demolition. The first and not the last time the family would get fucked on compulsory purchase. We lost the stalls because no one could crack the whip and everyone, well almost everyone, had their own jobs and their own lives. Beforehand it was all down to Grandad. He owned and ran the lot.

People told tales of my Grandad in his heyday. It turned out he wasn't the gentle James Cagney lookalike who picked me up in his arms and took me to the sweet shop. As well as my Mum, I really loved my Grandad. He'd given lots of people credit and was also a money lender. To friends it was a favour with a favour returned, to family like Uncle Albert Martin (Mum's cousin) it was the done thing to help them "get on." To strangers it was a business. This resulted in being able to recover debts with minimum fuss but might also lead to treading on another money lender's toes. In those days poor people never had access to banks, never mind a loan.

Uncle Albert sat there until he died a couple of years back dressed in a Saville Row suit, Fedora, double cuff shirt, cufflinks, handmade shoes, reading five newspapers every day one of which was the Sporting Life. To this day I still don't know how he made his money or where his lifestyle came from. At least he never bored me with tales of being in the Navy. That's because he never served anywhere!

I asked why and he told me "Flat Feet." He recanted many tales of his early life in Bethnal Green and growing up with the Kray Twins. I won't bore you with the details because it's been done to death. But in a way it was like a second education. I'm a great believer in being just as street-wise on a football field as you need to be in life. On the international stage we are far too English. It's about winning and getting the job done. When I see some other national sides they seem to take the Malcolm X mantra "By any means necessary" to the enth degree and meanwhile we are not even "also rans."

My cousin Sandra was a pseudo intellectual who drank too much, went to college and spent most of her life being selfish and totally indulged. Her Mum my Aunt Nell worked hard and had the strength of most men. She left most of Sandra's upbringing to my Mum. I returned home from school one day soon after Grandad's death and the stories kept coming. Along with that I heard my Dad and Uncle had spent all day recovering money owed to Grandad. It was still being counted out and covered the whole dining room table in piles of £500 at our new house. But it was the stories that I couldn't get enough of. Grandad vs one team of four, another team of seven brothers against my Grandad, his brother (Uncle George) and Uncle Alf, and as they got ironed out, my Uncle Albert (Martin) turned up at the Bricklayers with his future wife Norma to see bodies flying out the door, bottles and glasses raining down on them and Grandad on seeing George's son Albert and Norma, doffing his trilby and saying "evening boy" before carrying on. Madness!

Once the madness showed up at our door. Grandad was called and a team of hounds wanted "compensation" for a so called victim who'd started the fight in the first place. Smelling either a threat or blackmail Grandad asked what side of the man's face he'd scarred. "The left" he was told. My Grandad said "well if I see you again, tell him he's got plenty of room left on his right side and you've got room on both sides." As they walked away he shut the door. It was intimated to me by Aunt Nell he'd done worse between the wars and paid off Police. Apparently he'd calmed down since then! We never heard from them and was never disturbed again.

Playing football almost nonstop started early for me with my first school. Brettenham infants next to Brettenham junior school. My Mum got me and my brother Chris matching shoes, socks, shorts, shirts, v-neck grey sweater, Brettenham tie, navy blue raincoat and Brettenham navy blue cap. It was raining, so my Mum bought us both wellington boots. I combed my hair in the mirror and put my cap on. My Mum made us wear wellingtons, I didn't want to. She said "you'll see, all the other kids will be soaked and their feet will be wet." I hid my shoes inside my coat anyway. We kissed our Mum and I held my brother's hand as we walked to school. It was his first day. I'd been there a year already. By the time we got to school my brother's nose was running. We both had brand new freshly ironed hankies. I told Chris to wipe his nose on his sleeve.

By the end of the day apart from noticing not one other kid had fucking wellingtons on and even though my Mum had proudly bought us shoes and wellies I'd decided I wanted to wear my shoes. So I killed two birds with one stone. At school I discovered a football and during morning break, lunch break and afternoon break I played so much I'd worn a hole in the toes of the wellingtons. When we got home I took the sting out of the ruination of my new wellies telling my Mum I'd tripped and stubbed my toe on this very high, steep, stone staircase and a teacher saved me from falling down the stairs. Saving her little General Montgomery. "Oh, long as you're alright babe" she said. I thought she'd changed her mind as she then went apoplectic as she hung up our US Navy issue raincoats. My brother's sleeve was covered... "What's this?" She asked. "Mum it's down to me" I said although I knew neither of us would get a slap. All the way through my young life my Mum hardly ever told me off and never raised her hands to me once.

My wife feels however that this should have happened on a far more regular basis.

"Why do you think I spent Sunday night ironing all your clothes so they're fresh for you Monday morning, including a hanky each?"

She asked. "Mum I know" I said. "You do our breakfast, you cook dinner, you tidy the house and you go to work. I thought you work so hard while Dad's away I'd try and save you some work so I told Chris not to use his hanky, to save it and keep it clean and wipe his nose on his sleeve." Typical Mum she said "oh bless, alright pet" and kissed me on the cheek and cuddled me into her pinafore. Truth be told I should have kept it going. The bullshit that is. As you'll read I was told time and again by one of Orient's so called directors "bullshit beats brains." I think it was his way of trying to convince me to place the accent more on kidology instead of structure and organisation. Since then I concede you need all three. Most of the time you are dealing with a little boy in a man's body. It's only my opinion but "man management" isn't applicable to men. Men manage themselves.

Since then I've probably gone from that extreme to the other, the charm that is, whilst balancing myself precariously between the people in percentage terms that probably make up society and football in particular. The categories they fall into are normally people who either don't want to hear the truth or insist on hearing it then can't handle it. The other problem is, even if someone insists on the truth you're then judged by how you word it. So you shouldn't be surprised when someone's self-protection mechanism kicks in and they become evasive. Me? I've never had that problem. If you ask me a question you'll get an answer.

From twelve years old to thirty-seven years old all I knew was football. Since I could walk, all I knew was football and I grew up in an era that compared to the previous generation with kids being evacuated was an era of relative calm and innocence. The trouble was most of the calm and innocence was the world outside not at home. But you get through it. All I thought of was to make sure my brother and little sister were alright and play football at school with my mates at Brettenham.

My best mates were Tom Loizou, Ian Jauncey and Anton Osbourne. One Greek, one Jamaican, one English and me supposedly from the rough family. Playing football over the park with my mates and my Dad led to the only time I was ever chastised. It was my Dad who duly obliged. It was only the once which is just as well because he had hands like a baseball catcher's mitt. I remember it well. We called it "Wembley." We played multiples of one vs one with my Dad in goal. I sussed that he kept throwing the ball to the other kids. No doubt to test me. How much did I want It? Defend, retrieve the ball, dribble, score then you could sit out having gone through to the next round. I'd had enough and said "I'm not playing anymore." I took the ball in my hands and my Dad said "where are you going?" I said "you keep throwing them the ball you cunt." As I ran he caught me and gave me a clump. As my Mum put a cold flannel on it I decided I never wanted another one off him.

Uncle Alf Mum's brother, it has to be said was a bit simple. In his day he was built like a brick shithouse but was distinctly lacking in social graces or any sort of street wise worldliness. Why? Well at the time and Sir Michael Caine tells a similar story about his own brother, my Nan kept him away from school and all that goes with it because he suffered from epilepsy. At the time, post war, it was socially taboo and deemed a mental illness. As a consequence he suffered. Once it even cost him a good hiding at the hands of a local family supposedly tough enough, but as he held his own against Johnny a boxer, Barney, whose claim to fame was as a piano player at a Kray party and their other brothers whose names I'm not sure I give a fuck if I know or not, the epilepsy kicked in and these tough guys kicked him senseless.

When my Aunt Nell and Mum told me the story I couldn't help thinking "how tough do you have to be to stoop that low and do that?" That's pack animals, plastic gangsters and make believe tough guys for you though. I've always thought only cowards hunt in packs.

As a family we were tight knit and mainly self-sufficient. At the time my Dad held down two driving jobs. He had HGV class 1 from his national service. From what he told me this service basically constituted policing post war Berlin and what he called "The Blockade of Berlin." So while my Dad was telling me tales of Germans taking scraps from the dustbins outside the NAAFI Uncle Albert was telling me how he spent 1940 - 19 whenever, getting rich from the black market and various other activities like gambling and long firming back in Bethnal Green.

I think some of it was steered Grandad's way to feed the poor in North London. Anyway the money collected kept coming after Grandad's passing and my Aunt Nell assumed control. My Mum was loving, giving, and as far as I'm concerned too trusting and submissive to those around her particularly her older sister. Because her own home life was shit my Aunt Nell practically lived with us. The burden of holding it all together fell on my Mum. There were now her own three kids, Mum giving birth to my little sister Kay in the same hospital as me and my brother on January 19th 1969. I went with my Aunt to collect them both, my Dad was nowhere to be seen. At first I took no notice then as my Aunt Nell told my Mum what had been discovered I noticed. It didn't help hearing Uncle Albert say "I've never known a firm go to pot like this one."

My Dad had given up one of his jobs supposedly to be at home more. He was always away to Wales or Scotland and we saw him for the first time on a Saturday. Sunday night he was off again. Then he committed a sackable offence by grabbing the foreman at his other job and chinning him. All I knew is my Dad and this geezer Gorman hated each other. Gorman the Foreman. He'd given a load promised to my Dad to another driver and the result was a slap and a ripped shirt covered in grease where the old man had got hold of him. So at the tribunal he loses and he's out of work.

My Mum, three kids, no prospects and out of work. Who says lightning doesn't strike twice in the same place? Anyway, he turned to a bit of ducking and diving and some mini cabbing. This is where it went from bad to worse as it was explained by Aunt Nell to Mum she'd caught him with some blonde slosh pot called Patricia. The fallout was unbelievable. Not something I'd recommend for a nine- year-old with a seven-year-old little brother and new born sister.

As my Mum tucked us in that night I said "sorry Mum." She said "for what?" I said "about Dad and that other woman." She kissed me and Chris and walked out crying. They'd tried to keep it from me but I was a nosy little bastard and heard it all. What I didn't know was that a cunning plan was about to be put in place and carried out.

I found out about the plan after it was executed. I wandered into the kitchen as my Mum, Albert and Aunt Nell were just sitting down with a cup of tea and the inevitable accompanying cigarette. "Do you feel alright Belle?" My Aunt said. She always called Mum Daisy or by her nickname "Belle" as in Daisybelle. I said "what's happened?" "Never you mind longboat" was my Aunt Nell's reply. Mum's adrenaline was still going. "Mum what happened?" Nell told me they followed this Pat to her house in Tottenham, let her get settled in, then knocked on the door. Pat's Mum answered and called her daughter. My Mum and Aunt pulled them outside and left them laying there according to Albert. My Mum chided in "I told her to stay away from your father."

We never heard from them again. So it was back to what you would call normal. At least normal for our household.

"Oh well," I thought and took my plastic ball out the back door and started kicking it against the wall. That night I remember walking up and down stairs as my Mum and Dad sat on their bed talking. "I swear I never touched her." My Mum took him back. Not before someone played the idiot I thought. Either my Mum had to believe the "friendship" was platonic or my Dad actually never got a shag out of it.

There were varying degrees of happiness and ups and downs after all that. Almost immediately my Dad got one of his two jobs back. He'd worked two as I said one was a firm called Hipwood and Grundy the other was Greenwood's. With Greenwood's he would go backwards and forwards to Wales and Scotland and he took me once or twice. I remember going to some dockside on the Clyde and thinking what a shit hole and that hard working people deserved better than this. On those two trips it was the first time I'd ever felt anything like close to my Dad. It would be better for a while but that was well into the future.

Then a few weeks later it kicked off again. It was a Thursday. Pay day. The back door opened, my Dad walked in. My Mum asked him why he was late because she was waiting to dish up dinner. My Aunt Nell was holding my sister Kay who was still a babe in arms. "Mind your own fucking business, here's your wages." My Mum opened it and I'll never forget it until the day I die. She read the wage slip "you've been gone all week for £42 and there's only £18 in here. Where's the rest?" He told her he'd lost it at cards just before he came home. My Aunt Nell made a sarcastic comment, my Dad told her to "fuck off out of my house." My Aunt passed me the baby and as I walked into the front room to keep my baby sister safe I turned to see my Aunt chin my Dad and my Mum pull him down by his hair and tip a saucepan full of boiling gravy all over him. He broke free and threw a cup that hit the door to the cupboard under the stairs. The cup made a dent and left a scar on the door. My Dad eventually got the polyfilla out but it was never repainted right up until I left home.

All I could think of was to hold my sister and put my arm around my brother who had started crying. He was only seven years old. My Dad ran out and would you believe it came back with a copper who he'd found on the beat and had my Aunt thrown out. My Aunt turned on the copper until my Mum calmed her down. I had to sit with my little brother and sister whilst the copper interviewed my Mum and Aunt.

As you might appreciate it took me a while to settle down to sleep that night. I lay there thinking what my Dad had told me and how he had acted around my Grandad. Everyone trod lightly around my Grandad.

"Once he gets started he can be a little fucker." I thought about Grandad and how he had worked, built up his bankroll and businesses and always put family first. I concluded I'd rather be a man like my Grandad than the type of man my Dad was. As you read this you could be forgiven for thinking "why tell us all this?" It's simple really, other than my Grandad I don't suppose I've really ever had a role model like lots of people, but in the end you learn as you go and make your own mind up on how you should be and how you want to live your life. I'm sorry but I can't get all misty- eyed in admiration when I hear stories of people in football and their "work ethic" and the fact that their father may have turned up to do an eight hour shift in a coalmine, shipyard or docks. I was bought up around men who never had a guvnor and did sixteen to eighteen hour days. Men who were their own bosses and stood on their own two feet. There was a lot of jealously around my Grandad and the family. While others looked for handouts, kept their Mrs short and spent their money in the pub, we had money coming in and built on it.

My poor Mum then had to deal with what I thought was even more bullshit. On top of working, running a home, looking after three kids, trying to rebuild her marriage and pander to her sister she now had to deal with the cash collected after my Grandad's passing going missing. Not only that she had to swallow a "story" from her own sister in one of the most hare-brained, ignorant things I've ever heard. I promise you couldn't make it up. All I know is our household suffered and Aunt Nell never. Sandra got married, had a lavish wedding and reception and she and her husband bought a house for cash in Buckhurst Hill. I've put two and two together and I might be so far wide of the mark it's untrue, but you make up your own mind.

The cash owed to the family was all finally called in. I know banks and bankers latter day have had dubious practices and headlines but fuck me! Listen to this. Mum was holding my hand, Chris was in the front room with Sandra (our cousin) and Uncle Albert at their house number 10, Lansfield Avenue. Believe me I never got much older than I was at this time before I even started to question why everyone lived in these houses. The reason is simple. Cash! Bundles of it! Before I go on let me give you just one for instance when it came to the type of cash my Grandad was always holding and consider the prices back then. They never thought to buy houses for the family or have one massive one built for everyone. Although Grandad started to veer that way before his life was cut short. I remember we all went for a ride down the A12 and viewed what I thought looked like a mansion. Big enough for the whole family, a cottage in the grounds and a working nursery standing in acres and acres of land. Guess what? My Nan didn't want to move! So we go back to our two up two down then walk down to Nan and Grandad's shop. Everyone was congregated in the back room, seated around the fire. Grandad had ripped the pocket on his suit trousers and asked Sandra to sew it. My Mum, Aunt and Nan were in the kitchen getting dinner ready for about eight or nine of us. Sandra said "I'll do it tomorrow Grandad." He then says "charming, the work I put in and you'll do it tomorrow. Fuck the trousers!" And he throws them on the fire with over £3000 in the pocket. This was early sixties. I never saw my Dad move so quick. He pulls them out of the fire and says "Alf, calm down she'll do 'em." Anyway, back to the story of the buried treasure...

I stood slightly behind my Mum as if it was explained by my Aunt Nell that she'd divided the money into three equal shares, wrapped them in plastic and pointed out three rose bushes that she'd buried the packages under. "The one on the left is yours Belle, mine's the one in the middle, Alfie's is the one on the right." Can you believe my Mum actually stood for it?

She trusted her sister and they all agreed to let the dust settle with probate, solicitors and the tax man. Not long after I remember a conversation between my Mum and Aunt and my Mum walking around the house in shock, crestfallen, stunned. She was told that the money had been stolen. No burglary, just stolen. I'm a kid but I'm thinking "did a neighbour hear it all?" "Was it Uncle Albert?" He was a career spiv, criminal and general ne'er do well. Aunt Nell once put on a charade in front of me saying to Albert "I know you took it, you no good..." More relevant to me at that time was asking for some money for sweets and my Mum saying there wasn't any. She went upstairs to make the beds and I sneaked a look in her purse, there was a couple of coppers, some halfpennies, no silver and no notes. I still remember to this day thinking "this ain't right." Maybe one of the reasons why when I had children I always made sure there was money and I tried to make sure they had everything they wanted. I've tried to deny them nothing.

Anyway a little while later excitement was building. My cousin Sandra was about to get married and me and my brother Chris were to be page boys. In the build up I remember sitting by Sandra as she planned the service and reception with her Mum. Sandra said "what about the cost?" My Aunt said "don't worry I'll manage." Sandra's husband-to-be drove us to see the house they'd bought in Buckhurst Hill. Ironically just down the road from where I live now. At the time I thought it was in the countryside. I'm wowing at the fact it's detached, nice garden, front drive, garage, next to the forest. Then over sausage, mash and onions, Tony, Sandra's husband-to-be says to Sandra "thank your Mum and tell her I'll give her a lump sum every month or if she wants I'll give it to her weekly." I piped up "what's that Sand?" "Oh the house, Mummy lent us the money for the house." I said. "What? you never got it from the bank?" Tony said "no way, we're not paying the interest they want..."

Frank Clark my manager at Orient once said to me "Sitts one of your problems is you find it hard to trust people." If the money my brother gave to trace the family tree is to be believed, we came from traders in silk from somewhere in France. My ancestors were probably running around a forest with the arse hanging out of their trousers. Apart from that I chuckle and think about how I got through that first part of my life. If it was now I'd probably have my own social worker.

CHAPTER THREE
Be Young, Be Foolish, Be Happy

It seemed like half of North London was at Sandra's wedding and reception. The wedding itself was at St John and St James church situated in Fore Street. The reception was a sit down three course meal followed by a band, a disco and Sandra along with various friends of Uncle Albert and Albert himself belting out a tune as the night wore on. I remember seeing a buffet laid out for more guests arriving and crates and crates of empties in the corner of a small yard just outside the kitchen of the venue we had. Dad was at home more and it now became a regular thing for him to take me, Chris and Kay to Pymmes Park. We'd leave early enough to watch the Sunday morning football then have a kick about and on the way home we'd stop in the garden of the Pymmes Park Inn.

My sister had her bottle with some milk still just about drinkable, me and Chris had a Pepsi and a packet of crisps and my Dad always had one, just one, half a lager with a dash of lime. My Dad had his vices booze wasn't one of them. Some weekends me and Chris got to stay at cousin Sandra's. It was on the edge of the forest and it seemed like we were in the countryside and we made the most of it. Momentarily it seemed like better times. Mum, Aunt Nell and Uncle Alf were now waiting for finality on the last piece of the financial package my Grandad had left them. I was aware but as a kid I never seemed to bother until I saw that the people around me were bothered. When the details surfaced it ended up having another massive impact on us and a resonance with me that played on my mind for years. In the immediate aftermath of Grandad's passing developers were interested in the purchase of our twenty-two acres of land. They offered the equivalent of one eighth of what had been stolen by the Great Train Robbers. A tidy sum in the region of £350,000. To put it in proportion pro rata in today's money it's said the Train Robbers' haul would be worth £55 million or so. Therefore back in the early to mid-sixties even an eighth would have made a nice windfall. It's funny when I look back and realise that it's alright for the establishment to take from you, but you can't take from them.

The family rightfully so in my opinion agreed to hold on to the land. One, we didn't need the money and two the land would increase in value. So for a while it was put on the back burner. In the meantime life was good at school, good at home and we now owned a car and a brand new caravan for our holidays based at Highfield Holiday Park in Clacton-On-Sea in Essex.

I've got to say I loved it. We'd go at Easter, a long weekend at Whitsun then every year the same last week of July and the first week of August for our annual two-week holiday. Every summer holiday as we pulled away from the house my Mum would get us to sing along with her "we're all going on a summer holiday." The Cliff Richard record. It's still one of my favourite songs to this day. I felt free, I loved it outdoors all the time. Maybe I'm wrong but the summers seemed warmer and longer back then and all I know is I felt totally spoiled and it felt more like what a childhood should be about. A typical day would be woken by Mum with tea, cereal or egg and bacon then pack a picnic and set off to the beach. The choices were Clacton, Frinton, St Osyth, Holland-On-Sea. Sometimes after the beach we would have a wash and brush up then go straight onto the fair at Walton-on-the-Naze. I got what I asked for ice creams, nougat, coconut ice, honeycomb, popcorn, then a game of football on the grass with my Dad or on the beach and in the sea to cool off after.

To me it was fantastic. At night if we didn't go to the fair we'd book a show on Clacton Pier. The drinks order was always the same. Uncle Albert was conspicuous by his absence, Mum and Aunt Nell would have a gin and bitter lemon, Dad half a lager and lime and me and Chris the inevitable bottle of Pepsi with a straw and a bag of crisps. We used a pub right opposite the pier at Walton- on-the-Naze. It had a family room and I remember seeing a black and white programme with Dad. It was called "Match of the day." The noise, the crowd, the players, the goals, the excitement. I was buzzing. Or maybe it was the Pepsi! Since then I've never passed up an opportunity to tell my kids now in their mid-twenties, that with the money for the trips I've paid to take them on to the mountains of Granada and Mijas in Spain, and the Highlands of Scotland, four trips to Majorca, two to Menorca, eight times to Cyprus, twice to America, twice to the Bahamas, Kos twice, Corfu, St Maarten, Dominican Republic and British and U.S. Virgin Islands, I could have bought my own caravan by now.

Anyway I asked my Dad could he take me to football? He said "on one condition, I'll only take you to the Arsenal." He said Arsenal was his team, he'd been brought up in Queen's Crescent, Kentish Town so it had to be Arsenal. From then on every Arsenal home game we were there on what was known as the North Bank. On the way he'd make me stand on the corner of St Thomas's Road and Seven Sisters Road where there was a bookmakers. Sometimes I'd be outside for over an hour. If I'd told my Mum she'd have gone mad. The reason I never told her was if he won I'd get sweets, a match day programme and wimpy and chips. If he lost, I'd get home and make light work of the dinner she'd cooked.

I remember a lot of the games. One that sticks out was a game played over the Christmas and New Year period versus Manchester United. It was an occasion for a number of reasons. I went with my Dad, Uncle Arthur, who was my Dad's brother and my cousin Paul. We got there early to see United get off the coach: Stepney, Crerand, Charlton, Law, Best. Then we went into the ground and my Dad and Uncle fucked off and left me and Paul on our own down at the front of the North Bank. As the crowd got bigger, I'm a kid getting squashed and I think my Dad's lost so I start crying. I'm shitting myself. My cousin Paul who I last saw at a funeral, never fails to bring it up and torment me. Probably to deflect the attention from his distinct lack of hair. Anyway the game was fantastic. The crowd were packed like sardines and the noise was unbelievable. What an atmosphere, I loved it all. For the record, I'm almost sure the game ended in a 2-2 draw.

At Brettenham Infants and then juniors any sport was I'd say, pretty organic. I feel like Peter Cook as Ron Manager when I say it literally was jumpers for goalposts. The facilities were negligible on sports day or if there was any sort of competition in PE you were identified by a coloured sash. Apart from a couple of ropes and a pummel horse to encourage gymnastics there were half a dozen mats, a couple of plastic balls and bean bags and hula hoops for the girls. So in the infants it was the stereotypical eighteen to twenty kids swarming around the ball, marauding around the playground, trying to get the ball between the aforesaid jumpers, or two coats or two blazers. It's always the way, or it was back then, it goes nowhere and never progresses to anything meaningful unless a teacher goes above and beyond the call of duty.

The first two teachers to do that for me were Mr Dix the headmaster and Mr Parker who taught PE as well as his classes. Mr Parker played all the "houses" off against one another as a form of trials to pick a school team. I remember mine and all four houses to this day. I wore a red sash representing my house which was Florence Nightingale, Yellow was Albert Schweitzer, Blue Gladys Aylward and Green for Montgomery. I got in the team and Mr Parker took an immediate interest in my progress. He guided me and played me up against older kids and said "try this" or "today try this," moving me around the pitch, getting a feel for nearly every position. When I played well and when I scored Mr Dix would highlight it in assembly and I'd get a round of applause. It's funny the teachers you remember. Another was Mr Spicer, he was my Geography teacher also there was Mr Bundok who taught Maths. My English teacher was a Welsh lady Ms Simmonds. I enjoyed school and the commitment at weekends to playing in the school team.

I was always met from school by my Mum, if not my Aunt would pick me up or if he was visiting Uncle Albert Martin in his flash car. He seemed to have gone from strength to strength since he borrowed £300 off my Nan and Grandad to buy his first lorry. Now he had land, a yard, a few lorries and a nice house. It's relevant to me in that he had started out with a minimal amount of start-up money, although in those days it was a nice few quid and as a kid from a position of relative wealth compared to most of our contemporaries our family has slipped back. Without Grandad there was no leader, no ingenuity, no initiative and no balls among the remaining so called men in the family. In their own individual ways they were a hindrance rather than a help. That left the women, all with different agendas and what would now be called "skill sets."

Going from infants to juniors was no hardship because it was the building next door. By now I had three or four close friends, Anton Osbourne, Ian Jauncey and a dark skinned kid who was dragged kicking and screaming into the playground on his first day by someone I thought was an attractive looking woman. Fifty years on I now know him as my brother-in-law Tom. I said come and play football and he stopped crying and joined in. It's easy when you're six to adapt. One English, one Jamaican, one Greek Cypriot and me, the kid from the rough family. We were like the United Colours of Benetton before the company was thought of. That's the beautiful thing about kids, innocence and no thoughts of prejudice. It's ironic because I came from an era where prejudice and racism were commonplace and if I wanted to be a victim I'd even come to experience it myself, sometimes from the unlikeliest of sources, which at the time broke my heart.

Call it fate, a pushy parent, or some things are just meant to be. My Dad lost his only income driving backwards and forwards to Wales and Scotland. I don't suppose the previous episode involving the foreman helped things, but he was "laid off" as they called it. I remember it being the early 1970s and not a lot of work was about at the time. For a while the old man eked a living cleaning drains. Not to denigrate any job done by anyone earning an honest living, but not for the last time in my life I thought how did it come to this? Part of the local redevelopment in our area involved the building of a youth club, Craig Park Youth Centre. My Dad put himself forward as a youth worker and seized on the idea of forming a few initiatives. As well as their jobs now working for extended family as greengrocers my Mum and Aunt took part time jobs serving at the bar of the youth club. My Dad set up circuit training, weight training, table tennis competitions and football teams. There was a men's team that fizzled out so he concentrated on a boys' team that played Sundays in the Lordship Lane Sunday Football League. In the first year at under thirteen level we got hammered every week. Slowly but surely good players were added and as we progressed we got stronger because we stayed together. By now I'd started as a first year at senior or secondary school. Everything got better and a lot of happy coincidences started to come together. I think they call it serendipity.

The lads at Craig Park I'll never forget. How can you? It was part of the change from childhood to puberty to youth. The men's team had disbanded. Angry young men who worked when they could and divided their time between chasing women, drinking and supporting their football team of choice and fighting on the terraces. People of a certain age will remember that time and rarely a week went by without headlines being made because of the tribal warfare between rival supporters. Some of the tales filtered through to the youth club. My Dad wouldn't let me go to a game if it wasn't with him. My Mum and Aunt kept a tight rein on me when he was away so all my mates were vetted and known to the family. I remember our team to this day. The lads were John Lampe (son of Derek Lampe ex Fulham centre half,) Derek Jolly, Paul Brown, Kevin Morgan, Steve Hagerman, Gary Patterson, Chrissy Wright, Simon Wilson, Mervyn Weeks and Bobby Double, whose Dad was the sponge man. In goal was Alan Lewis whose son went on to be a pro at Wycombe after being at Arsenal and Spurs. Dave Till was our coach and helped the old man run the side. I remember any mail or documents involving the side was opened on our age group's club night which was a Friday night. My cousin Sandra screamed to my Dad "it's here! I've got it!" I didn't know but my Dad had written to Arsenal recommending they look at some of the lads including yours truly. At the time all I was interested in was my Ska music and choosing a Ben Sherman shirt to go with either a pair of "Levi Sta- Press" or Rupert two tone trousers and my Solatio Woven shoes.

My Dad and cousin showed me a letter on headed paper with Arsenal's crest inviting me in for evening training signed by someone called Ernie Collett.

I'd never experienced being out of a home environment before. I was used to the comfort zone of playing football with the boys from the local and surrounding neighbourhoods. When I first turned up at Arsenal I've got to admit, it was daunting for a twelve-year-old and I was only just twelve.

The Sunday side was under fourteen by now but my Dad threw me in anyway and I coped. When I was invited in by Arsenal my Dad added nearly two years to my age and told me "get in there, it'll do you good." It was called "coaching at the college." That's the name given to it by one of the coaches, an aggressive, loud, brash, arrogant man, at least I thought he was by the name of Ian Crawford. Despite following football for a few years at this stage and having all the football annuals and magazines money could buy, I'd never heard of him. Knowing what I came to know as coaching, didn't really happen under Crawford. With him it was a couple of drills then a nine a side.

The premises known as "the college" was an indoor facility behind the clock end of Arsenal Stadium known throughout the football world as Highbury. The surface was a red coloured grit and the goals were painted on the walls. I remember my first session like it was yesterday. I ran up the steps of the main entrance, through the double doors that were opened by a commissionaire in uniform and up to an office window on the left. I was shown where to change by a big man called Alf Fields. It was the home team dressing room with marble and granite everywhere and as I put my trainers on I felt the warmth of under floor heating. As I walked back out I was told to turn up the tunnel and jog around the red cinder track behind the coach.

The session lasted about an hour and in the dressing room Alf Fields had a form and a plastic bag full of change. Expenses were offered and you signed your name next to what you had written down as your return journey. I found the other coach we worked with had a more gentle way about him, was humorous and seemed more knowledgeable stopping sessions to actually coach. He also gave me my first taste of a more intense form of work and being isolated in a grid. The guy's name was Dave Smith. At the time both he and Crawford were on Arsenal's staff. In the future I think Crawford went to Norway and Dave Smith had one or two coaching jobs and a stint as Southend Manager. I told Alf Fields that I didn't need expenses as my Dad had driven me there.

I saw on the way out a bust of one of Arsenal's former managers, Herbert Chapman. It seemed to me that at Arsenal everything looked and felt like it had been built to last. It also showed touches of a quality finish, class, tradition, and a style that was somewhat formal. It felt to me that without the under floor heating it would have been too formal and even dare I say it cold. Still the good part about formality I thought was being formally taught something, particularly by Dave Smith. Ian Crawford's sessions were more like drills. I remember a passing one and he gave demonstration. It was how to address the ball and strike it so that the ball swerved. He said "now, did you see a definite curve on the ball?" Thinking he wanted the truth I put my hand up and said "no." Without a doubt from that moment on his attitude towards me hardened. As I've said I was twelve and I didn't quite know how to handle it. That's why subconsciously with younger players, say 10-16 I've always been firm but fair and tried to put them at their ease whenever I've coached, with bundles of praise. It's not my fault Crawford couldn't play and provide a decent demo or example, but I suppose he thought I was a little upstart. I don't know to this day if he had any sort of playing career or background.

Within a season the coldness and almost forensic attitude and selection of youngsters reared its head and I received a letter saying that I hadn't come up to the required standard. I had been playing for ten months with a condition called "Osgood Schlatter." I wouldn't know the causes, reasons and remedy for the condition until many years later as I delivered modules on "Growth and Development in Young Players" and "Physiology and Anatomy" whilst staffing UEFA "B" courses for the FA via the LFA. All I knew as a twelve- year-old was the pain and trying to cope with it as I continued to train and play.

From what I'm told by a couple of acquaintances who have sons in academies at clubs now, the kids are monitored, measured and after a certain amount of hours playing and training they are given a significant rest period to help with a growth spurt that may have been detected and recognised. Part of the module I delivered on courses informs would be coaches to look out for the signs in growth and development and the accompanying debilitating effect. A male has growth spurts between thirteen and eighteen but could take until twenty-one to reach their full adult height. For females it's a spurt between thirteen and sixteen reaching full adult height by the age of eighteen. In the not too distant future I had a lot of football coming up and little did I know that within six years I'd be playing for Chelsea against Arsenal's first team with no time given for rest, to grow or to mature.

Back then that's just the way it was. Goings on off the field of play didn't exactly help at the time either. But as I approached the start of my teenage years through ability, hard work, determination and a love for playing football, I would soon have the choice of nine clubs. In the meantime I'd done well academically receiving rave reviews on parent evenings that normally only my Mum attended. I had put down three choices for secondary school and I was placed at Chace School for Boys. It was there I met a great, if not the best mentors I'd had in sport, football, and life in general, our PE teacher who actually joined from one of our school's main rivals Bishop Stopford's, Mr John Rouhan. In the run up to changing schools the youth club team had a trip to Belgium and Holland. You may find it hard to believe but in the two games that were played there were no "Cruyff turns," no "total football" and no "tiki taka," we were kicked to pieces. I remember the Dutch kids and the Belgian kids couldn't get near us. I got the ball passed to me and as I got it out of my feet to pass I was kicked cross both knees and being already sore and tender I cried out and went down holding both legs. My Dad ran on with spray and a cold sponge calling out to this honey monster of a kid, obviously auditioning for Sugar Puffs "you little fuckpot" and told the referee "to get a fucking grip or I'll take my team off." After winning a couple of league and cup doubles our Sunday team conquered Europe winning both games conceding only one goal.

At school I'd only just sat down for my first lesson and a classmate came up and said Mr Rouhan was having a practice match after school as a sort of trial to start a school team. I attended and got selected. There were plenty of hormones and testosterone as you'd expect when we played against older kids in the playground and games against other schools. It was a good toughening up process as we usually won or at least held our own which usually led to some mug or older wannabe tough guys putting in some heavy challenges. Having played six a side with men at Craig Park Youth Club and then for a couple of seasons against older boys, you could say I coped.

Like most schools, especially boys only or girls only you had the stereotypical pecking order and the odd scrap in the playground but nothing sinister or unmanageable. Unlike today in my opinion where nobody knows the boundaries anymore. Or if they do, brain dead morons keep pushing them further and further. It seems respect is kept to a minimum. I've got no qualms in saying before lily livered do gooders who have done no good at all started to err on the side of caution and put wrong uns before proper people there used to be an acute sense of right and wrong and some standards. Back then nobody spoke in some kind of concocted street dialect and it was no hardship to address the teachers as "Sir" or "Miss." But it has to be said there were times when as pubescent boys we did fuck about and on one or two occasions maybe even went too far.

One such occasion was in Religious Education. I sat there with my mates Gary Patterson, Dave Street and Steve Turner. Patterson did a blinding Les Dawson impersonation. Turner coughed and shouted "Helmet." Dave Street sat there laughing and I declared that I had an erection. Patterson said "let's measure it!" So I got my ruler and I have to say I was quite pleased with the outcome. The problem was it had a mind of its own and wouldn't go down, so Patterson smacked it with the ruler as David Street went red as he cried with laughter and Turner's cry of "Helmet" led to Mrs Simpson walking up the aisle and standing over us to see what the fuss was all about. She never batted an eyelid and carried on reading a passage about some miracle or some geezer who wrecked a temple and getting his hair cut. The bell went, Mrs Simpson said "see you next week," and we were off. Years later it was a joke more personal to me than he ever knew, when I got out of the shower as youth coach at Leyton Orient, and Trevor Putney would say "I'd like to see that with the choke out!" Not very sophisticated I know, but they are the sort of things that made us laugh as thirteen year olds.

Just like infants and juniors I remember my secondary school teachers as if it were yesterday. They all made an impression for a number of reasons. Physics, Mr Porter, Maths, Mr Van Graan or Mr Polly, English, Mr Evans or Mr Mortimer, History and Spanish, Mr Jordan, French, Mr Wilson, Chemistry, Mrs Achillea and Mr Barrand or Mr Rouhan for PE. My favourite lessons were PE, History and Spanish. I was in set two. The sets ran from one to six. One was the intelligentsia, so academically I was doing ok. But as sport and in particular football took over my life, I did just enough to scrape by. This led to one or two disappointing feedbacks on parent's evenings for my Mum. John Rouhan seemed to go above and beyond the call of duty. He put a couple of us forward for district trials. Again I got in. After Enfield he informed me of Middlesex trials. At aged thirteen it was not only to change my life but it put me in a professional football club environment up until the age of thirty-five and set my life in stone for nearly twenty-three years.

CHAPTER FOUR: CHELSEA 1974-1976

You can get it if you really want

Behind the scenes and without my knowledge at the time, my Dad had written to a host of clubs on my behalf asking for a trial. I had entered the marble halls of Arsenal and after a year I'd be shown the door. I never won a keepy uppy competition to earn an advertising contract or been spotted at a high profile international's soccer school. My real start was more inconspicuous than that. After school and district Mr Rouhan put me forward for county trials. My county was Middlesex. His only insistence was I attended, be punctual and turn up in my school blazer with a collar and tie. At the same time as remembering in finite detail the whole day   I was totally oblivious to the who's who of scouts in attendance on behalf of their respective clubs. Dickie Walker (Spurs,) Arnie Warren (Palace,) the boys mentioned someone from West Ham and Arsenal, Fred Ricketts (Fulham,) Chris Gieler (QPR) and others milling around asking for the names of boys playing under the watchful eye of two teachers who would manage the team once selected. I played in four games across the whole day on breakfast cereal. I was at the back of the queue when some jugs of orange squash was put out. I got half a cup and unlike quite a few of the boys who had money, I had just my fare to get there and back home. My stomach was rumbling and within minutes it had a relevance to at least the next six years.

The last game was between two teams consisting of boys deemed good enough to play it out for the right to end up in a squad of fifteen or sixteen to represent Middlesex. The age old probables versus possibles. I was in the possibles. In the other team were boys who all seemed to know each other, the nucleus from the East End who played for a Sunday team called Senrab. Down the years players from Senrab read like a who's who of London footballers who made the grade. It's unlikely that it happens like that anymore. By "like that," I mean organically, as big clubs and the FA have dictated training times, hours played and when they relinquish control of players. You now have an elite player initiative. One problem I have with it is who is the person or persons that determine who the elite players are? The person or persons might not be that elite themselves and don't particularly know what they are looking at. It's just my opinion on the National game, but I think more is taken away from a player when at an early age he is labelled elite. Even more is taken away from players who are not labelled elite because the programme assumes there are no players who might take a little longer to develop. I'm sure if you ask the people concerned at the F.A you'll be given a long and comprehensive answer that actually doesn't answer anything. Just like a politician. They've all mastered the art of saying a lot and answering nothing. We've gone through more England managers more regularly than some people do with their socks and underpants, chosen latter day by someone who has never probably done more than the occasional gin and tonic in a boardroom, one who admitted to "not really (being) a football person," and one who has never laced a pair of boots on at first team level anywhere. How the fuck do these people get these jobs? Maybe it's by not using the ocassional curse word.

Towards the end of the book, without giving anything away, I'm convinced that my theories on any coaching initiatives or syllabus would blow out of the water what has been in place at the F.A. for years now. Put in place incidentally by people, and I can't stress this enough, who have never kicked a ball. I have even been advised by someone to put in place intellectual copyright. Senrab is Barnes spelled backwards, which is where I believe the team was started. Barnes Street in the East End.

Whether it was coincidence or not, I don't know, but on a family holiday to Clacton a man stood and watched as I played football with my Dad and a group of kids. He introduced himself as Malcolm Lewis, I came to know him later on as "Lew." He said he liked what he saw and would mention my name to the coaches at Chelsea's evening sessions for schoolboys where he lent a hand. His full time job was as an engineer for British Gas. Fast forward to the final trial game and as I waited to go on, starving hungry, thirsty and fast running out of steam, I saw a bloke in a long coat take out some sweets. I said "give us a sweet mate!" He laughed and gave me a tube of those mints with the hole in. I didn't have a clue at the time but he was the man who not only discovered an immense amount of talent, but after procuring them made them welcome and kept them happy on behalf of Chelsea Football Club. He was probably the original Youth Academy Director or Youth Development Officer but without the fancy title or big pay cheque. His name was Eddie Heath.

I've said to my kids all their life to work hard, apply yourself to the task at hand, if you get a knock back, bounce back, don't take no for an answer, never give in when it's something you want and you'll find lots of good things can all come at once. A car, a house, a job, a partner, a qualification, a promotion. With persistence and seeing the back of a debilitating injury, that's what happened to me. Letters and representatives of nine clubs came through the family's front door. I've told my children "that's how quickly things can happen." And for me it did.

I had progressed from school team to district and now represented Middlesex under fourteens. I mentioned the age group because it has a relevance for two reasons. Firstly compared to now when clubs are getting kids in as young as eight everything had been organic with no real coaching other than Dave Smith at Arsenal. Secondly fourteen was a threshold whereby promising players started to become attached to clubs by signing "associated schoolboy forms." I was offered untold amounts of kit by Chris Gieler at QPR along with a bit of money for a holiday. I accepted neither. I trained once at QPR where the session was taken by one of the famous Morgan twins. Between them they had played for

QPR, Spurs and West Ham. I can't remember if it was Roger or Ian who took the session. I was invited in by Spurs, Palace, Colchester, Fulham and Ernie Collett got back in touch at Arsenal. I trained at Chelsea's training ground on a Monday and Thursday night which at the time was Mitcham.

Years later when different coaches and managers said at half time or pre-match, or during a physical workout which was normally a laborious cross country run "how much do you want it?" I smiled to myself. It was a knowing smile because from day one I think I'd shown how much I wanted it. A lot of the time I was in a team where I wanted it more and down the line it led to trouble and my services being dispensed with. But that was in the long distant future. What you don't realise when you are training and playing every day as a professional footballer is the future quickly becomes the present. I remember two family holidays to the exotic climes of Jersey. Which as a kid was the closest I got to going abroad with my family. We were playing cricket on the beach at a beautiful place called St Brelade's Bay and my Dad wanted to pause for a rest. I took the micky and he said "leave off, I'm forty-two, I need a break." I remember thinking it'll take me ages to get to forty-two.

The way I saw it and so did Mr Rouhan, I had two years of football to convince the decision makers at Chelsea that I was worthy of being signed apprentice professional. In those two years to come I played so well I added two more clubs to the list, Aston Villa and Manchester Utd, who ended up wanting me to sign as an apprentice. Now let me explain my commitment and you decide if I "wanted it."

John Rouhan spoke to the Headmaster Mr Madoc and got me off my last lesson so I could travel across London and make it in time for Chelsea's evening sessions. The W8 bus wasn't particularly reliable so I walked from Chace School to Enfield Town Station about a mile, got the train to Seven Sisters, changed and went down to the underground and got on the Victoria Line almost to the end and changed at Stockwell. I changed again and got on the Northern line to Morden which was the last stop. I got out at Morden and got a 118 bus that stopped on the corner opposite the training ground at Mitcham. Then across the road and up the drive of about five hundred yards to the old wooden pavilion. Altogether on a good day just under two hours and that's before I kicked a ball. So having been asked on numerous occasions "how bad do you want it?" I can cite a four hour return journey to do one hour's training. Of course today it wouldn't happen but looking back it never did me any harm. At Mitcham there were three grass pitches, a tarmac area under floodlights and a car park. I did that twice a week for over two years.

All the boys who were already there came from more local areas and represented a team called Mitcham Royals. On my first night I got a not very nice welcome from a kid with a big nose and loads of spots who approached me asking where I was from. I said "Enfield, North London." As I walked to get changed he kicked my legs to try and trip me. Nice welcome. I just swivelled round and glared at him and his sidekick. Even though I was peckish and I could have eaten them both, I kept my cool as I didn't want to be seen as a discipline problem. I wanted to jump on him as he came nose to nose with me and bite his face off. One of the things that stopped me was his acne. I couldn't do it, not on my first night. It's fair to say that I have had quite a few street fights and I think it's because I saved up a lot of rage from a catalogue of insults, belittling and incidents that I had let go previously. This being one of them. I didn't want to let Eddie Heath down and have the Chelsea staff and coaches asking what kind of kid are we signing here? So I let it go.

In time to come we'd be team mates in the youth team. His name turned out to be Gary Chivers and his sidekick was Micky Fillery. Chivers later told me he had changed his name to that from Charalambous and his Dad was Maltese. I'm not sure of the reasons why. I know one thing, you should never forget or be ashamed of what you have come from.

Although I had no money and hadn't eaten since lunchtime I was anxious to get stuck into training. That first night was a short session, the rest of the time we were shown a film with the highlights of the FA Cup Final between Chelsea and Leeds. The following week they showed us the replay. The players on both sides quite clearly hated each other and at times it was fierce. In the preceding four seasons Chelsea had won the FA Cup, the European Cup Winners Cup and been losing finalists to Stoke in the League Cup Final. All the while they were in and around the top six or eight teams in the First Division as it was known. So Chelsea seemed the place to be as far as I was concerned.

The sessions were taken by Ken Shellito and Dario Gradi. I enjoyed it. I enjoyed being coached. I loved the attention to detail and the help it would give me in games. The holidays were the best, especially Easter. That first Easter all the schoolboys were invited in to train in the afternoons after the pros and apprentices had left. Up until now I'd refused any expenses from Eddie Heath who doled them out in his office after training. I used my school train pass. I don't know why or how I got away with it but I just did. I couldn't keep going without food and at night when I got home I noticed my Mum seemed to get more early nights as she seemed to tire more quickly. I have never cooked and I wouldn't disturb her to do it for me so I went without.

The Easter break meant you could go in, train, then train again in the evening session. I was bang up for it, then fuck me my train's cancelled, I'm now running late. I lived between two stations. Edmonton Green and Silver Street so I started my journey at one of the two and did the same journey I've already spoken of. I got off the 118, ran up the drive and after changing, I explained my tardiness to Eddie Heath. He said "don't worry, you're in Dave's group." The session was being taken by the man himself, the manager Dave Sexton. I'm not embarrassed to say I shit myself and jogged over embarrassed that I was late. I remember the session to this day. It was a phase of play in the middle and attacking thirds coaching third man runs. We sat on the grass as Dave Sexton did his summary and at the end of it he asked who was late. I put up my hand, Dave said collect the balls, bibs and cones. As I did he walked over to me and said "good boy for being honest." I told him a train was cancelled and the next one just went through the station and I apologised, saying I was never late. He said to me "don't worry, never mind, it couldn't be helped. But take my advice, as you go through life, don't be on time, be early." I've never forgot it. His other favourite saying which has been repeated ever since and was coined after a discussion between him and a player with both giving forthright opinions was : "Don't tell me, show me..." It's something else I've never forgotten.

My age group all came through together and we all trained twice a week for two years. The age groups above were the same and only a year separated two groups who went on to be professionals. Derek Richardson, Steve Wicks, John Sparrow, John Bumstead, Trevor Aylott, Ray Wilkins, Tommy Langley, Ian Britton, Graham Wilkins, Gary Stanley, Lee Templeman, Lee Frost, Teddy Maybank, Clive Walker, Ray Lewington and Gary Locke. Within a couple of years most of them would be blooded in the first team. Not long after meeting him and being coached by him, Dave Sexton left to manage QPR and Manchester United.

The vibe was good and I was at a club that gave its youth a chance. The great side of the late sixties, early seventies was breaking up and I'm led to believe some of it was acrimonious. Stories filtered down about the greats of the side and their social habits. Peter Osgood was a legend, so was Alan Hudson. Both criminally underused at international level and pure class. I remember seeing footage of the 1970 Mexico World Cup squad coming back to the hotel from a shopping trip, Ossie wearing a trilby, whistling as he walked past the cameras. He never played, he never even got on as a sub, and Jeff Astle did, missing a one versus one with the Brazilian goalkeeper as we lost 1-0. I eventually got to play alongside Ossie and I'm in no doubt he'd have buried that chance. My opinion is you couldn't put a price on Peter Osgood if he was around today. He had everything. Unlike some of the players who have fortunes spent on them in transfer fee's and wages. When he came back to Chelsea and I played alongside him in training and games, he was without doubt a footballing God.

Back home Dario commented to Ossie on his running action and got a curt fuck off. Dario had played amateur for Sutton Utd, been a university graduate and owned a sports shop. The sports shop was to have a relevance over the next couple of years as he juggled it all with his job as reserve team manager and coach at Chelsea. When you needed new boots you went to Dario and he knocked off a pound and the pence, so my new Pumas at twenty- one pounds ninety-ninety pence cost twenty pounds, instead of free if I'd joined QPR.

If you were lucky after one of the day sessions and if they saw you, Ken Shellito would stop in his mark two Cortina at the bus stop and give a lift to Morden Station, Dario would sometimes do the same in his navy blue Aston Martin. We'd heard there was a fall out on the training pitch between Dave, Ossie and Alan Hudson. They parted company. Ossie went to Southampton, Dave to QPR and United and Alan Hudson to Stoke.

After the evening sessions the vibe continued to be good with post training table tennis, a game of pool and a lift from Eddie Heath in the minibus. On the bus the jokes, impressions and general fucking about nurtured a good spirit among the lads. I got off first at either Brixton or Stockwell and rode the Victoria Line to Seven Sisters. There I got off and got the bus. Being late I got off the bus a stop early because I was now holding my £1 expenses and there was a well-known chicken shop where I got chicken and chips for 99p. On the theme of "how bad did I want it" I continued to train Monday and Thursday. I trained Wednesday and Friday with the Youth Club. I played Saturday morning for the school and Sunday morning with the youth club side, but not for much longer as Chelsea had the nucleus of boys who were on schoolboy forms playing for a Sunday side called "International." Based would you believe it in Basildon and run by one of my group's fathers, Ray Kean. His son Russell was in my age group so I switched.

At home it looked like things had taken a turn for the better and then again for the worse. And believe me the news couldn't have been worse. After being in pain my Mum was referred by our doctor to a consultant. Following tests she was diagnosed with cancer and admitted immediately for surgery. I had only just turned fourteen, my brother two years younger, my sister would have been about five and the woman who held us all together and did everything was gravely ill. I was praying she didn't die and leave us in the hands of our Dad who couldn't, wouldn't or wanted to have coped. I knew even as a kid he was too selfish for that. The evidence as I grew up was overwhelming and underpinned by the most recent episode. Who knows? Looking back maybe it's what has helped shape me as a man and a father.

Post-surgery I remember running with my brother and sister to my Mum's bed as my Dad stood back, then walked slowly. I think secretly he was shitting himself as to the possible dire outcome. The hospital was a small unit at High Cross in Tottenham. My Mum lay there post-op, helpless, tubes coming out of her and I distinctly remember her colour, which was grey, tinged with a jaundiced look. As I held her hand I thought of a couple of years back when I went with her to Inner Temple, off Fleet street. All those years later I had to learn it for the Knowledge. Inner Temple, Outer Temple, Middle Temple, inhabited by solicitors, QC's and their ilk. The lawyer we saw might as well have been fucking Shirley Temple as he sat and explained all the deductions from Grandad's estate. What a fucking joke, the biggest joke was on us, our family. We had been back doored and the local council had slapped a compulsory purchase order on our twenty-two acres of land to the benefit of property developers. To this day it is occupied by a small housing estate. There is a common thread that runs through our family history. We've always been money getters but we seem to have had a problem holding onto it.

There's no doubt in my mind someone's palm was greased. Anyway the family settled on £100,000. I sat with my Mum in front of Rupert Tristram Fuckwit Shaftyou-Smythe as he told of the deductions like his firm's final bill, death duties, capital gains tax and anything else he and the government could think of to fuck us and relieve us of monies for my Grandad's lifetime's work. By the time he was finished, there was little over seventy grand divided between my

Mum, her brother and her sister. See what I mean when I say we're expected to find it palatable when they take it from you? My Mum immediately bought our council house for £8,800 and my Dad relieved her of most of the rest of it when he suggested opening a haulage contracting business, taking and bringing back goods all over Europe and the Middle East The failure of the business would have a relevance later on.

I remember the representative from Volvo which was the lorry my Dad bought, as he drank the tea my Mum served him nearly choking on it and falling off his chair as he started to discuss finance packages. My Dad said there will be no finance, we'll pay cash. The sum was fifteen and a half grand, a lot of money in 1974. As I helped my Mum with the housework while she recuperated my Dad went missing two weeks at a time returning with a tan from Spain, Greece, Italy, France, Germany, Iraq and Iran. My Mum said to me she started to feel better and I should concentrate on my football. I've got to say training and playing was a relief.

I'm not trying to win any sort of sympathy vote, far from it, but it seems that there was a never ending sequence of dramas and events that crept up and encroached upon my wellbeing, happiness and as a kid, a part of my life I should have been enjoying. One of the biggest things at the time caused a lot of tension around the house which must have ultimately led to my Dad looking forward to being away in his lorry. As usual my poor Mum was stuck in the middle and apart from me ended up doing the most. Her brother, my Uncle Alf as I've said was a bit simple and led a somewhat sheltered life. He was hardly going to go to the Playboy Club or dress up in a dinner suit and go to Aspinall's and meet someone. Against my Mum's and Aunt's advice and their personal feelings towards it all Uncle Alf ignored them and took up with a blonde slosh pot from Harold Hill near Romford. She already had a reputation so Uncle Alf was warned by Mum and Aunt Nell to steer clear. He'd found out his appendage had other functions and went on the missing list. Needless to say, the female fell pregnant. It was a life lesson on what could happen if a lying, scheming, cold, callous piece of scum can do if they marry into your family. Uncle Alf returned to Edmonton with a letter which he couldn't read because he was illiterate. My Mum read it before he sat down as a guest to Sunday dinner and it said to him he wasn't wanted, wasn't loved and he was now homeless and as a consequence of her ways rather than Alf 's, he returned penniless. I'd hazard a guess it was more than likely the female in question who had gone through every penny of my Grandad's inheritance. Well at least my Uncle Alf 's share.

For quite a while I had to give up my bed for Uncle Alf and share one with my brother. No picnic when you are fifteen and trying to train to become a footballer. I'm convinced that what seemed like a never ending sequence of events might well have contributed to me having quite a wild period. I also think it's fair to say it can help shape you as a person. There was loads of shit I had to tolerate and wade through and I was sometimes "called out" just because of my family or for being quiet and keeping myself to myself. Sometimes I'd think "what the fuck? where did this come from?"

Even one of my best mates at school Dave Street sheepishly confessed to me once that his Mum had told him to stay away from me saying I was from a "rough family." She was a 1970s carbon copy of Hyacinth Bucket (Bouquet.) Loiza and I as a couple also had to put up with disparaging remarks. It wasn't nice for either of us because we got it from both sides. Loiza got it from the English and I got it from the Greeks. I got stick from everywhere.

They say time flies when you're having fun. I can verify that it certainly seems to. Things were good at school and so was the involvement in all the football. Training at Chelsea, with the school and youth club was always enjoyable, then at the weekend I sometimes got to play three games in two days.

The growth spurt injury was well and truly behind me so it was train, rest, play, school and in between I ate like a combine harvester. So apart from having to take a bit of responsibility at home and help my Mum it was a nice little existence. This is where years later it helped form my opinion that sport, not just football, is an absolute must for kids and adolescent youths. It's healthy, gives structure, takes discipline and even if it's only good timekeeping, is a good commitment. The positive influences on me can never be underestimated. Just to reinforce it I have to say football helped me turn and live my life right.

And so I assume it can only do good for present day youngsters. My Dad returned home normally for a couple of days in fourteen and usually returned with a tasteless, tacky gift for my Mum. He was new money flash. A flash wanker How did I know? Well, two examples would be I bumped into the park keeper across the road from the youth club, his name was Norman, he said "what about your Dad? He's doing well. I couldn't believe the wad of notes he pulled out, he gave me a £20 note and said there you go, have a bet." The second example was on a rare visit to one of my Uncles on my Dad's side, Uncle Arthur. As we left my Uncle said "see you tonight for cards." My Dad said "shhh!" I had already climbed into the lorry and heard it anyway. Then I put two and two together. For months my Dad had left home straight after Sunday tea telling my Mum he wanted to avoid traffic. Traffic on a Sunday night to Dover. At school I'd had a few ups and downs and the odd scrap, not enough to disturb my lessons, but there was the odd chastisement when it was allowed. Unlike now where kids seem to run riot and teachers pander to their every whim.

As I wondered, wanted and more to the point liked the thought of being a footballer I became increasingly distracted.

This resulted in the cane from the headmaster, the slipper from Mr Van Graan, again from Mr Evans and with a run up, one from Mr Polly. Evans and Van Graan wanted me to leave football for rugby and behave. I did neither. I wasn't really angry but I wouldn't take a slap down, even from older boys. This led to a couple of confrontations that came out of nowhere other than the fact that people had heard that I was on Chelsea's books. I had two fights with someone who I thought was a mate and I have to go on record and say he started both of them. The first one was like the first round of Hagler v Hearns. I ended up on top of him to be told by Gary Patterson "quick the teacher's coming." I let him go.

The second time it started in the middle of the classroom and he caught me once which gave me a black eye and a split across the eyelid even though I'd punched him all the way into the blackboard at the front of the class. Classmates jumped in I think out of shock and alarm at the damage we were trying to do to each other. The only other time I had grief at school was as I played football during break and I was approached by someone from a group of plastic gangsters and was told "Paul so and so wants to fight you at lunch time." They were two years older than me so obviously I asked why because I didn't even know him. When the time came he was pushed forward by the so called faces in this team of wankers. I didn't hang about and got it over and done with. Shocked that their Joey had been beaten, two more jumped in, one raining blows on the back of my head and one kicked me in the mouth. My brother, future brother-in-law and a family friend Vernon Hart jumped in and covered me. As I came up I asked who had kicked me in the mouth. I stored it and waited.

One of the younger ones, a certain Paul Whitehouse took a kick up the arse from some of the older boys once as he impersonated Python's Ministry of Silly Walks as we were about to have a game of football in the playground. Years later I just laughed my nuts off when I've seen him on television because he was not only funny but he had a good living from basically doing what he did at school taking the piss, funny faces, funny voices, impressions and general buffoonery. He was two or three years below me. In the last six months before I left school which turned out to be the Easter of 1976 everything seemed to get crammed in.

All the stuff going on included sitting ten mock O' Levels as they were known at the time, a parents evening with this time both Mum and Dad in attendance, football in abundance and one game that included a double tetanus shot for me. Chelsea started to give an indication of the new intake of apprentices in readiness for the 1976-77 season. My partner at centre half for Middlesex Paul Miller had already been given a clue that he wouldn't be signed and set about doing a mini tour of London clubs settling on Spurs where he had a very good career. All the boys knew each other and we played against each other or with each other at county level, club level, or for our respective Sunday sides. I have to say without knowing any of them really well, apart from the Chelsea boys they all came across to me as not only top boys, but good players and fierce competitors. Three out of the back four for Middlesex alone all had professional careers. Myself, Paul Miller and Tony Gale. Not many people know but "Galey" started life at Chelsea as well. In midfield we had Jerry Murphy and up front Paul Goddard. On a Sunday and at club level as schoolboys I came up against Billy Hurley who was built like a man at fifteen, he was on Orient's books Then there were the Palace boys like Vince Hillaire and Billy Gilbert. Good players, charismatic and they all played to win. When we all eventually signed apprentice they were added to Stevie Lovell, Ian Evans, Terry Boyle and Peter Nicholas. When you played these boys you had a game on your hands. I could have been one of them.

Season 1975-1976 was a pretty amazing year for me. I actually think it would be an amazing year for any kid let alone someone from a council estate in London. At the time though and I think it was probably the same for my peers at places like Crystal Palace it's what you think you were born to do. You work hard, you get on with it and the rewards like nine or ten clubs vying for your signature become a by-product. My Dad was now one year into the business my Mum had financed and it never came as any real surprise to me that my Dad would have the time of his life and the worry, burden, detail and responsibility would be down to Mum. In the end unknown to anybody apart from my life partner it would seep into, encroach upon and have an impact on my life.

The teachers in school in the meantime, encouraged me to sit all of my exams. They also encouraged my Mum to try and influence me, dangling the carrot of my likelihood of success in at least eight subjects. This would enable me to push on and take a minimum of two A' levels, possibly three and I could be the first person in my family to go to and even complete university. This was back when attending university was based on your academic capabilities rather than just being able to afford it. At fifteen I thought I was the man of the house while my Dad travelled and guess what? I said "fuck the exams, I'm going to be a footballer." I walked out at the first available opportunity which turned out to be Easter. This coincided with being sent to Loughborough University for England schoolboy trials. There were kids from elsewhere but it was a who's who of London schoolboy football.

As usual I never had a pot to piss in. We got the early train and after we got off I was one of the kids who got a bus and walked the rest of the way to the university campus. People like Paul Miller and Jerry Murphy got taxis. We were there for four or five days with trial games every day and some uninspiring training. I remember being hungry most of the time and struggling to fill the downtime between training and playing. It was good grounding for the future though as it usually consisted of either listening to players talk bollocks, or playing cards, or both. The other thing I struggled with was listening to kids who acted like former day divas, talking of the chore of attending trials and that they "hated it." I thought then and still do now representing your country is the pinnacle of any sports person's career. How bad can it be to get recognition as one of the best in whatever you do? I think it's an absolute honour. Sadly for me it wasn't to be. I was injured as I slid a ball out of play right in front of one of the selectors who stood on the touchline. Whilst others flattered to deceive I trained and played like a beast. Commanding, talkative, bossing people, winning tackles, headers and passing sensibly. I heard my thigh rip as I stretched. I tried to play on after a fuckhead northerner told me to run it off. In the end I was on the periphery, hobbling around like a wounded extra in a war film. Aforesaid numpty said "you'd better come off." A couple of days after arriving home, I received notification thanking me for my attendance. It was a "thanks but no thanks."

As a coach many years later I would always trust a player and

his integrity. If he's injured and he says so that should be it. It's funny until someone actually gets a fairly bad injury themselves I've known a lot of coaches and managers who think you should "run it off." For the record, I never trained for over three weeks after it was discovered I had a partially torn abductor in the groin area. As a coach I would always put a player's welfare first.

At home Mum was still getting manipulated by her sister who thought she smelled money and asked to buy in fifty percent of my Mum and Dad's haulage business. My Dad had pulled in a lot of work and the business started ok. I remember him clocking up the miles as he did runs to Spain, Italy, Portugal and a couple of short ones into France, always returning with a tan. Then he ventured further afield and the problems started. It was a double whammy. My Aunt never saw the thousands she anticipated and pulled out asking my Mum for her half back. I was a kid so I couldn't step in to protect my Mum because at the time I'm sure anything I'd have said would hold no sway. It's relevant because history would repeat itself with my own brother years later. I then experienced what my Mum had as I always tried just like she did, to please the world around me. Looks and physique wise I'd taken after my Dad. In terms of nature, disposition and family, I'd taken after my Mum. That's my opinion and it will never change.

My mate Miguel recently remarked and I perhaps have learned too late that if you want a good life or what is perceived as a good life, you have to be selfish. The trips farther afield held a number of sinister overtones for quite a few reasons.

My Dad got long runs to Turkey where once you crossed into the Asian part life was made hard for you. My Dad told stories that defied belief. Adults would send their kids to hassle the drivers for money and cigarettes. A favourite trick according to my Dad was for the kids to mime "cigarette, cigarette" and if you never threw a pack out of the window, they would throw rocks at your windscreen and BANG! My Dad would remonstrate "ok, ok, calm down," then throw an empty pack out of his window and as they ran over to divide the pack of twenty, he would change gear and speed off before they'd sussed it. Other tricks where it seems survival took precedence over decency would be the siphoning of diesel while drivers slept. The main victims according to my Dad were the Dutch and Scandinavian drivers who indulged in a glass of ale or twelve. Whilst they slept it off they were either relieved of their diesel or coming in through the sunroof with wire, their money, passport and documents. As a kid with fuck all I couldn't help thinking there had to be an easier way to utilise Mum's share of £100,000 less the bumfluffery I've already spoken about. But the old man was in his element. Just around the corner though was a major setback after he did two runs to Iran, which in terms of danger alone, never paid enough. Watch a film called "Argo" that will explain what I mean.

Closer to home, the highs and lows of trying to make it in football continued. The highs were being invited in with other prospective "apprentices" as they were known at the time, to train with the youth team over the Whitsun Bank Holidays. I also got to play in a youth team friendly with Gary Johnson and a skinny kid who was deceptively strong and also very quick, called Michael Nutton. Dario loved him. Even as schoolboy you could see Micky being pushed on. He was even invited to do cross country runs around Mitcham with Dario and the young professionals. I always got on really well with Nutts. We were both October birthdays and had a similar sense of humour. I actually came to envy his pace but I never envied him trying to keep up with Dario and Tommy Langley in those cross country runs.

Call me overly sensitive but one of the lows came via some verbal piss taking from one of the youth team and another was getting bitten by a dog. They (the second year senior apprentices) could have been forgiven for thinking who's this upstart but also could have made me feel a bit more welcome. I think it's called banter but sometimes it can overstep the mark. Believe it or not I've rarely subscribed to it, and when it gets too personal or spiteful, it veers away from any atmosphere, feel good factor and team spirit. I've always believed in courtesy, respect and harmony. One time it did overstep the mark was at an end of season awards party and before we all left our Sunday side to sign apprentice for Chelsea. I'm sure someone who has since reached what might be called the pinnacle of the game wouldn't want to be seen as a drunk, racist, bigot or loud mouth. As an eighteen-year-old he was at least three out of four. This particular person along with Ray Wilkins had been invited to hand out the medals. The person concerned showed that everyone at one time or another in their life says things they shouldn't. My girlfriend and I made the most of a bit of freedom from her parents and family, had a good dance, a giggle and a little smooch. As I stood at the bar to get us a drink this mouthy little cunt asked "who's that pikey you was snogging?" Peter Bradley who incidentally was not a very good goalkeeper and was lucky to be there, got brave and piped up "Sitts' bird is a refugee!" Hurtful, spiteful, nasty and unnecessary.

I've never gone out of my way to be like that and I like to think I've conducted myself appropriately in front of team mates' wives and girlfriends showing the utmost respect. I was two age groups younger than this lairy loud mouth who now gives off an air of upmost respectability but back then I had the same three choices I've had all my life; ignore it and leave them to their ignorance, have a verbal battle or put them in A and E. The last two could have spoiled a nice atmosphere. Besides it would have been like kicking a puppy. Ironically where this player was concerned I was the only one in my age group who had respect for the age groups above and I never took the piss out of his stature, physique and running action which was like a two-year-old who'd just learned to walk, running in quicksand.

I've matured now and prefer to use words but for years I was angry even though some stuff was harmless, I did, or was on the verge of always reacting. Where the anger came from I still don't know and I didn't always contain it. When I did contain it, as arrogant as it sounds, nobody knew they'd had a pass for taking things too far. I just smiled and nodded which was a nice little tactic I'd picked up from my wife's side.

I trained and played well over a long period and I already felt

I was better than some of the defenders at under eighteen level. I wasn't yet sixteen and I had the jump on people like Paul Hammond, Danny Godwin, John

Sparrow and Paul Miller who had been released to find new pastures, eventually settling at Spurs. I don't know to this day if it was a form of acceptance or Francis Cowley being spiteful but he declared in front of a large audience "you've got some gear Sitts" to quite a few chuckles. My only clothes were my school uniform, some training gear, a Gi for Jiu Jitsu and what I had turned up in on this blazing hot day. We got off the 118 bus and I was walking up the drive in a pair of beige Farahs, brown moccasins, a brown checked sports jacket and a very hot, itchy roll neck sweater. I looked like a rough villain in a 1970s cop show usually played by ironically a Chelsea supporter Patrick Mower.

So far apart from a couple of scrapes at school, I'd kept my head down determined to keep a clean record. I chose to ignore it just like I did on the first night when Chivers -Charalambous tried to kick my legs away as I got changed. I thought, and still do, that it's strange for people to go out of their way to be nasty. I just went red. Cowley who was one of the most skilful and talented players I'd seen was released. I once saw him take the ball up to Arsenal's left full back, tread on the ball with his right foot, pirouette in mid-air and as he completed three hundred and sixty degrees, use the sole of his left foot to spin past and accelerate away. Even his own team mates clapped as they laughed at his audacity but if truth be told, I don't think he took a career in football seriously enough. He became like so many, a walking cliché, just another flash fucker from the East End but a talented player without doubt who I looked at, admired and thought never made the most of it.

I got what I came for which was the offer of a two-year contract as an apprentice professional with Chelsea Football Club. First mission accomplished. In the meantime I think unknown to Chelsea, I was spoiled for choice. The same clubs who had wanted me to sign schoolboy forms had kept tabs on me for two years and now invited me to sign as an apprentice. Because of the distance involved in travelling every day Colchester was a nonstarter, plus the facilities were poor. That left Villa, whose lack of personal contact and interaction that I thought equalled arrogance, in the same boat. All I got from them was an invite to view their facilities and a brochure with information and pictures of a hostel they had for boys who signed from outside the local area. Man Utd were more personal, sending a representative to talk to my father at all the Middlesex and Inner London games. The boundaries had changed. So now we were called "Inner London." Spurs actually approached me and my Dad after I'd signed for Chelsea. Keith Burkinshaw was at a Spurs vs Chelsea Youth game and said he was very impressed and there was a place for me there, at Spurs. My old Middlesex and Chelsea team mate Paul Miller was doing really well there and getting rave reviews. His dedication was praised by Mr Burkinshaw on TV in an interview I saw saying how they "couldn't get the likes of Paul Miller out of the building as he was always back in the afternoons doing extra." I thought good for him that he bounced back after leaving Chelsea as a schoolboy. When he was released only Paul would know what was said but he went on to have a very good career and I respect that.

Because of our progress and the fact the club got wind that other clubs were sniffing around us me and Jerry Murphy got a couple of games in friendlies for Chelsea's youth team as fifteen-year olds. At the time it was virtually unheard of and it was deemed an honour. I thought it was, or maybe the coaching hierarchy just let me think it was. As a coach years later it's something I never hesitated in doing. If a kid was exceptional or too good for his age group, I would rapidly promote him to the age group above. I always felt that it would constantly be testing the player, technically, mentally and physically.

One day we were playing a friendly and at Mitcham in those days it wasn't like the training grounds now. These days you need a pass, a personal invite, a visa and a passport, then you have to negotiate a barrier and one or more security personnel. One man and his dog were walking around the pitch. As we played the ball ran out of play, every player shouted, as you do "our ball" and the referee gave it our way. The problem was what looked like a cross between an Alsatian and a grizzly bear took ownership of the ball and guarded it fiercely growling and barking at anyone who made an attempt to get near it. I mistakenly tried to play mini macho man and ran over and with a growl of my own, told the dog to fuck off. A bit like my Nan used to when I annoyed her a few years earlier. It was as a gurning cockney I said "GERTCHA, fuck off." The dog backed off, I picked the ball up and turned to throw the ball to the full back to take the throw in. Turning my back was a mistake, the dog leapt and with a paw on each of my shoulders bit into my back, just below my shoulder blade. The retarded owner had by now walked the fifty yards he was behind and he and a very angry Eddie Heath got this mutt off me. I remember the pain and the stinging sensation. Agony! Because there was only about ten minutes to go I was asked if I wanted to come off. I said no trying to hide the pain. I was taken to hospital straight after the game by the manager of Mitcham Royals, Johnny Sparks, who steered good kids Eddie's and Chelsea's way. It wasn't the nicest way to end the day with two tetanus shots in the cheeks of my arse but the fact that I'd had a good game took some of the sting out of it.

I laugh at myself sometimes when I look back to me as a young man. Particularly as a fifteen-year-old. Arsenal came back in and even offered a small inducement. Much to my Dad's disappointment I acted churlish saying "no fuck 'em they had their chance." I think it's fair to tell you the supporter, with my opinions based on true events, that decisions either well or ill-informed shape your fate. Your future sometimes is in the hands of and lies with the opinions of coaches or managers who see enough in you, to trust you as person, a player and a professional. Sometimes it's the opinion of a muppet who is clueless and just does not like the look of you, the cut of your jib, your perceived disposition and consequently they decline to put faith in you as a player and move you on. There's many times when I was totally perplexed as I slid down the divisions when I looked on and questioned what a certain player supposedly had that I didn't. I can even give several examples which I will in chronological order as I tried to work out why either inferior players were better rewarded than me or were brought in on higher wages and signing on fees when I was delivering good performances week in, week out instead of rewarding me when I absolutely deserved it. Usually someone in charge with delusions of grandeur concerning their managerial ability and psychology ended up just shuffling their pack or squad of players just for the sake of it. It's another thing in a list that rankles with me. At the time it could have been soul destroying and disheartening as well as being unjust, which I thought it was. I ended up re-doubling my efforts but staying poor.

Many years on and I have to say this, an old one-time team mate at Middlesex, Chelsea and Inner London who then moved onto Fulham, Tony Gale snapped it all into focus. He stood with me and commentator Jonathan Pearce in Arsenal's press room at their Emirates Stadium and gave examples of decisions he'd made on his career, who paid good wages, who didn't and how it all becomes an intricately woven web of fate that ultimately determines the club you play for and your career outcome. Tony is not one to mince his words. He is an astute guy and yet he reminisced on the choices he'd made concerning certain clubs at different times in his career. Having known him for years I could see even with a good broadcasting career, a Premier League winners medal with Blackburn, a good run of games at a great club in West Ham and early recognition as a kid at Fulham that he made the most of to earn his stripes, he looked into the distance with almost a tinge of regret as he gave me times and dates when he actually could have gone to Arsenal and Liverpool. Then there's his observations on my career that he'd kept an eye on from a distance. He's a good mate Galey. He put to the test immediately if I was up for telling it straight (and how bullish my mood) by asking if I had the same opinion as him about a certain player and if I thought this particular player was better than me. I replied "that's an emphatic no." Galey had identical theories to mine on luck, fate, choices and decisions out of one's own control. He then remarked that the player in question and myself were similar types of player but the difference was he won the ball and rolled it five or ten yards to an international team mate or one of two world class midfield players just in front of him. Galey then added that I shouldn't be so hard on myself and it's just a quirk of fate that the other player concerned was lucky enough to play at Wembley eight or nine times. That conversation was in 2012. This is what happened in the meantime...

CHAPTER FIVE: CHELSEA 1976-1978

Dancing Queen

My last decision to make before I signed apprentice for Chelsea came at me post-match after one of my last representative games. I remember it like it was yesterday. I was picked to play against Berkshire and as I've said three out of our back four had careers in professional football me, Tony Gale and Paul Miller. In midfield we had Jerry Murphy who by now had left Chelsea for Crystal Palace. At centre forward we had Paul Goddard who played for so many top clubs he ended up with the nickname "Bundles." It was a pretty good spine to the team.

The occupants of the Mercedes that pulled into the car park next to the football field it turned out had come to see me and speak to my Dad as I warmed up. Out of the Merc came Arnie Warren, Fred Ricketts a scout who had previously been at Fulham and tried to sign me for them and lastly Malcolm Allison manager of Crystal Palace. I'd only known "Big Mal" as he was called from guest appearances as a pundit on "The Big Match" on Sundays and as a guest panellist for ITV during their coverage of the 1974 World Cup. From a kid till now I thought he was the bollocks. Charismatic, flamboyant, but above all innovative and knowledgeable. He predicted forty years ago the back pass rule and the first £100,000 a week footballer. I remember his other prediction which was the football field would be marked out into three thirds with offside only given in the respective end thirds. The stories right back to his West Ham days were sometimes legendary, sometimes profound, always colourful.

Even when he took his coaching badges he was two classes above the staff coaches. One story goes he and his followers including Alan Harris, Ron's brother, would indulge in the night life while at Lilleshall. When asked "I suppose you lot are off to abuse your bodies again" by I think someone high up like Walter Winterbottom, Big Mal just replied "hopefully! See you in the morning." I'd heard he came in just as everyone else was going to breakfast and still did the best session.

Malcolm Allison was in my opinion and I'm stating the obvious here, a deep thinker, innovator, great football man, coach and supreme psychologist and he wanted to sign little old me! I must have been doing something right over quite a long period because he was blatantly open and very forthright about it all as he walked straight up to my Dad who was standing alongside and talking with Eddie Heath, Chelsea's chief scout. Eddie walked away.

My Dad relayed the story in the car on the way home. Mr Allison introduced himself, Arnie Warren and Fred Ricketts who we already knew. He then gave a running commentary for the first hour of the game telling my Dad what I did well, what I had going for me and more relevant to him as a coach, what he thought my weaknesses were and how he and a young coach he had coming up called Terry Venables would help me. He then outlined the plans he had put to Crystal Palace's chairman who I think at the time was a Mr Raymond Bloye, which was to get all the best kids and from apprentice at sixteen years old, within four years by the time they were twenty have them ready and knocking on the door of the first team. He wanted to build a young, exciting side. He then said he had made his own mind up as well as hearing good reports and wanted to make an offer of £3000 in cash for my signature. He then added "but now I've seen him play, I think your son's worth more. So let's say £4000 with weekly wages and living and travelling expenses on top, or we can put him in digs." My Dad thanked him and basking in the reflected glory said to Mr Allison he'd speak to me and give a decision as soon as possible.

What people outside football don't know is that twenty-five years before Arsene Wenger was even aware of it, Big Mal was already introducing dieticians, stretching programmes, plyometrics and even hypnosis. He was as I've said a visionary. It's shame on the English game that he was allowed to fade. I think it's an embarrassment that a list as long as my arm, with big Mal at the top, of coaches and managers who haven't had their experience and knowledge called upon by the F.A. and football in general. If I had been in football for any length of time as a coach or manager I'd have paid the likes of Allison, Lyall, Moore, Gradi or Cartwright an arm and a leg just to have them alongside me on a consultancy basis. As I've said shame on the English game. It's tragic to think that his knowledge was not used to consult or advise younger coaches and the national set up. I think he made enemies high up who were afraid of his colourful nature.

One of the best books I've read was "Colours of my Life" by Malcolm Allison. He even introduced other sports, including martial arts to solve a discipline problem at Porto. I thought he was a genius but the people in power at the F.A. and the people who owned clubs obviously didn't. It's funny how people are afraid of big personalities. In the car my Dad said I could probably push for

£5000 or even £6000 if I fancied it which was a lot of money in 1976. Big Mal parted company saying in the meantime come as our guests to a first team game at Selhurst Park next week, speak to Fred or Arnie and everything will be taken care of. Arnie Warren gave my Dad his card as they all left.

Through the counties and Sunday football I'd already heard the stories of young players being offered inducements. A lot of kids and their parents were well looked after. I then remember watching a kid a bit older than me look and play magnificently for England schoolboys at Wembley versus West Germany who was already at Palace. His all-round game and pace stood out as did his smart suede head haircut and I thought he was a player to aspire to. I thought he looked the nuts in his England kit and for me although wrongly utilised by various coaches and managers at club and international level, just shades Ashley Cole as England's greatest ever left back.

Obviously I'm talking about Kenny Sansom. Around his year give or take were two Welsh kids, Peter Nicholas and Terry Boyle. After them Vince Hillaire, Jerry Murphy, Stevie Lovell and Billy Gilbert. I liked Billy, we always had a ding dong at county level but we got on and he made me laugh.

After us and our age group the next wave were the likes of Sean Brooks who was to become a team mate and Neil Banfield who would become a friendly acquaintance. I went to the Palace first team game, met Arnie Warren and Mr Allison officially and I was introduced to the first team. Then Fred Ricketts took me and my Dad to a canteen and I had was a plate of chicken and chips and a match programme. We watched the game and told Fred we'd be in touch. The season was drawing to a close and at the time Palace were in the third division and had a bit of a ramshackle ground. As I ate my chips I could smell the damp in the area where we sat. At Chelsea, who only a few years earlier had won the FA. Cup, the European Cup Winners Cup and were League Cup finalists it seemed there was more of a buzz. In the equation were Eddie, Ken, Les, Lew and at the time Dario. By now I felt bonded with and part of my age group. We were to be the next set of apprentices at Chelsea Football Club so why leave? The obvious answer was money but I've never been that fickle, shallow and disloyal. I trained, played and felt strong, like a hero. One of the heroes I used to watch at Saturday morning pictures. It was usually either Zorro or Tarzan who was the hero. I said to my Dad to ring Palace out of courtesy and tell them that even though I was very proud and flattered that they wanted me, I was very happy at Chelsea. He said "you sure? What about the money?" I told him that at the moment money didn't matter and it was more important to me to be happy and enjoy my training and playing. Looking back the only problem that seemed to arise was there was nobody to tell me what happens when Zorro and Tarzan get old. Naive or what?

As the season wound down all the new intake of apprentices were summoned to a sort of open day at Mitcham with one or both parents. I went with my Dad, had a chat with Ken Shellito and an appointment was made for me at Stamford Bridge. The boys were split into two groups, we went in, signed, got a handshake and that was it. We were taken along the Fulham Road to open a bank account at Barclays Bank so our wages could be paid straight in the bank to encourage savings. My apprentice contract read that I was to be paid £12 per week for the first year, £16 per week for the second year, travelling expenses and £2 per point for South East Counties League Games. If you got in the reserves you automatically went on to a football combination bonus which was three pounds for a draw and six pounds for a win. Obviously after achieving due recognition as a schoolboy and signing schoolboy forms then achieving my ambition and reaching my next target which was to become an apprentice, my next targets were to achieve full professional status, get in the reserves and then ultimately the first team.

We then went to a very pompous club doctor affiliated with Hammersmith Hospital and Chelsea Football Club who had his own private practice. He must have been very comfortable financially but this spilled slightly towards arrogance and pomposity, two things I abhor. Because I was in football over a fairly long period I got to meet a lot of medical people who I think normally fall into two categories, they are either very humble or think they are God. Eyes, ears, knackers, jump up and down with your knickers in the air, cough and that was it. Well almost. He hit me across the knees with a rubber hammer and I never moved. He did it again, I never moved. I asked him what was supposed to happen and as I did I said "let's have a look" and took the hammer and hit him back. Luckily, he laughed, Ken laughed, and he never moved either. So I said I must be alright. Ken added "it's nice to know you've got a clean bill of health John." I was given a letter telling me what day to report back for what would be sixteen consecutive seasons of pre- season training. I always called it "the necessary evil" when players moaned, myself included, I said to look at it as a brief downpour of rain, nobody likes rain, but I think you'll find it's a necessary evil. Sunshine follows the rain. As a player, the ray of sunshine you're looking for is to be picked for the first game of the season. That's what I told myself anyway.

I went back to Chace to say goodbye to a few teachers and pals who I knew I probably wouldn't see again and stay in touch with one or two which I would. Just before I left school there was another problem. This time involving more bullying scum who were making my brother's life a misery. My brother was virtually in tears and asked me if I could get them to stop. I've always had a fairly high threshold, but where family are concerned I've always drawn a line in the sand a lot sooner. I'm not just saying it to justify anything because my time has been and gone, but this kid although a year younger than me was actually bigger than I was in physique and towered over my brother. I timed it so that I confronted him when he had his little gang around him and asked him politely if he could leave my brother alone and let him get on with his lessons. He came out with a cute piss take answer to try and make his mates laugh. I hit him and laid him out to some nervous laughter from Gary Patterson. As he laid there I stood over him to tell him I was leaving school for the last time but if he didn't leave my brother alone I could always set aside a day to come back.

As I explain all the incidents please don't think I am being an arrogant braggart. Every time something happened it was down to provocation or in retaliation. I have never started trouble in my life. I was born and brought up humble, polite and courteous, but I wasn't born yesterday. I can never understand someone going out of their way to cause trouble. Unfortunately there was a period in my life where it never seemed to be too far away. I always preferred to be left alone and blend in as part of a warm friendly group.

On the last evening at the schoolboy coaching sessions word went round that help was needed to tidy up our Mitcham training ground. The surfaces were very poor and apparently it was because of poor drainage. Nearly all of the first year apprentices volunteered to turn up every day for expenses only to help Eddie Heath. The second year lot lasted about two days. It could have been seen and used as a form of conditioning over the summer but after a couple of days the young pros and second year apprentices couldn't be seen for dust. As it turned out I don't blame them. For about four weeks we all helped Eddie Heath dig trenches, move the excess soil, put sand and top soil on the training pitches and the hardest bit of all, tree felling! All around the trees and shrubs were so dense it stopped the pitches drying naturally because there was no breeze. So there's Eddie with a chainsaw taking out thirty feet trees, then cutting it into logs which we had to cart off. The main trunks got dragged off with a chain and the tractor which we all got a turn to drive. It was hard work and towards the end a few got tetchy and irritable.

He felled a tree that came down the wrong way across a little country lane at the back of the training ground. Call it the opposite of serendipity a geezer comes along in a van, jumps out and starts going mental. He's having a pop at us kids, Eddie walked over and asked the guy to turn around and bypass this bit of road. The bloke wouldn't have it saying "can't you move it?" Eddie, 6'6" with a chainsaw in his hand said "if I could, I'd be in a fucking circus." The bloke turned and got in his van and drove off. Eddie just winked at me, Iori Jenkins and Clive Penny as we all laughed.

The only break I got that summer was three days down at my family's caravan with Gary Johnson and Jimmy Clare. What else was we going to do on £12 a week? Mind you someone in football was still getting rich even if it wasn't us. At the top of the game I suppose pro rata compared to the boys in today's game you had the superstars of the day at clubs like Man City, Leeds, Liverpool, Man Utd, Arsenal etc etc. Then and it's only my theory no one else's I have to wonder who else was cashing in. I'd attended games at Arsenal where the attendance at Highbury was 62,000 standing. Bob Wilson recently wrote in an interviewed article that he was paid £2 for a draw and £4 for a win the year Arsenal did the double. In my house my Dad had to repair a chandelier as we both jumped up when Charlie George got the winner against Liverpool to clinch it. So only a few years on I got exactly half of what Bob did for winning a youth team game. Talk about perspective.

That first day at training as an apprentice I'll never forget until the day I die. The whole place at Mitcham was buzzing. The manager following the departure of Dave Sexton was ex-player Eddie McCreadie. All of the apprentices had to report at 8.30 am to Stamford Bridge, load the kit into a skip, put it on the minibus then we'd be taken to the training ground to lay it all out for the pros after we'd got changed ourselves. The intake for my age group was a pretty full one. In goal was Peter Bradley. Full backs Clive Penny and Micky Nutton, centre halves, me and Iori Jenkins, midfield, Chris Sulley, Russell Kean, Jimmy Clare, Steve Wallington, forwards, Gary Johnson, Bobby Tapping, Richard Wilson. Also in the squad were Gary Chivers, Mike Fillery and later on Colin Pates and Peter Rhodes-Brown. Everyone was paired off to do duties on a rota basis. I remember being paired with Gary Johnson. When it was your turn you laid out the kit and boots and collected it back in again after training.

Back at the ground, two pairs did the baths, bathrooms, showers, toilets, dressing room floors and cleaned everyone's boots ready for the next day. We were allocated for the whole season one pair of studs, one pair of moulded and one pair of trainers. If you wore them out before the end of the season you had to find a way of replacing them yourself. In the meantime you had to try and impress and not be mugged off in training.

The summer of 1976 was a hot one and that first day was no different. After everyone changed we were told to congregate and sit on the grass on the side of the pavilion that faced the entrance and driveway. Chairs were set out for Ken, Ron Suart and Eddie Mac. Ron Suart spoke first telling us do's and don'ts and finished by saying everyone will address Eddie McCreadie as "Boss."

The speech given by Eddie Mac was the best I heard in a sixteen season career associated with a professional environment from 1974-1991 and altogether a twenty-five-year association with the game from 1972-1997. It was inspirational, visionary and made everyone feel wanted and ten feet tall. He outlined his plans for how we would play, should play and the importance of sticking together. He added that any misdemeanours would be dealt with in-house and that we are family. "You are my babies and no one I swear to God will be allowed to speak against you without me to deal with. Any questions before we go off and do great things this season?"

I thought having seen him coach that knowledge and confidence oozed out of him. We then broke off and the pros loaded into cars and the minibus and went for a run at Epsom Racecourse. We trained on a patch of grass by the drive into Mitcham. Ken broke it down nicely, which you appreciate as a player and only came to know the planning when you start to coach yourself. It was a nice mixture of ball work and fitness work. Just before lunch the first team came back and Eddie Mac had the minibus stopped on the drive, got out and came and watched as we finished the morning session with a small sided game.

His face was red from a mixture of too much sun and running the Derby course with the pros. As the ball ran out of play he yelled "so! how do my new babies like training on a day like this?" Almost in unison we said "it's good Boss, all good," He pointed at me and said "come over here son." I thought for some reason I had done something wrong, the kit maybe, or someone had been given the wrong boots. "You ok son?" "Yes Boss lovin' it" "I've seen you play, now I've seen you train." I thought oh fuck here it comes! "Ya know what?" "No Boss, what?" "You should've been born a Scotsman, You've got too much passion for an Englishman." "But I'm proud to be English..." I answered. He laughed, ruffled my hair and said "go on son, get back in the game." I looked at Ken Shellitto who smiled and winked at me. Eddie Mac made me feel ten feet tall.

Even now at fifty-six as I write it, it makes me smile, it was a lovely gee up. It was nice like it is for any player or employee to feel valued and wanted. In all honesty the only other coach or manager who was that open and honest with me, telling me the truth, a well done when it was earned, a bit of help if required and a bollocking when not very often called for, was George Petchey at Millwall. I've got to add contrary to popular opinion, I didn't spend my time as a coach like a raving lunatic. Or as one comedian put it, asking "why do leaves fall off trees?" Supposedly getting upset about it. He probably thinks he is a funny fucker. But I'd say it probably explains why he is rarely on the TV. I openly and very honestly showed many players my true feelings towards them and never held back any praise. I saw a speech or motivational talk, call it what you want, highlighted on a news report that Sir Alex Ferguson gave in America. It was either a university or business school and he stated that his most frequently used phrase as a manager was "well done." It's fair to say in my time in football with the many coaches and managers I've come across, no manager has ever held the copyright to either "well done" or " the hairdryer." I picked up later that myths are easily created in football and normally come about to give people something to write about. After some foundation had been laid to their fitness the young pros were normally taken by minibus for a week long training camp in Dawlish, Devon. Pre-season back then was about five and a half to six weeks. It was always tough especially if you're not a natural athlete. Then the league was up and running and on the opening day Eddie McCreadie introduced everyone at the club from top to bottom including backroom staff and all the coaches, onto the pitch to the supporters. At one of the early season midweek fixtures at home I sat where the apprentices had seats which as you look at it would be to the left of the tunnel. I was on duty and had completed my tasks, I sat and watched as Ray Wilkins and Ray Lewington came out to check their studs on the turf. It was a warm, balmy evening and Dancing Queen by ABBA was blaring out over the tannoy. I'm struggling to really explain how I felt, maybe the word I should just settle for is content. I felt excited, warm, relaxed, happy, calm, positive and along with what a lot of people must have felt at a time in their life, looking forward to what seemed like my whole life in front of me. It was either the football or the change in my domestic situation, or both.

I regarded Tom as my best friend. We had been to the same infants' school, junior school, senior school, youth club and Sunday football team and we'd always looked out for each other. Tom had two sisters and the one closest to us in age was Loiza. I thought she was pretty and had a lovely smile and we got on well. As Tom's mate I was a guest to his house quite a few times and his parents who were Greek Cypriot were called Andreas and Georgina They were always very hospitable and welcoming. One night as we hung out, Tom's Mum went into one in Greek. When she left the room I asked Loiza and Tom what was said thinking I'd betrayed some sort of etiquette. To be fair to my mother-in-law nothing ever gets past her. Before this particular episode she even asked Loiza why I visited so often.

Loiza told me her Mum told her to "watch out... You're talking with your eyes!" You know what they say about women, you chase them until they catch you! Her Dad for some reason nicknamed Louis which was his Dad's name, just laughed. He had known me from the age of twelve when he watched the Sunday team play. Years later Loiza confessed while we were at school, even though Chace School for Girls got out after us at the boys' school, she raced to the train station so she could get the train home with us and she and I could talk. The first time it was just fate, even the connecting bus was on time. We got on well, I made her laugh and I was even a bit protective of her. Before reporting for pre-season Tom asked if it was alright for me to come with him on a family day out as his mate. Tom's Mum and Aunt said bring him along. Four adults and seven kids in two cars to Shoeburyness and then a couple of hours at the funfair in Southend which was down the road. There was a massive grass car park where people had their picnic. I went off for a walk and a kick about with the boys. We got the call to come back to eat. My future mother-in-law had laid out a spread and the portions would have had an American running for cover. We sat on the floor and it reminded me a little of how my family used to be with everyone well fed and happy. Louis lit his customary Senior Service and said "all I have to do now is find two nice Greek girls for you and Tommy." I said "I think I've already found mine Lou." You could have heard a pin drop on the grass. My future mother-in-law exclaimed "OH NO!" Louis smiled a sort of knowing smile. He'd used his intuition, dangled the bait and I bit. I thought there was no sense in wasting time. Loiza's godmother and Aunt said "let him speak." Future ma-in-law got me out of tricky situation by stating "you must have your own house and £4000 in the bank if you want to marry my daughter." I thought I could have done with that few grand offered by Big Mal at that time but due to a combination of saving and events in the not too distant future, by the time I was twenty I'd saved £7000 and put it down as a deposit on mine and Loiza's first house.

As I've matured I've come to know what my father-in-law already knew, you can't stop nature. Nature also had quite a bit to do with the opposition and fences we've been given to jump in the fourty years since, thirty-four of them as man and wife. Human nature that is. You wouldn't believe the shit that one or both of us at one time or another have had to listen to or put up with. Without a doubt there are people I've met or come across who make me look like a cross between David Niven and Shakespeare. There's lots of times when my courtesy, kindness and tolerance may have been mistaken for weakness. I just let stuff wash over me, after all, you can't correct, fight and argue with everyone. Some even included relatives and so called friends. It was quite enlightening learning that racism and ignorance is not confined to one colour, race or nationality. I've got to say I bore the brunt of it. At the time I could have reacted and easily sent one or two ignoramuses to A and E but restrained myself with the knowledge that it was a few hyenas cackling about a lion.

In our first year as apprentices I played in both the South East Counties Division's one and two. Chelsea had teams in both. The second year apprentices earmarked for professional status by now were ever present in division one or in the reserves playing in the football combination. I couldn't have asked for better coaches or role models. But me being me I did it my way and within four seasons I'd blown it. In the meantime, Ken and Eddie Mac were different class. Players I looked up to were the likes of record signing from Celtic David Hay, the Wilkins brothers Graham and Ray and two accomplished and crafty East End boys who were good defenders, Ron Harris and Steve "Polly" Perkins. It's fair to say that Steve Wicks was also making good progress. He was in the first team at eighteen and would probably come under the heading of one of the best uncapped centre halves in the country. They could all play and the common denominator in all of them was they were all great trainers and very dedicated.

Polly hit a rough patch with a diabolical injury, a fracture of the vertebrae in the lumbar region of his spine. At the time the surgery was deemed risky and he declined it. A diabolical shame he was never the same. I couldn't believe how hard it was to train full time at first. To help himself Gary Johnson bless him, did extras like cross country runs on Wanstead Flats and as a guest of Les Brown at the famous Peacock Gym, still there to this day. Gary said in all of the training we all did the hardest he found was to do one minute at thirty second intervals on the punch bag at the Peacock! I wouldn't know, the closest I got was focus mitts at Jiu Jitsu as a thirteen and fourteen-year-old which was the other path I'd considered taking. The energy was such that during lunch the young pros would go to their cars and play the latest tapes they had bought.

I remember laying on the grass watching Ray Wilkins, Teddy Maybank, Ian Britton, Derek Richardson, Gary Stanley and one or two others stand around as Graham Wilkins danced to George McCrae's "Rock your Baby" as it came out of a door speaker on "George's" Mark Two Escort. "George" was Graham's nickname, which I think was their Dad's name. He played for Brentford I believe and they were a football family with Ray, Graham, Steve and Dean. I was still laying on the grass when a mixture of apprentices and young pros played cricket and as I was falling asleep I caught Garry Stanley in the slips who screamed "he's not even playing." Ken gave him "out" as he cracked up laughing. Would you believe we would not have had a lunch if it wasn't for Eddie Heath? We got a salad and tea or squash. The pros had a roll, chocolate biscuits and tea. A bit different to now.

Without a goodbye and not knowing the reasons, apart from speculation that he didn't see eye to eye with Eddie Mac, Dario left. In the meantime, all of Chelsea's sides were competitive and usually victorious from S.E. Counties Divisions one and two to the reserves and ultimately the first team. Eddie Mac had created what Big Mal and Terry Venables were striving to do at Palace, an exciting young side. I dare say the coaches were very happy because the training was always competitive with everyone training at full speed, tempo and with an edge that kept all the players on their toes determined not to be second best. On Fridays we normally reported to the Bridge. After a practice match on Thursday, Friday was usually short and sharp. After a not very sophisticated warm up especially compared to now there was normally a small sided game and some sprints to finish. Apart from the first team squad everyone else was mixed in, apprentices, young pros, pros coming back from injury, so it was a good if at times steep, learning curve. The small sided games became so competitive Ken had to step in and ban them. The day it happened I caused it by tackling Richard Wilson then doing the matador bit, using my body to shield the ball. Out of pure frustration Richard just kicked my legs away. Ken stepped in and until further notice banned small sided games.

As a youth team we had some cracking games and put in some superb performances. Ipswich was always a tight game and without research I'd hazard a guess we came out even with Terry Butcher and Russell Osman holding the fort at the back and Alan Brazil up front. It was always a good test and they were well coached and well organised. I remember Bobby Robson at a youth game that he came to watch before their first team home game. He couldn't stay out of it and he got more and more frustrated with a centre forward they had called Alan Bond. Going by the way he moved I don't think he was James' brother. Bobby Robson screamed at him to "move his fat arse" and called him "a lazy bastard." Not the prim and proper behaviour you saw as an England manager I'll admit but I could feel the passion and a little frustration oozing from his every pore. I was a first year apprentice and on this occasion I was a substitute so I got to hear all the information given from the coaches and Mr Robson himself. As a sub I always made the most of even that situation by trying to watch the game through the coaches' eyes and relate it to what they were saying.

In the return fixture at home Terry Butcher was stretchered off after breaking his cheekbone. He went for a header with Iori Jenkins who was as hard as Portland Stone. Iori had represented Wales in football and rugby and was competent at both and played both with the same intensity. As a loose ball came between the two of them you couldn't envisage Butcher or Iori pulling out and Big Butch got stretcherd off. Orient had good kids but we turned them over. Spurs was always hard especially as Mark Falco started to come through. Portsmouth was a nightmare, up at 6.30am, leave the Bridge at 8 o'clock, stop for a cup of tea, kick off at 11 o'clock then back to the Bridge hoping it didn't coincide with a first team game and loads of duties. That was inevitably a long day especially for a kid, usually fourteen to fifteen hours. Ken got the ball rolling with the cutting back on duties so we could concentrate on football. I personally loved Ken and wanted to play for him and not let him down. It was the same with Eddie Heath, Les Brown, and Malcolm "Lew" Lewis. Dario I was always wary of, he seemed less warm, harder to fathom, not as relaxed as Ken, and more forensic.

The first thing to go thank God was sweeping the terraces. What a filthy mind numbing horrible bastard of a job. Filth, litter, dust, puddles of urine, it was a nightmare. Can you imagine today's academy "stars" sweeping the Shed End after 40,000 against Leeds or Arsenal? Anyway it got phased out thank Christ.

Coaching wise, Ken was I'd say and definitely as I came to know, particularly in 1990 then 1997 when I converted to the UEFA "A" ahead of his time. He could coach by command but as I learned later in '97 he used "question and answer" and "Guided Discovery." He made sure you advanced quickly to autonomous thinking by using the powers of suggestion to help you suss it out yourself. As I've said myths are easily created in football. One of the biggest is a so called productive youth system at West Ham. Latter day it's not just them, but most clubs, who spend fortunes on academies, coaches and scouting without producing home grown players. For me over the decades they haven't produced enough. Latter day everyone can recite the names of Joe Cole, Frank Lampard, Rio Ferdinand, Anton Ferdinand and Michael Carrick but players only came out intermittently before that and not very many since. When I came up against them we spanked them 6-0 and spent the last twenty minutes having a keep ball. The balance of power in turning out kids had shifted to Chelsea and Palace in the 70's, along with Arsenal and Spurs, who particularly in the 1980's were very productive, and West Ham came good again in the 90's. In my humble opinion this is usually down to a combination of three ingredients. Good long term planning at a club (usually accompanied by stable management,) a bit of money spread around and of course quality coaching. These things had a relevance on more than one occasion during my association with football as a player and a coach.

I've always felt it should be normal practice for a club to turn out one or two promising youngsters every season even in the lower divisions. I also feel there is enough talent in the UK and I have questioned on numerous occasions why multi millions are spent on youth policies, coaches, facilities and scouts only to have one, two or more barren seasons without home grown talent in a first team. After all, particularly at Premier League level there never seems to be a shortage of average or slightly above average players from the Far East, the continent of Africa, Europe and Scandinavia. Surely it shouldn't all be about the sale of TV rights and replica shirts to the detriment of the Home Nations National sides. But I suspect it is. Give me the Bundesliga blueprint above ours any day of the week. This is where I was spoiled rotten. As a kid, Ken, Dario, Dave Sexton and later on watching and listening to Eddie Mac set a template that was rarely if ever matched later on in my career and I would do well to keep my mouth shut and stay focused just so I could get a living.

I have to say there were numerous occasions I could have exploded at the embarrassing ineptitude of some coaches and managers I played for. Nice enough people but absolute fraudsters and it was never the same. This is where if no other fucker would do it I have to reach behind and give myself a pat on the back for my exemplary professionalism throughout. Dario and Ken taught me habits that as a defender would stay with me for life. Later on, Ken as our youth manager gave us and taught us the importance of working as units within a team, team strategy, patterns of play and set pieces. This is a sad indictment on the coaches and managers I played under after Ken Shellito but I never experienced any sort of structure again until I was twenty-eight years old. I was training and playing so well and my physicality recognised and appreciated that I was played up front alongside Gary Johnson for what turned out to be my biggest disappointment over two seasons. It was the F.A. Youth Cup against guess who? Crystal Palace. For 65 minutes we ran them ragged. We went 2-0 up and then a combination of things happened all at once. Me and Johnno hit a brick wall of fatigue, the back four was weaker without me and Palace's patience was well rewarded. We lost 2-3. It was at home at our brand new training ground in East Molesey in Surrey. The clubhouse and changing facilities were nicely tiled and the bar and function area beautifully carpeted. There was a viewing balcony where Eddie Mac and Terry Venables watched along with Alan Harris, Venables' sidekick. I heard that in the end Eddie Mac had to walk away as Venners was winding him up so much. Knowing Eddie he would have taken defeat like it was a first team game, he had Chelsea blood running through his veins. Ken was ready to rage but held it in. I dare say he thought we had it won along with the rest of us. I actually could have clinched it. I made a run in between Billy Gilbert and Peter Nicholas as our winger Steve Wallington cut inside from his right wing position. Wally slipped in a reverse pass with his left foot and it sat up as I ran onto it. Bang! I hit it first time on the volley right on the eighteen-yard line, it rose and hit the top of the bar and went over. We took several positional gambles that day but unfortunately none of them paid off. Even on their time off Ray Wilkins and Ray Lewington came to lend their support which I thought was a fantastic gesture. Afterwards we were crestfallen and I looked on a fair bit jealous as Palace went through the rounds. I remember reading a match report Leeds versus Palace in one of the national newspapers. It was either the final or semi- final and both teams' competitive streak spilled over into a mass brawl which came as no surprise. Molesey was a nice change from Mitcham though with better cleaner facilities and far better pitches.

The game against Palace opened my eyes to a few things and it was testament to my all-round ability and not least, physical presence. It was also testament to the coaching at Chelsea. When I became a coach myself I was of the opinion that a well-educated footballer like me, could and should be able to play most positions, could slot in and play in any formation and invariably as any system was being coached and rehearsed, would only need to be told once or a maximum of twice for the sake of revision or a reminder. Since I could remember and was aware of as a kid or as aware that a kid could be, it all added to my football intelligence and understanding of the game. It's tribute to Dave Sexton, Eddie McCreadie, Dario Gradi and Ken Shellito that all I was ever guilty of later was trying to replicate that. Sadly not every player I came across, even ex England Youth Internationals, had the grounding, education or foundations laid that I did.

As a coach or manager there will be many who can confirm that it only ever makes your job harder. In my case it manifested itself in acute frustration that shock, horror, probe, I was perceived as being unable to handle. Unfortunately, selective editing made me look a temperamental idiot or as one lazy, fuckhead journalist put it "a pitiable ogre." Believe me my perceived incompetence pales to insignificance. It was and has been prejudiced bollocks. I also think I'm the victim of a sort of other prejudice against Cockneys. How many Cockneys can you name at any level of the game? It's the most penalised regional accent because we all sound as if we're running a flower stall outside Waterloo Station, even though it's the same game, the same coaching points and the same habits that you are trying to articulate. It could have been worse though. I could have got a team promoted instead of helping one at first avoid relegation and still got shown the exit door. That's what happened to Eddie Mac. He got Chelsea promoted and was then out of a job. The football under Eddie Mac was some of the best ever seen at the Bridge and some of the best I've ever witnessed.

But not everything in the garden was rosy. I don't know who sanctioned the deal but the newly completed East Stand and the ripple effect it caused even made the news. It had run massively over budget and the consequences both little and large, reverberated around the club. Little cutbacks became to me personally very annoying, although I never voiced it, I definitely felt it. Slowly things started to unravel that were to have a massive and undeniable impact on everyone at the football club, not least Ken Shellito.

I felt it a few ways. Some more painful than others. A woman called Millie did the washing of the kit in the very new, modern and expensive laundry room. The problem was, most of the time she didn't and the dirty kit was put straight into the massive dryers. So if the conditions were not too muddy, you got a kit and a towel that stunk of BO. It didn't help that she permanently had a cigarette hanging out of her mouth. I quickly christened her fag ash Millie. She looked and spoke to the apprentices like a pig. After a while and I still to this day don't know how the numbers would dwindle, there was a shortage of jock straps. So coming from the furthest to get to training I went without one on, of all days, a Friday. Anatomically I match up quite nicely, and as a younger man, my temperament and personality matched my anatomy. But it's no good if there are no jock straps to hold it in and protect it all.

I warmed up and played our customary small sided game but dreaded the sprints. My worst fears were confirmed when in pairs it was "on the line, backs to me, turn to your left when you hear a clap" there was a clap, then a second clap as my balls got twisted and squeezed between my thigh. Aargh! The pain! I went in after and was diagnosed by physio. Eddie Franklin who had left Harley Street to come to Chelsea joked that I might not be able to have children. Next up was the news that our expenses would be paid fortnightly. So we as apprentices had to budget and wait to get paid normally after a home game that brought in the prerequisite receipts.

Christine Mathews was like a friend, big sister, mother hen and my favourite Aunt all rolled into one. A top administrator as club secretary she often worked over and above her remit. There was no dough and we had an away game in the Southern Junior Floodlit cup at Derby. We had beaten my old mate Tony Gale's Fulham at home and someone had forgot to draw a line at Watford Gap as I don't see Derby as particularly Southern. Big Tony was running the game but unfortunately got a knock and had to go off. As I tackled him he tweaked something and as I apologised to Galey, Fulham's manager Bobby Campbell ran on the field like a protective Dad and bollocked me. Anyway before, during and after a bastard journey to Derby's ground in the middle of what looked like the set for Coronation street, there was no money for a stop off for tea and toast or any sort of pre-match meal. Not for the last time, with no food or water, never mind some posh isotonic drink we lost 2-0. I remember feeling so weak I was shaking like anyone does when they've had no food or drink. On the way home Chris Mathews had provided some sandwiches and a couple of quiches to eat on the way home. It looked what it was, six hours old and not very appetising. I didn't touch any of it. My Dad had two slices of quiche as I glared at him. You could say so what? But little professional touches that help to create a professional environment started to go missing. Things like clean kit, clean towels, jock straps, pre-match meals or at least water on the coach should be a given. I wasn't particularly worried about the expenses, even then I helped the club by hopping over the barrier and paying 10p at the other end.

At the time it was a friendly club from top to bottom, most of the time anyway. The chairman Brian Mears used to have a run with the lads, normally after having returned from Italy or somewhere in the Caribbean and he seemed totally unconcerned with the finances as the first team were absolutely cooking. I actually stood on the North Bank at Arsenal with Chelsea the better side, as we went out of the League Cup. Ray Wilkins said don't do it again and told me to ask him for a ticket which I thought was nice. I remember a ding dong between David Hay and Malcolm McDonald. Dave wasn't in the mood and left him laying there having treatment for what seemed like ten minutes. That night Arsenal got away with it and I think it was a 2-1 win for the Gunners. A few years earlier I might have been pleased, but not now, I was a Chelsea apprentice.

Steve Finnieston turned who I thought was a poor centre half and rolled the ball across the second six-yard box with Ray Wilkins and Gary Stanley coming in on it. Ray opened his body and as it came across him he side footed it wide with his right foot. That would have made it 2-2. The next day he confessed to being caught in two minds and he added that he might have been better off letting it run for "Stanner's" to bury it. I don't mean to be disparaging but when you see certain players playing especially as a young player yourself with aspirations of making it, sometimes when they perform poorly it reinforces your belief in your own qualities as a player. You automatically think I can do better than that.

A few years earlier watching Arsenal with my father I had thought the same about a player and I came away from the game thinking I must have a chance. Apart from David Hay and maybe Ron Harris who was substitute quite a lot under Eddie Mac, the very young first team had grown together and acquitted themselves magnificently. They were also consistent which is a massive plus for a young side. This was reflected in the superb football and our league position. The vibe throughout the club as you can imagine was awesome. My personal reward for having a good first year was to be selected by Ken for a six a side tournament at a holiday camp on the south coast somewhere. It was a coming together of all youth teams from the South East Counties and one or two from the Midlands including Aston Villa who was managed by an ex-Chelsea player Frank Upton. Even that didn't pass off without incident. I was told by Ken to keep an eye on the lads and make sure there was no trouble. One night Gary Chivers is getting at it with a team from Portsmouth. This was after Chivers had spent the best part of an hour comparing his abdominal muscles with an Arsenal player. They actually took turns punching each other in the stomach as I stood there shaking my head in disbelief. I said "it might be time to call it a night..." then out of nowhere the team representing Portsmouth started to have a go at him, a bit of pushing and shoving, some verbal and singing "Pompey aggro." As I put my arm around "Chivs" to usher him away I got sucker punched. I took one right in the eye. I turned round and launched myself at the dirty bastard that did it. I remember being pulled off him by Russell Kean, Clive Penny and Gary

Chivers. I had gone in as peacemaker and woke up the next morning with a black eye. Ken Shellito just looked at me and shook his head.

I got to meet West Ham coach Ronnie Boyce and got on well with the West Ham lads, particularly Alan Curbishley's younger brother who I think was called Paul. If you have seen the film Quadrophenia Paul has a walk on part and a couple of lines as a Mod. When we got back to the Bridge, Eddie Mac was still around and there was no inkling whatsoever that he was about to part company with Chelsea. We all had to muck in and help repaint the dressing room corridors, clean up, leave everything packed away and tidy for the

summer.

Then all of a sudden after clinching promotion the bottom didn't just fallout of my world but also Chelsea's. It was a situation that on and off the field would take the club almost a decade to recover from. As a player you tend to try and get over things quickly, adapt, look forward and try and do your job and impress the next person in charge. The real reasons for the departure of Eddie McCreadie never filtered down as far as the youth team. All I know is he juggled and used a fairly small squad, blended the majority of youth that was home grown with experience that was also largely home grown and knitted it altogether with some innovative formations, tactics and a brand of football that would not only stand up today but paid homage to the total football previously coached by Dave Sexton as players came through the ranks. Sexton's love for Ajax and their footballing brand in the early 1970's was something that was often spoke about by Dave and Dario who both had unswerving football philosophies and principles. Eddie Mac made it his own, honed it and brought his charisma and personality to it all. I have to say it was a pleasure and privilege to watch. I can recite without research the squad.

Wolves went up as champions, we went up in second place and the other team promoted was Nottingham Forest. At that time I was nothing to do with the first team and it was nice to see the celebrations from a safe distance. It's worth noting that under Brian Clough and with a stable well-structured club, within a few seasons Forest would be first division champions and European Cup winners twice. I suppose with the benefit of hindsight and experience that appetite, determination and will to win is what separates the men from flash young boys. I looked on mute, as quite a few of Eddie Mac's young side, with the odd exception who would always remain the same, walked around thinking they were film stars and God's gift to football. After all who was going to crack the whip? The next eighteen months would prove to be a disaster for the club and a career defining disaster for me. Things were about to get very interesting starting with pre-season back at Molesey.

CHAPTER SIX: CHELSEA 1978- 1979
Uptown Top Ranking

Chelsea had good defending and in particular good overlapping full backs long before other clubs. Other clubs at the time thought "overlapping" was either a style of haircut or something to do with tailoring. One of the best was Ken Shellito who was part of a golden era age group that formed Docherty's Diamonds. The Harris brothers, Ken, Terry Venables, George Graham, Jimmy Greaves, Bobby Tambling et al. But for a career ending injury although now a cruciate ligament injury tends not to be, Ken would have been part of the England set up and I'm sure with his ability, style, intelligence and athleticism he would have been number one in the pecking order for Wembley in July of 1966. A one club man who came through the ranks as a player and had coached at every level in the club Ken Shellito was named manager. "The King Is Dead, Long Live the King" a phrase that was used constantly during my time at Chelsea. It would seem nothing has changed.

I ended up having seven managers in six seasons. If I compared Ken to any number of managers today I'd say he was very much like Arsene Wenger. Studious, calm, erudite, softly spoken and compassionate towards players. He was also very understated, but funny with it, as he regaled us with tales from his playing days during any down time we had when he was my youth coach. The stories and personalities involved just endeared me more to Ken, the club and the big players and big personalities involved.

One story involved Ken and Terry Venables as they both came from the same neck of the woods and as young players they travelled home together. I thought it was funny, clever and typical Venables. They travelled home together on the underground and Terry always got off first. It was an era when homosexuality was more covert. Venners got up from his seat to walk towards the door then turned and came back to Ken then leaned over and kissed him. Then in a loud effeminate voice said "see you same time tomorrow sweetie." Leaving Ken to complete his journey beetroot red and fit to burst with embarrassment.

Anyway with the constant change of managers I was experiencing, having lost Ken as my youth coach I had to re-focus and concentrate on trying to work my way up through the ranks. As a school boy it doesn't affect you, after all nobody looks that far down. As an apprentice, then a professional it can, and with me it did, as different people have different opinions. After promotion and all the other qualities Eddie McCreadie brought to the table he left so we were led to believe, because of a row over a club car. There's no doubt in my mind and I'd have my mortgage on it there was more to the story. The car was supposedly a Jaguar. Incidentally the car driven in the not too distant future by

Martin Spencer the man brought in to sort out the club's finances as we lurched towards administration.

I even remember the concourse in the new East Stand with oil drums chained to the floor so that supporters could drop money in. They were kept in place long after the appeal set up for a great winger and servant of the club Peter Houseman who was killed in a car crash to help his family. Pre-season at Molesey didn't get off to the best of starts for the youth team because we now no longer had our coach and it was Eddie Heath who picked up the pieces and tried his best to prepare us for the coming season. The training was flat and not particularly planned or organised. This wasn't Eddie's fault at all and he did his best to keep it all together, after all he was chief scout not a coach. Ken had been promoted, Dario had long since left, Eddie Mac so I was told, resigned and went to America. For a top club like Chelsea the foresight and planning by the club's hierarchy was nothing short of shambolic. Unfortunately it wasn't to be the last time I found myself in the middle of a shambles due to lack of forward planning and organisation. No excuses either here or further down the line but the ranks were thrown into confusion and disarray and no good to me as a second year apprentice learning the game and desperately wanting to make it as a professional. I thought in the time that he was in charge Ken handled what was quite a bit of turbulence superbly. Looking back at it all, considering what was going on at the time, between Ken and the players they pulled some nice results out of the bag. It was only towards the end of his time as manager that I began to see Ken get stressed which was probably as a consequence of being told he might have to part with one or two of his best players and not being given any of the money to replace them.

In the meantime he was his usual calm, dignified and informative self. It's not the first and it won't be the last time, but some players saw it as I thought a possible weakness and a chance to have a fuckabout and a pose. Maybe, just maybe, the tell-tale signs were starting to show that there were quite a few players who were just not good enough and married to a questionable attitude with players training at less than one hundred per cent are the ingredients that probably led to the poor results towards the end of Ken's tenure. At the start of pre-season Ken had Ron Suart by his side. The seniors returned from their holidays looking resplendent, particularly Graham Wilkins who had returned from Barbados, his blonde hair now white and with a magnificent golden tan. The poor approach to training started almost immediately.

I remember to this day a keep ball where players were showboating, taking the piss and a load of general hooting and hollering. Short of numbers, Ken sent for me and Micky Nutton to inject some urgency which I think was achieved. Basically me and Micky at that time only knew how to train one way and with two young centre backs adding to the numbers putting in their ability and hard work determined not to be mugged off, all of a sudden a few started to take it a bit more seriously. Next up, me and Micky Nutton in some two versus two, plus the goal keeper. The ball served to the eighteen-yard line for the pros who obviously were in pairs. Only Clive Walker and Lee Frost gave us a problem. So in actual fact, two apprentices at the time, me and Nutts were doing ok.

At the time and it wasn't a realisation until later on in my career, I played in a lot of teams with no real potent goal threat. At the time I just thought "job well done" but nobody could find a way past me and Micky. Steve Wicks to everyone's laughter, took to just running at me and smashing me to the ground to create a two versus one on Micky. I got up beetroot red and angry but what can you do? Welcome aboard rookie! The main goal scorer Steven Finnieston had left for £100k to Sheffield United. The reports didn't take long to filter back that it wasn't the same as the Bridge and Steve wasn't happy but he'd gone. Steve was diminutive in stature but had incredible goalscoring ability and fantastic football intelligence. He was to prove a major loss. Before Steve, Teddy Maybank had been sold for the same money to Brighton. Someone must have got a good deal because I could never work out how Steve who was prolific, went for the same dough.

If they could be bothered the experienced pros and the younger ones that Eddie Mac had blooded should have been a nice blend. A midweek night game at the Bridge was always a buzz but as a player, coach or manager you can often get a gut feeling for how things will go. I was only a kid but to me it didn't bode well as I watched the players warm up prior to kick off. I used to love watching all the players' different approaches to how they'd prepare, try it for myself, see if it fits, then either keep it or not bother with it if I thought I couldn't use it. To be truthful I was still maturing but it wasn't until I was twenty five years of age and it was almost too late in my career that I realised that even though you are part of a team you must have your own agenda. At Chelsea I have to go on record and admit some of the bad habits at the club started to rub off on me. I realised too late that I needed to be single minded and have my own agenda with regards to rest, diet, training, strengthening, mental focus, discipline and performing. I looked over to see two players laughing and dancing to "Uptown Top Ranking" by Althea and Donna. I said I don't judge and I don't, but in many ways even though different players have different strengths and the two players concerned would lean more towards the creative side of the game, football is somewhat "Gladiatorial" and you have to be psyched up. Each to their own and all that, it's just that I couldn't see players at Arsenal, Liverpool or Man Utd doing the same. One of our more creative players was Clive Walker who is now a respectable and respected broadcaster. Back then he was a phenomenal talent and I thought a physical phenomenon. Like a few before him he could drink into the early hours of the morning and still run everyone into the ground the next day over any distance. I've seen him sink fifteen pints then the next morning win a seven mile cross country by a distance. When we did a cross country run there was always water and ice cold watermelon at the end of the run. Probably indicative of the team spirit inside the club was the fact that unless you finished in the first third, the water and melon was all gone by the time the rest got over the finishing line. All I know is I wouldn't have fancied being in the trenches with some of them, I'd have probably starved to death. Clive was bright, talented, likeable and a funny guy but had overstepped the mark according to a police caution for flashing his todger at some schoolgirls. I'd hazard a guess he was the worse for wear. The Shed used to sing certain players' names and Clive had "Flasher Walker" reverberating around the ground prior to kick off. "Walks" had pace, trickery and is probably one of the few back then who could still get a living if he was playing now in the present day game.

Walks was very capable and if he was "at it" he was more than capable of being one of Chelsea's match winners. During Ken's tenure I saw him almost single handedly tear Liverpool and Joey Jones in particular apart in the F.A. Cup. It was a great game that I think ended in a 4-2 win for Chelsea. I was on the South Bank standing just in front of the clubhouse Eddie Heath had set up for us as both teams ran out with Joey Jones shaking his fists towards some great Liverpool support. I'm sure Joey would have kicked Walks if he could have got near him.

It was a fantastic team performance with everyone up for it and having a go for Ken. I think everyone was willing him to do well. Ken made a couple of appointments to the backroom staff. Norman Medhurst was still physio, assisted by Reg Byatt but we now had Frank Upton from Aston Villa taking the reserves and Brian Eastick who had done a little bit at QPR was now our Youth Coach. I think Brian didn't know how to handle quite a few of the young lads. If you were unquestioning and subservient you were ok. So you can probably work out that we didn't get on more or less from the off. Stories that I have heard since like managers or youth managers inspecting completed tasks and duties by apprentices with baseball bats make me laugh. The mind set I was in at that time I'd have probably taken the bat and stuck it up his arse. I had a major attitude at times. It didn't help matters with the goings on we had on a tour towards the end of pre-season in Spain.

We were invited to an under eighteen tournament to play a couple of Spanish teams and Inter Milan. I got sent off in the first game so apart from training I was like a spare part. The tour was in Lloret de Mar and the journey was a nightmare. The plane was delayed, then as a consequence our transfer vehicle had left so we had to get a fleet of cabs. I jumped in with my roommates who were going to be Clive Penny and a kid from QPR, Tony Gummer. The driver set off and drove like a lunatic. As we conversed he started having a pop at the English. I dare say some of it might well have been justified but I was fraught, hungry and in need of a shower and a shit, so at first I was happy for him to step on it.

We were on a sort of dual carriageway or motorway. Clive Penny was in the front and pushed himself back in his seat as the Spanish geezer got up to about 110. It was a nice Mercedes and shifting along nicely but the geezer's still nausing me about the English. Gummer was behind Clive and I was behind the driver so I put my hands over the driver's eyes and said "guess who?" We went down to about 40 MPH, and now the driver says "you see! you English!" Gummer had an infectious laugh and he's pissing himself for about half an hour. When we got to the hotel Brian Eastick paid him off and said the driver had complained about me. I said I should be complaining about him, all he did the whole way was generalise and slag off the English. When I told Brian he saw the funny side as I explained I covered his eyes at about 110 mph to calm him down a bit. Brian said "Sitts there's something not right about you..." that set Gummer off again.

We were told to go to bed, be up for breakfast and report for training at ten o'clock before it got too hot. Me, Gary Johnson, Tony Gummer and Clive went for a walk and ended up in a club until about 3am. We had a giggle with the DJ, club owner and promoters. They offered champagne but believe it or not we stuck to fruit juice. When we got back Eastick, Les Brown and Lew were all waiting up for us. Brian could see we never had a drink but gave us a bollocking anyway.

After the first day's training I got a bit of a talking to from Les Brown as well. We'd showered back in the hotel and we were on the balcony, me, Gummer and Clive with the rolled up wet towels playing "Flick the Cock." If you get caught it doesn't half sting. I lost because the other two had a bigger target to aim at but we never took into consideration families around the pool on their holidays. Les told me off but in a nice way, saying how families on their holidays deserved better and that they'd worked hard all year etc. etc. I didn't need telling twice, especially by Les who I had a lot of love and respect for. I took it upon myself to walk up to some Mums and Dads and apologised for the noise. The Dads just laughed and offered me a beer. I said "I'd better not, but I'll buy you one by way of an apology. "

The next day we got ready in training for our first game which was against Inter Milan and what dirty bastards they were. I was given the captaincy and when it kicked off with the tackles and the violence all I tried to do was act as peacemaker. We started tremendously well, the passing and movement was good. Milan couldn't get the ball and the tackles came in. From the first few free kicks particularly in the middle third, Brian had worked on getting your hand on the ball, spotting it, and taking a quick free kick. Not the usual "lump it forward into the box." We played across the back and as the ball went wide to Clive Penny I dropped out for Pen to come out so I could go out the other side and switch the play. The centre forward about 6'3" came across and tackled Pen across the thigh. He was "topped." In the end after treatment he was carried off. Everyone kept their cool. The Italians were bang at it, leaving their foot in, spitting, pulling shirts, hair, and no doubt calling us choice names. Up front Richard Wilson built like a pocket battleship was getting kicked to pieces. He flipped as he was kicked again. We'd got the free kick and I was on my way up into the box and Richard is getting at it with the two centre backs. I waded in to pull them apart and the ref blows his whistle walks straight to me and gives me a red card. Maybe Liverpool winning the European Cup had given them the hump who knows?

I was in the toilet and who walks in as I'm standing there in my kit trying to pee, Liverpool captain Phil Thompson. He had been given extra time off and he's relieving himself as he held a bottle of lager in his other hand. "You the lad who got sent off?" "Yeah" I said. "I thought I'd watch a game when I saw the posters advertising the tournament, the sending off was a bit harsh." I said "I'm glad someone else thinks so, now I miss the rest of the tournament." "Never mind son, keep your chin up." "Cheers Mr Thompson see you later, all the best for the new season." "You too son."

After the game the hardest thing was having to share a coach with the Inter Milan youngsters. They were all sat round one kid with a guitar. I've got to say they looked the part in new trainers and matching tracksuits in their colours. There must have been some piss taking as Pen sat there with his leg up, heavily strapped with an ice pack. Even if there was we couldn't be offended because we never had a clue what they were saying. I ended up training for the week and helping with the kit. Eastick didn't say much to me but Les and Lew tried to keep me involved.

In life, if you have regrets they're either big ones or little ones. One of my big ones is not maintaining a link with Les and Lew.

They were both great old school men. I looked up to Les a lot. He trained at the Peacock, was built like a brick shithouse, he loved his family who he regularly toured with in his VW camper and he had a lovely manner about him. I thought he always looked well- groomed and stood out as a handsome, clean cut old school bloke. Nice suit, braces, double cuff shirt, tightly knotted tie, shiny shoes and not a hair out of place. That was Les Brown. If he spoke to me I listened and in the time I knew him he tried to help me a great deal. I suppose we are all different but Les would be a shining example of it's not what you say, but how you say it. Something I would suffer from later on. Sometimes Les would give me a lift home and put on his eight track tape and he introduced me to a band that I became a fan of "The Mamas and Papas." Brian Eastick told me when on the odd occasion we conversed, that he was a qualified teacher out of Loughborough University had one game for Plymouth reserves as a goalkeeper and took his coaching badges. Some years later maybe I made some of the same mistakes as Brian did when I first encountered him as a kid at Chelsea. I was a testosterone fuelled eighteen-year-old too loud, too aggressive, too acute in my sense of right and wrong, too impetuous and Brian came in all guns blazing handling everything in black and white, determined to impose himself and assert his authority and carve out a coaching career for himself. Coaching wise he was at that time ok, but nowhere near Ken's, Dario's or Eddie Mac's class. I wanted and needed to push on and wrongly I challenged him.

It's not until years later that I appreciated as a coach myself, but before that as a more experienced player under Eastick for a second time at Orient, that you should want to push on but also dedicate time to rehearsing and going over the basics. This is where after a gap of ten years having no contact with Brian when I left Chelsea, I have to give thanks and pay tribute to his professionalism, talent and organisational skills in leading me to the only success I had as a player which was promotion at Orient. In the meantime I was with my first love Chelsea and if I was to give a list of advice to any young players, which I honourably tried to do, and was questioned and ridiculed for by Terry Howard and Gary Bellamy in their observation of a meeting we held, it would be this: If "I" could have my time again I'd be constantly taking a personal inventory. It's something I never did or thought of until I was on my third club. You need to be single minded enough to stay on top of your own game and don't worry or get distracted by anyone or anything else. I made the mistake of thinking I would always be the hare. Remember the story of the hare and the tortoise? Between the ages of fourteen and eighteen, metaphorically speaking I'd been the hare. By not staying on top of things I'd slipped back. I'd also added to that being surly, loud and not training appropriately.

I can categorically state to any player young or old, even if like me you had ability, decent technique, wanted to win and could cope physically, when things in the minus column start to stack up and even outnumber what was in the plus column you are bang in trouble and at a massive club like Chelsea there is only one outcome. Only the super talented players are regularly forgiven their misdemeanours and tolerated and even then it's only up until they can be replaced. I didn't yet know but after briefly flirting with first team football, my own shortcomings and an amalgam of circumstances some beyond my control, would mean that in less than two years I would leave Chelsea and have to start all over again. When we got home, Ken pulled me and said Brian had told him

I'd gone like a bull in a china shop. I told Ken my version and he said "just learn from it." That was Ken. No histrionics, he believed my word and showed a trust. At the time with me and Brian it was either me or my perception of him but everything between us seemed confrontational. Not long after I think Brian more or less washed his hands of me and left me to find my own way.

My relationship with Brian constantly ran hot and cold. The characters around at the time probably didn't help but that's my fault. With experience and hindsight I just wish I could have been as focused and single minded in the first half of my playing career as I turned out to be in the second half. Some of the best of me was at Millwall, the first two years at Gillingham and the six years as a player at Orient. After all the hard work I'd put in for four years at Chelsea I was starting to spoil things and hinder my own progress. I passed my driving test at the youngest age that it's legal to do so and bought a lairy looking car. Believe me having wheels can suddenly make you popular. I started to keep poor hours and get out and about socialising. I've never even really liked the taste of any alcohol. Nevertheless it didn't stop me indulging so that I felt like one of the lads. When you are not what one might call a natural athlete this becomes a problem. Some years later with the benefit of experience I realised I needed to be training and playing at my optimum level every day to give myself a chance. The training to some players became nothing more than an irritation, an interruption to the day's social plans. There was many a time when straight after training players would either go to the races and drink, it was usually Sandown, Kempton or Windsor, golf and drink, lunch and drink or just drink and drink. Some senior pros didn't bother training at all and were almost constantly injured or they would pick their days to train.

My example should have been Ron Harris. Ron was diagnosed with an untreatable arthritic big toe. The options were rest with no guarantee of it getting better, have it lobbed off so no more pain, not ideal for a footballer because he'd have probably kept falling over, or plough through the pain barrier which is exactly what Ron did, training and playing for weeks with an arthritic toe. At the opposite end of the spectrum were players like John Dempsey. Once a magnificent servant and a defender who Ken told me to study. Ken said "Demps" was the cleverest defender in the club. Sometimes though, and I'm not doubting for one minute there was a problem with either his knee, ankles or back, you can elect to be too clever for your own good. Out of the six years I was at Chelsea, although the first two you don't really have any contact with seniors, I hardly saw Demps train. Even the head physio Eddie Franklin used to walk around saying "I can't find anything wrong with him." Demps was usually behind him pulling faces as everyone cracked up. On the odd occasion Demps trained, if he scored in a small sided game he'd scream "ATHENS" in reference to him scrambling home the winner against Real Madrid in the European Cup Winners Cup Final replay as everyone fell about laughing. Demps was one of the funniest men I ever came across in football.

Micky Droy would do his bit and be off to keep an eye on his car front in Clapham and he then ventured into an electrical wholesale business. You can't blame him. The money paid to players at the time was negligible compared to now so Micky was clever enough to start preparing for life outside of football as well as adding to his income. For me Micky was a massive underachiever in footballing terms. Six feet four inches, built like a brick shithouse, heading ability, natural left footer which is a value added premium, good talker, good reader of the game, passed well and no slouch if he could be bothered. He was quick for a big man. If Micky had punched his weight he could have eaten every other England centre half for lunch. I think I'd have gladly sacrificed a testicle to be the same size as him. In the end I had to make the most of what I had to eke a living. Sod's law isn't it when you want something so badly. In the stat filled modern era there's no way any "performance director" would ever be able to come up with a stat to show how much I wanted to make it at Chelsea and how much I loved the game. My mother-in-law has a lovely saying "sometimes the crunchiest biscuits go to those with no teeth."

If I had known then what I know now which would very much be the case on so many things during my career, it would be easy to categorise the 77-78 season as at best, inconsistent. Big results against European Cup winners Liverpool and Nottingham Forest aside the season withered and died. We lost a leader in David Hay with a detached retina that would blight his career at Chelsea. That left two leaders in Ray Wilkins and Ron Harris. With all due respect to everyone else it seemed to me that they were the only two who took on more responsibility than just themselves and their own game. Others I thought did the bare minimum and I think it was reflected in the results. After drawing away to Orient in the F.A Cup 5th round the replay was midweek at Stamford Bridge which we lost. Ironically the venue for one of the semi-finals that year was Stamford Bridge. Orient went out to Arsenal in that semi-final. Not before they made us look ridiculous at the Bridge though. I was on duty that night and being so close to the pitch I heard Micky Droy scream at John Sparrow to "get tight and fuckin' deal with him" as Orient's winger John Chiedozie and their midfield ran the game. It was a shock and an embarrassment to say the least. None more so than when I heard John Sparrow say he couldn't get near him because quite frankly Chiedozie had too much pace for him. Micky Droy said "get tight and kick him" It wasn't going to happen as "Spadge" had long since taken a bollocking off physio Eddie Franklin about his weight gain. Chiedozie went past him again and Micky Droy drew back his left foot. I thought "here it comes, John Chiedozie is gonna land in my lap." Micky stubbed his toe, took up about a metre of turf and did his ankle ligaments so bad he had to limp off with his arm around Norman Medhurst. We struggled with their ability, athleticism and in one or two cases physical presence and pace. Ironically Steve Wicks used to dig out one or two of the youngsters saying "if you don't buck your ideas up, you'll end up at a club like Orient." Now they had put us to the sword, leaving us beaten and embarrassed.

The bare minimum for any side which I often said as a coach, is to be fit, organised, motivated and hard to beat. I thought Ken was let down towards the end of the season. In March and part of April I think we lost something like six and drew four with two wins. In actual fact we only won twelve all season, two of them cup ties. Even with the faces in the side who had won promotion under Eddie Mac the club hovered precariously between mediocrity and relegation. There was a different vibe and it was a poor mix of players who did the minimum, hid, cheated, posed, and in some cases, looked the polar opposite of what they were in the promotion year.

Off the field antics consisted of some of the usual stuff, some of it comical, some deluded, some embarrassing. One player had his training gear segregated, all his body hair shaved and his naughty bits area painted with a chemical that was a funny colour as a result of crabs because he loved a groupie and it would seem he wasn't fussy. Another player's family used to scream down the tunnel "so and so, you've got to leave, you've got to get away, the club's killing your career." So much for sticking together. Kenny Swain was his usual enigmatic self as one day he pulled up alongside the minibus and shouted. "The Sweeney! Pull over." We were in Richmond town centre at the time on our way to the training ground. The younger lads who were first year apprentices said "what the fuck?" As Swainy waved a shotgun in his left hand and a revolver in his right hand at all of us. It was before Dunblane and Hungerford so firearms licences it would seem were easier to come by. Swainy did a bit of shooting and he'd cover the cost of his cartridges by selling the pheasant he bagged to Ron Suart. I loved a bit of pheasant, partridge and wood pigeon in season. My father-in-law to be was a head chef and laid it on for me when I had a meal at Loiza's house. Kenny Swain at Chelsea started life as a midfield player and was then moved wide right midfield. Then he had a few appearances at centre forward before he became a European Cup winning right back for Aston Villa. Up front he had other tricks up his sleeve when I marked him in practice matches. The movement is the same but the coaches word it differently for a forward to get a yard so that he can receive the ball. Some say "one run for the defender, one for you." I've always seen it taught as "threaten the back, then come off the defender sharp and at an angle." As he got no joy off me in training Swainy added a bit by pushing me off with his furthest arm. The best player I ever saw use his arms and upper body over the long association I had with football was I think, the greatest midfield player ever produced on the British Isles, Paul Gascoigne. When you need a yard little things mean a lot.

As I approached eighteen I was pushing up against forwards and reversing the process so I had a yard. If the ball was clipped into space behind I had a yard start. Swainy took to flicking me in the balls with a backhand slap. I remember thinking that it couldn't be right if a mixture of reserves and youth team were keeping clean sheets in practice matches against the first team. Where would the goal threat come from? In the following season or two this would become a self-fulfilling prophecy, especially as an eighteen to nineteen year old having a small run of games in the first team. It's no picnic when any small mistake we made was punished. Even if you and your team mates defended well and competently, I played in a few teams where the best you could hope for was 0-0. I also ended up having the dubious pleasure of coaching and managing one. You absolutely must have a goal threat. Preferably more than one.

As the end of the year approached I was performing well in the youth team but now more often than not I was performing just as comfortably in the reserves. The old football combination was a superb league in which to learn your craft. Frank Upton made me captain. As I hovered between youth team and reserves I adapted well but it unfortunately never passed without incident. I ended up on Arsenal's shit list for a couple of incidents I was involved in. This was probably the first two glowing examples I experienced of the outright hypocrisy in the game. I had been an Arsenal fan as a kid and right up to the present day I could recite the combative, physical, uncompromising defenders who would, to put it politely, make life uncomfortable for opposing forwards and players. The first incident involving me was in a South East Counties game at Molesey where an Arsenal midfielder was growling, snarling and kicking anyone within tackling distance. We had a fifty-fifty challenge and I won the ball cleanly, or so I thought. Brian Eastick declared "What a tackle that was! Well in Sitts!" The ref stopped the game immediately. I think it's relevant to say it wasn't to award a free kick. Alf Fields ran on glaring at me as the Arsenal player was carried off. Years later I was referred to as the Neanderthal man on websites and press articles ran in the North London local press about me ending this particular player's career. For my part all I can say is I always tried to make life uncomfortable for opponents and try and be physically dominant but I would never set out to purposely end anyone's career. You would never have thought I'd seen Bob McNab go over the top on Billy Bonds in the F.A. Cup sixth round at Highbury or the likes of Adams, Bould, Keown, Winterburn, McClintock and Peter Storey in particular never went in hard on anyone to let the opposition know life was going to be uncomfortable for at least ninety minutes. I watched every game on the North

Bank with my Dad as Peter Storey put in tackles that on the street would be GBH. That's what I mean by hypocrisy.

After turning down quite a tidy sum from Palace you could say I then made the next mistake of my career in not furthering my football education but I didn't know any different. Ken was the boss but kept an eye on all the club's teams and he watched as I had two outstanding games in the reserves away to Luton and away to West Ham. David Pleat enquired about buying me and John Lyall offered to take me on loan. I was sitting with Jimmy Clare and I think Micky Nutton as I took my boots off and Ken walked in at Upton Park and asked me outright if I fancied it. I just said no I didn't fancy it, I'm a Chelsea player. Ken just stared at me and said ok and that was it.Only with experience and maturity did I realise it might have helped all concerned and Ken was looking to help my football education. Maybe it was a hint or I looked like I was in a rut, who knows? Looking back, who in their right mind would pass up an opportunity to work with John Lyall?

As the summer approached I was looking forward to watching the 1978 World Cup hoping Scotland as a home nation would do well in Argentina. I had also allowed myself a smile of satisfaction and I was immensely, massively and overwhelmingly proud in the summer of 1978 at the end of my two-year apprenticeship to be offered a full professional contract by Chelsea Football Club. It was now only twelve years since we had won the World Cup and we had already failed to qualify for two so for a couple of weeks I cheered on Scotland as ultimately the home nation Argentina was victorious. Stand out players were in abundance in that World Cup along with some great goals. In the Autumn of 1978 I got tickets this time and watched Spurs versus Chelsea at White Hart Lane and a 2-2 draw as Spurs' new boys coped easily and admirably with the English game. The new players Spurs had managed to bring in were Ricky Villa and Ossie Ardiles part of Argentina's World Cup winning squad. In the close season there wasn't quite as much transfer activity at Chelsea. I distinctly remember one of the main talking points that summer being the first team's new suits. I overheard the discussions amongst the players as they were left to decide their preference of either single breasted or double breasted. I think the casting vote went to Ray Wilkins. A few of his peers said "it'll be double breasted then." Ray and the lads looked resplendent and thoroughly professional as they got off the coach at White Hart Lane in their brand new single breasted suits ready for work.

That summer along with Gary Johnson and Micky Nutton I had been offered a four-year professional contract. I spoke to Micky Droy and he said the club obviously think you three might do something. The good part was being given time to develop. The not so good part was the money. By now legislation had been adjusted and previously as an apprentice I had my second year £16.00 per week underpinned by travelling expenses and £20.00 per week keep money. Despite my Mum's best efforts to take nothing I managed to force her to take £6.00 a week and I kept the other £14.00. It was paid monthly so it was a nice lump sum to look forward to. The problem was my first professional contract being offered was £95.00 a week for four years. A couple of the other lads got offered one year, one or two got offered two years. After tax I wasn't much better off than I'd been as an apprentice. I could have taken the security of four years and with what ended up happening, perhaps I should have. I elected to talk to Ken and Ron Suart and rather sheepishly said I only wanted to sign for two years and if I did well it might give me the opportunity to renegotiate better terms with the club if and when the club might want to re-sign me. After a few days I was called in and I signed for two years taking me up to the end of the 1979-1980 season. I signed, shook hands with Ken and Ron and that was it. I didn't ask but I had a strong feeling that Micky Nutton and Gary Johnson might have been offered better terms which was heavily ironic as they both hardly played either now or in the future. The bottom line is you just worry about your own career. Meanwhile as I travelled home I was totally perplexed and struggled to work out why Ron, Ken and the club had a high enough opinion of me to offer an initial four-year contract but contradicted that by offering shit money that earned barely fifteen to twenty pounds more than my apprentice package after tax. I convinced myself I did the right thing in refusing four years and signing two years hoping to do well enough to get improved terms next time around. Little did I know that the club was about to implode yet again and enemies I'd made lay in wait.

Ken Shellito had a terrible run of results after a period that had initially shown promise. Results were inconsistent bordering on at times disastrous. By now I was a regular in the reserves playing in the football combination and picked by Frank Upton to captain the side. I remember a few occasions when after the game the first team results came in and following any kind of defeat, some of them heavy defeats, players who had a taste of first team football and were now out of the side took the blatant piss out of the first team's result. Frank Upton went ballistic. I watched as he verbally chastised players and rightly said "the first team is everyone's bread and butter and where does that leave you? You're not in the first team, you're in the reserves!" I watched and tried to be influenced by the likes of David Hay. When I was a second year apprentice in the youth team, before Brian Eastick came along, the youth team were taken by Eddie Heath and David Hay as Dave recovered from a detached retina. I've got to say Dave's coaching was invaluable and first class. Now I sat with him in a communal bath as he was on the comeback trail. He regaled me with tips and do's and don'ts. Do you think I listened? Looking back it's fair to say I had only total respect for David Hay, Ron Harris and Ray Wilkins, the rest .....

Off the field I had one or two upsets and one day eerily, uncannily, I was driving home from training and I was no more than two hundred yards from the murder of Conservative Minister for Northern Ireland Airey Nieve. I left the Bridge and always enjoyed the drive along the Embankment on my way home. Strictly speaking not the shortest route but I enjoyed it. I remember braking as I approached the lights at the junction of St Margaret Street and Parliament Square. I was listening to Michael Aspel on Capital Radio, then BOOM! The car shook, the windscreen seemed to ripple, I looked over and thought what the fuck was that? I saw smoke rising up behind the gates where the politicians entered the grounds of the House of Commons. By the time I had driven around the square to go forward towards Westminster Bridge to turn left on to Victoria Embankment the whole area was cordoned off. By the time I turned left onto Queen Victoria slip just before Blackfriars underpass Michael Aspel's programme was interrupted with the news that a bomb had gone off and Airey Nieve was dead. A slightly smaller bomb had gone off in my Mum and Dad's haulage business. My Mum's sister pulled her money out and my Dad was knocked for payment on two big jobs running bulldozers to Iran. His response was ongoing which affected the household because of comings and goings to a shady crew in Staffordshire. I offered to help. My Dad said "leave it to me and your Uncle." We were owed thousands but my Dad didn't want it to interfere with my football career. I know for sure if I had been a bricklayer I'd have gone up north with him and my Uncle and as far as I am concerned even though the man had two sons, we'd have got our money. When my Dad came back with one of their trailers and relayed the story it just made me more angry when I found out they lived in a big detached bungalow in massive grounds with a freehold yard on the side. The anger manifested itself three times in quick succession. On the way to training I was on the train going towards Seven Sisters underground. I got a feeling that someone was staring at me. I turned round and guess who I saw? Standing there in a smart suit, shirt and tie was the pack animal who kicked me in the mouth at school. I followed him down to the subway and tapped him on the shoulder. He turned round and I said "do you remember me?" He went red and said "yeah Chace Boys." I said "I remember when you stuck someone up to fight me and I didn't even know any of you and I'd never crossed you. I remember giving your Joey a clump and you jumped in and kicked me in the mouth with that other wanker GW." He said "ah that was a long time ago..." I said "I remember it like it was yesterday." A couple of men tried to step in and women started screaming because I left him against the wall bleeding on his suit, shirt and tie.

There's no doubt as I look back I had a few demons. I had an acute sense of right and wrong. My Mum and Dad's business was going down the toilet, my Mum was ill, my professional life seemed constantly in turmoil, I was putting up with snide remarks at work and still putting up with petty shit and snide, sarcastic comments from Loiza's extended family. What with my age I confess I was almost permanently angry. We were a self sufficient hard working family that were being shit on, going on the evidence, by pikey plastic gangsters from up north. I came to the conclusion that if my Dad couldn't or wouldn't take drastic action why should I?

Not long after I was on a night out with Jimmy Clare and Micky Nutton. We did some shopping, went for a bite to eat then on to a few drinks in a pub on the Kings Road called The Trafalgar. It's still there to this day with exactly the same layout. As you walk in the bar is directly in front of you and forms a semi-circle. We stood to the right in conversation. On the far side were two old boys having a drink after work. Behind us at a table were four girls sharing a bottle of wine. To our left about ten yards away were five blokes. The rest of the pub was completely empty. After about twenty minutes the five blokes started some play fighting. They came right across the room and smashed into me and Micky. At first I said to Micky and Jim "let's move up." The play fighting carried on and some drinks were thrown. I got barged again and covered in lager. I said to Micky and Jim "if it happens again I'm going to have to say something." Out of the five, two of them came crashing into me and some drink went over the three of us. I turned and said "calm down a bit, the pub's empty, if you want to fuck about go over the other side and stop throwing drink." I got a half hearted apology and a sarcastic remark. I told Micky and Jim to move up a bit more. Like I said there was plenty of room. Lo and behold the wrestling starts again, I've got my back to them and more drink rains down on me. I turned and said "What did I fucking say? if you want to fuck about do it where you were standing." They were all lumps, but a silverback standing in the middle walks towards me and starts with "what's your problem? You want some?" He walked straight onto it and he was out before he hit the floor. He ended up slumped against a juke box. Micky jumped up and I turned to see Jimmy bright red and shaking slightly. I was just hoping they had my back as I stood my ground and asked "anyone else?." I got the reply "no mate, we don't want any trouble…" I said "pick your mate up and fuck off." As I turned round the governor of the pub came up and I apologised. I couldn't believe his reply: "Don't worry about it, they've been making my life a misery all day. The next rounds on me." I just said "if it's all the same to you we'll have these and go." To be truthful I wasn't sure of Micky and Jimmy's capabilities and whether the five would return, maybe even tooled up.

In the meantime, my Dad part exchanged his new lorry, only four years old for another new lorry this time not for cash but

H.P. which turned out to be a mistake. The repercussions in the household and between me and my Dad as I tried to protect my Mum were going from bad to worse and usually out of sight of my brother and sister who were at work and at school. After doing two trips with bulldozers and JCB's to Iran my Dad failed to get most of the money he was owed. He resorted to various threats and brought home and hid this firm's trailer. While he was away on another trip it was snatched back by a finance company so now my Mum and Dad had a debt they had to write off and suffered the double whammy of being in debt themselves to meet the repayments on the new lorry. Even though I hardly had a pot to piss in myself I remember with the permission of my fiancée who later became my wife, and during the first part of married life, bailing my Dad out with cash on at least three separate occasions. I handed the money over as my Mum's eyes filled with tears but felt it was my duty as their eldest son to do what my brother and sister couldn't do and help them.

This was probably one of the main reasons that led to me losing respect for my father. I think in the end as other people selfishly went about their own business I became angrier and angrier because I couldn't refuse giving help particularly to my Mum. In the end for a number of reasons the haulage business failed and apart from the purchase of our council house my Mum's inheritance had been squandered by my Dad. Just as poignant there was nothing to show for the work of three lifetimes, my Mum, my Dad and my Grandad. I had recently sold some assets and had spent three summers working without any rest and scraped together a tidy little sum. It involved working for relatives in fruit and veg wholesale and working on extended families' stalls which took quite a few by surprise as I was seen as some sort of young football starlet with a big future. I also worked for a friend of my future father-in-law where I actually earned good money, more than what I was getting at Chelsea, relaying some pavement and drainage in Green Park and the other side of the fence in the grounds of Clarence House which at the time was the residence of the Queen Mother. I remember every morning meeting at six thirty and by seven forty-five we were presenting police with our security passes to gain access to the grounds of Clarence House. We normally went straight through with an eight am start and a four p.m finish. I sacrificed all the money I had saved to set my Mum and Dad up at an indoor market on the corner of Buckingham Palace Road and Ebury Bridge. Even the thickest of footballers these days, although they are good athletes and it gets them through, earn ten's of thousands a week and don't have to get up and lay new pavement.

For a change and for a little while things were quite lucrative and my Mum was able to set money aside, this didn't last for long though because the owners of the market relocated to Clapham. More trouble was on the horizon because unfortunately you can't legislate for scum. I'd just got home from training and the telephone rang, it was my Dad asking me if I could come and get my Mum. I immediately said "what's wrong?" It turned out that while my Dad went for a break my Mum was mugged for their takings. When I got there I got to meet a lovely Jewish man who owned a shop selling curtains and he had seen it all and had given chase. He was so annoyed that he never caught them he offered to loan my Mum and Dad replenishment of their stock money. I immediately stepped in and said thank you for such a lovely gesture but it won't be necessary. So everyone including myself was back to square one. As a footballer I had plateaued slightly. Too old for the youth team, quite enjoying the reserves and performing comfortably and consistently, but not yet ready for the first team. As the results declined Ken's tenure looked more and more precarious. Things quite plainly were not right on and off the field, but come match day it was a lovely escape to focus solely on the opposition in the reserves, especially playing alongside the likes of Peter Osgood. What a player he was! When I see the sums being paid for players now not fit to lace "Ossie's" boots, it's fair to say I'd be hard pressed to put a price on him. He had everything in my humble opinion.

CHAPTER SEVEN: CHELSEA 1979 - VALENTINE'S DAY 1980

Those were the days

If you listen to the words of each song that is the title of each chapter it probably explains the goings on and the way I was feeling at the time better than I ever could. It might be a word, a line, a verse or the title that I might have used, sometimes sarcastically to draw an analogy. "Those were the days my friend we thought they'd never end..." Trouble is, in football they do, and all too quickly. My acrimonious departure was still some way off and I was to suffer my own Valentine's Day Massacre at the hands of Geoff Hurst and Bobby Gould crafted behind the scenes by Brian Eastick who at the time I was constantly at loggerheads with. I've got no qualms in saying it was all my fault. It was all self inflicted. In the run up to Christmas 1978 Ken Shellito left as manager after about seventeen months in charge. On the plus side, a club legend Peter Osgood returned and I was fortunate enough to be able to train and play with Ossie. The majority of it was in the football combination, but one or two outings in the first team with him was a wakeup call believe me! I don't think you'd be able to put a price on him in his prime. He broke his leg as a youngster but was still a good athlete. Playing with him I was spoiled he said "good service son, keep it coming like that" as we turned Arsenal over at Highbury in the "stiffs" or reserves. "Ping it in" he'd say. He'd control it on the ground, off the ground, right foot, left foot, chest, thigh, he killed it stone dead. How was I spoiled? Well with all due respect to some of the players at some of the clubs I went to, in comparison some of the forwards couldn't trap a medicine ball. This means a clip, a chip or long lofted pass to slow the ball down which in turn slows the attack down. At Chelsea it was always a "ping" with the emphasis always on quick passing and movement. Then for me personally came the culture shock of the third division.

I went out once with Ossie, Clive Walker and Lee Frost once to a club called The Pantiles off the A3. As we went in I paid Walks paid, Frosty paid, Ossie walked in. A bouncer the size of a brick shithouse, no neck, shaved head, grabs Ossie by the arm. I almost shit myself. Ossie looks at the boss of the place and says to the bouncer to "take your hand off son, I've never paid to get in anywhere in my life." The manager told the bouncer to wave him through. Then at the bar I call a round in and he says "I'll have a bottle of Chateau "

"I've only got a week's wages on me!" I said. He starts laughing, puts his arm around me and calls for a short and a mixer. He says "work done, time for fun" Ossie clinks glasses and says "nice to be in your company Mr Sitton" and the night went on from there as he told me tales of some of the goings on with the personalities involved in that great side of the late 60's early 70's. One thing I detected about Ossie, which I'm not sure a lot of other people did, was he could be a very deep, profound man. I asked about the bouncer and Ossie confessed to knowing the manager and that he was teasing the bouncer who looked like he could have carried Walks and Frost under one arm. I said "do us a favour Os, can you tease someone a similar size to me next time?" He just chuckled. A Man Among Men.

I never went to this particular fixture but Micky Nutton came back pissing himself with laughter at Ossie's audacity. There was a few injuries, bodies all over the place, guess where? Old Trafford! Ossie gets the call from the bench to drop back and fill in at centre half. United pile on the pressure, it's in our penalty area, scrambles, melees, it's like a pinball machine, the ball squirms up, Ossie catches it on his instep and as he is closed down by a forward, nutmegs the forward in our eighteen-yard box, runs round him and calmly rolls it forward to a midfield player. I'm sure they nicked a 1-0 away win.

After I'd left and gone to Millwall I met up for a social with Micky, Jimmy Clare and Chris Sulley after a Millwall home game and it was explained to me that Nutts's next brush with Ossie wasn't so enjoyable. It was a second testimonial for Ron Harris. Just to set the scene on a couple of fronts, Ron elected to have Chelsea's first team play Chelsea's Old Boys. The team that Ron captained to a couple of trophies, a League Cup final and a top six finish most years. They met for lunch and spent all day drinking right up until the testimonial kicked off. Guess what? They ridiculed, beat and played Chelsea's current first team off the park. Ossie received a throw in and took offence to Micky Nutton's closing down and pressure from behind. Ossie's arm comes back and his elbow leaves Micky carted off with a broken nose. This in a testimonial! But that old school side liked their territory and the right to play. I remember a game not long after Norman Hunter was declared one of England's hard men and went on to trade punches with Francis Lee in the middle of the pitch. He whacked Ossie from behind in Chelsea vs Leeds at the Bridge and Os just forgot the game and offered Hunter out. It's probably one of the few times anyone would have seen Hunter back down, looking like he was concentrating on the game and not fancying a proper tear up. Ossie had returned from the USA after the glory days at Chelsea and a good time at Southampton, including that famous cup final win over Manchester United. Ossie's return unfortunatley coincided with Ken Shellito's departure.

Ron Suart was caretaker for the second time since I'd been associated with Chelsea. The dominos had started to tumble. Kenny Swain went to Aston Villa, returning only to collect his boots and tell everyone about the car he'd picked out and give an indication of the signing on fee, then Steve Wicks saying he wants to further his career, went to Derby. On the horizon were two more departures Stanley and Wilkins and a strange signing of a goalkeeper who was to become a bit of a cult figure for a couple of years. The club was in a dire and I mean dire financial mess. The so called family silver was being sold off. Although knowing what I know now and it ties in with my instincts at the time, out of the four who left I only thought two were worth keeping anyway. Out of the four, one of the players sold came back and openly bragged that he wouldn't leave unless he got a briefcase full of money from Chelsea as well as a signing on fee from his new club. "I know how it works and I'm going to make the most of it" was what he said.

It gave me a broader indication of the existing cynicism at the club and not a lot of love and respect for a club who had coached, nurtured and given this player his chance. It's funny I thought how supporters automatically assume some players love the club as much as they do. In the end I thought this ordinary, functional, nothing special player was out of order, cashing in on the misery and financial state of the club. In case you haven't sussed it in the thirty- five years since that's football. On the flip side, he was to receive in a briefcase what I was to earn over the following three years. So, that's why look after number one prevails in football and society in general. It left me wondering recently why someone who in his career probably played a third of the games that I did, earned ten times the amount! There has got to be something wrong somewhere. It might have been my poor skills as a negotiator over the next ten or eleven seasons because enough managers saw enough in me to pick me every week. For some it's about the money, for some it's about playing every week. I like to think I put playing first. I remember a conversation with Frank Clark who told me: "You're just like I was Sitts. It means everything to you to just play." I replied, a little sarcastically "Yeah but it would be nice to get paid for it."

Ona personal level Iwas finding reserve teamfootball comfortable to deal with. I think I only had uncomfortable afternoons against what were two extremes. Austin Hayes at Southampton was elusive, perpetual motion with good habits. We later became team mates for a while at Millwall. The other one was Colin Lee an opponent who had everything but failed to really fulfil his potential at either Spurs or Chelsea. Big, strong, powerful, good habits, good first touch, two good feet, a strong threat in the air, we had a right couple of ding dong battles. He looked thoroughly upset at being in Spurs reserves after getting off to a good start there.Years later I came across Colin again when he was number two to Mark McGhee at Reading. Both good football men who know their stuff.

After an amazing playing career and dabble in coaching and management, Chelsea's next manager and my fourth in three years if you count Ron Suart as caretaker was Danny Blanchflower who lasted nine months. He came in hot off the press! He had worked for a while as a newspaper columnist and after his brief stint as Chelsea's manager went back to his column. I actually remember an article I read which he wrote just after leaving Chelsea. It was based on an imaginary board meeting at an imaginary club, akin to the "Mad Hatters Tea party" in Alice in Wonderland. I wonder what gave him the idea? Danny was a playing legend for Spurs, Northern Ireland and early in his career Aston Villa. When he took training he vowed to include the majority of ball work. He said at Aston Villa as a youngster he had experienced the opposite and come Saturday he and his team mates were fit, but didn't recognise each other or the ball. I refuse to speak ill of Danny Blanchflower or Ron Suart who gave me my debut and a small run in the first team. Out of the youth team and reserves who came through together, and married to the fact that more senior defenders had left the club or were injured on a perennial basis, and their only consistency was to consistently underachieve, I was thrown in.

Initially I acquitted myself well. I was nineteen. I weighed twelve stones two pounds and was now a tad over six feet tall. I had been measured and recorded once when I signed apprentice as five feet eleven inches tall. As most people will agree an extra two inches can make a difference. Over time the game has come on leaps and bounds in its protection of youngsters. If they come in and hit the proverbial brick wall physically they are rested, counselled, put back to reserve football, put on special diets, weights programmes, stretching programmes and gradually reintroduced. Back in the day it was "in you go son, sink or swim." I ended up sinking with probably a fifty percent return on good games which at any club, at any level, never mind a club of Chelsea's size, is unacceptable. Yet again off the field goings on didn't help matters either. I was wrung out physically and mentally, as well as hung out to dry as the playing structure around the club went from bad to worse and it was almost every man for himself. I think the term they use now is "thrown under the bus." Supporters didn't care that I was a kid and that I was wearing the shirt. Any mistake that I made was seized upon while experienced players who were just as poor, if not more so, were given a pass. Either that, or one or two used their experience to keep their head down, hide, and be anonymous.

The club was a mess, the finances were a mess, the management and coaching structure was also a mess. It was a cross between a Chinese fire drill, a Marx brothers film and a scene out of The Crazy Gang starring Will Hay. It was almost impossible not to be affected. My debut came at home to Coventry City and I didn't have a clue. I had only reported in plenty of time by accident, out of respect and professional courtesy. I turned up with my fiancée and we headed for the mini youth club headquarters and young player base created on the South Bank by Eddie Heath. As the ground started to fill up with almost a knowing look, Eddie told me to report to the first team dressing room. The side was named and I was a substitute.

Ron Harris was asked to play at centre half and believe it or not struggled to cope as we came in at half time 3-1 down. Coventry's centre forwards were Ferguson and Wallace, both had represented Scotland at full international level. Ferguson was a big, powerful unit. Wallace was the smaller more mobile one. I was brought on for the second half and as we started City rammed the first ball down my throat as a tester. I cushioned it with my head for Ray Wilkins, a ripple of applause from the crowd, good start. It seemed to go at a million miles an hour, a blur. Forty-five minutes was over in no time. I had passed sensibly, won my headers, got in some decent tackles and interceptions and rightly in my opinion delayed, bought time and shepherded Ferguson and Wallace into the channels and towards the corner flag. We had no real firepower and couldn't pull it back and the game ended in a 3-1 home defeat.

Since the departure of Steve Finnieston various forwards had been tried and although one or two were full of running, I've got to say I'd have loved to have played against them. They couldn't score in a brothel. It was an ongoing problem providing no respite. Unfortunately for me I experienced it at every club I played for at one time or another. A dearth of forward talent, no goal threat, pressure brought to bear on an already stressed back four and in the end the best you can hope for is a 0-0 draw. After the game Ron Harris and Ray Wilkins said "well done." Ron went on to add that I would find that I'd have more time on the ball than what I'd been used to in the youth team and reserves and more importantly to try and make use of it. It was Wednesday 21st February and as I took off my boots and banged them out to get rid of the mud from a quagmire of a pitch, I looked around at people senior to me who seemed battered, dejected, almost forlorn, resigned and devoid of any confidence. What became apparent to me that night and blatantly obvious in the following few months was nobody, apart from Ray Wilkins demanded or wanted the ball. I was in the side from the start on Saturday 24th February away to Bolton. We had taken the lead through recent signing Eamon Bannon. Eamon was a welcome antidote to the atmosphere and did his share with Ray in wanting the ball.

Frank Worthington one of a front three that also included Gowling and Whatmore dropped short, got on the half turn and sprayed a ball wide. I got an almighty bollocking off Ray Wilkins "WE SAID GET TIGHT BEFORE THE GAME, SO FUCKING GET TIGHT!"

I felt embarrassed and angry at the ridicule. My answer was to go in on Worthington who spun round saying "you little bastard, you've been in the game five minutes and you fucking KICK ME?" A long diagonal ball from just inside our half was hung up at the far post. The other problem at the club was being surrounded by small goalkeepers. The shout went up as usual "away." I deflected a header for a corner at the far post. BLACK! I was knocked out cold by a thirteen stone Frank Worthington that had channelled all his weight through his elbow that in turn, connected with my temple. I was brought round by Norman Medhurst. I'd been knocked out, but still went back for more. As the game went on certain players were fucking useless, hiding, not up for a battle and Bolton wore us down. Trailing 2-1, two more incidents came about and resulted in Peter Osgood retaliating on my behalf. Two team mates had pulled out of challenges and it was on our right side, a loose ball resulted in a fifty fifty between me and a Bolton midfield player who looked and ran like a chimpanzee. He went over the top on me and I ended up with a gashed shin and ankle. Norman Medhurst covered it up and I just got on with it. We were defending for respectability and Bolton got a corner. I'm at the near post jostling to get in front of Alan Gowling. Ossie appears from nowhere gets in front and I didn't even see it. CRACK! He sploshes Gowling across the nose. "Fuck me Os, what's that about?" Gowling protests with claret pouring down his shirt. "Well someone's got to look after the kids." We lost 2-1. The following Saturday we had Liverpool at Stamford Bridge. Recent European Cup Winners, League Champions, a who's who of current British footballing talent. If they had entered they'd have probably won the British Grand Prix, Wimbledon, the Derby and the Grand National.

A new signing had appeared in the form of Petar Borota a goalkeeper. He cracked me up every day as he turned up for training saying "ooh my head" after getting on the whisky in the hotel where he stayed with Eamon Bannon and a centre forward who made no impact, no progress and was completely out of his depth, Jim Docherty. The other keeper was Bob Iles who was a victim of the disharmony, piss taking and cynicism at the club at that time. After a couple of torrid training sessions and poor performances in the combination Clive Walker and Lee Frost started a trend around the club that had a lot of players saying "call me anything you want, but don't call me Bob Iles." I think he came from non-league and was another one, some of whom had become established with a lot of games, who was out of his depth. Liverpool at home, over forty thousand which can make you run a yard faster and up against Kenny Dalglish and David Johnson. The pitch was cutting up and I remember four or five things from a game that we drew 0-0. Firstly, Petar Borota comes up to me and Micky Nutton and says "today, no goals, no shots, no chances ok?" I said to Petar "of course Pete, you relax, have a whisky and a cigarette." Nutts started laughing. Borota smoked like a chimney by the way and had come out of the Yugoslavian army after his national service. Secondly, as we waited at the dressing room door ready to go into the tunnel, Ray Wilkins spins around and says to me, Nutton and Bannon "watch out for so and so, he's a dirty bastard, if you get a tackle with him he goes over the top."

Not a lot to contend with. A spiteful dirty bastard, a goalkeeper who can't speak English and Kenny Dalglish. Full backs were Dave Stride and Graham Wilkins. Up front I think we had Tommy Langley and Gary Stanley, so I anticipated Hansen and Lawrenson having a cigar and the afternoon off but Tommy was everywhere. Midfield was held together by Ray Wilkins and Ron Harris and I'm not sure, but playing wide were I think, Bannon and Walker. It was a bit of a dour game with the odd highlight. Micky Nutton hit the top of the post from a corner which apart from a rasping shot from Ron Harris was as close as we got to scoring. On the commentary on the Big Match next day Brian Moore gave the credit for Micky's magnificent header to someone else. A ball over the top led to me getting kneed in the head by Borota whose starting position wasn't good enough. I tackled Dalglish, got the ball to safety and a corner for Liverpool and my thanks was to be knocked out again. I think it's fair to say that centre halves do take a bit of a battering. Neil "Razor" Ruddock recently said to me "we're centre halves, to play there you've got to be a bit of a silly bollocks. There's not really any glory." Ron Harris was everywhere. He must have gone home on Friday afternoon and gone straight to bed. He protected Wilkins at right back, he protected me and Micky, he supported Ray Wilkins on the ball and even found time to whack David Johnson up in the air right in front of Liverpool's bench.

I noticed the pseudo hard man Ray had warned us about steered well clear of Ron Harris. On the Big Match next day I laughed at the studio guest who was Alan Harris, Ron's brother. When the programme highlighted Ron's tackle on David Johnson Alan said "what a lot of people don't know is that Ron is short sighted. He probably thought he saw the ball." A Liverpool player interviewed on the same programme made a very relevant point saying if we played like that every week perhaps we wouldn't be near the bottom. He intimated that a team shouldn't raise its game just because they were playing Liverpool. It didn't apply to me. I was a newcomer to the side and I approached training and playing the same every time regardless of the opposition. But I knew exactly what he meant.

One little footnote to the game came on Monday as I rode in the minibus to training with the apprentices and other young pros. It was driven by Norman Medhurst who said "John, I just want to say well done for Saturday, a lot of people thought you'd get roasted and we'd get hammered. You proved a lot of people wrong." I just replied "cheers Norm." I thought it's nice to know team mates and staff have got your back and have faith in you!! Following Saturday away to Norwich City, Fashanu and Reeves up front. Even though we lost again I acquitted myself well. On the day I was one of Chelsea's best players and easily our best defender. Micky Droy out injured again, and not known for expressing his feelings, came in ruffled the back of my hair, put his arm around my shoulders and said "well done Sitts, well done." As Justin Fashanu declared in the bar "I never do any good in the air against you pal, youth team, reserves and now first team!" I tackled, headed and started to feel more comfortable bossing team mates more senior. I even found time to ping a couple of decent cross field balls. In case you haven't noticed, a pattern was forming and would continue with the opposition I came up against. Every centre forward was currently or had been an international centre forward. The common denominator among the teams at the bottom were that none of us had one. Following Wednesday, West Brom away Cyril Regis and Alistair Brown up front. I was faultless until a split second when I wasn't. Ally Brown ran me under the ball, pulled away behind me and nodded in a winner with only a few minutes to go.

Again, the best we could hope for was 0-0 and up until then we looked like we might get it. Confidence throughout was lower than a sunken submarine. I was to enter the slump that left me tarred, scarred and more or less discarded as not good enough... QPR at home. A local derby and we lost 3-1. I remember a quagmire, Dave Clement trying to top me, he went in so high he caught my hip, a mishit clearance that went out of play on the opposite side of the field, tens of thousands letting out a collective groan, being embarrassed, nobody wanting or taking responsibility for the ball and Stan Bowles declaring on camera that it was the worse Chelsea side he'd ever seen. I was part of it, ashamed and embarrassed. The problem in the club was, I got the feeling that not many were.

Home again to Wolves. Front two John Richards and Billy Rafferty. I got bullied by Rafferty and rolled in the penalty area when I got too tight to John Richards and he smashed it in the roof of the net. It was direct from a throw in and I was screaming for someone to screen the front. I never got the protection and compounded it by failing to do my own job. The most humiliating experience was still to come with a 6-0 away defeat to Nottingham Forest who were on the crest of a wave and challenging for European honours. Graham Wilkins got topped in the first couple of minutes by Trevor Francis as Graham clipped a ball forward. I don't think our midfield hardly touched the ball. I'm not sure, but working from memory I think neither did the forwards. Forest had Larry Lloyd and Kenny Burns at the back who on the night could well have indulged in a brandy and a good cigar it was that easy for them. It was nonstop pressure for ninety minutes. Up front were Woodcock and Birtles with Francis on the right and I think Robertson on the left. To add injury to insult as I cleared a ball out of our box late second half, Francis stamped down on my knee. I was in so much pain and after a scan two days later I'd been diagnosed with ligament damage as well as the bruising. To make matters worse, on top of the injury I'd received, as I limped past Brian Clough (holding court in the corridor outside the dressing rooms with reporters,) with a bandaged knee now bigger than my head, Cloughie says, "it was men against boys I'm afraid, men against boys."

Out of emergency, urgency and the need to, I returned to play alongside Micky Droy away to Arsenal just under three weeks later. Micky Nutton was injured again. Later on he seemed to have a short injury prone career. In football and it was something I probably realised too late where my Chelsea career was concerned, it's about looking after yourself. Although I couldn't help noticing that some players almost seemed to take turns in being injured and out for two or three weeks at a time. It was a bank holiday morning kick off. I was allowed to drive straight to Highbury. Micky just walked to the ground from his house on Highbury Hill. I was determined to play despite being hurt in a training game. After seventy-two hours' intensive treatment I had a fitness test on the track around the pitch at Highbury. Added to the squad that day were Gary Chivers and a slightly younger Micky Fillery. They both went on to have a good few games and long runs in Chelsea's first team after I left.

Liam Brady ran the game, David O'Leary was in his pomp as a great, pacy defender reading the game and snuffing out any semblance of danger if we managed to mount a rare attack and me and Micky Droy were like two retreating soldiers under siege in our trench that had been overrun. Liam was picking up the ball everywhere. That led to a disagreement between Ray Wilkins and Micky Droy. I pushed in to try and stop an attack at source. Ray said it was the right thing to do, Micky wanted me to back off. Frank Stapleton who was as cute as they came was one of the centre forwards. Even though his first touch was immaculate, if you brushed up against him he went down like he'd been hit from behind with a pick axe handle winning numerous free kicks. His side kick was Alan Sunderland who was always mobile and busy. The midfield was passed through like a dose of salts and I questioned why I was trying to press the ball and make tackles in front of an under siege back four in areas between us and the midfield that you could have driven a fleet of Sherman tanks through. Micky was proved right, I should have backed off, delayed and bought time. It was another avalanche, we lost 5-2. As a kid I tried to take responsibility for the ball but gave it away too often. In the dressing room after I remember Mike Fillery trying to commiserate, Gary Chivers laughing, Ron and Danny trying to raise spirits and most poignantly of all Ron Harris who hadn't played saying "there's no doubt about it, the whole place is in a rut." I'd driven my Aunt and Mum on my day off to the London Hospital Whitechapel for my Aunt to receive the news from the surgeon that despite her previous operation she was terminally ill. Her husband met us there from a pub in Cambridge Heath Road. My Aunt came down the steps with a look on her face that told me all I needed to know. That she was dying and didn't have long to live. Yet all she did was give Uncle Albert a bollocking for smelling of booze. She said to my Mum she wanted to be with us and spend her last days with the only people she had really known as family and took my sister Kay's bedroom. My Dad, now on the last of my Grandad's money and his business hanging by a thread, took my sister abroad with him. My Aunt passed away less than the time it took my Dad to get to Greece and back in his lorry.

I missed the funeral after a call by Ron Suart to play in a game at Fulham. I can't remember whether it was a testimonial, a charity game or some sort of centenary. I do remember Fulham's centre forward getting at it with Ron Harris. Ron told Chris Guthrie to "fuck off back to your cockles and mussels in Southend. "This is the club Fulham had paid one hundred thousand pounds to for Chris. It didn't matter to Ron that big Chris was a six foot three inch Geordie.

Arsenal again, this time at home. I was part of a more solid looking back four. I played right back up against Graham Rix. The two Mickys, Droy and Nutton had to contend with Stapleton and Malcolm Macdonald. This time it was a more respectable 1-1 draw although it was no good to us and we were already condemned to relegation. The promotion, nurturing and feel good factor under Eddie Mac were a dim and distant memory. Two years plus had lapsed and through poor planning, foresight, players having no leadership, no organisation, no discipline, managers changed like you'd change your socks and underpants, the club being virtually insolvent due to a new stand running over budget, players left to their own devices and the better ones sold off or being injured when they felt like it, had us arrive at this juncture. I was caught in a juxtaposition of being blooded before I was ready, and through personal ambition and desperation for first team football, thrown in at the deep end of a division where my predecessors far more experienced had either struggled or bailed when the going got tough. Unfortunately as football entered an era of honey monsters and flying machines and if you were both you played for Arsenal or Liverpool, I was found wanting.

Football will wait for no man. Barring extreme exceptions a centre half after a run of games against various opponents providing lots of different problems to solve, a fair few mistakes, and being educated on a daily basis in training, does not really mature until his early to mid-twenties. If I had known what was around the corner maybe I'd have elected to sign for four years instead of two. Who knows? Maybe I still wouldn't have been big, quick or physically powerful enough. What I can state for sure is the nineteen-year-old John Sitton was a massive difference from the twenty-one to thirty- one-year-old John Sitton. My time was about to run out at my first love Chelsea Football Club.

Last game of the season it couldn't be any bigger or better, Manchester United away. More injuries or fucking about, who knows? I got reinstated at centre half. I roomed with Ron Harris after lunch and he said if I wanted to, leave the radio or

A Little Knowledge is a Dangerous Thing. A Life in Football - John Sitton

TV on because I couldn't settle down. "I'm used to it at home with my two boys" he said. Out of respect and courtesy I switched them off. We both had a kip and got up for our pre-match meal. Joe Jordan and Jimmy Greenhoff up front. I'm glad I had that sleep. Both superb, both mobile, both immaculate in technique, both hard as nails but old school fair. I played very well, as did a few others. We drew 1-1 but scant consolation with relegation beckoning. Pre-season at Imber Court was almost nonsensical. After a punishing morning session, it was lunch of a couple of cheese rolls and mugs of tea. Petar Borota walked in fully clothed having showered. Ron Suart says "what are you doing?" Petar says "I'm going home, I'm tired."

Ron, with the lads pissing themselves with laughter says "NO! it's pre-season. We train morning and afternoon get your kit on, good lad." "But back home, we only train in the morning." The lads are still cracking up. Ron again insists "get changed again, good lad."

I could have called the chapter "Where have all the young men gone?" Ray Wilkins was shortly off to Manchester United for eight hundred to eight hundred and fifty thousand pounds after much speculation towards the end of the season before. That's what happens when a club is in a downward spiral. Other clubs cherry pick your best players. One less leader, one less good, if not great player. Danny Blanchflower left not long into season 1979-1980. My association with Chelsea began as a schoolboy with Dave Sexton as boss. A well run, well organised club full of good coaches. Ron Suart caretaker, followed by the sensational Eddie McCreadie with the team promoted. Then it all goes tits up over a car! Promotion from youth coach to first team manager for Ken Shellito. The rot starts to set in and sabotage Ken's opportunity as boss. Stadium over budget, club sinking towards administration, no transfer kitty. Players being unprofessional and mistaking humanity and kindness for weakness. What chance did he have? Ron Suart caretaker again. Danny Blanchflower comes in, the pick of the squad sold or want to leave. What's left? A lot of young, immature, not yet ready for action players and older pros on good secure contracts none too fussed about the world around them. Except for one or two who I have mentioned. My second from last outing was to come on as sub at half time away to Newcastle. We were already 2-0 down, both goals scored by Peter Withe who I pulled down just inside our half as he broke away to try and register his hat trick. He was incensed, I was booked and just under forty thousand Geordies wanted to lynch me. Season 1979-1980 was well underway and Danny Blanchflower left in the second week of September, just under two weeks after the 2-0 defeat at Newcastle. I thought that even though pre-season consisted mainly of friendlies and behind closed doors practice matches I personally felt fit and strong. I was approaching twenty years of age and starting to mature.

Chelsea's new manager, my seventh in my six-year association with the club and my fifth in the four seasons since I'd signed apprentice took a different view. Geoff Hurst and his assistant Bobby Gould openly stated that they thought none of the playing staff were fit enough. With now extensive experience in life and football I've come to the conclusion that's what they usually say when they can't think of anything else to do. As a coach even if I did think that I'd be capable of being a bit more subtle and I've always felt fitness can also come as a consequence of ball work at a good tempo rather than just mind numbing running.

I had three more incidents that were the three final nails in the coffin as my career at Chelsea was brought to an end. I had set myself up for failure and was duly obliged by the people in charge as my conduct played straight into their hands. It was the opposite of serendipity, a perfect storm as far as severing my connections with Chelsea Football Club were concerned. I have to go on record and state quite openly, emotionally and categorically that I'd been there boy, youth and young man. I loved the club and along with later on Millwall F.C it had got under my skin. If I had been asked at Chelsea or Millwall, I'd have dressed up in drag and stayed at either club happily for life as the laundry woman. I'd have been kit boy, boot boy, water boy or taken a physio course to have stayed at either. Unfortunately I wouldn't feel the same say at Gillingham or Leyton Orient because I felt betrayed. As you might recognise I felt betrayed twice at Orient. When you read it I'd like you to imagine how you would have felt, or maybe as a professional athlete I was a bit naive getting emotionally attached to any club. I might say the same thing two or three times in that men are easy to manage, they manage themselves. As a reference for coaches or managers it's not the men you need to worry about, it's the boys and young men at your club. A similar situation happened to a kid that I had high hopes for at Orient. As youth coach then first team manager I knew I had to stay on top of, keep an eye on, nurture, coach and work with constantly a lad called Lee Shearer who was a very promising centre half. Due to the revolving door of management the same thing happened to Lee that had happened to me. This is my own self-searching, self-awareness, experienced take on it all, a bit like the rest of the book really. First of all for young players comes confusion. This comes as a consequence if like myself and Lee you have early recognition and a successful promotion to the first team and then discarded. Next comes anger. "Oi what about me? I was doing ok." Then resentment. Resentment of the fact that there's no interaction, explanation, or recognition. Then and definitely in mine and young Lee's case, self-loathing and a don't give a fuck false bravado attitude manifested by hurt pride. The pride by the way that made you a player in the first place. Away to Cardiff reserves I'm completely out the picture and slippery, skinny, muppet cunts who had watched, waited and despite their constant gossip, moaning and bad mouthing of the club and all that was around them, are in the first team frame.

"Report to the Bridge 10am for a football combination game away to Cardiff, have a good breakfast." Nine and a half hours to kick off Eastick says "I've been given twenty quid for tea and a slice of toast each." I give Eastick both barrels, not even water on the coach, just a machine giving out lukewarm piss water coffee, never mind a posh isotonic drink. No lunch, no pre-match meal, the team are as competitive as a sheet of kitchen roll in a hurricane. I say during the inquest of a 1-0 defeat "no fucking wonder, who can leave their house at eight thirty, be expected to eat a big breakfast which nobody does as soon as they get up, spend nine hours in the run up to kick off with no water, no Lucozade, a slice of toast, a mug of tea, and lukewarm pisswater brewed an hour ago (an age old trick of small minded opponents) when we get to Cardiff?"

No doubt it got back as I declared "the bones have been picked clean at the club and who suffers? The youngsters, the future of the club and players trying to get back from injury, it's a fucking joke." Another lesson, this time for players. If you're in a hole stop digging! Or more to the point if there is more in the minus column than there is in the plus column you are in trouble, even more so if you open your mouth. Even if it is justified. Since then, Chelsea supporters have known the era as "the dark days." Newsflash! It wasn't just dark days for supporters.

I was thrown in as left sided centre half against Plymouth Argyle in a home defeat in the League Cup. I invited my Mum, Dad, fiancée and future father-in-law and mother-in-law to the game with the idea of a family meal and drink afterwards. Walking to the car my mother-in-law said "Chelsea were not very good tonight, you didn't play well either." I needed it like a third bollock. I said "I just want to go home." We weren't just beaten, we were well beaten by a lower division side.

Every single player who represented Chelsea Football Club that night was a disgrace. Mind you the preparation was just as disgraceful. The team and the whole club were rudderless. It seemed like every man for himself. As for any sort of togetherness, fighting spirit and the things they derive from like attacking and defensive strategies or set pieces to help us win a game, forget about it.

Plymouth wasn't part two but it didn't help. Part two was more of a combination of things that culminated in me mouthing off again and getting called into the office. First by Brian Eastick, the next and last time before my departure by Geoff Hurst and Bobby Gould. As a young player, still a month or two away from my twentieth birthday I had slipped back and apart from Brian I was never coached. I needed help and the only guy offering me help I was at loggerheads with over doing things properly. A joke again coined by Clive Walker and Lee Frost was an ironic, double meaning piss take. When we went in to get a drink or breakfast or lunch at Imber Court a magnificent facility one of them would say "let's skin the club." How can you when it's already skint? You want morning tea? Buy it. You want breakfast? Buy it. You want lunch in pre-season? You get a cheese roll and a cup of tea or orange squash. Anything else? Buy it. Chelsea had been a successful club but rumours had it that we had left Mitcham because the rent was too high and we were now at a facility owned by the Metropolitian Police.

I started to overdose on the way to training on water and tropical Lucozade. After one of our many forays to Richmond Park for a seven mile run interspersed with "doggies" and "shuttles" Bobby Gould even remarked at lunch one day as he pushed in at the front of the line "you ran well today Sitts." I thought I'd turned a corner although my only communication was to say "yeah, I've had a service and MOT Bob." That training! You'd think a former West Ham player and World Cup winner and hat trick hero could coach standing on his head, with an eye patch on, while playing the mandolin. We were assembled on the track at the Bridge and Geoff said "there are not enough players putting in one hundred per cent during our running, this is how I want you to run. Off you go Bob!" Bobby Gould runs a lap at the pace the manager wants as a demo. He summarises by saying "If Peter Osgood ran like that he might still be at the club." I can recite to this day the training for the last five months I was at the club. Warm up, 1 x 800 metres, 2 x 400 metres, 4 x 200 metres, 4 x box to box, four sets of doggies, nine a side to finish. As Geoff lay on the grass at Imber Court chewing a blade of it, the first team are struggling to cope with third man runs and penetration and numerous chances created by the reserves. Can't condense the play, then drop out to pick off the run? The shout went up "get Brian over to deal with it." Another shout this time from Micky Droy "this is a fucking joke." Phase of play to create space and passing and support in the final third? " Get Brian over." Crossing and finishing? "Get Brian over." etc., etc., etc. If not, it was a seven mile run in Richmond Park. Fucking clueless.

On TalkSport not too long ago, Johnny Vaughan sarcastically remarked, "well I suppose you can do that when you've scored a hat trick in a World Cup final." He also spoke over my right to reply which was or would have been "not when it's your job to coach and improve young players and organise experienced ones to win football matches you can't." I agree wholeheartedly with something Don Howe said years ago. "The best coach in a football club should be the manager or the first team coach." After all, who is everyone's point of reference or go to guy? That's when he was there, because Geoff was quite open about some grief he was having with a pub that he owned in Telford. At this point I'd like to make reference to Roy McDonagh's comments in his book about his time at Chelsea. We can't all be wrong. My take on it is and it's how I approached the job I had for ten months at Leyton Orient, you are not just there to work for a business, particularly in a responsible position in a football club like first team manager. You should look to care for the business, improve the business and grow the business as part of your remit as coach or manager.

Sadly, down the years apart from two or three who one could easily recall it's not the case. Football and football clubs are it has to be said, partly to blame. Maybe short termism and the time given is the enemy. If only directors and supporters could see it. Final nails in the coffin Part Two:

Arsenal reserves at home in the football combination. We start well. Good tempo, defended well when we had to, when we had the ball we were passing Arsenal all over the place and took an early lead. It's 1-0 and contrary to popular belief over the years, like most high achieving football clubs, Arsenal could mix it. They've got the hump, the tackles are flying in, they are trying the age old adage of "earning the right to play." Another way of looking at it would be to get physical, spiteful even, try and physically impose yourself, wear your opposite number down, put in a few challenges, dish out a few bruises. This day they couldn't. We stood up to that as well. You only had to see the self-satisfied, smug look on Brian Eastick's face to confirm it. Jimmy Clare does a flick round Jim Harvey and nutmegs Paul Davis. A third player comes in, whack! Free kick to Chelsea. It's a happy meeting of we are outplaying you, 1-0 up, coping physically and let's get you at it a bit more by taking the piss. Whack! Another free kick. Handbags at ten paces, pushing and shoving, verbal. I stay out of it as usual. I spot the ball, looking to take a quick free kick. There's another scrap, I'm minding my business. Kevin Hales who was a master at a wind up calls Paul Davis a not very complimentary name. Paul thinks I've said it, an Arsenal player, not Paul, spits at me.

Totally selfish and unprofessional I know, but having been spat at I'm ready to go schizo. The half time whistle goes. I don't even listen to Brian at half time and his call for "discipline, retain your shape, keep the passing and movement going, clean sheet" etc. etc. I'm meant to be right back as Arsenal kick off, I'm standing at inside right and I lunge two footed at Paul who rightly never spoke to me for years. As soon as I did it I regretted it was Paul, but the man hadn't been born who can spit at me and get away with it. Paul Davis wasn't the culprit, but anyone would do as retribution and he was the closest. I was totally wrong. Straight red card, Arsenal's bench are trying to get at me, I think one of them was a geezer called Paul Barron. Chelsea's crowd behind the dug outs shout "You fucking leave him alone." Believe it or not it calmed the game down. I was sorry that Paul was out for about eight weeks, I'd seen red and been a nasty bastard. It took years for Paul to even start saying hello again. I'm not condoning what I did, but at the time I wouldn't have given too much of a fuck if it was Muhammad Ali who gobbed at me, I'd have chinned him. The fallout was terrible.

Another comment on radio in the interest of balance is that rarely in football is anyone beyond reproach. Ray Wilkins said he is Chelsea through and through but if he could have played for any other club it would have been Arsenal. "They've always had a touch of class." In this case selective memory loss, which I don't suffer from tells me that every club has had its share of players who have seen the red mist, been physical, even spiteful. The list is endless. Paul himself years later, was banned for I think nine months for punching Glen Cockerill during Glen's Southampton days from the side and behind and breaking Glen's jaw. I saw Viera spit at Neil Ruddock and get sent off. Bob McNab go over the top on Billy Bonds as West Ham beat Arsenal in the cup at Highbury. Don't get me started on Peter Storey! Let's not forget I was an Arsenal fan for years on the North Bank standing with my Dad. I'm only mentioning it because guess what? Arsenal's manager sends a letter according to Gouldy, complaining about my disciplinary problems and my assaults on Arsenal players. Well now you have both sides of the story which Mr Neil and Gouldy never had until I had to try and defend myself in Geoff Hurst's office. The moral of the story is except for Bobby Charlton, Gary Lineker and other gentlemen of the game who haven't been booked or sent off, nobody in football is beyond reproach, hasn't retaliated, seen the red mist or had a hack at someone at some time or another, especially if you have misguided pride, are a competitor, and you came from the walk of life that I came from. Can you not see the hypocrisy?

Part three: the final nail, the final showdown. It's a Friday first team picked and I think there was no reserve team fixture or if there was a few of us were ostracised and left out. For years at least ten to twenty players traipsed down to a pub (recently renamed) called The Black Bull on Fulham Road, about two hundred yards from the main gate at Stamford Bridge, turn left out of the gates and you're there. It was a Friday ritual that after training consisted of cottage pie, chips and beans, a pint of blackcurrant and lemonade and a game of pool or darts. Totally innocent and something to help engender a team spirit that was already at best hanging by a thread. We've had our lunch and are playing doubles in a second game of pool for some or a game of darts for the others who hadn't already gone home. I'm standing next to Chris Sulley, there's Clive Walker, Lee Frost, Jimmy Clare, Micky Nutton, I think Chivers and Fillery were also there. The door to the part of the bar where we all were opens slightly, a head pokes around, it's Bobby Gould. Straight away I hear Sulley gulp. I looked at him and he went beetroot red as Bobby said "what are you lot doing in here?" Me, Chivers and Walks all took turns in explaining that we had done our normal Friday thing of having lunch, a harmless blackcurrant or lime and lemonade and a game of pool before we go home. Besides, we haven't got a game tomorrow. "But what if someone falls ill and cries off? You might be needed" Gouldy says. "You should all be home resting" he adds. "You and you leave NOW! You, you, you and you (pointing at Nutts, Jimmy, Sulley and me) manager's office three o'clock." The door closes, unfortunately after Gouldy got his head out of the way. I look at my watch and declare "it's another hour, we might as well finish the game." I think, conscience clear, not inebriated in any shape or form it's going to be a bollocking and maybe a fine.

I didn't realise the bottom was going to fall out of my world and previous misdemeanours had been used in a totting up process against me, some of which Hurst and Gould could never have known about. That left only one person responsible. Still, I thought let's wait and see what is said. My mind drifted to a few years earlier when Eddie McCreadie had caught nearly half the first team in a pub directly opposite the main gate to Stamford Bridge. Maybank, Stanley, Ray Lewington, et al. Steve Wicks told how Eddie Mac asked "what sort of impression do you think our supporters would get if you lot are all drinking next to the stadium?" He declared it unprofessional and as the young pros shifted nervously awaiting an almighty bollocking from Eddie Mac, he actually said "I could fine you, but I was young once. Has anyone heard the expression don't shit on your own doorstep? Don't let it happen again. Off you go." Fast forward to now, I'm called in after Walker and Frosty come out giggling and Sulley is red with nervousness and embarrassment. "Close the door" says Geoff Hurst. Geoff gets up out of a chair and now they're both standing. Most often players assume it's one good cop, one bad cop. They both went for bad cop. Rat-a-tat-tat. "What were you doing in there? You're too loud, you're a troublemaker, you cause problems, you're the leader and an integral part of a drinking culture at this club and a group of bad professionals." I replied calmly, which in their psyched up pseudo hard case state wound them up even more. "No I'm not. I'm not trying to wriggle out. I'll take my medicine, fine, whatever, but I'm the last one you need to worry about as a drinker. There's far worse than me, two halves of lager and I'm three parts pissed. I can't drink to save my life." Gouldy pipes up "it's not just that, we've been contacted by Terry Neil" "Yeah so what?" I come back at him. Admittedly I was as surly as fuck but I wasn't about to shit myself at the thought of a letter or phone call from Terry Neil to Chelsea's manager and his assistant, currently both trying to play bad cop, but all my life I had walked the line between academia and the street and would have been more intimidated by the fairy cop. "First of all a kid a few years back in the youth team, now (which Eastick had already rightfully bollocked me for) another incident in the reserves and you leave the team a man short, to hang on for a 1-0 win and let your team mates down." Coincidentally more or less word for word what Eastick had said "I agreed with Brian wholeheartedly and apologised. What more do you want?" I then added "do me a favour Bob, yeah you notched a few goals, but I grew up an Arsenal supporter, I saw you play, you've got some front. You ran around and made a career out of being physical, leaving your foot in on defenders, so don't tell me I'm out of order for being physical. Even you did stupid things. I remember a game against Leeds, you ran under the ball, Gary Sprake came and caught it and you did a backwards donkey kick to try and catch him. He chinned you and you held your face like you'd been hit by Joe Frazier. The moral for you and anyone else, is don't give it out if you can't take it."

Hurst's turn to start on me. "You say you're not one of the drinkers at the club. Then you'll tell me who is." "Geoff, I never said I don't like to go out. I go for a social with some of the lads because they're my mates now. I've lost touch with school friends. They're all I've got. But I can't hold liquor, I'm not a heavy drinker. Fuck me, even Gouldy said the other day I was training well, running well, I can't if I'm always pissed." Hurst insists again "If you're not at the middle of it all, you'll tell me who is or suffer the consequences." They both stood with their mouths open as I said "fuck off, no way. Who did you play for in the East End? I'm no grass. You played for West Ham and ask me to be a grass?" It was my turn to stand with my mouth open. "In that case, you have it your way, if you're not going to tell me, from Monday you will report to Stamford Bridge every day and train on your own. You will have no contact with anyone else at the club and you can train on your own until I can get you out. You train every day on your own until you find a new club." I just said "fair enough, anything else?" I then went out and told Jimmy and Micky what was said which I think suited Geoff and Bobby as it set a precedent. Needless to say the PFA was in it's infancy. They wouldn't get away with it now.

I was crestfallen. I'd worked my bollocks off, had some recognition and the reward of captaincy of the reserves and a call up to the first team but through being surly, hot headed, too loud, overly aggressive and outspoken I'd blown it all. My hormones must have been going mental. I got home and my Mum immediately saw something was wrong. She was tidying and making the beds with the radio on, the light programme, whatever that was. As I explained briefly what had happened she cuddles my head as I'm sitting on my bed and starts singing along to what's on the radio "you're a silly little bull, you're a pretty little bull, you're my little bull, so please don't ask me why little bull you just ain't black." Tommy Steele singing "Little White Bull." The bottom's dropped out of my world and I'm laughing as my Mum sings along to the words. "Never mind babe, you'll be alright." I said "what do you mean, how can I be alright?" She said "you have got to show 'em that you can't be beaten. You're not beaten until you're buried and you've always got the option of coming back to haunt them!" I started laughing. " Want a cup of tea?" "Nah Mum, I'm going to have a lie down before I go round Loiza's house." I lay there wondering what was in store for me. As I lay on my bed, the only thing I knew for certain was that Arsenal wouldn't be in for me. Halfway through the following week, Micky Droy turns up at the Bridge to get treatment and train on his own. As we ran together, which is all you can do, Micky just said "the place is a joke. I had to get away from the training."

I took each day as it came and did a programme of weights, body exercises, terracing and interval running and a long aerobic run to finish. Within a week or two I turned a page and moved to Millwall. I had to snap out of any thought of apathy, self-loathing, depression and self-destruction that can sometimes come from a stark realisation that I might not have been good enough and if   I was I'd blown it with my prickly disposition anyway. I'm more at peace with it now as I look back and see what happened to the hard drinkers at the club. Four of them had combined appearances that add up to less than a fifth of my career total. So much for me not having the ability, professionalism and endurance. To help rid Chelsea of its drinking culture, not long after Geoff Hurst went out and bought Roy McDonough from I think, Walsall. At the time Roy was averaging between seventy to eighty pints of beer a week according to his autobiography or I might be wrong and at Chelsea it was only thirty-five pints a week. I'm afraid in a game where there are very few guarantees and more variables than in any other sport, the only certainties are there are people who tell lies, people who tell the truth, people who start trouble and when they get ironed out choose to become a victim, people who are fraudsters and people who should be nowhere near a manager's job especially at a club the size and magnitude of Chelsea.

Looking back the timing with regards to me leaving Chelsea was probably perfect for all concerned. The main reasons on the field I have given. Off the field I was torn between telling the club or keeping it a secret that I was due in court charged with Actual Bodily Harm. Yet again I was picked on and the man who started it ends up becoming or turning himself into the victim. I had returned home from training absolutely shattered after one of our jaunts to Richmond Park. My car had previously been a target for vandals coming out of a local youth club and I was wasting fortunes on constantly getting it resprayed. My Dad built a ramp and created a parking bay in our front garden. When I arrived home the driveway was blocked even though the rest of the street was empty.

My brother's girlfriend was visiting and she informed me it belonged to someone visiting across the road. Actually they were neighbours I was quite friendly with. I knocked on the door and it turned out the car belonged to one of their relatives.

I politely asked if it could be moved so that I could pull on to the drive because I wanted to go to bed. The neighbour's brother-in-law came out and said "I'll move it when I'm ready. Who do you think you are? I can park where I like. I've heard about you footballers..." all the while poking me in the chest, walking towards me which made me walk backwards. I said "it will take you ten seconds, my car keeps getting scratched, I want it off the road. By the way I wouldn't do that if I was you. Stop poking me in the chest." He said "I'll be leaving in an hour, you can pull on your drive then, go away you silly boy, just because you're a footballer ..." Still poking me in the chest, I'm now down in the curb. He then pushes me into the road. I left him laying on the pavement.

After returning from Loiza's house I was arrested that evening. At first I played stupid then the arresting officer shows me pictures as evidence along with a statement from the man and his sister-in-law who he was visiting. The officer said "he's had twenty nine stitches as you can see over both his eyes, nose and mouth." I pled guilty at court, was fined and had to pay the man compensation. As I walked out of court someone jumped out from behind a bush and takes photographs of me as I'm taking my tie off. He jumped into a sports car and sped off. Next day there's a paragraph in one of the tabloids with the headline "Chelsea Star Charged." I was hardly a star. At the time I was a reserve team muppet who'd had enough. Family business skint, Mum dying, Aunt dead, father a useless businessman and gambler, fledgling career all over the place, snide remarks about my woman, snide remarks to me from some of her family and on top of all this a bloke trying to act the tough guy and thinking I was a kid who could be pushed around. Still I bet there's still people who'll tell me that's not how you should handle it. Now I'm older and wiser, who knows? Maybe they're right. Certain people would turn a blind eye to someone insulting their mum, bullying their brother randomly attacking them, have someone presented to them as an opponent, even though you don't know them. Then in a pub, because they are outnumbered, allow pushing, shoving and beer to be showered over them, their mum's house trashed and all manner of bullshit and still not raise a hand. I was different.

CHAPTER EIGHT: MILLWALL VALENTINE'S DAY 1980-SEPT 1981

Little White Bull

I was oblivious to the fact that before I had been ostracised from all of the playing staff and ordered by Hurst to train on my own, I had been watched by a great football man Arthur Rowe who was working with George Petchey at Millwall. There was interest at the time from only two clubs. Dario Gradi who was at Wimbledon working for Ron Noades at the time, was first on the phone. I was told not to report to the Bridge and meet him. I had wasted a season at least and I was now twenty years old. Dario took me to Wimbledon's training ground on the A3 and introduced me to Ron Noades and offered me £120 per week. For the first time I spoke up saying I was saving up to get married, my fiancée was working in a bank, and I need a deposit for a house so I want a signing on fee. I didn't get Dario's attitude. He said Noades was in property and might be able to help or alternatively I should choose my house, he would tell Noades and he'd make a maximum of £3000 available to help as a deposit. I said in reply that with no signing on fee written into my contract I'd have no control over what could be perceived as my own money. Dario asked me to show trust. I said it's not that I don't but what if something happens to you? I then added I'd like the chance to speak to Millwall. I could see that it gave him the right hump and his attitude changed.

Eddie Heath had been sacked by Hurst and even though he was taking Chelsea to a tribunal for constructive dismissal, he resurfaced at Millwall as a scout alongside Arthur Rowe and Bob Pearson. At the time Millwall had just been relegated from the old second division to the third. To me it seemed a no brainer to stay as high as I possibly could now that everything I'd worked for had at best, stagnated. I was contacted by George Petchey and asked to come to the Den, Millwall's ground. I got there, announced myself, and was shown to an office where I met Arthur Rowe, Bob Pearson, George Petchey and received another warm welcome from Eddie Heath. Arthur Rowe told me of a fairly recent game in the football combination away to Southampton and in front of everyone, told me that he'd reported back to George saying that me and Micky Nutton had been so outstanding on the day we'd won the game on our own. We kept them out at one end and I set Micky up for the winning goal at the other. It was nice to feel wanted again. I remembered the goal Arthur was talking about, which was an over hit corner beyond the far post. I headed back across goal right on the six-yard line and Nutts came in and buried a header.

Hurst asked me what was happening and I told him I wanted to join Millwall. He asked,"why not Wimbledon?" Within eight years Wimbledon would go through a few promotions, a couple of relegations, unless my memory is playing tricks, and famously win the F.A. Cup by beating Liverpool. I turned up next day with my boots and was driven to a training ground miles away the other side of Catford. When I got there I thought what the fuck have I done? There were no toilets, no showers, two goals and only one goal had nets. Terry Long a lovely man who was George's number two and first team coach took training. From day one, believe me, I had to get back to being mentally strong because every day was to become a battle. If there was ever any doubt about me being highly self-motivated it was about to be extinguished. Believe me I'd found out the hard way how much I loved and needed football. Because of the facilities or lack of them, the choice of three poor training grounds, the training compared to Chelsea was laughable. Only George Petchey, the lads in the squad and the supporters stopped me from pining for Chelsea and wishing I could turn the clock back as well as sinking into a self-defeating depression over what I'd done and where I'd ended up.

Just after I signed for Millwall I took Loiza to a cinema in Haymarket in London's West End to see the much publicised and greatly anticipated film "Raging Bull," a biopic of Italian American World Middleweight Champion Jake La Motta played by Robert De Niro. It's still to this day one of my top ten all-time favourites. In one of the opening scenes De Niro as Jake says to his brother Joey, played in the film by Joe Pesci "I've got these small hands, I've got hands like a girl." "Yeah so what?" "You know what that means? Don't matter who I fight, how big I get, I ain't never gonna fight Joe Louis." "That's right so what? He's a heavyweight, you're a middleweight." I've got to say I nearly crumbled. I could feel my eyes welling up. It's almost as if I knew how he felt. I suppose the right word would be a feeling of inadequacy because I wouldn't be playing among the "heavyweights" in football's top division. It would need massive luck or something gargantuan and unexpected for me to appear in the first division again. The realisation engulfed me.

It has to be said the things that kept me going were the supporters, the spirit and camaraderie and trying to maintain a foothold to get a living out of the game. It also has to be said that for a while I was a confused, angry, footballer who had gone off the game and the living that I talk of was barely that. I'd hazard a guess I'd have got more as a bricklayer. The training was comical, farcical and not anywhere near what I was used to at Chelsea before Hurst and Gould, but it was a welcome relief from seven mile runs around Richmond Park along with other running that seemed to be all they could think of. "Longy" had us jog around the pitch, then after a few stretches we did a lot of standing around which according to the physiology side of things is counterproductive and Longy played Simple Simon with us. "Do this, do that." At first if he said "do this" we did it, which normally consisted of touching your toes or the top of your head. If he said "do that" and you did it, you served a penance. Then it was opposites. To be blatantly truthful the training was a joke when George wasn't there. Do this meant do that and vice versa. John Jackson then broke off for a bit of work with youth team goalkeeper Peter Gleasure and later on there would be a third with the ascendency of Paul Sansom.

From the back there was Paul Roberts, myself, Barry Kitchener, Mel Blyth, Phil Colcman, Tony Tagg, Paul Robinson, Tony Towner, Dave Mehmet, Tony Kinsella, Dave Martin, John Lyons, John Mitchell, Bobby Shinton on loan from Wrexham, John Seasman, Nicky Chatterton who was our captain, Chris Dibble and one or two youngsters who were making headway. Longy had everyone chipping the ball into him and he bravely caught it knowing it was fifty fifty as to whether it was covered in dog's shit. We then ran towards him as he threw it up for us to volley the ball to try and score. Then it was a small sided game. Only when George was on the training ground did we do any set pieces or a practice match to rehearse any patterns of play. I have to say it was a massive culture shock and the obvious highlight after a tough week was running out to a few thousand fanatical Millwall supporters.

During the week, after a lack lustre Monday with the warm up and session I've spoken of, Tuesday would be another day that goes totally against the grain of modern training methods that consisted of weight training that tends to shorten the muscle, followed by a track session. Unless there was a midweek fixture. Either way we had Wednesday off, did a practice match Thursday then a good session, probably the best of the week on a Friday. Good long warm up, team games, sprints and a small sided game. I chipped the ball into Longy for him to tee me up for a volley and as I did, a shout came across the dog shit park training ground for me to go for my medical.

I passed with flying colours and went to see George in his office. It was time to talk terms. I've got to say that George was one of the nicest guys I ever met in football. He was honest, genuine and had a nice gentle manner about him. For the first time in a long while, I felt relaxed in his company and at ease when I spoke to George. He was gifted in allowing you to express yourself and he was always keen to know and was inquisitive about a player's feelings and welfare. I couldn't believe it when he actually said to me I want you here as part of our future, sign a long contract if you want, take three or four years. In the end he said if you're happy with two years, it's up to you. When he offered the money available I went with two years.

George obviously had a budget and it seems it was all taken up by the players he had previously brought in. A technically good but ageing John Mitchell from Fulham, a good, bustling, goal hungry John Lyons from Wrexham, George's tried and trusted core which was Mel Blyth, John Jackson, Tony Towner and Nicky Chatterton and the rest were Millwall through and through. Barry Kitchener and the young lads who had just won the FA Youth Cup. He offered the same as Wimbledon and expected me to sign. I piped up and told him they had offered a signing on fee. He asked how much and I was totally honest with my answer. He said we'll match that and give it to you in three instalments of one thousand each. He budged when I told him of my wedding plans and agreed a two-year deal, fifteen hundred immediately and fifteen hundred at the start of my second year. I signed, we shook on it and I went straight in the side for my first game away to Hull. What happened to them? My memories of that game were getting a good write up in the newspapers, including one or two nationals, Mel Blyth calling it a day after an innocuous challenge along with some strong verbals from Seasman and Chatts for doing so, eventually losing the game 1-0 and early in the game peeling flat and wide to receive a throw from John Jackson. I was playing right back on the day and as I clipped the ball short into Tiger Towner or one of the forwards I was upended by Hull's left winger. Welcome to the third division! Normally defenders are accused of being overly physical with forwards, I was now in a division where wingers tried to iron out the defenders.

All the way home on the coach all I heard was quite a bit of bitching about one particular player who unless things were absolutely perfect and everything in place, either wouldn't play or would start and if the going got too tough or we were getting beat, would limp off. Considering what George and the couple of player friendly directors had done for them, I couldn't understand the partial lack of spirit. Thankfully the main core of the side and the youth cup winning boys seemed to be together.

Prior to my arrival and it's just a case of bad luck on my part, Mr Martinelli one of the directors tried to help incentivise avoiding relegation the previous season along with one or two other board members by promising two weeks with the wives for all the players in Jamaica. As things became desperate and relegation looked a distinct possibility, Mr Martinelli said the lads could be unlucky and it might be a case of hitting the post or the crossbar instead of a goal to win the game that could be the difference between relegation or maintaining second division status. The two weeks in Jamaica was booked anyway and it would seem that the ultimate relegation and all it entailed was rewarded with a fortnight in the Caribbean. How's my luck? It was a long way from there to a cold wet February in Hull that's for sure.

Things took an immediate turn for the better for me when I played well and scored on my home debut in my Millwall career. It also helped that in one game my commitment was highlighted to go along with my ability. The goal was in a 3-0 home victory against Oxford with the same personnel that would see them go through the divisions, eventually playing their football in the first division and doing well in a cup competition. We got a free kick just in from our left touchline, Nicky Chatterton was on the ball. We gave each other eye contact. I threatened the back of the defender, I got across him and Chatts whipped the ball in head height with pace. I doubled the pace of the ball with some head, neck and shoulders to put it in the top corner. During the next home game, I was played short by I think Dave Mehmet, so it ended up a fifty fifty. I went through my opponent and the ball squirmed out, I got up quickly to go into another fifty fifty. I won that, and the ball went forward taking me into a third successive fifty fifty. I won that, and Chatts picked it up short off me as I recovered for a breather. The Den erupted as if we'd won the European Cup. The fans loved it. I loved it and I loved them for loving it.

At the time I thought just as Micky Droy had predicted, me and Millwall was a match made in heaven. The other way of looking at it would be to say it was a laconic piss take by Micky, as in I wasn't good enough for Chelsea but I was good enough for Millwall. So what? Looking back, the massive, overwhelming differences between the two clubs suited me down to the ground. At Chelsea it was false, fake, plastic, and full of people just looking out for themselves. The spirit was non-existent. There was no togetherness, just players and people who were too paranoid to speak honestly but had no hesitation in chipping away at somebody behind their back. By contrast Millwall was real, full of real people, proper, down to earth, with no agenda. Everyone was in it together and the spirit and camaraderie was the polar opposite to the club I'd left. Given the choice, looking back, I'd have played there for the rest of my career. After all, what was stopping me? I was made to feel welcome by the supporters, my team mates, the manager who was as close as I ever got to someone who was one hundred percent honest with me and as I looked at the playing staff I couldn't help thinking there must be a place for me. I was close in age to the boys who'd won the youth cup and it was a pleasure and a privilege to tap into the experience and play alongside Barry Kitchener, John Jackson, Johnny Lyons and John Mitchell.

The off field spirit was good and I knew I should be getting a game allowing for suspensions. Ability, consistency, form and fitness wouldn't be a problem. Roger Cross who was youth and reserve team coach even complimented me on my improved fitness over the first few weeks and the condition that I returned in for the pre-season of 1980-81. The defenders were what I was obviously looking at and Paul Roberts was the F.A Youth Cup winning captain who played mainly right back. He had got in the side but plateaued like I had at Chelsea. I was brought in to help replenish a back four of two extremes, one young and inexperienced the other towards the end of their careers. Big Kitch was a club legend and still capable as well as being helpful to the youngsters, that left Mel Blyth who missed training or a game with the niggles normally associated with a player his age. I looked around and saw more strings or assets to my bow that certain others didn't have and to put it bluntly one or two others and I knew I was just a better player. There seemed to be plenty of cover but any player will tell you that it's about getting your name on the team sheet then worry about who else is playing after. Another defender who played centre half was Tony Tagg who apparently came from QPR. He was knock kneed, pigeon toed, ran like a baby giraffe and his knees had so many scars they looked like a map of the underground. For some fixtures I actually played alongside him, but I have to say, if he was a horse they'd have shot him.

The training ground situation never, ever improved. It was pot luck when we turned up every day at the Den to get changed. Some days it was dog shit park the other side of Catford, sometimes a windy litter strewn place also covered in pet droppings in Lewisham, sometimes the astroturf in Southwark Park, sometimes the main ground. It was an era when the playing surfaces were little better than some of the training grounds so at least there was a familiarity about it come Saturday. The downside was being the owner of a new car. I went

Charlie Bigtime in relation to my pittance of a wage. At Chelsea I had an Opel Commodore Coupe then after a bit of vandalism and a mechanic who turned out not to be one fucked it up, I sold it a lot cheaper than I'd bought it for. I then put down a deposit on a Renault 18 GTS which at the time was a new model and nice car. I got it on H.P and spent a lot of time hoovering it out to get rid of the mud from the kit and boots of team mates who I'd given a lift to the training ground. It's a long way from the state of the art training grounds now and the concierge service provided for players so they don't have to walk to the car park.

The spirit and banter though was something I looked forward to every day. Tony Towner did the same song every morning as we got changed, "Brass in Pocket" by Chrissie Hynde. Paul Roberts walked in and said "morning Sitts son" or "morning son" to Jacko, Blythy or Kitch all of them almost twice his age, with a Burberry, deerstalker hat and a Sporting Life under his arm. I'd had two lots of aggro away from football, even though I think, I have never instigated or started trouble in my life, so I was nicknamed "Jake" by John Mitchell. I've already mentioned the film of the day was to turn out to be one of my all-time favourites "Raging Bull" a biopic of Jake La Motta, a stubborn Italian Middleweight Boxer with a very questionable code of ethics, a dubious take on being an Alpha male, manhood, an acute sense of right and wrong and his perceived masculinity. "What's up now Jakey?" Mitch would tease me and we had a laugh, or maybe I've just got one of those faces that says I'm angry when I'm not. My Secret Santa present at the 1980 Christmas party was a pair of boxing gloves which raised a laugh and tormented me, but I like to think I took it in good heart. It probably came as a consequence of me having to attend court again on a second charge of Actual Bodily Harm. Yet again I was in the wrong place at the wrong time... home. We had Wednesday off and I promised my Mum whose health was getting worse by the day, that I would take her up the West End for lunch and buy her something nice. I was thinking of as many things as possible to try and raise my mum's spirits, cheer her up and re-energise her in her fight against cancer. I had a new car and I said to her she could choose whatever she wanted. I would treat her out of my signing on fee. I went out to start the car up and there are two youths in my Mum's front garden on their way to college, pelting each other with rotten tomatoes, potatoes and bits of fruit. The pathway and my car were covered. I said "what the fuck is this?" they both started laughing as they walked away. I picked up a potato and launched it and hit one of them in the back of the head. They both turned round and came walking towards me. Here we go. I remember one being about my size and the other being six feet four. The bigger one says "did you throw that?" I replied "It wasn't a fucking poltergeist. Fuck off round your own neighbourhood and throw all this rotten shit there. Look at the fucking state of my car and my Mum's garden." He swings for me, I duck under it and ping him three times splitting his mouth and sending him into my mum's porch. His mate tried to grab me from behind so I turn on him. As I'm throwing punches I felt my hair being pulled. I turned round and it was my Dad pulling me off. He just said "get in the house."

My main concern was that I had upset my Mum. They returned with about twelve mates from Tottenham College. One threw an iron bar at the window splitting the lead above it. The rest were trying to turn my car over. One of them opened the door and started looting it. I go to get out there and my Dad throws me on the armchair like a scolded puppy. He said "stay there, I'm ringing the police..." Within a couple of minutes the Police arrive and after enquiries I'm thrown in the back of the van and carted off to be printed and have mug shots taken. This particular incident was thrown out of court and I was found not guilty. I made a note from a copy of the charge sheet of the bigger one in case there were repercussions. I'm just being honest.

Trouble seemed to follow me and arise out of nowhere and I remember having to jump up and turn it on a bit after a midweek home game against Brentford. Big Kitch was trying to get an extra few quid and prepare for life after football and I had tried to keep in contact with blokes in my age group at Chelsea to maintain what I thought were strong friendships. Over time it seems both me and Kitch turned out to be wrong. Kitch got a lease on The Shard Arms which was on the corner of Old Kent Road and Peckham Park Road. Over time it would be demolished, rebuilt as accommodation, then offices and lastly turning complete circle it was quite recently up for rent once again as a bar. I ended up making all the telephone calls to mates I had left behind at Chelsea and it was rarely if ever reciprocated. I'd been shown the door and the lads left behind tried and ultimately failed to carve out a career there and but for the odd exception anywhere else. On the one occasion my call was returned it seemed as if the writing was on the wall for a few at Chelsea and my invitation to come to Millwall vs Brentford was accepted.

I've got to go on record and state emphatically there are two or three things I've never done in my life. One is, I've never taken liberties, been too loud or disrespected anyone, particularly erring on the side of caution with strangers. Two I've never looked for or started trouble or a fight. Three, despite all you see on the Channel Four documentary, born of my hate for losing and trying to save a club and my job, and despite all the handbags at ten paces you see in football, the verbal, the threats, the pushing and shoving, I never ever got involved. I think it's because I felt it was wasted energy, false aggression and the fact I had nothing to try and prove. Over time and I include any era and any player in any division, I've never felt threatened, intimidated or thought I wouldn't fancy messing with him. Why? because I knew at the time I had too much pedigree and I knew too much for them because of my other training. As a consequence I always stayed out of things. But sometimes when someone takes a liberty or in this particular case when you are chilling out with a drink post-match in the upstairs bar at The Shard that Kitch had decked out exclusively for the players as weakness, you are forced to react. I've still got the knowledge and know how, but I no longer have the exuberance of youth. Back then I had both as a Millwall supporter came and sat next to me as I sipped a beer. Kitch's players bar was full with all the Millwall and Brentford lads mixing, enjoying each other's company and I had invited three mates from Chelsea. "How do you like Millwall?" "Yeah I'm enjoying it, I think I've settled in and I love it here." "Well I'm telling you, we fucking hate Chelsea and you're not welcome here, you're a fucking King's Road Poof" Pretty shocked I just said "what you on about? I'm a professional and I'm a Millwall player now." This guy who shall remain nameless pulls out a flick knife and clicks it open and says "I'll cut ya." Decision time. You either run and try and get as far away as you can or wake up and take the initiative. A few people started to look over as they heard the "cut ya" part and there was a fracas. We wrestled over to the doorway and top of the stairs and I was in pole position to punch, throw or kick him down them as I was pulled away and about ten of my team mates and the company there got between us. It spilled onto the street. Kitch stepped in, asked what happened and told my new sparring partner he was out of order. I said to Kitch "fuck this, I don't need it." I suppose I was lucky. Kitch knew that it would jeopardise his new pub business and if it got back to George there would be a ban on players going there which would also indirectly affect Kitch's custom because it was nice for players to socialise with supporters.

Anyway, where some of my so called ex-team mates at Chelsea are concerned you can only make the effort so many times. Seeing as I was constantly putting myself out and nobody else did, I lost touch with my age group at Chelsea and decided to concentrate on my new friends at Millwall. What a nightmare! My day off after a game, I want a lie in and the telephone rings at eight o'clock in the morning. The guy with the blade rings up to apologise saying, "I'm out of order, you're one of us now, I shouldn't have done it. I apologise." I just said fair enough, apology accepted, forget it, let's move on. Personally I've got to say, despite the adrenaline and getting through it, I didn't fancy making a habit of it, so I was pleased that it was resolved amicably and I became a regular in Kitch's and down the Old Kent Road which at the time with the likes of Jimmy Jones, Jim Davidson and places like the Dun Cow was buzzing. The players there that night were shocked, on my side and didn't have a lot of time for the guy concerned. They just conducted themselves politely in his presence and drew the line there. After all I suppose you never know when you might be socialising and you're standing with your back to him. One of my favourite, straight talking, good guys was Alan "Jock" McKenna, a centre forward from the youth cup winning team. He just said "och, he's a fucking idiot mon." We laughed and sang on the Karaoke together at Kitch's after the next home game. He was a good lad Alan Mac, they all were.

Despite the lack of training ground, George did all in his power to give a comfortable existence to the players. George Petchey was top drawer when it came to player welfare, but some of the diet might not go down too well these days. There was no giant dining room with round tables and crisp white table cloths. The players' lounge at the Den was old, dark, dingy, dusty and full of what looked like old brown pub furniture. I look back and prefer to remember the noise, life and banter rather than the surroundings. Robbo and Chrissy Dibble screaming at the telly as they watched the racing trying to cheer on the horse they'd backed. Chatts having a quiet conversation with his wife. Kitch standing with a cigarette behind his back hoping George wouldn't see him or smell it. Mitch taking the micky. Dave Martin winding up Tony "Tubbs" Isaacs the kit man. Johnny Lyons saying "that's those G and T's sweated out." Dave Mehmet talking out of the side of mouth like a cockney villain cliché. Although all he was saying was "any spare tickets?" rather than planning a bank job. He made me laugh Mehm, but I could see him coming a fortnight away. Jacko taking stick over his Parka as he walked in. Blythy with his acerbic wit or pithy put downs. I loved it. Then for away games, above it all you'd hear Lily the tea lady call over whoever had just ordered one ham roll, one cheese roll or as Robbo would say "gis one of each Lil darlin" to have with a cup of tea before we got on the coach. The coach I might add was the one used supposedly by the England squad. I think the coach company was in the vicinity somewhere so we got it allocated for away games which was nice. I think the only thing it didn't have was a helicopter landing pad. It was George again, making sure we had the best of everything to prepare for games.

With a mixture of youth and some experience the results were at best inconsistent. Chief scout Bob Pearson loved to see as many of the youth cup winning side in the first team which obviously reflected well on him and the club's youth policy. But as I had learned at Chelsea where I had acquitted myself very well and performed very consistently at youth and reserve team level, the jump to first team level was another thing altogether. In the case of the Millwall boys the third division was particularly unforgiving. Never mind the battering Tony Towner received, our other right winger Chris Dibble was kicked all over the place. Tony Kinsella looked and was built like a fourteen-year-old and got battered regularly. John Mitchell was technically proficient and brave but not particularly combative, which left Johnny Lyons as our main physical presence and contributor of goals. In midfield Nicky Chatts was fearless, a good athlete and never got the credit he deserved for his undoubted ability. We could have done with him at Chelsea when I broke into the side because he made life easy for his team mates, always available, always wanting the ball. His short and medium game was comparable to anything I saw or played with at Chelsea and his move from Crystal Palace to Millwall highlights perfectly my take on opinions of coaches and managers and a player's fate. Apart from Ray Wilkins, Ron Harris and David Hay I can't remember a single player apart from maybe one in my age group Jimmy Clare, who came towards me as a centre half demanding the ball. One player in particular who I played with in the reserves and first team and had a lot of games for Chelsea never asked for it once in three years during a competitive match. He played midfield and was not at all creative, wasn't an enforcer, didn't carve out a niche protecting the back four, so what was he? Straight up and down between the penalty boxes, being diligent, competitive, but not particularly dominating and definitely not doing anything creative or extraordinary. Nicky Chatterton could do all of the above but played in the third division for Millwall.

Some of the players at Chelsea in midfield hid, never upset the status quo, placed demands on the club, team mates and hardly on themselves. Just enough to get by and play in a central tranche between the eighteen-yard boxes.

Therefore I saw Nicky Chatts as a breath of fresh air. Although Captain he always canvassed the lads and listened to the experience of Jacko, Kitch, Lyonsy and Mitch. We had some good results and not so good results and I think it was reflective of our youngish side and as the game evolved with the coaching side of it with opposition teams organised and harder to break down and beat, playing off the cuff, freely and organically like they had to win the youth cup was no longer cutting it. Knowing what I'd had at Chelsea under Eddie Mac, Dario, Ken and at the time to a lesser degree Brian Eastick, made it harder for me because Terry Long's "do this do that" and "Simple Simon says" wasn't cutting it either.

Then there was the social side of things which probably shaved a few per cent off performances. The social started post-match in the Jubilee Lounge which as you came out the tunnel was at the top of the stand to the left. I was introduced to it after scoring on my home debut in the 3-0 win over Oxford and some supporters who were ex "Treatment" and "F Troop" Millwall's hard core, said "you're out with us tonight." They took me to a pub in Bermondsey and said "you're not paying for a drink and if anyone looks at you cross eyed or upsets you let us know, no one can touch a hair on your head."

I could just about keep up and read the script. I was going to end up that night either in a police cell or in the gutter because my capacity for drink wasn't as great as some people had thought and the supporters were pumped up from the game. So I gave it an hour then made my excuses and got off back to North of the river where I lived. The post-match drink always started in the Jubilee Lounge and it was a good friendly crowd, as long as you were Millwall. I remember some good wins and some big incidents that year. The fracas in Kitch's pub came after a 3-1 home win over Brentford and to win a London Derby was always nice. We hammered Swindon 6-2 and I did a Gary Mabbutt, who I thought was a well-intentioned, but at times an unlucky defender who had the uncanny knack of closing down an attacker to block a shot, which either clipped his knee, boot or backside and flew in the top corner.

That's what happened to me against Swindon. I chased a half clearance from Taggy to the edge of the box to close down the ball, someone took a touch, had a shot and it clipped my knee and flew in the top corner. The press gave it as an own goal. A 1-1 draw with Sheffield United was just as lively because United brought a lot of away support and a combination of ten thousand Millwall and Sheffield United made as much noise as I'd ever heard at any grounds around the country. The supporters were segregated but Sheffield tried to take over the Ilderton Road end. I remember defending a corner and struggling to concentrate as the fighting continued for virtually the whole ninety minutes.

In the Jubilee Lounge we were still talking about it all and in walks one of the lads, Davey Rann. He was a smart guy, a little smoothy. He's got on a lovely leather jacket, top drawer, big money, and it's ripped to shreds all down one side. I turned to order his drink and as I handed it over, I walked in between four or five of the other lads as he held court. "Dave, what happened? How comes your jacket's like that?" He replied, "the fighting, I was in the middle, they tried to take us at Ilderton Road, my jacket got ripped 'cos I wouldn't back off and I ended up fighting a police dog." Davey might have only been about 5'6" but I thought he was fearless. The home form was decent, but we blew hot and cold on our travels. We eventually finished fourteenth on I think forty-five points. Who knows? Maybe George spoiled us.

On the coach for away games we had an old boy whose name I've forgot. He was a chef and George paid for him to come along and make sure we had what we wanted on the coach to eat. George even allowed card games and after doing my bollocks once, I never played again. One away game one of the lads lost so much money including some that he'd borrowed that as we pulled into our opponents' stadium he was practically crying. Barry Kitchener said with a dud hand, "if you win this pot I'll give you your money back as long as you promise not to play on the way home. "The youngster won it and Kitch gave him his money back which was Big Baz all over. It probably saved a nervous breakdown and a nightmare game. That season ended with quite a long close season and I joined my fiancée and future in-laws for my first visit to Cyprus for three weeks.

We had an apartment in Paralimni just outside the resort of Ayia Napa and Protaras. Back then I thought it was an unspoilt paradise of immaculate beaches, crystal clear seas, great hospitality and exceptionally reasonable prices. Within ten years the same area had become neon city, with clubs, discos, lap dancing clubs, strip joints and the sort of owners and patrons that go with that. The last time I was there I just thought it was a shame it had lost its genuine old world charms. On that holiday I ate and drank to my heart's content, but as soon as I got back to London I started to do some light training. I did some running, stretching, body exercises and weights and returned for pre-season raring to go. In the running I was unlucky enough to be paired with Nicky Chatterton but was complimented by Roger Cross on how strong I looked as I pipped Chatts on some hill runs and a race up some steps in Greenwich Park. As usual, Chrissy Dibble won the cross country by a distance as we finished on the brow of the hill facing Greenwich Naval College.

I'd had a good pre-season. I've never really bigged myself up. Truth be told, I had a magnificent pre-season. I was strong, fit, acquitted myself well in pre-season friendlies and chomping at the bit for the start of the season. Roger Cross ("Crossy") didn't go around handing out praise, but he saw the work I'd put in and gave me few well deserved compliments. I have to go on record and say that the John Sitton from ages twenty-one to thirty-one was a vastly different one to the young captain of the reserves at eighteen and then thrown under the bus in the first team between eighteen and nineteen and out on my arse by the time I was twenty. There I was, making strong, sure, steady progress and circumstances including cheats who didn't want to play for a struggling Chelsea first team, feigned injury, put in a transfer request and left, led to me getting my chance. Although it was well earned, it was also well before my time.

In the end fifty percent efficiency is not good enough in the ruthless world of football, not good enough at a massive club like Chelsea and I spent too long operating at sixty to seventy per cent of my physical and playing capacity. In reality it took a couple of more seasons to get back to what I was capable of and realise any sort of potential and ability. It was an era where some players got away with it, but I couldn't. That is to say you had to be either a six foot three honey monster or rapid quick. I was in between at a tad over six feet tall and not particularly quick. If you had both you played for Liverpool, think Hansen and Lawrenson or another good example would be David O'Leary who kept things simple and defended well. In fifty percent of the games I'd acquitted myself well against centre forwards, every one of them an international at one time or another. But I'm not at all deluded. Fifty percent is unacceptable and I was physically and mentally fatigued and it felt like off the field things, some outside my control, started to interfere.

In the end its opinion and conjecture, but the Chelsea team photograph of a supposed first team squad for season 1979-1980, of that group who I left behind hardly any had a career of any note in any division. Being told what you can't do rather than what you can has a debilitating effect. Not tall enough. Not quick enough. All I can say is I could have done with some help in polishing my strengths and working on my supposed weaknesses, although I have to take massive responsibility for my off field lifestyle, contempt for so called coaches and managers, and aggressive outspoken nature. Funnily enough most managers say they prefer their players to be strong characters. That is until you question them. It broke my heart to leave Chelsea, a first love, a love of my life, supposedly not good enough, someone who didn't fit in, and then be named years later by supporters in Chelsea's worst ever team. Although they don't know the half of it. In a total self-belief sort of way, apart from one or two who fully deserved their places like my old team mate Colin Pates and the likes of Doug Rougvie I can rattle off the names, they roll off the tongue, a list of players who came after me and were lucky enough to be in a side and at a club in the ascendency but I'd have eaten them like jelly babies in my time at Chelsea. Millwall on the other hand had a feel good factor and togetherness about it. And if you are doing ok it's always reassuring to be told by your coach or manager. I'd got my mojo back and as long as I could steer clear of injury, stay match fit and sharp, I would play.

I'd arrived at Millwall dejected, rejected, depressed and confidence lower than a snake's belly. Thanks to training hard to get rid of "reservitis", good team mates and camaraderie, the staff and great supporters who seemed to appreciate me, I felt totally rejuvenated.

This I thought might mean I could work my way back up. Funnily enough, a couple of years later at Gillingham we played Chelsea in one of the cups and it was the only time in the thirty-six years since I've left that I went back to the Bridge. On that occasion then manager John Hollins, or he might have been player coach, remarked to an ex team mate of mine, I swear it's true, that I was the only one in the Gillingham side who had any idea. It was Colin Pates who told me as we had a beer together after the game. It was a nice way of taking the hurt out of an emphatic defeat from a Chelsea team playing in second gear. While I think of it, in that game as I kept getting the ball off Ron Hillyard our goalkeeper, I looked up and saw the same picture I'd seen on the same pitch years before, which was some people hiding and not demanding the ball.

The other things I remember were Keith Peacock starting me in my best and preferred position at centre half, then asking me to push into midfield to help Dick Tydeman, then playing me right back to try and nail Pat Nevin, then getting a semi-bollocking and disapproving look from Peacock after the game as I launched myself at Nevin to make him pass the ball, as he and the left back had a piss take two versus one against me to run the clock down. I replied I had to try and force an error or make him pass inside where we had bodies. The other very good reason for not getting injured at Millwall was the nonexistent medical department and rehab there. There was one ultrasound machine at the main ground and two couches, all manufactured I think in 1897. The ultrasound machine had then been serviced in 1898 and left alone since. On the odd occasion I reported with a knock I had to report with whoever else to the Queen Elizabeth the Second Military Hospital in Woolwich. I have to say, it put things firmly and humbly into perspective. Our "dead legs, bruised shin, or bruised instep or tweaked ankle or knee ligaments" were fuck all compared to seeing a soldier with a leg or arm blown off, or half his body recovering from burns doing his rehab.

Our physio was Sergeant Ricky Adams. Dave Martin, my roommate at Millwall called him "Peanut" because Dave thought he had a head like one. One day at the Den having prearranged it with Ricky, Dave brings in his mate to have treatment on his knee. He introduces me first to his friend and says, "Sitts this is Carlton Leach one of West Ham's ICF." I shook his hand and started laughing at Dave and his audacity. I then said to Carlton, "fuck me, you've got some front, West Ham ICF getting treatment on his knee at the Den!" We all had a laugh, after all, it's only football. Dave Martin and Paul Roberts were both in a similar situation, they played for Millwall but loved and supported West Ham. Carlton asked me who I supported. I just told him my brief life story of starting with Arsenal, playing for Chelsea, liking West Ham and John Lyall asking to take me on loan and now supporting who I worked for. Carlton seemed to love to talk about football. Then it was my turn to get treatment. The season started and apart from getting into the realms of buying my first house and planning my wedding, I didn't have a care in the world as I looked forward to being on my own with my wife Loiza.

Off the field I'd started a small business to pull in some extra money as it seemed evident that I wasn't about to get rich from playing football. I opened a couple of outlets to start retailing Mediterranean foods thirty years before any ethnic food supermarkets were thought of. If we had a Wednesday off I did the bulk of my stock buying then. If we were at home, I did it on a Friday afternoon. I got up on Thursday, Friday and Saturday at six thirty am to set up and paid a friend of the family called Mary to staff it for me. If we had an overnight stay and an away game my Dad helped out. After building it up for a year, a retailer saw how busy I was and made me an offer which was sufficiently generous enough for me to sell. I took a lump sum and moved on.

Things seemed to be going fairly well but there was always an undercurrent with my future wife's family and my Dad's behaviour. Football was an escape. This was reflected in my performances, a renewed appetite for training and matches and a compliment from one of my few footballing heroes. I don't really have heroes, I'd rather try and be one. We had drawn 0-0 at home to Blackpool, their player manager was Alan Ball. It was the first, but wouldn't be the last time I was praised by a pocket battleship redhead with a whisky in his hand.

As I walked into the Jubilee Lounge I looked up as I got to the bar and standing there with a whisky, extending his right hand to shake it was Alan Ball saying "well played son, you were tremendous." To be fair, that night in a war of attrition, I was, as I'd decided to whatever the circumstances, enjoy defending.

During the game I could see occasions where Alan Ball had to actually protect the ball and wait for players in the Blackpool side to catch up and get on the same page. I told him I loved watching him at Arsenal when I was still a kid and I said "I don't care about Hurst's Hat Trick, you were my man of the match in 1966." He asked "do you want one of these?" Pointing at his scotch. I told him I could just about handle a beer, a scotch would knock me out! He said "you've made an old man very happy, you could come to Blackpool, play centre half and be my PR!" I swigged my beer, went to the bar, ordered a double scotch, put it in his hand and said "thanks Mr Ball, have a safe trip back, I'm off out with my mates." "See ya son." I felt ten feet tall and John Jackson said "Sitts, I'll tell George," joking that he'd seen me tapped up.

The vibe was good. I was training and playing well, the social was good and I made some fantastic friends who were fanatical Millwall supporters. Two of them were Ted Lynch and his wife Eve, with their two sons, Tony and Danny. Sometimes if I'd had a social south of the river, Ted and Eve would put me up and I'd sleep there. Other times after a game, I'd send a car to pick up my wife to bring her to us in the Old Kent Road and we'd all be together having a nice time. I was as comfortable in company in an old school boozer having conversation and a sing-song as I was in a club or disco with the boys. Ted and Eve's youngest boy Danny was to be a page boy at my wedding and all these years later, I've seen Tony who like me is a London Cab Driver as we have been out and about looking for work. So, what could possibly go wrong?

One thing was results which were at best inconsistent. We beat local rivals Charlton 2-0 at home and drew 0-0 away. I started at right back at the Valley and one of our centre backs, it would have been Tony Tagg or Mel Blyth, went off injured and I was moved over to centre half against Paul Walsh and Derek Hales. Again I was outstanding and as I came off got a fuss made of me by Bob Pearson with well earned praise. However I didn't like what I was seeing or hearing. As George Petchey struggled with a young squad, no money, no training ground, an increasingly impatient crowd and above all his health, the club seemed to be lurching towards a crisis. George had missed training and the odd game and the first team was taken very briefly on a caretaker basis by Terry Long, assisted by Roger Cross and Bob Pearson. The club was in debt to the tune of £500,000 and the chairman, a Mr Leonard Eppel, was high up in a property company that eventually sold the Den for housing and developed the New Den.

I'd sort of read the script as I'd already lived through diabolical times at Chelsea. What gave me the hump were the politics and self-interest and self-serving people who had revealed themselves. It was another in the long list I'd seen over the years of paranoia, ring fencing and mini empire building, to put oneself before anything else. I won't name any names, but I think I know in no uncertain terms who wanted, tried and thought he could get a stranglehold on the club by bad mouthing George at every available opportunity and particularly after a bad result.

In the meantime the chairman had the coach drop him off at his mansion in Hampstead before considering anything else, including dog tired players after a long away trip. I couldn't help thinking if he was that rich, how come he and the club relied on a nonexistent commercial department and not a lot of gate money from a dwindling crowd and on the face of it, never seemed to put money in? He might have been at loggerheads with George who wanted things done properly. We didn't even have a training ground. We were away to Carlisle and as ever George put the players first. He said to cut down on travelling time we'll go up by train, have lunch, get some sleep in the hotel, play the game, do the business, have a night out, stay overnight, breakfast, then home on the train the next day. At Carlisle we actually played really well, took the lead I think through Nicky Chatterton, but a couple of mistakes and no breaks meant a 2-1 defeat. George was quite benevolent, praising and philosophical afterwards. I looked around at one or two who I thought took the piss out of the supporters, the club, their team mates and above all George's respect, decency, humility and attention to detail and concern for player welfare. It's funny how kindness is mistaken for weakness.

Believe me George could have a temper but it rarely surfaced. I felt like I wanted to protect him for the faith he'd put in me. I refrained from handling it the only way I knew how at the time. Try first with words, like Nicky Chatts ably did, but I knew if I got a load of bollocks aimed back at me it might have escalated. So I did what everyone else did, put £5 in the players' whip round and went out after the game. There was only one player who didn't put in the whip but it didn't stop him ordering drinks at our expense. It got messy.

There was a basement club under the hotel and full use was made of it. At breakfast Lenny Eppel says "George are the lads always that noisy on an away trip?" Eppel was on the same floor as the players, but George asked "why Chairman was there a problem?" "I hardly slept." "I'm sorry Mr Chairman, I never heard a thing, it couldn't have been our lads." Right then I knew and I was only twenty-one, there's a good chance George is a dead man walking. How's my luck? I turned up to the Den with the lads to be told George was moving "upstairs" although he eventually left altogether and Longy would be caretaker manager.

Then not much later on, someone appeared from nowhere. To be more specific, Tampa in Florida USA, where he had played for I think Tampa Bay Rowdies among others. His relationship with the English game was to have played for

Luton and this is where he knew Lenny Eppel from. He then played in Belgium when Belgium was more famous for chocolate and flavoured beers than it was for football or producing players. He knew fuck all about English football, couldn't coach, spoke in a mock American accent saying "Oh Man!" every ten seconds, had a big nose and eyebrows that looked like two caterpillars mating. I said to the lads, he looked like Virgil Tracy on Thunderbirds.

His name was Peter Anderson. My timing couldn't have been worse because due to the totting up procedure at the time, I was up before the F.A. disciplinary committee at Lancaster Gate to be heard and of course suspended. It was an occupational hazard to try and be a good defender, want to play for Millwall supporters, put in tackles and sometimes getting booked. The winds of change were at first more of a gentle breeze as a man by the name of Alan Thorne was seen more and more around the club. Some of the debts were paid off by him and our Christmas function was held at one of his properties on the A2 called the Beaverbrook Club which externally had its own greyhound track for training and trials. I wanted to be part of it all and played accordingly. But yet again I was in between the old guard of Jacko, Blythy, Kitch, Chatts, Mitch and Lyonsy and the majority of a squad made up of Millwall's youth team. I feel strongly that a behind the scenes power struggle, paranoia on the part of one person involved and then speaking out against me, led to Peter Anderson saying to me "I'm looking to change things around."

Talking of Thunderbirds, Peter Anderson might as well have been Sylvia Anderson because he didn't have a clue in either what he was looking at or how to run things and I thought I had more to me and more in my locker than some of the defenders in the youth cup winning side. Behind the scenes for the sake of self-promotion and justifying an existence, certain people would always endorse them over me, an outsider, better player, better coached from a bigger club. I was coming back when it all came to an end. I was in for extra training and to play one hour of a reserve game. The side was already picked, it was in the afternoon before a first team game and the side was being taken by Roger Cross. Crossy knew I hated being out of the side but then he said to me "do well today, you can help yourself, someone's coming to see you." I said "what? I want to fight for a place. " Anderson had given me false hope at the F.A. saying in front of the disciplinary committee my conduct, training and approach had been exemplary but it seems his mind was made up. Barry Kitchener was to receive a telephone call at his pub asking him to report urgently to the ground to play centre half where I was told I was already playing. I was moved to right back at the behest of Ted Buxton who was back from America, knew Anderson, knew me, knew Millwall, and knew my next manager Keith Peacock who'd worked with Ted under Gordon Jago in America.

I played well, never put a foot wrong and never looked like I'd been away on suspension. Anderson told me to report for the first team game to talk to Keith Peacock ex Charlton winger, now manager at Gillingham. Anderson then said "he has asked what money you're on, I think I told him £150 per week." Adding sarcastically, "if you don't fancy it stay here, you never know Manchester

United might call for you." I'd hazard a guess there has been a seismic shift to how managers suck up to players these days. I just stared, dumbstruck, but thought, "you horrible sarcastic cunt." I wanted to lay him spark out. I had done nothing whatsoever to disrespect him, trained hard, played hard and I was to be eventually sacrificed for lesser players and an overweight northerner who openly bragged about what he'd received for coming down south. A player who got more than three times my salary and ten times my signing on fee. I know it's over simplistic but I often questioned throughout my career when I found out a player was earning a small fortune whether they were three times, five times, or in this case ten times the player I was. Fucking No Chance. It would seem he only had a bigger slice of luck, a bigger head and a bigger waist. Still if that's what Anderson wanted I'd have to pack my boots again.

That night I spoke to Keith Peacock who had on first impressions an easy going nice manner about him. It didn't hurt that he massaged my ego with his favourable opinions on how I'd played and the good reports he'd received from Ted Buxton. He offered me one hundred and eighty pounds per week. Anderson had told him I was on one hundred and fifty pounds but I had signed for George for two years for one hundred and twenty pounds per week, so Keith thought he'd offered me a thirty pounds per week rise when in actual fact it was a sixty pounds per week rise. I said I wanted travelling expenses, we agreed on the five pound per day in petrol, I'd need to get to Gillingham Football Club from my home in North London on production of petrol receipts. Maybe it was my upbringing but I was made to feel greedy and awkward.

I then asked for a signing on fee. I was offered two thousand pounds in four payments of five hundred. Little did I know at the time that Keith's ex-team mates at Charlton got three times that amount when he signed them. This along with what he ended up doing to me only added to my eventual resentment. We shook hands and having called my Dad to bring my fiancée to the game I went back out and sat with them for the second half. It didn't help that the team seemed to be playing ok. I started filling up as I turned to my Mrs and saw her crying. We both got emotional. I was absolutely choked that I was leaving Millwall just as I had been when I'd left Chelsea after six years there. I had been at Millwall for approximately eighteen months and it had got well and truly under my skin. Loiza cried and we spoke of the friends on and off the field we were about to leave behind. I stared ahead and thought about some good times, good games, good people, good supporters and as a soon to be married man, I had to jump quickly to how I needed to take care of the future. As my mind wandered to what the immediate future held, Millwall supporters started roaring and singing. I was gutted, totally devastated that I was leaving supporters who I'd have sweated blood for. Any player who couldn't play when he ran out in front of these people, quite frankly shouldn't be playing.

It has to be said though for a long time I really was like some sort of love sick teenager struggling to let go. At every opportunity I went back to the Den to watch a game, have a drink after and sometimes a fully-fledged social. One night the company was awesome. I went to a club in Deptford, owned, or part owned by a group of brothers called Heywood. There was me, Paul Roberts, Dave Mehmet, Sam Allardyce, Dave Martin and Tony "Tubbs" Isaacs who was kit man. It was a good night and I only broke off because I had to get back north of the river. The thing that always struck me around those boys, the supporters and people that came into our company was the humour. I carried on going to Kitch's pub for quite a long time after I left for Gillingham.

The characters were funny, quick witted and let's say resourceful. Full of grafters who loved to turn a pound note. You could do your shopping with them. Stereos, TV's, Ghetto Blasters, shoes, suits, shirts, you name it, someone always had a parcel. One of the guys there turned up on the front pages of a well-known Sunday paper. As I read the article I called out to my Mrs. "Here, do you remember him?" He was on the run in Spain and remarked that the only thing he missed about London was "Millwall on a Saturday." He drank with everyone in the Jubilee Lounge and Kitch's pub and now he was trying to avoid extradition after being a suspect in one of the big robberies of that era. I've got to go on record and say that even though there were some right herberts, villains, career criminals and plenty who could have a proper tear up, these guys were good company around the players and polite and respectful to my fiancée. I can honestly say, I don't even think I heard any of them swear. They seemed very particular about how they behaved around women.

Slowly but surely even though my wedding was a year or more in the planning, things were coming together and taking shape. We bought our first house just after I moved to Gillingham nine months before the wedding. It was a three-bedroom end of terrace with front, side and rear garden and cost twenty-seven thousand pounds. We'd saved seven thousand for the deposit and I elected to only borrow twenty thousand with interest rates of fifteen percent.

For years Loiza and I were content to be near close friends and a very close family. The daily round trip to Gillingham, to train and play that I was about to embark upon for four years, made it nice to come home to.

CHAPTER NINE: GILLINGHAM, SEPTEMBER 1981 - JUNE 30TH 1985

Don't you forget about me

Have you ever had a hastily arranged barbecue, dinner party, impromptu drinks or night out and it turned out to be one of the best you have ever had? That would explain my first two years at Gillingham.

Have you ever had a show, dinner date or party that you gave been looking forward to for ages and it turned out to be disappointing? That would explain my last two years at Gillingham.

As Keith Peacock drove me to a training ground he told me that Ted Buxton had spoken very highly of me for quite a while now and that the side being rearranged at Millwall's reserve game was for his benefit to see if, quote: "I had a football brain." What I didn't tell Keith was given the choice I'd have preferred to stay at Chelsea for fifteen years and if not, Millwall for fifteen years. The other thing I did not mention was that I would put up with the three to three and a half hour return journey every day because in my old schoolteacher John Rouhan's words, "you have to keep the cheques coming in." The squad that I met was what made it all worthwhile for the first couple of years. In goal Ron Hillyard, a bright straight talker out of York. His wit was as dry as my mouth after the one- and-a-half-hour drive to get to work. Full backs John Sharpe, Colin Duncan and a young player full of himself with plenty of front and the dedication and ability to match, Micky Adams.

Keith told me I was brought in as a right back which is where he played me in the first practice match. Although my all-round ability as a defender would help me acquit myself, I preferred centre half. The other centre halves were Mark Weatherly who doubled as a centre forward and Steve Bruce. Brucie had been let go by Burnley as a failed midfield player and he had resurfaced at Gillingham coming in as a second year apprentice.

In midfield left to right Colin Duncan would sometimes play in front of Micky Adams as a left midfield player, Dick Tydeman, Dean White and Richie Bowman were centre midfield with Colin "Paddy" Powell wide right. Richie had started life at Charlton then played for Reading where Keith got him from. Up front it was normally Trevor Lee and Kenny Price. Keith's number two was Paul Taylor who regaled us with tales of his time as a young player at Sheffield Wednesday during the time of the bribe scandal in the sixties. He landed in America during the MLS soccer boom of the seventies and early eighties as the Americans paid fortunes to former top players, has beens and never wases to try and promote the game over there. At the time I think it was the NASL. This is where he hooked up with Keith Peacock. Behind the scenes was chairman and club doctor Dr Grossmark who would later relinquish power to a Mr Charlie Cox whose trade was a caterer.

His main contract so he said was Kent County Cricket Club. After Doc Grossmark retired the new club doctor was his son Dr Michael Frank. I asked for a clue about the different surnames and was told "don't ask." Charlie Cox's brother-in-law was Bill Collins known around the club as Buster. He was a former player when players trained in roll neck sweaters and boots that looked like Dr Martens with studs. He had roles as a coach, youth coach, sponge man and physiotherapist. The medical side was worse than Millwall's. There was a small medical room with two benches and an eighty-five-year-old ultrasound machine. I had a fall out with Buster which he never forgave me for. No one ever questioned or dissented where Bill Collins was concerned, he was an institution inside the club. It wasn't the smartest move but I always thought things should be done properly.

Later on, much later on John Gorman who came to Leyton Orient from Gillingham as youth coach confided in me that Buster Collins had warned him about me and told John to watch his back where I was concerned. I told John he had no worries because I was not going to change the habit of a lifetime. If I had a problem with someone I would tell them outright and come at them head on. For the record I was out unnecessarily long for nearly six weeks for a deep cut in the crease where your knee bends. I was playing right back and had a poor, frustrated, fat winger in my back pocket called Willie Naughton who topped me as I slid the ball out of play with added praise from his manager Gordon Lee. I was nonplussed as I lay on a bench in the medical room. I was quite philosophical as there was a lot of pushing, shoving and usual handbags at five paces between Gordon Lee, Paul Taylor, Naughton, Bill Collins and even Gills secretary Richards Dennis got involved. I thought that after all, if on the odd occasion you live by the sword there might be the odd occasion when you die by the sword. The wound was deep and in a very awkward place and just as I made progress the stitches pinged open again.

Injuries were left at the main ground for treatment when the lads set off for training. The problem was the only one there to administer the treatment was Bill "Buster" Collins. Bill had no medical qualifications whatsoever and masqueraded as a physio and match day sponge man. It was ludicrous, unprofessional and without a shadow of a doubt totally jeopardised players' safety. Like the expense that resulted in a lack of training grounds most lower division clubs had the same outlook on qualified medical staff, medical facilities and equipment which was totally wrong.

Back then you just got on with it.

On the first team's return from training one day Keith Peacock came into the medical room and asked how I was getting on and when I would be back. I said a lot sooner if I could get proper stitches in this gash and proper treatment. I'd already remonstrated with Bill as well as nearly hitting the ceiling much to everyone's amusement when Bill, standing with a cup of milky coffee, apart from Guinness his favourite drink and the ever present roll-up in his mouth, put the ultra sound rod in an open cut.

Two things you don't do, is put ultra sound on an open wound or directly on bone. As he did I jumped up and got an ice pack to take away the pain of the treatment I was supposed to be getting to take away the pain! Keith went red as I told him the goings on and I added that although I'd fucked Bill off and spent the rest of the morning in the gym on my own I would appreciate it if you as manager could have a word.

Things between me and Bill were never the same after that. That's the true, factual version of what happened despite what Bill may have told John Gorman.

Even with pace already on the ball it takes a lot of power and technique to punch a defensive header forty yards. Both me and Steve Bruce were capable of it. I have been accused of having a long memory, holding a grudge and capable of being vindictive. Well I have to say it depends on why and what for. If it's a small professional fall out, I prefer to bury it and move on. A while later, away to Walsall I was defending a throw in. I was totally dominant over the centre forward and as I rose to win another header, I jack knifed to punch a header into the corner to run the clock down.

When you get injured you don't legislate for a pretend physio who I felt became vindictive. Either that or I was right, someone unqualified shouldn't be blagging it and jeopardising players' safety. I completed the header and my momentum led to me hitting my face at full speed and full power into the back of the forward's head. I think they heard the crack in Birmingham. It turned out I broke my nose on the back of the guy's head. There was a split on the bridge of it and claret everywhere. As I walked along the touchline, dazed and wondering what day it was. Bill Collins whacked a cold sponge on it and said "yee'll be alright," then sat down again. I squatted and heard a couple of voices. Not the usual ones in my head that I'd been accused of hearing, but the lads telling me to "get back in" (position). Keith walked on the pitch, cupped my face, saw the blood, that I was boss eyed and that my nose looked like a scenic railway and said "you'd better come off."

Bill was sat in the dugout, breathless from having to run on a couple of times. it was either the roll-ups or the fact that he held a grudge that he left me to my own devices. St John's staff took me back to the away team dressing room, cleaned it up and gave me an ice pack. Walsall's doctor checked for fragment by putting his little fingers inside my nostrils. The pain! I nearly bit him. By the time we were on the train going home I looked like I'd done ten rounds with Jack Dempsey.

Butterfly stitch across a cut, swollen bugle, whacked off centre and two black eyes. I couldn't breathe for a couple of weeks after and slept with my mouth open. To highlight how bad it was and dismissive of me the people were who were supposed to look after me, at Orient I continued for a couple of seasons struggling to breathe, then on examination Bill Songhurst referred me to Dr

Beasley who found a blockage and I was admitted to hospital for a procedure called a Rhinoplasty.

The small bone and mainly cartilage that constitutes someone's nose was found to be all over the place and blocking my airway, so until I had the surgery years later I couldn't breathe properly. Still, it was only four or five seasons discomfort.

The other thing that I was less than happy with was that sometimes after negotiating the mess that was Blackwall Tunnel and completing the one-and-a-half-hour drive to Gillingham from my home in North London, I arrived to find Bill on his way out of the door on his way to London to attend a Lodge meeting. Bill was quite open about being a Freemason and being from his part of Ulster, an Orangeman. Over the years I had on many occasions a Guinness or two with Buster. We made each other laugh and spent a lot of hours talking politics and Question Time was something else we had in common as one of our favourite TV programmes. If you had Bill snookered on a political point or he didn't agree but couldn't articulate it, the room would erupt in laughter at his favoured riposte. In a broad Northern Irish accent he'd shout, "oh away ain fuck!!" It's a shame my talent for diplomacy was at beginner level. I have to say though, like the rest of this book, this story, I want to make it clear that I'm not complaining. I am just telling you how it was, and rightly or wrongly, how I reacted to it all.

The other thing and it's a big umbrella, for at least the first couple of years at Gillingham everything was enjoyable and in the everyday trials and tribulations of a football club about as good as it gets. I can't stress enough that as a player, coach or manager all I ever wanted was an excuse free environment. With Keith Peacock, Paul Taylor and the squad at Gillingham it was almost exactly that.

Apart from a three to three and a half hour return journey every day, what did I have to complain about? The vibe was good, the humour and banter was good, the lads were great and the training with Keith and Paul was among the best I'd ever experienced. You just had to make sure you steered clear of injury. It seems that it wasn't only Gillingham who sometimes didn't take things as seriously as they should have. I remember once turning up for an away game at Scunthorpe United. On arrival we used to go out for a stroll and look at the pitch. Standing in the centre circle was the famous cricketer Ian Botham drinking a pint of bitter. We kicked off and Ian Botham was centre half for Scunthorpe! To be fair he gave Tony Cascarino a hard game.

Talking of injuries again, my team mate Steve Bruce had a couple of bad ones. One was a broken leg. He came in from behind on a player, Tommy Tynan I think, when we played Plymouth. Tommy lifted his foot and Brucie broke his own leg. The other was a bit more light hearted where the lads were concerned. You might find it hard to believe, but Brucie actually broke his nose. The lads creased up as for at least the next four games he got whacked in exactly the same spot. Then Buster ran on and whacked a cold sponge on it. On one occasion it was at Doncaster and their manager at the time was the legendary Billy Bremner. By now we had a tight knit capable squad. Keith canvassed a couple of the more experienced players, namely Paddy Powell and Dick Tydeman on me plugging a gap made by a couple of injuries and whether I'd be able to cope with another change of position.

I had joined the "London Bus" as we called it and on the way home, Paddy told me I had trained well, Keith was pleased with me, then went fishing for a response by asking if I thought I could cope with a change of position to help the side. In training games and small sided games, I expressed myself and tidy capabilities to the enth degree. Paddy asked, "do you think you could do a job for Keith in midfield?" I was over the tantrums and adolescent angst of my time at Chelsea, well almost, I was twenty-one, as fit as a cross between a footballer, middle distance runner and a boxer and I was playing well. I said bring it on, no problem. Looking back I can't help thinking that if other players were meant to be so much better than me, how come's they weren't asked to play righ back, left back, centre half and midfield?

At Doncaster I got the ball off Dick Tydeman and pinged it wide, there was a diagonal ball into the penalty area, I made up the ground for a knockdown, there was a half clearance, I walked onto it. Bang! Left foot, half volley, top left hand corner from just outside the box. It would have pissed a goal of the month and been a contender for goal of the season, but wasn't seen by anyone other than the small crowd. That's the price you pay for being in the third division. After the game I was in the player's bar and just like Alan Ball in the bar at Millwall a year or two before, I'm told by a football legend, winner and larger than life personality, Billy Bremner "well done son, what a strike that was for your goal!" He stood in a top drawer, medium length, dark brown sheepskin coat, he had a whisky tumbler in his hand and took a sip from it. I just said, not sure how to address him, "thanks Mr Bremner, that means a lot." "Och, call me Billy." Then a handshake from Keith for Billy Bremner and we were off to the coach, Keith saying we can't afford to miss our train.

On the train as the usual group of Keith Peacock, me, Dick Tydman and either Paddy or Ron Hillyard played hearts, Keith said Leeds were a nightmare in the nineteen sixties. He spoke of how Billy Bremner raked his studs down Keith's back as they competed for a loose ball. Nobody should underestimate a player's capabilities when he is talked up and praised, especially by the likes of Alan Ball and Billy Bremner. I always thought any praise I received was hard earned and well justified when I got it. The training as I've said was different class. Long before the mid-nineties revolutions supposedly brought in by Arsene Wenger there's no doubt Keith's experience as player, what he liked and disliked, forging ideas in America, and putting his own stamp on it all, definitely benefitted the players. Paul Taylor's warm ups and sessions were equally enjoyable and dare I say it, informative. Paul Taylor's warm ups and ball drills were gradual in intensity and always very thorough. The only time it drove me mad was when Keith added to his collection of ex Charlton players by signing an IT graduate Peter Shaw.

As we warmed up to get ready for a running session, Paul would ask, as a qualified teacher would do, "does anyone know the shape I've marked out with the cones?" Peter Shaw would look over, put his hand up and say "I do, it's a quadrahedron." Whatever the fuck that is. On the plus side it was a fourth member to add to the London Bus. Me, Richie Bowman, Paddy Powell and now Shawy, which meant only driving from a pub car park where we met, the Dover Patrol, every four days. The first season flew by and but for some disappointing results at home where we drew instead of winning the game, we'd have got promotion. A plus for me though was finishing above Millwall, still managed by Anderson at the time, but it wouldn't be long before he was on his way. Something me and Anderson eventually had in common was that neither of us would ever work in English football again. What we didn't have in common were the fortunes given to Anderson by new Chairman Alan Thorne. Some of the signing on fees and wages were astronomical. To give you a clue Sam Allardyce actually chose Millwall over other clubs higher up because of the money and a free house.

That season Burnley, Carlisle and Fulham got promoted. We finished sixth, Millwall finished ninth, just above Brentford. It was important for me to finish above the London clubs especially Millwall after Anderson let me go. Relegated were Wimbledon who were doing their own version of boing boing and within seven seasons would be in the top flight and FA Cup winners. The other three were Swindon, Bristol City and Chester. We finished on seventy-one points and Fulham were promoted in third on seventy-eight, so optimism for closing the gap was in the air. We drew with and beat Millwall which was good for me, beat Wimbledon at home 6-1 and 2-0 away. I got the second from a free kick rolled to me by ex Millwall team mate Dave Mehmet. I pinged it in the top right corner past Dave Beasant from twenty-five yards at the old Plough Lane. Despite hard warm up balls, cold showers, cold tea, a bobbly pitch and other amateurish small minded shit, we played them off the park both times. We done Brentford away 1-0, but dropped costly points at home by drawing 1-1.

See what I mean? The problem with football, one of many, it's not an exact science. The squad was being constantly refreshed, results were good, training was meticulous and enjoyable so for a while with Keith Peacock and Paul Taylor it was a players' dream. Keith ran everything on a clock and it was all game or match day related. Drills, phases of play, practice matches and small sided games with a theme. Everything footballers enjoy or should enjoy doing. My room mate for away games was Richie Bowman a great bloke, good pro and good player. Unfortunately he was having a hard time having injured his cruciate. Eventually it forced his retirement. Keith brought Dave Mehmet back from America where Millwall had sold him, brought in Peter Shaw from Charlton's reserves and had a nice little windfall by getting in a six foot four-inch centre forward from a glorified Sunday side in the Kent League, Crockenhill, called Tony Cascarino. I got on really well with big Cas, he was as easy going as you like, and his Dad Dominic.

The transfer fee and it's a true story, was twelve tracksuits for the team Cas was leaving behind. Because of the vibe, the mutual respect and feel good factor, the near-ish miss on promotion and the relaxed social aspect when we were all together, Steve Bruce and an old Chelsea team mate of mine from Chelsea youth and reserve teams Dean White, convinced Keith and Paul to take us away on an end of season break. It was a bit clichéd but we went to Benidorm in the summer of nineteen eighty-two. Keith took his wife and two kids and stayed in a separate hotel which was just as well because we shared a hotel with a rugby team. I think they were called Hull or Hull K.R.

One of the lads met a female at one of the many discos and introduced her as Jackie. The player, a big strapping boy was basking in the kudos of attracting a member of the opposite sex among the lads when I asked "what's her surname, Charlton?" She towered over him. Dean White and Brucie suggested a stag night after I got up late one morning as I was to be married when I got back to England. It became a stag day as the drink flowed around the pool and a few of the rugby lads were surprised at some of our lads' capacity for drink. With Dick Tydeman, Colin (Paddy) Powell and Paul Taylor pacing everyone it moved on to lunch, then early evening, where we ended up in a bar in the old town. The owner was delighted to have us there as the drink flowed.

What struck me most was the lads were funny, friendly and merry without being obnoxious that sometimes appears as a result of drink. With music blaring the lads sat around a couple of tables and along a bench and belted out "American Pie," Paddy turns to me and says "this is what I call a night out Sitts." We had a great sing song and a good drink then we moved on to a disco and again everyone was drinking, merry and dancing. The player I spoke of saw Jackie Charlton and joined her on the dance floor at her request. I don't think he was about to argue and I was suspicious of her deep voice and Adam's apple, so I gave it a wide berth and after a good drink with Paddy, Dick Tydeman, Colin Duncan, Ron Hillyard, the last two things I remember were having a bop on the dance floor, then being held up by Richie Bowman and following about seven or eight of the lads to a fantastic bar. It was massive and full of Spaniards at about four o'clock in the morning.

They must have had some siesta that's all I know. I had a couple of coffees and along with it drank in the atmosphere and envied their lifestyle of early rise, coffee and breakfast, work, a snack, more work, lunch, a long sleep, back to work from four to seven pm, shower, change, out to dinner and meet friends. There seemed to be a great sense of community. I was three parts pissed but awestruck by the size of the bar, the mahogany, tiles, Moorish architecture and noise.

After me and Richie Bowman polished off a chicken between us with all the usual trimmings we got back to the hotel. The police had been called because one of the lads was so drunk he couldn't get the attention of the night receptionist to open the sliding glass doors. He was seen trying to climb to his balcony and the security thought he was a burglar. About six or seven of the lads had to explain and apologise on his behalf and the law just walked off shaking their heads. Next day the hair of the dog. The lads hit it hard again and we went on the beach afterwards and hired some pedalos. I got mugged off as we went out to some rocks to the left of where we had plotted up in the beach. A few of the lads said "Who's up for skinny dipping?" Like a silly bollocks I'm one of the first to drop my trunks leave them on the pedalo and dive in. As I resurface I see three pedalos with about eight or nine players heading back to the beach. Brucie and my roommate Richie Bowman are playing catch with my trunks. "Rich! Deano! Brucie! lads! Come on lads, stop fucking about. Lads." It was a forlorn cry for help as they pissed themselves laughing and showed no mercy. I could just about make the swim back, then it was the problem of the walk back to the plot on the beach. The lads even moved back to make the walk longer. As I came out of the water I hid my undercarriage, sparing my blushes, but out of nowhere as I put my trunks back on a guy in a g-string comes flouncing over and says "hi, my name is Louzaki!" Brucie had an infectious giggle and sussed straight away our new friend is gay. "I noticed you, are you all together?" I asked him if he had binoculars, he said "no but I noticed you come out of the water." Now it's on me, so I explained that we are a football team on tour, he explains he is here with friends and I ask where he's from "Mykonos." Paul Taylor was a good looking man, fair hair swept back, blue eyes and a nice smile with a big bushy Magnum moustache. I used to keep singing "YMCA" but he never sussed it, what's more I never had a clue whether Paul had been to Mauritius, Mykonos, Madeira or Minehead on his holidays but I said to Louzaki "this is Paul, come and say hello he goes to Mykonos every year." Paul gives me a look, but starts laughing as he shakes the guy's hand. I turn to Dean White, Richie and Brucie and ask, "anyone for a Harvey Wallbanger?"

To protect the innocent, like quite a bit of the book involving stories like these, I have to draw a line somewhere. You never know, some of the people concerned might even still be married! So in the interests of decency, none of which was shown when certain players indulged themselves I have elected to only tell a few of the more relatively harmless ones.

I returned to London to get married at the age of twenty-one and as we all parted company at the airport Keith came and wished me all the best for the wedding and my honeymoon which he'd found out was a tour of the south of France. I turned up in a white tuxedo and with a nice tan to marry Loiza at the All Saints Greek Orthodox Church in Camden Town. In the three quarters of a season I'd been at Gillingham I constantly returned to Millwall to watch games and have after match drinks with my old team mates and maintain friendships with some of the supporters like Ted and Eve Lynch and their boys Tony and Danny. I didn't want them to forget about me and what they all meant to me. Loiza and I were blessed and married in the eyes of the church with the presence of most of my old team mates and my new ones at our wedding and reception. At the time it was considered quite small for a Greek wedding with four hundred and sixty guests. The reception was at a hotel called The Bloomsbury Crest in Coram Street between Tavistock Square and Russell Square in London. All my team mates new and old helped make it a day to remember as they indulged in a bit of Greek dancing and I did a turn with a belly dancer.

What was important for me and Loiza apart from sharing the day with friends, family and all those team mates was the fact that my Mum was able to attend even with her deteriorating health. Not too long afterwards my Mum was readmitted to hospital for treatment on her second lot of cancer. This involved surgery at a small hospital unit in Tottenham which is no longer there. After the operation my Dad asked me to come with him to see the surgeon. The guy who did the operation said that the last lot of surgery hadn't taken away enough bad tissue and that the cancer had spread. I'll never forget the words "it's peppered all over her stomach." My Dad asks if she's going to get better. The surgeon replies, "I think you should prepare yourself for the worst." My Dad asks, "how long do you think she has got?" I had to jump up out of a chair and hold my Dad up as his legs buckled under the answer "eight to ten months."

I remember having to juggle a lot of balls at that time, one was the welfare of my Mum. Unknown to anybody, barely over a year into what should have been the happiest time of my life, me and my new wife are working to build a home and life and even though we bought our house a year before we got married we still only had two partially finished rooms in our house as we moved in after our wedding in June 1982. The rest looked like a building site. I now had a situation where even though everybody else around was getting on with life, I had once again assumed responsibility and with my wife's support I made sure my Mum never wanted for anything even if it was to our detriment. I put off quite a lot to make sure that my Mum was taken care of. I needed a newer car, the house needed finishing and furnishing, all of which was delayed. Loiza carried on supporting me as I constantly switched from the terrible situation involving my mum's health and the shambles that was my father, to being a footballer and back again. But you know what? I'd do exactly the same again. There's a lot of things in my life I wouldn't do again but making sure my Mum was comfortable isn't one of them because it was the right thing to do.

I still made the side a lot more often than not. The way I saw it, I was always worthy of a place in the starting eleven. It got ridiculous on a couple of occasions though when I was asked to play left back. Keith was less than impressed in a pre-season friendly against QPR managed by Terry Venables. I started ok because they were working on their defensive plan of shutting the line off and showing teams inside, which meant I could come inside on my stronger right foot, play it off the front man and let fly with a couple of shots. The problem was I got too full of myself as I grew in confidence and tried to nutmeg Tony Currie which Keith castigated me for at full time. I was played there instead of centre half against Southend away who were managed at the time by Bobby Moore and his coach and number two was Malcolm Alison. Two of the greatest football people ever. Pure class, charisma, and full of knowledge. Look what the English game did to them. It would have been nice to play well at centre half and get a result, but the whole team was dire on a burning hot day, there were too many positional changes and we lost. Another downer, which also highlighted the diabolical medical set up came when I got back in at centre half. We were away to I think Rotherham and as I got up to win a header my knee locked at forty-five degrees and the pain was phenomenal.

I came off, got checked by the opponent's doctor, went home on crutches and after my Dad got a call from Keith Peacock he met me at the train station to be told I'd torn a cartilage. I lay in pain at home until Monday over forty-eight hours until a place was found for me in a private hospital somewhere in Kent. I was prepped Monday night, operated on at seven am Tuesday morning and released Wednesday. The surgeon came in with my cartilage in a jar. He said it was a "bucket handle tear." I was told to walk as normal as possible immediately. I had it checked on Thursday and by Friday I was jogging box to box in some straight line running. The last bit I didn't have a problem with. What I did have a problem with was laying in agony for over forty-eight hours because the club couldn't arrange to have me admitted to hospital immediately.

Whether it was lack of money or lack of insurance I'll never know. What I do know is I think I was treated more like a sick animal rather than a supposed professional athlete. I hope and I can probably guarantee that clubs have finally got their act together and players are now better looked after, but at the time I was the only one with the balls to complain and all it got me was viewed with suspicion and perceived as a troublemaker and turncoat.

My stance was over simplistic really, I trained hard, showed that I wanted to be a footballer, wanted to be in the first team, but please don't take the piss. Talking of taking the piss, after I lost my room mate Richie Bowman who had to retire through injury my new roommate for a while became ex Crystal Palace centre forward Dave Kemp. As sharp as a carpet tack Kempy was. He was looking for a club after returning from America where he had played for Chicago Sting. You've got to love the names they give their clubs. He also returned with an American wife Debbie who was fantastic company. Dave knew all the angles and one night we are in the West End, we've had a meal in Tony Roma's and ask for the bill. As the waiter comes over, Debbie asks for a second cup of coffee. The waiter picks up the bill, Deb says "what are you doing with the check?" "Adding on the second coffee madam." Debbie protests "I thought this was an American restaurant." The waiter replies "it's only a pretend American restaurant madam." Kempy pipes up. "Well everybody's happy then, 'cos I've only got pretend money." I didn't know, but during dinner Kempy and slipped off and made a call. He came back to the table and says "Sitts I've got a nice surprise, but you've got to help me front it." He puts in a call to Stringfellows, gives his name as some agent, says Crystal Palace's Dave Kemp and Chelsea's John Sitton want to attend Stringfellows this evening, they would like immediate entry, a table and a bottle of champagne on ice. They'll be attending the disco part of the club with their wives. I couldn't stop giggling as we walked straight to the front and we were all ushered in. We clinked glasses and I said "Kempy, you've got some fucking front." Deb shrieks, "oh my God, there's Godzilla!" we were standing in a section full of transvestites, one of them six feet four inches in a lime green dress and high heels. She (or is it he?) takes a shine to us, but after a couple of dances with our wives and polishing off the champagne lively, we left. Kempy left the club not long after, but what a good player and good pro he was around the place.

I'm not in the least bit surprised he has done so well as number two to Tony Pulis. He's a good sounding board Kempy. Forensic, erudite and very knowledgeable. After stints at Wimbledon and Plymouth he's served Pulis well for quite a while now. One thing I can almost guarantee Kempy wouldn't recommend is the same training we went through on a couple of occasions. Sorry to keep repeating the fact, but like most lower division clubs and most certainly the three I played for, training grounds were pot luck. You could be training anywhere on any given day. I remember being in Kempy's running and circuit training group when we trained at Chatham Docks with the Gurkhas. Firstly they didn't talk to anyone. If you made eye contact they looked straight through you and training wise they were on a different level. It's almost as if they never experienced pain, fatigue or lactic acid. Forget entertaining the thought of losing a team game!

No more than five feet six or seven, some smaller, each and every one of them was built like a pocket Hercules. They ran in boots, vest and combat trousers and they looked like they'd have no problem whatsoever slitting your throat. I just though thank fuck I'm not Argentinian! The time frame was either just before or just after the Falklands. Tough, resolute men, and there's me complaining about the time it took to get back from a gashed knee.

By the summer of 1983 I had been married a year and I was out of contract. Peacock took the piss by offering me the same money. I refused because by now I'd got wind of what other people were earning and what they had received in signing on fees. The PFA was in its infancy and being offered the same money was sufficient enough for clubs to criminally in my opinion have a hold over you. To me it was all contradictory in that I was thought highly enough of to be retained by Peacock but on less money! He offered the same basic with no expenses. I wanted a rise and to keep my expenses. There was never any talk of a signing on fee. I said to my wife " we'll sort it out when we get back off holiday." Apart from the honeymoon a year previous and being constantly chaperoned in Cyprus in 1980 this was our first break as a young couple.

We went to Rhodes for two weeks. Even that went tits up and turned out too good to be true. The holiday company went bust and we had to be chartered out, flown to Manchester and brought down to London by coach. Still, it was the least of my worries as I was out of contract. In the end Keith wanted to up my basic by including my expenses. What a piss take. The warm feelings I had towards him were evaporating fast. I'd had a go for him and this was my reward. I ended up signing a contract in the summer of 1983 taking me up to the summer of 1985 for the same money to carry on playing. My fault or his? I'll never know if it was me as a poor negotiator or him as a diabolical liberty taker. Two things I can definitely state for sure are that my performances and professionalism never diminished but my feelings for Peacock and the club definitely did. After all, who wants the piss taken out of them as a reward for good service? Towards the end of my third year by hook or by crook I helped get the money together to take my Mum and Dad to Florida for three weeks. I'm convinced to this day that holiday contributed in my Mum's fight against her illness. She lived for three more years after we were told she had eight to ten months. Whilst there we saw Tampa Bay Rowdies play QPR. The visit to the U.S.A was to have a relevance not long after to my own career path and choices I would have to make. It's another regret of mine that I never took the plunge and chose a new life, a different life in America.

What has never ceased to amaze me in football are some of the decisions and transfer policies of clubs and managers. Some I saw first-hand, some I suffered from as a consequence and right at the end, some that led to a shambles that contributed to killing off a fledgling coaching and management career because of piss poor, barely thought through purchases, financially beyond the reach of the club concerned. I fully understand a manager's need to turn playing staff over to improve, replenish and refresh. One thing I think you shouldn't do is penalise your most habitually consistent performers, good professionals and good trainers. Those are the categories I came under. I had served Gillingham and Keith Peacock on an almost exemplary basis, but because of turnover of players and good players being replaced with either not so good players or not so good professionals it led to us becoming the nearly men.

I didn't know it at the time but the first season near miss was as close as I would get to promotion with Gillingham. To me it's no coincidence that apart from a goal scorer that was missing and would have made the difference, during the first two years it was the best group of players, best professionals and best men that I was involved with in my four years there. We acquitted ourselves well in the cups against West Bromwich Albion, Spurs and most notably Everton over the course of a couple of seasons, but the supposed difference in quality tells in the end in one or two positions.

In an overview and synopsis of my career I came to the conclusion that in football you can fall into one of three categories. You can get what you pay for, you can get less than you paid for, leading to disappointment, or you can get a lot more than you paid for, where the player brought in exceeds all expectations and you are pleasantly surprised that he can play well in three or four positions. That's also the category I fell into, and yet in Keith Peacock's memoirs he only remembers me for a fight in training with centre forward Ken Price. On a one to one basis he said to my face that I was "an enigma" and "a poor man's Steve Bruce." That's football and it's all about opinions. Take Tony Cascarino who said in his book his eight hundred thousand pounds' career earnings didn't leave a lot of jam to spread. By comparison I could barely afford the butter. Cas readily admits after a career spanning some of the top clubs in the UK that at times he left a bit to be desired.

The back four, particularly Brucie who dominated Andy Gray was outstanding and Peter Reid was over run, out muscled and out passed in midfield. We got a 0-0 and a replay at Priestfield. It was rumoured that if they lost the manager would be sacked. Ninety minutes 0-0, extra time 0-0, two minutes to go Everton get a corner, it's under hit and I hit a magnificent fifty-yard clearance that is helped on. I look up and couldn't believe it. Everton have left big Cas on his own on the halfway line, Cas is 1v1 on Everton's keeper Neville Southall. If he scores it's all over for Everton and Howard Kendall. What's more it sets a precedent that quite possibly would mean no FA Cup win, no Cup Winners Cup win and the team breaks up. Tony Cascarino admits to, as he's about to shoot, closing his eyes and striking the ball and hoping for the best.

For the record Cas hit Southall's legs and it went to a second replay. I got topped at Brentford with a karate kick from the side across my knee by Gary Roberts and resulted in me missing the game. Everton went through and nobody knew that Cas's finishing involved him closing his eyes. My memories and Peacock's memoirs seem more sinister by comparison. I was on my way back from injury and a practice match meant I was in the reserves providing opposition for the first team. Dean White rolled two or three balls into Ken Price and I either intercepted it, drove Pricey back into midfield or affected his touch to the extent that we pinched it off the first team. Deano gives Pricey a bollocking to "get hold of it." Pricey blames me and calls me a not very nice name. The by products would be for me to react to the not very nice name and my discipline and concentration being affected. For fourteen seasons I never got involved in, reacted to, or was affected by verbal. Pricey fell into the same trap as most others I had come across who indulged in this most futile and energy wasting past time and couldn't take anywhere near what he dished out. For once I sarcastically said "don't blame me Pricey, it's got nothing to do with me that you couldn't fucking trap a bag of cement."

I saw the signs and the signals after being warned by full back John Sharpe that Pricey could get tetchy and flip at any time in a keep ball, practice match or eight a side. This resulted in his eyes glazing over and followed by a head butt. At one time it led to a big gash over Sharpey's eye and across his forehead. On his realisation that I was right and the assumption the truth hurts, Pricey turned to come at me and nut me.

Contrary to popular belief I am the opposite of losing my temper in a physical confrontation so as soon as Sharpey told me Price's eyes glazed over etc. I was ok with it. I pinged in a shot and as he reeled backwards, I put in two more shots and knocked him back into Dean White's arms. As I went in to finish him Dean White screamed, "quick get hold of him" and about eight team mates got hold of me and Pricey and kept us apart. I dropped my arms but never took my eyes off him. Peacock sent me with Dick Tydeman and three or four others to the other end of the field for me to cool off. I said to him I'm fine, but he insisted, feeling Pricey might react to his mouth being split and bleeding. Like a lot of others before him, I wasn't fussed if it carried on or not. That afternoon Keith insisted we forget it and fined us twenty-five pounds each. The turnover continued.

Richie Bowman was on the brink of retirement through injury. Dick Tydeman wasn't getting any younger, Dave Mehmet came in from the USA. We signed Russell Musker, Jeff Johnson and had Mel Sage coming into the first team squad via the youth ranks. There were the imminent departures of Micky Adams, Steve Bruce and Kenny Price and the loan signings of in my opinion, two players that ensured an upset to the status quo and two permanent signings that led me to think I might get a move but in the end only resulted in Keith Peacock playing games with my career. I think he was paranoid about selling me to a competitor. In the end no good whatsoever came out of it. Gillingham never received a transfer fee. Peacock thought he had two replacements and I was an unhappy player that Brentford, who had started to put together a decent side, couldn't add to their squad.

We played Brentford. Paul Roberts who had by now left Millwall comes bowling in at Priestfield "he fancies you Sitts son, he's gonna bid for you, you'll do well for us at the back with Bob Booker." The "he" was Fred Callaghan ably assisted by Ron Harris as player coach. The Brentford lads got off the coach and the officials followed. One of them was Christine Mathews and as she walked in she gave me a hug, Ron just winked at me. "Alright John?" With the nucleus of the side built around Robbo, Ron, Bobby Booker and Terry Hurlock I must say I fancied returning to London. I can guarantee subject to terms I would have jumped at the chance to move closer to home. I wouldn't have missed the daily return trip of three and a half hours and that even though all this was going on my training and playing standards never once dropped. Keith invited me into his office to tell me that Fred had enquired but he never disclosed the fee offered by Brentford. I was told the fee by Robbo and became a little angry and perplexed because what Peacock did defied logic.

He let Dean White go to Millwall, a reliable, steely, determined, good professional whose passing, movement and goals from midfield made for a great contribution. Where I was concerned Peacock could have sold me for a sum that would have meant Gillingham had received my services for three years for nothing. After my first two years I was offered the same money to re-sign which in those days meant the club had met the minimal legal prerequisite and could hold your registration, determine your future, your movement and in Keith Peacock's case, stop me from moving onto another club. In those days there was no such thing as a "Bosman," which has to be said would benefit lower league players, particularly back then. Quite honestly, the only way for a lower league player to earn any money back then was to move every two or three years, get a signing on fee and a rise in your basic wages. What angered me was Keith Peacock had seen fit to sign Keith Oakes, a centre half, a decent enough pro, but one who made me look like Valeriy Borzov. I'm not saying he was slow, but he turned in instalments.

Keith also signed Joe Hinnegan, a good all-round defender, predominantly a full back, Joe had bad knees and was in constant rehab after surgery, never passing up an opportunity to work on his quads, (quadriceps). He was also short sighted and blind as a bat. There was also Peter Shaw and Mark Weatherly so after two to three years' good service I questioned what it was all about. When you add to the mix wages, signing on fees and relocation expenses for Oakes, Hinnegan and the loans of Terry Cochrane and Duncan Shearer from Middleborough with hotel fees alone costing a mint, I started to get angry and resentful at the situation. To add to my anger at Keith Peacock, I was asked to drive in on Christmas Day on dangerous icy roads through snow storms for a twenty minute warm up and twenty minute eight a side. Then all the way home again in diabolical conditions with Christmas Day virtually over. He then insisted I train on the day of Eddie Heath's funeral because we had a midweek game and I never got the chance to say goodbye and thank you to a great man, mentor and friend.

Most of the old school Chelsea boys were there and I've always felt ashamed I never went even though it was beyond my control. The team put together by Keith towards the end of my time at Gillingham never got anywhere near the promise, togetherness, enjoyment, camaraderie and sheer joy of training and playing that I felt existed in the first two years of my time there. Good Men, good footballers, equals a good environment.

During one of my disciplinary lapses I got a lot of help and guidance from Paul Taylor and the senior lads even though they could see I was tired and frustrated at being fucked around and played centre half, right back, left back and centre midfield. It was in midfield that I presented a silver lining for Harry Rednapp. He told the story a few years later in the coach's office at Leyton Orient. At the time he was West Ham manager and as a guest of Bernie Dixson he recognised me and said I had done him a turn when he was manager of Bournemouth.

At the time they were on a diabolical run of results which was reflected in their over physical approach to me and Dick Tydeman as we entertained them on home soil at Priestfield. We're on a run, playing well, looking to make a breakthrough when a loose ball bounces between me, John Beck and Nigel Spackman. It was a little bit Roy Keane on Alf Ingerhaaland, only higher. I got a straight red card and from 0-0 with Bournemouth hanging on and us looking like getting a breakthrough at any time, Bournemouth ran out 5-0 winners and Harry's a hero who's stopped the rot and goes from within a gnat's pubic hair of the sack, to safe in his job. My take on my time at Gillingham and after a lot of miles on the A2 and four years on the same wages, I went from being sought after for a fee to not having a new contract offered to me.

Somewhere along the line Keith Peacock and Gillingham could have got my services free of charge by selling me to Fred and Ron at Brentford. The alternative was for Peacock and Paul Taylor to keep asking me and pestering me on whether I'd be interested in a move to "Dallas Sidekicks" in the North American Indoor Soccer League. I was told by Ted Buxton they'd agree a deal with Gordon Jago for me to be transferred there. The fee was twenty thousand pounds which was ten thousand less than the offer made by Brentford. I was offered fifteen thousand pounds signing on fee, an apartment, a car and a basic wage of eight hundred dollars per week. I said no because I didn't want to be in Dallas with my Mum dying of cancer. I thought what if she took a turn for the worse?

Eleanor Roosevelt once said "No one can make you feel inferior without your consent." All I can say is Keith Peacock had a fucking good crack at it, buying players to play ahead of me after the service I had given him yet refused to sell me so that I could get on with my career. Instead I left on a free transfer to Leyton Orient.

CHAPTER TEN: LEYTON ORIENT JULY 1985-1990
Pleasuredome

The mid-eighties meant dark times for English football. Attendances were down. On a personal level I had been fucked about for two years after Keith Peacock brought in at quite a bit of expense another centre half and full back, the two positions where I had acquitted myself just short of superbly for two years prior to that. The clubs in those days held all the power and as long as an offer was made, even if it was for the same money, they had jurisdiction over where you played, when you played and if you played. If I was surplus to requirements I should have been allowed to leave. Not for the first time and it most certainly wouldn't be for the last time I found myself in the wrong place at the wrong time. All of a sudden the powers that be at Leyton Orient realised they had spent a lot of good money on not very good players.

Unfortunately it was just as I came through the door and because funds had been eaten away and I was dealing from weakness, I signed for Frank Clark for less money than I would have earned as a labourer. All of this was put in perspective with the likes of the Heysel stadium disaster that claimed thirty nine lives, mainly Italian when Liverpool contested the European Cup final with Juventus in a run down, dilapidated arena, not fit for purpose. Closer to home over fifty lives were lost as fire took hold of the main stand at Bradford City on the last day of the 84-85 season.

With experience, hindsight and my own opinion ably formed, I could never understand a manager standing in the way of a loan or transfer of a player seemingly surplus to requirements. Actually I could, I still think it's down to the lack of self-belief, paranoia and conviction on the part of the manager himself. If I made up my mind that I had bought and brought in a player, in this case players, to supposedly improve on what I already had at my disposal I would never impede a man's right to get a living, support his family, ply his trade, and take his career elsewhere. Unfortunately because of the number of self-absorbed, self-important, paranoid, small minded wankers in the game, passing off as pseudo intellectuals but totally unconvinced by their own ability and decision making, football does not work like that.

One man who for a second time did fantastically well for me was Ted Buxton. He arranged and staffed as manager for the day a game between Gillingham reserves and Orient reserves to complete the fixtures in the reserve league at that time. No offer came from Peacock to retain me and Ted told then O's Manager Frank Clark to have a look at me as I was in Ted's words "playing to get away." Luck would have it that on the day I was outstanding. Orient as they were known at the time fielded virtually a first team and with me surrounded by kids defending well, bossing, organising and being very vocal, we beat them. As I walked along the corridor to some showers Frank asked "is that right you're playing for a move?" I said "am I? News to me." He said to come in at Orient for a chat in the summer. So after four years at Gillingham, two of them very enjoyable, I did. There was a major problem for me in that apart from Cambridge there were no other offers. The Brentford ship with Fred Callaghan as manager and my old Chelsea comrade and mentor Ron Harris as player coach had well and truly sailed.

I was yet again dealing from weakness. Frank didn't know it, but after telling me he'd take a punt on me but could only offer me two hundred pounds a week, I signed for two years and was one of the best signings for many reasons of his managerial career. In the distant future I would be castigated, criticised and ridiculed as an Orient manager. That's because football and football supporters when it suits them have short term memory loss. It wasn't only dark days for football in general but Orient in particular as they suffered two consecutive relegations. Firstly under Ken Knighton with Frank as his number two and then in eighty-five with Frank Clark as manager. When I reported for pre-season I could see why. As a pick me up for the squad Frank snapped things into focus and put some perspective on the O's relegation citing that things could be worse and made reference to the poor souls at Bradford who lost their lives. At the time you could have been forgiven for thinking never in a million years could you see Frank going on to manage Nottingham Forest and Manchester City with two relegations on his C.V.

I attacked pre-season with my usual vigour and enthusiasm alongside three other new signings as part of a new look squad. Frank brought in a goalkeeper Peter Wells, full back Kevin Dickenson and centre forward Paul Shinners. Later on it transpired that Shinners told Tony Cascarino to do the same as him to earn himself a contract in France. Cas mentions it in his book. Cas followed suit after Shinns told him he knocked three years off his age to get a contract. Can you believe it? Shinns fronted it, no background check was made, and he got away with it. Our first pre-season friendly was at one of our many training grounds behind closed doors, our opponents were Gillingham. Keith Peacock came up for a chat to ask how my knee was.

I just replied "fine, it stood the acid test of Epping Forest" and trotted off. For most of the game I had a chat with Derek Hales about the upcoming shooting season, something we shared an interest in. I got on with Halesy when I was at Gillingham he seemed right up my alley. He had his family, loved his country pursuits and his circle of mates was tight knit. Yet again the training facilities were pot luck. Would it happen now? Every day we reported to the main ground. Frank got on the phone and it was in the cars to either Ive Farm, Low Hall Farm or Nutter Lane in Wanstead. The best surfaces were at Nutter Lane. The other two were muddy, rain soaked, covered in dog's shit and as bleak as anything because there was no shield or cover from the elements.

I'm sorry if it appears that I keep justifying myself, but I suppose it comes from a lifelong habit left over from football. Anyone at Chelsea or anywhere else for that matter who called into question my motivation, commitment and dedication to a career in football and my love of training and playing only had to look at the training facilities of all my clubs particularly the last three after Chelsea's facilities at Imber Court, which incidentally belonged to the Met Police anyway. Despite all this Frank Clark made the best of what he had and I found him a good man to work for. For decades now I'd watched and listened in disbelief, smiling wryly to myself as not just my four, but countless clubs who asked so much of their players, to train daily with dedication, for you to show how much you want it, perform consistently, do the basics well, when clubs couldn't do the basics themselves and have a base, a headquarters, a training ground to call your own and the facilities and consistency of having somewhere to report every day. The situation didn't really change for a couple of years at the O's and although Frank was nudging towards it anyway, Brian Eastick highlighted the absurdity of having no regular training ground and insisted on a base.

My opinion formed from experience and a good cross section of facilities is instead of an excuse free environment it can lead to training and playing becoming almost nonsensical. Then again I suppose it depends on the players and personalities involved. Over a couple of seasons Frank Clark had quite a turnover of players and their personalities, ambitions and professionalism sometimes varied a great deal. Paul Shinners who previously played non-league for Fisher Athletic was at first tremendously popular with the crowd and seemed to enjoy and make the most of being a full time footballer. A big strapping boy, he had a good first season and pitched in with his fair share of goals. Having knocked three years off his age to earn a contract his real age and off field lifestyle started to catch up with him and he started to pick up numerous niggly injuries. Even with all the injuries he had, he made the most of it with the physio Bill Songhurst.

While the rest of us were knocking our bollocks out on the training ground or doing a five mile run in Epping Forest, Bill often suggested a referral to a specialist in Harley Street especially when Shinners was injured. It would mean leaving late morning which conveniently for Bill meant he never had time to treat anyone in the medical room. He and Shinners would leave, keep the appointment, do a bit of shopping in Selfridges, have a late lunch, then disperse. Shinns would go home and Bill would return to the ground where in the evening he held a private clinic. I did the same thing with Bill once myself. The difference was I was coming back from a ruptured achilles not a dead leg or stiff back. I thought the whole thing was a piss take, unprofessional and penalised players like me who stayed fit and players who needed treatment and had a chance of being fit short term.

It's funny when I look back that Shinns never seemed to have a short term injury, the old chestnut of a bad back would surface again and anything from a calf strain to a dead leg would keep him out for as long as I thought he felt he needed a rest. On the flip side I remember walking into the medical room prior to training and asking Bill Songhurst if he would rub some gel into my calf muscle and on match day asking him if he would massage my hamstring. His reply? "I don't do massages." I said " I don't believe this place. Are you the physio or not?" Bill then said "I've got a simple rule when it comes to massaging players... good players don't need it, bad players ain't worth it." Tommy Cunningham erupted into laughter. I said "no wonder you've had two fucking consecutive relegations..." And I walked out. I suppose that's what people mean when I've been accused of a prickly disposition or not sucking up to the elder statesmen in situ.

Sometimes on a Monday Chris Jones would say to me and Brooksy "this is bollocks, if we win and play well, we run in the forest, if we lose and play poorly... we run in the forest." The run he spoke of was called the double loop which was two walkways that crossed over in the middle of Epping Forest. Peter Wells and one or two others used to hide in the trees after doing a part of the first loop then join in with the rest of the lads for the last part of the second loop. I was middle order in the running, probably because it's hard to do a cross- country while you're laughing. Nobody grassed Wells or the other lads. Frank actually said to me in front of Bill Songhurst that he sometimes despaired over Shinner's conduct adding "he makes my life a fucking misery but the crowd love him." The cries of "Rambo, Rambo" reverberated around the crowd as he bowled over opposition centre halves with his combative, subtle as a pick axe playing style.

He was in stark contrast to the Jersey born, skilled, cultured and intelligent Chris Jones. You could argue that Chris had the first touch of a heart surgeon and Shins had the first touch of a blacksmith. I looked upfield as good service was pinged into him and came to the conclusion he would struggle to trap a bag of cement. Sometimes though it was a good combination with Chris linking the play up nicely with Sean Brooks or Andy Sussex and as play developed Shins provided the physical presence in the opposition box as the crosses came in. Kevin Godfrey provided pace, trickery and fantastic ability but to me always appeared to have a lack of ambition. He had come through the ranks and remained at Orient for years, clubs higher up may have looked but never bid. Peter Wells in goal had been at the likes of Southampton, Forest and Millwall and was vastly experienced. He said he'd had a problem, quite a serious one with his heart while at Southampton, and it had totally changed his whole outlook on life. He confessed it had scared him and he swore to enjoy life to the full.

His logic defied me somewhat as I listened and observed his off field lifestyle and how he liked a good drink and a good curry. It probably explained what he had done the night before as he tired long before the seventy-four-year-old goalkeeping coach Dickie Moss in a pre-season warm up. Kevin Dickenson was the best left back I ever had alongside me during my whole career, including some of the vastly overrated ones at Chelsea. He had a turn of pace, a physique like a pocket battleship, a sweet left foot and could defend. He was also intelligent, read the game well, and always giving out good supportive information. There was Kevin Hales an ex-Chelsea team mate of mine, John Cornwell, Colin Foster, Tommy Cunningham Peter Mountford, Pat Corbett and Ian Juryeff, a centre forward from Southampton who would make up the rest of the squad. Tommy

Cunningham who had previously been in the side and captain for a few seasons before I arrived, suffered a broken toe just before the opening day of the season by dropping a barrel on his foot as he carried out chores in his pub in Bethnal Green.

Frank made me captain of the team.

Obviously I thought it was the right choice. Apart from the goalkeeper, a centre half gets the best view of the game and the football field. When you add that I was a good trainer, good professional, could read the game, a good talker, could dominate aerially, control and pass with both feet, committed, determined, could tackle and boss the people around me as a leader should, it was a no brainer. Immodest I know, but apart from Chelsea's first team I thought I should have captained every side I played in. Pat Corbett could play centre half, Tommy Cunningham was an experienced centre half, but the best pair at the time was me and Colin Foster. Frank tried me and Tom together once away to Swindon in one of the cups and it didn't work out. We both lacked pace, Tommy more than me, and on the coach on the way back Frank saw the disappointment on my face as the captaincy was given back to TC on account of seniority and time served. He came and sat next to me and said he was quote: "looking to make me the cornerstone of his side." There always seemed to be two problems. We either struggled to score, or got bullied and overrun in midfield. Brooksy made up a song based on Johnny Cash's, "A thing called love." It ridiculed John Cornwell's talent for shrinking from 6'2" to 5'8" when competing for a header. I had a good start then it went tits up. I got summoned to Frank's office after getting sent off three times in a month.

The first time at home to Tranmere when I got in between Ronnie Moore and Colin Foster. The ref took exception to me grabbing Ronnie Moore by the throat. Not long after the referee evened it up by sending Ronnie off for leaving his foot in on Pat Corbett. Pat clipped the ball into Chris Jones then whack! To be fair to Ronnie, he poked his head around the dressing room door and said "we're both in the same boat big man, no hard feelings." I thought fuck it, no point in a grudge and shook his hand as he held it out to me. The second was away to Torquay. I was sitting with the lads after our pre-match meal in a beautiful hotel in a beautiful part of Devon, but I always had the ability to ignore stunnings surroundings and gradually build up towards kick off, and get psyched up, ready for battle. However it wasn't always the case with team mates. I was sitting on a sofa in reception and in walks Kevin Hales, signed from Chelsea, where he had a few games in Chelsea's first team, but had picked up a serious knee injury. He was known as son of Frank and for some reason, Frank loved him. Anyway, I'm focusing on the task ahead and Halesy is standing there with two boxes, gift wrapped, complete with little silk bows. I asked "been shopping Halesy?" He replies "Yeah, I got a couple of bits for my wife and mother-in-law, we're in Devon, so I'm taking them home some clotted cream."

I was thinking yet again, no wonder they've had two consecutive relegations, with me getting ready to try and pillage three points and a team mate acting like a tourist, I'm wondering "what the fuck am I doing here? What's it all really about?"

The centre forward kept stamping on my toes as he backed in, so I let him get on the half turn and came in too high for the ref's liking. Straight red. The third was for a long time, a record in the British game after thirty-two seconds. Away to Burnley they kicked off, out to their left back. Colin Foster got dragged short, Halesy, playing right back with a double hernia was taken short by the left winger Ashley Hopkins the full back bounced it off Ashley who spun in behind. It was a race into the channel between me and the winger, he got there first, I got there as soon as I could. I tackled him and he went down. At first it seemed like a yellow card, first tackle offence. Ashley's reaction said it was something worse, I got a red card and I went into Burnley's medical room to see if he was ok. He said "I can't believe it, they've sent for an ambulance, I think you've broken my leg." I just said "I don't know what to say, I just slid in from the side... I'm really sorry Ash" He was a small nippy winger but had a big heart and said "don't worry, it was an accident." Back at the ground, as I was summoned to Frank's office, Frank said "now say to his face what you've just said to me." Groundsman Charlie Hasler was standing there and said "all I said was, you've played well since you came in, but you're no good to us if you keep getting sent off."

I replied, knowing Charlie had established allegiances with other centre halves at the club, "what's it fucking got to do with you? You're the fucking groundsman, I only answer to him" pointing at Frank. "You can go now, I want to have a word with Sitts" Frank says to Hasler. I ask "Frank what's this all about?" "Sitts in case you haven't noticed, it's about a club where the groundsman thinks he can come into the manager's office and complain about a player. The walls talk and the corridors echo in this place." I just remarked it's fucking out of order. A classic example of agendas, politics, perceived off field friendships and people being busy outside their remit in a football club. Frank said to me, "however if I'm going to have a problem with you it'll be the parting of the ways for us son." I said "fair enough. I know where I stand." I went off to do some body exercises and stretches and Bill Songhurst, no doubt at Frank's request, came to find me on the pretence of getting my order for my pre-match meal for a game seventy-two hours away. "He knows you're having a go for him and the club Sitts, he's not looking to fall out with you." I said "Bill this place is like a fucking holiday camp, there's all sorts going on, and he can't tell the difference between a good pro, perhaps on occasions a bit too robust and politics and people taking the piss." I thought fuck this, when am I going to catch a break? I could see Frank had major problems behind the scenes and he was constantly juggling problems, opinions and putting out mischievous bonfires. Two blokes he never had to worry about were two of the greatest men I ever met in football, Jimmy Halleybone and Harry Spinner. Harry's death many, many years later caused an uncomfortable silence over a Christmas lunch I invited myself to just to say hello to Bernie Dixson, Frank, Bill and Mick Pentney. I'm not sure how he came into the equation but even Steve Shorey was there. Frank relayed the story that he'd been contacted by Carol Stokes to relay the terrible, diabolical news that Harry had passed away. I remarked, "NO! that's terrible, Harry was a great man, a lovely man." Frank replied, "he couldn't have been that great, there was only me and Pat Holland representing the club at his funeral, the only others were Carol and Harry's daughter." I said to awkward silence, "I'd have been there like a shot, it's not my fault you, Patsy and Carol kept it a secret. I'm sure Carol could have got my number." The other thing that nearly naused it, apart from me not having a drink because I had to return to work in my cab, was Shorey saying, "gis a bit of that cheese boy" after I ended my meal with cheese and biscuits.

Frank and Bill were deep in conversation at the end of the table, Bernie pissed himself laughing. Mick Pentney went red as I said "has someone ordered a cunt? I didn't know it was on the menu... because one's just turned up." I then turned to Shorey and said "don't fucking call me boy. Would you call Harry Rednapp, George Graham or Frank Clark, boy?" I looked to Bernie and Mick and then said "to think I gave him his first job in football, your old job Bernie and that's the thanks I get." What price credibility and respect?

Harry and Jimmy... where do I start? Between them they had at one time or another done everything at the club apart from chairman and manager. The best compliment I could pay them was if I owned a football club I'd look for, want and demand a Jimmy Halleybone and Harry Spinner. What's more I would have paid them a decent salary. Jimmy got no credit for it, but in a couple of short stints as youth coach he coached, encouraged and nurtured Orient players like Sussex, Nugent, Castle and Bart-Williams who all came through the ranks. When I got there he was the kit man. You could tell he loved being part of the club, although according to Jimmy I'm not sure his wife Flo felt the same when she saw his pay packet. I'm not even sure if Harry was paid. If he was it wasn't a lot to prepare lunch for the youth team and staff.

A little ritual on a Friday was for a few of us to stand around the kitchen, have a cup of tea and one of Harry's famous cakes. I used to ask him to make one of his coconut ones. I've always been mad for a bit of coconut. He made these lovely cakes and we stood around talking to "H" and about the game we'd just played or what was coming up. It was usually me, Dicko, Halesy, Keith Day when he eventually came to the club and Andy Sussex. In the end, years later, Peter Eustace banned it. I was sometimes accused of micro management and being a bit of a control freak as manager, which all good ones tend to be, although I prefer to call it paying attention to detail, but what harm can players being together talking football and their concerns about getting a result possibly do? My control freak part was wanting the best for the players and the best from the players for the supporters of the club. I can assure you I would never have been that paranoid whereby I'd have stopped players coming together to talk football over a relatively harmless mug of tea and coconut cake.

Dark days at Orient seemed cyclical. Harry regaled us with tales of his army days, his de-mob, career as a lorry driver and joining Orient when the club reached beyond its grasp and he and Jimmy were asked to walk among the crowd with buckets for the spectators to throw their loose change in to keep the club going. It seemed to me contradictory to the story told to me by Tunji Banjo who flew with another Orient player to represent Nigeria and the accompanying Orient official who returned with a brief case full of money. Someone was getting a leg up, but it wasn't Harry or Jimmy. I'm sure there are clubs who have people like those two who work for them especially in the lower divisions. If you haven't got a Harry or Jimmy you need one and I suggest you search high and low for men like these two. It might be a big ask because I think they broke the mould and men like these are in short supply. They were in short supply at Orient that's for sure. Frank was getting if from all sides. There were one or two highlights, but a good few lowlights as well. I remember the attendances dwindling when we failed to get promoted first time of asking. They were down to eighteen hundred or a maximum of two thousand two hundred. The trouble was on top of a small crowd, at least three quarters of them on the rare occasion they made a noise, it was to sing "Clark out, Clark out" as we did our pre-match warm up and then again as we prepared to kick off. The bigger problem was the bank who controlled the club's overdraft. If word got out how small the crowds were the overdraft facility would be reduced and the club wouldn't be able to function. This didn't stop one director from walking around the ground after one particular game saying "no one must know the gate." Thereby drawing attention to the gate! It's funny he becomes a recurring feature in this book. I'll leave you to make your own mind up if he never had all the tools in the shed. Training wise, Frank promoted Pat Holland to do a bit of work with the first team. Pat was one of many who I met in football who spent the majority of his career at one club, in his case West Ham, and supported another which was Arsenal. He had to retire through a nasty knee injury and wisely began to make plans outside the game to earn a living.

On one of the many occasions we spoke Pat gave me profound words of advice, that in the end for me at least became a bit of a self-fulfilling prophecy. "Make sure you get yourself sorted out for when you pack up playing, 'cos once you're out of the game, you're on your own, no one gives a fuck for you." So right, especially if like me you were a lower division player. I had a lot of time for Pat who was a good coach, affable, approachable, humorous and wanted to win. These ingredients would explain why in the distant future, when I thought I'd done a deal with Barry Hearn I wanted Pat as my number two. In the meantime, the club had hit hard times yet again and things in and around the place forced a change. From where I don't know, but Brian Winston had returned as acting chairman. Between them, Frank, Bill Songhurst and one or two directors who came by occasionally ran the club. In a land far, far away called Rwanda, a local boy who had made good through his entrepreneurial skills as owner of a coffee plantation and as honorary ambassador for Her Majesty's government, heard the plight of the club from the area where he grew up as results got gradually worse, which he listened to religiously on the BBC world service. He started sending cheques and Frank openly enquired and sometimes stated in disbelief "Who is this man? Does anyone know who he is? He keeps sending money."

Not long after he became chairman and it immediately helped Frank, Pat and Bill and gave the place a huge lift. Previously, Frank was restricted on what could be spent at the club. Never mind the thought of buying players, Frank called Mr Wood the new chairman and said "we can't run a club like this" as he (Frank) had to obtain permission for any purchases for over ten pounds from Brian Winston. The immediate short term future of the club was about to be put in place with a regime change and a new job title for Frank.

Things definitely seemed to be on the way up. Overnight stays were no longer a problem, Pat made training enjoyable and as a reward for the effort of most of the people around the club, Tony Wood gave all the players a Christmas card with two fifty pound notes in, a turkey and a Burberry Christmas Hamper. An unusual precedent had been set that was eclipsed during the ten months I was co-manager. I was not even into my first year as a player at the club and we'd already had three chairmen. Added to the staff after a visit to Cambridge was Bernie Dixson as "Youth Development Officer." He came into the players' bar and canvassed the lads on what we felt contributed to us currently being in a slump. Pat said to me that Bernie was credited by Frank for "hitting the nail on the head" after watching us just once and he was brought on board. Pat put on some great drills and very enjoyable sessions and had a good manner about him and Frank was the voice of any overview and came more to the fore on match day. Brian Eastick made his first appearance at the club as youth coach. After only a couple of months he turned it in and left. Frank said to me that he thanked Brian for his honesty as Brian had remarked "I've got nothing to work with."

For a little while the youngsters were helped by Jimmy Halleybone and Bernie which is not ideal because it's someone's potential career being messed with. I found it ironic that a club with an unbelievable track record in producing youngsters for their first team with some even sold to bigger clubs had put in place a youth development officer "the most important man in the club" according to Frank in the local press, but didn't have a youth coach prepared to set aside results and a few good hidings from bigger clubs to produce players for Orient's first team. Having been called an enigma by Keith Peacock at Gillingham I looked it up and was surprised to see it wasn't a piece of second world war machinery and more to do with explaining a smile in a painting. The word enigma could undoubtedly be applied to physio Bill Songhurst. He was funny, confident, charismatic, knowledgeable, profound, superficial, insecure, lairy, loud, astute and above all else, lost and contradictory. I laughed as he left his Christmas card on the coach and Frank had asked him "what he thought of the Christmas card from the chairman?" Bill Mumbled. "Yeah nice, why?" Frank says "there's three hundred pounds in fifty pound notes inside it!" I never saw him move so fast as the colour drained from his face at the sight of the coach pulling away at the end of the road. Bill could have been anything he wanted and although he never had a lot of competition at Millwall and Gillingham he was by far the most knowledgeable physio I'd come across, including Chelsea. At Chelsea the physios were Eddie Franklin and Norman Medhurst. Norman was thought of sufficiently high enough to be England's kit man.

"Songy" could diagnose, give an estimate of the time you would be out and very importantly for a small club, well any club really, get inside the head of a player who might not feel sure or confident of starting ninety minutes. People don't really know, but Bill mentored the current England doctor Ian Beasley through his sports medicine diploma when Ian was Orient's club doctor. Doctor Beasley had spells at Watford, Arsenal and I think one of my old clubs Chelsea. He then went on to England but started under Bill at Orient as a GP learning along the way when it came to football injuries and I'm sure the way footballers react to them and the many wide and varied pain thresholds. Bill over the years, if he could have been bothered to take, then top up his qualifications, could have worked at any club in the country but he was happy to poodle along the M11 from Harlow to the O's every day for nearly two decades. He always insisted, "I don't want to be a millionaire, I just want to live like one." And on the surface, the superficial outside, it certainly looked like he did. A big thing around the club was fashion and who had the latest clothes. I must say I took full advantage and tapped into the sales market to subsidise my meagre wages. A few of my close mates at the time had ready access to suits, jackets, shirts, ties, casual tops and I would sell a few to the lads.

My mates still have the shop in Haringey so the prices must have been quite good for a number of years. Not long after Brian Eastick left for the first time a new youth coach came in on a loose agreement called John Gorman. He was quite open about leaving as soon as a bigger, better offer came in. Not what I'd have or call a great strategy for a youth policy but as I found out later, the pay was diabolical so you can't blame anyone for keeping their options open. I must mention my experience of the first chairman I came across in that first year, Mr Neville Ovenden. I met him briefly a couple of times and the things I noticed as results were not that good and the finances took hold was how his health started to deteriorate and the stress etched on his face. Some welcome respite financially came in the form of a two legged Milk Cup tie against Spurs.

At home it was a guaranteed full house as fourth division played first division and to quote Frank "no one outside these four walls thinks we have a chance." Peter Shreeves, a London cab driver, had made good by working his way from youth coach to Keith Burkinshaw's number two and was now manager. At home it was possibly as strong a Spurs side as it could be. Hughton, Miller, Roberts, Perryman, Waddle, Ardiles, Hoddle et al. After a ricket early on when I got caught square and John Chiedozie was about to go clear, I never put a foot wrong. It was nice to play in a big game again. I pulled Chiedozie back and took the yellow card. I should have got man of the match after realising I needed to be exemplary and I was for the remaining eighty-eight minutes. Peter Shreeves saw fit to mention Kevin Hales in the national press, although I suspect it was a case of mistaken identity because Sean Brooks was superb. Shinners was a handful for Paul Miller and Graham Roberts and Kevin Godfrey at last, even though it was momentarily and short-lived, fulfilled his immense potential and tormented Chris Hughton and scored two goals. We came off 2-0 winners even though Spurs carved us open and Glen Hoddle instead of putting pace on the ball to finish properly tried to take the piss by cushioning a side foot volley so that it just about rolled over the line.

I raced back and made my recovery run complete by scrambling the ball off the line and away to safety. The only problem at the end was it was two legs. We had to go to White Hart Lane for the second game. After the game in Orient's small sponsors' lounge, me and Steve Perryman were invited in as captains of our respective teams. Steve was very praising, humble and an absolute gentleman. He was good company and easy to talk to in the brief time I met him and came across as a good professional. Obviously he not only served Spurs with distinction, but I found out that he could also tell people's fortunes and see into the future. I overheard part of his explanation for the defeat to a Spurs supporter "never mind, we'll get them at home."

As we handed the team sheets in at White Hart Lane, which as skipper you had to do in the referees changing room forty-five minutes before kickoff, Spurs players seemed to have a different focus. It was more intense and a long way away from most of the team surfacing from the away team dressing room a week earlier with a can of lager in their hand. Steve Perryman's fortune telling was proved correct as we were obliterated 4-0. I should have known as I ran on to the pitch for my warm up and saw the body language of some of my team mates. I looked around and got great energy from the crowd as I soaked up the atmosphere but unfortunately with only a few exceptions, the team was overawed and out of its depth.

The only semi-decent performances that night came from me, Colin Foster, Andy Sussex and one or two others. I don't think our forwards got a kick, the back four were constantly under pressure and midfield could hardly string a pass together. Apart from the result I remember Colin Foster getting topped by Graham Roberts after Roberts overran the ball and after the game Bill Songhurst saying that Graham Roberts beat us on his own which I thought was a bit harsh. Frank on a very rare occasion flared up at Halesy, as he remarked to Foster "you have got to learn to look after yourself." Frank said to Halesy "stop fucking chuntering on, it's a shame you didn't do all your talking during the ninety minutes." Pure frustration on Frank's part after squandering a two goal lead and not even remotely looking like we would pose any sort of goal threat ourselves in the whole game. I got a bit frustrated myself as I ran past our midfield to close down Graham Roberts on the edge of our box. I'd sussed there was absolutely no competitive edge, actually bordering on cowardice which was embarrassing. In trying to make up lost ground I overcommitted and Roberts touched the ball over me and finished with a volley from the penalty spot. Halesy might have had a point with big Colin Foster though, he wasn't at all aggressive and at times a bit naive.

That night a six-inch gash down his shin and part of his ankle down to Graham Roberts was preferable to and lucky not to be a broken leg. It came as no surprise to me as I looked around the dressing room that "Big Fos" as I called him was one of only two, at best three, saleable assets in the club at that time. A bit later on John Cornwell was sold to Frank's mate Willie McFaul at Newcastle for about seventy-five thousand pounds. I just said sarcastically to Frank " I thought McFaul was your mate." Frank laughed. Oh well, it's all about opinions. Andy Sussex was so laid back I nicknamed him Perry, after Perry Como. A good footballer, intelligent, decent athlete, natural left footer, probably explains why Dario Gradi liked him and took him to Crewe. The downside to Big Fos being a financial asset probably contributed to me playing when I shouldn't have. I had what started as acute tendonitis in my left achilles tendon. Colin Foster was on many occasions wrapped in cotton wool with a bruised big toe, dead leg, runny mascara, twisted eyelash, a dry bogie or poorly plucked eyebrows while I lay on the treatment table an hour before kick off with Bill Songhurst and the club doctor giggling as I screamed in agony with them taking turns with a six-inch hypodermic. "Bill! Bill!" He says "I've got to get the whole area," wriggling the needle around as he squirts in a cortisone injection. Memo to players: never take Hydro Cortisone.

I read up on it afterwards, it kills off the bad cells, but along with killing the pain, it kills and weakens the good cells. I had to ice it every morning before training and after every game just to walk. Fast forward to Brentford at home. Centre half for the opposition is Micky Droy. Free kick to Brentford for offside, we hold a line, I get up and power a header away on the edge of our box. As I land, I shout to "squeeze up, squeeze up!" I go to push off, BANG! like an air rifle going off, or if you've ever heard it, someone getting a right hander. I went down in excruciating pain. There was nobody anywhere near me and I knew it was bad, Songy comes on. "What's the problem Sitts?" I reply, "Bill I think I've ruptured my achilles." Bill gets my calf and squeezes it and my foot is just flopping around all over the place. "Sitts, I've got to say, that's a good bit of self-diagnosis." The signal goes up, St John's come on and stretcher me off and I'm put on a bench in the match day medical room. My wife comes down to see me, I tell her it's bad and got someone to give her my car keys.

She's at the game with my Dad and I ask him to drive her home. I get loaded into an ambulance and taken to Princess Grace Hospital in Marylebone. All the way there the attending paramedic doses me up on oxygen to keep me calm and ease the pain. That night I couldn't sleep without a jab to knock me out. Next day, I get a pre-med that leaves me floating about nine inches off the ceiling. I'm taken down, then the next time I become conscious, my Mum, Dad and Loiza are standing over me. The pain again, it was like a stinging, burning sensation. The nurse gave me another jab and it knocked me out after my Dad said "can't you give him something?" All this happened on my Mum's birthday. As I started to get drowsy my Mum said "we'll be back up tomorrow babe just rest."

Next day the surgeon appears and tells me I had a one hundred percent tear of the achilles and he has surgically repaired it by overlapping it and stitching it together. I ask how long and it tied in with what Frank was told by Bill Songhurst. Frank came to visit, have a pot of tea and a cream cake and as he left he tells me to expect to be out for six to nine months. I had four weeks in plaster from hip to toe, four weeks in plaster to just above my knee, and even though it happened in

December, I was back ready to play by April. Frank and Songy told me to ease up. There were four games left, so rest and be ready for pre-season. I ignored it and was relentless in training, strengthening and stretching. I lost count of the hours I did on a wobble board and stretching my achilles and calf muscle. Even though my contract was up, I was told to sit it out and not to worry.

Frank offered me the same money for another two years taking me up to the summer of 1989. I was badly injured only a few months ago, I was in the middle of rehab, and Frank probably could never be sure my achilles wouldn't snap again, so I don't suppose he wanted too much money tied up in one of his best players, best defenders and captain. Arrivals and departures would mean Tommy Cunningham released, Colin Foster sold to Nottingham Forest, Lee Harvey a good player and superb athlete progressing through the ranks with Steve Castle and the arrivals of Terry Howard, Steve Ketteridge, Warren Hackett and on the left a tricky, bright, intelligent winger with great ability Alan Comfort. So, I wanted in and to be part of what looked like a more combative, exciting team with a bit more of a goal threat. Steve Baker was added after over one hundred games for Southampton which would have a relevance later on because you'd expect a player from a supposed higher level to cope with tactics and strategy rather than just be able to run all day. As part of the deal for Colin Foster, Frank got Mark Smalley, lean, quick, intelligent, loads of ability but neither here nor there. He was too light and not physical enough to play centre half for forty-six games. I'd have played "Bert" which was a nickname I had given him, screening the two centre halves. "Bert" came from Bertie Smalls the infamous underworld super grass after I heard someone call him "Smalls" short for Smalley. I declared "fuck it, we'll go the whole hog" and I christened him Bert.

Frank didn't have a clue what I was on about. He also never had a clue about someone who asked to be on the board of directors. Not sure, Bill suggested to Frank that he ask me if I knew anything about this individual. I said behind closed doors, "don't touch him, he's been nicked for handling stolen cheques and I've heard he's going to prison." I had been told the story six months before it made any sort of news. The return of Colin Foster to pick up his boots came straight after Frank had taken him to do a deal with Brian Clough, "Fos" just laughed and said he found Cloughie quote, "a bit strange Sitts, he seems a bit strange." I asked "how so?" "Well I've just met him, it's mid-morning, he pulls his chair up to mine, offers me a lager, gives me a kiss and says "Colin, all I want you to do is come and head the ball for us."

A pre-season tour was arranged. Orient got relegated before my time and went to Majorca with the stories still being told six months later and I missed out. Before that Millwall were relegated and went to Jamaica, which I also missed out on, but this time I'm on board and we are off to, of all places Norway! How's your luck?

I couldn't wait to get started, so I did quite a bit of training on my own before we reported for pre-season. Then it was off to Norway. We arrived and got dished out the equivalent of eight pounds per day to pay for incidentals. The hotel was in a small town just outside Stavanger. It was clean and everything including the town centre was immaculately kept. The three meals per day were pot luck and a bit hit and miss. Breakfast was a good choice so I loaded up and preferred a lighter lunch so I could get my head down for a nap after training. The evening meal was ok but nothing special, consisting of a set meal with not many choices. After they got us out of the way Frank and Bill dabbled in the a la carte menu and Chablis.

On the way there striker Ian Juryeff was fretting over his father being diagnosed with cancer. Ian knew his Dad was due to have surgery but made the trip anyway. During the evening meal on the first night "Juke" got called out to be told the terrible, devastating news that his Dad had died on the operating table. The lads were stunned. Well most of them anyway, which has a relevance in that one of the more opportunistic ones used the sad situation to his advantage. Frank got a car laid on for Ian to be taken to the airport for the first available flight home. After a walk around town, I settled in for the night looking forward to the first day's training.

No player it has to be said, is a great lover of pre-season, but to me this was what pre-season should be all about. Sleep, eat, train, rest, train, relax, eat, sleep. Most days there was only one session because Frank wanted us fresh for the two games we had arranged to play. I've got to say, for me it became one of the most enjoyable periods of any pre-season I ever did. Covering sixteen seasons from the age of sixteen through to thirty-one. The only downside to a great country were the prices. It was very expensive, so inevitably having to top up on food, water, snacks, or a night out the eight pounds we got didn't go very far. I roomed with Micky Conroy who was missing most of the time which suited me down to the ground. No distractions, no disturbances, good training, good rest and where we stayed, you could have bottled the air and sold it.

The weather was superb and a nice relief for my legs was to have a dip in the lakes in the surrounding countryside. In the morning Micky came back to the room and served as the ideal wake up call for breakfast. Meanwhile elsewhere in the hotel Ian Juryeff's bad news was used to full advantage by another player. Ian's roommate was on his own, so player "A" says to his roommate, "you move in with Juke's roommate so I'm on my own..." In the downstairs disco on the first night most of the lads had a sherbet and got some sleep after a day's travelling. But not player "A" who I'll refer to as such because he was married. The lads all knew, and halfway through the week so did Bill, that this player had a young woman living in his room with him for the whole duration of a one-week pre-season tour. She even came down to reception to see off her mates as they left for home after their holiday at our hotel because she was staying put!

All the lads were given a coded knock, because if anyone needed to get hold of player "A" for a team meeting or to come to a meal or collect fresh training kit he didn't want to be opening the door to Frank or Bill. Halfway through the week the cat was let out of the bag when Bill was asking for this particular player to hand over some tape and strappings. So one of the lads gives Bill the coded knock. Half the squad waited excitedly behind Bill as he did the knock. The door opens and there's player "A" with a little blonde Norwegian bird laying there like the ace of clubs next to the ace of spades, giving away the fact that the hair on her head was dyed. This episode never ended there though. I'm not sure what Bill did with the information because in my time at Orient I always perceived Bill to be very loyal to Frank. Normally if Bill found something out about one of the players Frank would know not long after. But on this occasion I could never get my head around whether Bill had told him, and for the sake of not destroying the tour Frank left it alone, or whether Bill was stuck in the middle and withheld the information.

However, what happened at the end of the tour even Frank couldn't fail to suss things out. Anyway back to the football and after battering a local semi-pro side, it was on to the main course of Viking Stavanger. I think they took a leaf out of all the blokes in the bars we frequented and took their Viking heritage a bit serious because it got very physical. If you were stood at the bar waiting to order a drink, a local looking like an extra from the Barbarian hordes in Gladiator's opening scene would just barge you out of the way to get a place so that they could order an expensive beer. It was the equivalent of five pounds for half a lager. In the nightclub a few of the lads approached me on the third night rightfully pissed off that the Norwegian guests were helping themselves to our drinks. Every time someone was in conversation or went for a visit to the loo our patch was invaded and it was almost biblical.

There's one new team mate I haven't yet mentioned who was to turn out to be a perfect partner for me at centre half, we were almost telepathic. He did what I couldn't and I did what he couldn't, and he was the best centre half partner I ever played with at any club at any level, and I have always regarded him as my brother in battle.

His name was Keith Day who came to Orient from Colchester after starting in non-league at Aveley. He could do everything and had everything, and I loved him as a player and a person.

The training facilities excited me and every day I thought why can't we have facilities like this back in England? We were guests of a lower division club who had mannequins for free kicks, goals on wheels, significant in that in England when we had to move the goals six to eight players had to pick them up and walk them to a new spot and the dressing rooms and showers were spotless. The playing surfaces were like bowling greens which compared favourably to the three dog shit covered, tufted, windswept and muddy training grounds back home. I couldn't get enough of it, and with a new look squad, well newish, I was bursting for the start of the season. I wasn't the only one bursting with excitement.

I couldn't believe my eyes at the end of the tour as we waited at the airport to go home. There was about two weeks of pre-season left and we flew home to a couple of friendlies to get us ready for the opening day. A new and unexpected addition to the squad waiting at the airport was player "A's" Norwegian concubine who by now I had nicknamed Helga. According to player "A," Helga had phoned her family to inform them she was flying to the UK with the love of her life. Even back then as a younger man I still couldn't quite work out how two people who had only just met would do such a thing. It made for a very uncomfortable atmosphere and a bit of an undercurrent as we sat in the departure lounge. Everyone kept their mouth shut but as I walked past Frank and Bill having a meal in the posh part of the airport lounge with the ever present accompanying bottle of Chablis, I was munching on my cheese puffs or Toblerone, and I couldn't help thinking that surely Frank must know. Then to compound it all on the flight on the way home player "A" asked for one of the lads to stand guard outside the WC on the plane so that he and Helga can become members of the mile high club.

I couldn't believe my eyes when we got back that Helga continued to be a guest at the back of the stand and in the players' bar for the remaining pre-season friendlies and the home League Cup tie against Millwall. One man conspicuous by his absence on the trip was Pat Holland. Despite his enjoyable sessions, encouragement and feel good factor he never made the trip. I'm not sure of the time scale or the exact period when it happened but Pat eventually left for pastures new. It coincided with a bit of a save of face for Pat, that's just my opinion, when he took a job as youth coach at Spurs. After all why would you voluntarily leave someone's first team for someone's youth team? The season itself was respectable.

Results were fairly consistent but the team lacked one or two ingredients. I've got to say I'm glad I had Pat at my side as a coach and according to the feedback I got so were the rest of the players. He always put on fresh, enjoyable sessions and was a perfect go between for Frank. Pat would always encourage feedback and I think it was reflected in some of the performances. The disappointing end table, where we finished eighth was down to one or two draws that should have been wins. Away to Cardiff on the first day of the season and we got a respectable 1-1. The big hitters with stadium, crowd, money and good players were Wolves who went up as champions. We drew at home to Millwall in the League Cup and lost by the odd goal in the second leg. It was nice to bump into my old team mates Tony Cascarino and Teddy Sheringham, who was a kid when I was at Millwall but because he was already good enough trained with the youth team and reserves.

We hit a few teams for four and done Rochdale 8-0 but dropped some silly points that confined us for yet another year in the bottom division. After going out early in the League Cup to Millwall, we got a bit of pride back in the FA Cup. We beat Exeter, Swansea and Stockport, then got knocked out by the odd goal by Nottingham Forest. Mind you three out of the four games were at home so we were quite lucky with the draw. The last seven games of the season probably said it all, bang average. We drew one, won three, lost three. We drew against and beat Cardiff, who finished second in the league but Wolves done us twice. I missed the game at Molineux in front of a virtual full house. The noise was astounding and it made for a great atmosphere. Bolton finished third and they also done us twice. I looked at it and the difference always seemed to be a real potent goal threat. It's the same in every league.

Off the field, I had started to take my coaching qualifications and threw myself into a preliminary badge as it was known and loads of "prep" courses every couple of months on Sundays in readiness for my full badge. I coached on Sundays and picked up a bit of extra money to help the household and to help my Mum and Dad. With my wife's help and permission I had stockpiled enough money to help my Mum and Dad open a shop in the local neighbourhood. After the debacle and the human filth robbing my Mum of their takings in Clapham it was the least I could do.

My Dad had more or less single handedly wasted my Mum's share of her inheritance from my Grandad and financially they were on their knees. It was a quarter year's rent, some stock money and some readies for a redecoration and some fixtures and fittings. It's a good job I had set aside the money I'd made from selling the little retail business I had going. The only thing my Mum had to show for three lifetime's work, my Grandad, my Mum and my Dad was the council house she had bought outright. I thought "thank God" or my father would probably have lost that in the betting shop or at a card table as well.

This period, and as you'll have read it wasn't the only one, was a massive bitter sweet part of my life so far. To this day I still don't know how I got through it all. But I just got on with it. At Gillingham I had turned down the chance to go to America and play indoor "Soccer" in Dallas. My brother was a married man with two young children and my sister was to follow her fiancé to be near his family just outside Norwich. That left me, my Dad and my Mum to buy the stock and run the shop in the run up to Christmas of 1986. As we moved into 1987, a big decision is made by my Mum who declares it's time to move, and to kill two birds with one stone, it has to be semi-rural. So why not a place near her "baby" just outside Norwich. My Dad humoured her but I had a feeling that all was not well. The cancer, a most vile illness, returned and at first it was recommended she go on chemotherapy. Even at that fairly young and inexperienced age I thought on top of everything else, she's now a medical experiment. The shop and house were put up for sale and after a couple of messers, the shop was finally sold. It's just as well because my Dad couldn't cope on his own. I did my bit, but my Mum was becoming increasingly tired and ill. My Mrs and football were my only other priorities. To be fair, I don't think I had too much time for anything else. So for a while at least, we missed out Loiza and I, on some of the stuff you do with your peers as a young married couple. My brother came down and visited every day and I usually walked from my house to my Mum's every day to make sure she was ok. An offer was accepted for the family home and it looked like they were on their way to the countryside. I drove my parents several times for viewings and they agreed a deal to buy a bungalow from a lovely old couple located between Thetford and Norwich.

So, I was skipper, I'd seen off a ruptured achilles, I had agreed a new two-year contract in the summer of 1987 and after five years of being on our own as a couple Loiza and I received the news that she was expecting. Our first baby was on the way! I felt like I was walking on air, then smack! Boom! Lightning strikes and my Mum is told she isn't going to get better. We brought a bed into the lounge and as a final roll of the dice she is put on steroids to alleviate the pain. The sale of the house was called off, the purchase of the bungalow called off, the shop was sold and I told my Mum and Dad to keep the money to live off, despite what I had contributed. On the odd occasion my Mum got out for fresh air it was in a wheelchair pushed by my Dad.

The reception she got in the neighbourhood was mainly one of shock because of the extreme change in her appearance. She was swollen all over, bloated and her head was twice its normal size, even though she had kept her lovely thick hair through the chemotherapy. Loiza has been a great one for working around me and football, so she pitched in and often came with me after training to check on and say hello to Mum and help look after her. On one such an occasion my mum took Loiza to one side and removed her engagement ring which happened to be a solitaire diamond set in platinum and handed it to her saying "here I want you to have this. I know my John has picked the right girl for him and you will take over from where I have left off. I know you will look after him." My Mrs got emotional, gave my mum a kiss and cuddle and thanked her very much. It meant a lot to both of us.

After training one day we went to see my Mum and Dad and told them that tomorrow we would be late as we had an appointment at the hospital for Loiza's first scan on our baby and that we'll be around straight after. After the scan we went home for a quick bite to eat and the phone rings. It's my Dad to tell me that my Mum had slipped into a coma that morning and she had been admitted to hospital.

He asked if I would come to the hospital and try and talk to her. She was admitted to North Middlesex Hospital and we got there to find her lying on a trolley as they made arrangements for her to have a bed. Loiza leaned over and kept talking about the scan. I insisted she be around for "her first born son's baby, your grandchild Mum." She was unresponsive and after being by her bedside all afternoon and into the evening, me and my Mrs shot away to get everyone a bite to eat. She was never to return home and within the same twenty-four hours that Loiza had her scan to check on the life inside her, my Mum lost the battle for hers. My Dad and brother Chris joined us for a meal at home then we went back to the hospital. I left at around 9.45 pm. My Dad stayed on then left after being told he had already gone well past visiting time. He was told he'd get a call if there was any change in her condition.

I'm almost sure it was a Tuesday and me and Loiza were both exhausted and we went to bed quite early. The phone rang at about ten minutes past midnight. I ran downstairs and I knew it would be bad news. I was thinking ahead and I had an air of resignation. My Dad says that he got a call from the hospital and had been told my Mum's condition had worsened and to get myself over to the hospital. I lived not far so I was there within five minutes. I sat holding my Mum's hand, talking to her and she just looked like she was in a deep sleep.

My brother and Dad were pacing up and down and my Dad called a nurse. I remember her being a softly spoken middle aged black lady. She had a lovely, gentle way about her and seemed very dignified and tuned in to her duties and surroundings. I had only realised a few hours earlier that my Mum was on a ward whose inhabitants never went home. The nurse took Mum's pulse, turned to us and very quietly, very softly said "I'm very sorry. I'm afraid she's gone." It was 12.28am, September 9th, 1987. My mind was racing but outwardly I was very calm. My Dad and brother got upset but for some reason I felt it was my duty to be strong. One of my biggest regrets is not giving myself the chance to mourn as I tried to be strong for Dad, Chris and Kay.

The next day, which was a day off, I went into the ground at Leyton Orient, told Frank that I would need a certain day off for my Mum's funeral and he asked if I was ok. I said yes, and don't even think about resting me. I put a kit on, went for a run, did some weights and body exercises because I needed to escape and it was the only thing I could think of. Bill Songhurst came and offered his condolences, Paul Shinners did the same and added, "what the fuck are you doing here?" I just said to him I had to come away from it all, things like funeral arrangements and registry of death could wait or my Dad could take some responsibility for a change.

Carol Stokes asked if I was ok and to keep her informed as she offered her condolences. On the day of the funeral itself Mum got a good turnout of family, extended family, and a few old friends lined the pavement like they did for my Grandad. She helped a good few people in her life. Both Orient and my Sunday side sent flowers which was nice and something I'll never forget.

Some people are blessed with being able to work things out at a relatively young age. For me certain things have taken a little longer. Probably because I've just got on with living my life. I now feel that I'm able to look back and having thought about certain events, I have deduced that a lot of what I put up with as a younger man I wouldn't suffer for five minutes with the experience I now have. Bill Songhurst remarked on more than one occasion that I was "too sensitive." I think the opposite and I showed a mental strength, mental toughness and sometimes even a tolerance for the ignorance around me. One thing you learn as someone focused and quietly confident in his own ability is that in football you are surrounded by treachery, insecurity and a boat load of people which, like some of the rest of society, define themselves with bravado, a false front, a superficial plastic belief and trying to put down those around them to make themselves look better than they really are. In the end, none of it really matters at times like these. At my mother's funeral all I knew was I'd had a bellyful of bereavement. I'd lost my Nan, Grandad, Aunt Nell, Uncle Alf and now my Mum. I nearly piped up after the service at Enfield Crematorium when the vicar came over to commiserate and offer condolences. My brother and sister looked shell shocked and my Dad struggling for words remarked. "We had thirty-three bloody good years." I stopped myself from saying, "what you mean is, you had thirty-three bloody good years." I felt I was his son in name only as my mind raced over the twenty-eight years I had been around. As a man my Dad had juggled two jobs and yet still came home with a short wage packet.

Any holidays we had were down to my Mum and Aunt who owned our caravan. The nearest I got to going abroad was two trips to Jersey, down to my Mum's inheritance. The haulage business that basically meant my Dad had ten years of visiting most of Europe and the Middle East with a bit of driving in between, again down to Mum's inheritance. Our council house purchased by Mum, you've guessed it, down to Mum's inheritance. A cooked dinner every night down to Mum's work, foresight and planning of a nonexistent household budget. The stock money for Chelsea and Clapham markets? Fifty percent Mum, fifty percent me. The shop in north London? Me and Loiza and what was left over from the decimated haulage business. I even remember chasing my Dad's brother out of the shop as they discussed that day's race meetings and he asked my Dad, "If you can't get away, do you want me to put a bet on for you Reg?" If it wasn't for me and my Mrs, the rent on the shop was struggling to be paid. The holiday to America after being told that my Mum had eight to ten months to live was a mad scramble for cash. I found the bulk of it. None of this known by my brother and sister.

As a family it's about sticking together and trusting each other. It's no good being a grafter if fortunes are dwindled away through poor judgement, greed, selfishness and a trail of one disaster after another in your rear view mirror. This book is about me and while I am not that important, I think the story is. A lovely gesture by Uncle Albert Martin reduced my Mum to tears a couple of days before we left for a holiday a couple of years earlier to America. He visited, had a pot of tea and said "there you go, I want you to have this." He gave my Mum three hundred pounds to convert into dollars. He was doing well and I thought there was a poignancy about the sum he gave her, adding, "I want you to have a nice time." It was three hundred my Nan and Grandad had lent him to buy his first lorry. He was on the way up, we were on the way down. We had failed to build on what Grandad had done, he had built and gone from strength to strength. I asked "Albert, why? We'll be ok," he said. "I love your mother son, she brought me up and looked after me 'cos my parents were not around."

Within two weeks of my Mum being cremated, my Dad was out and about with his brother. Within six weeks, at fifty-six he'd met a woman of twenty-eight, the same age as me. Under a year later my Dad had sold, against my advice, the family home. Going on the information relayed to me the woman he was with, also had numerous assets. They moved to a bungalow in Clacton. Even though they paid cash, within a few years, with no visible means of income my Dad armed with just under thirty grand cash in equity and all the cash from his partner's divorce and assets they went through and eventually lost the lot. A few years back, I went to try and find him just a couple of years after being sacked at Orient.

I was curious and a little worried over his welfare. I stuck up for him when my siblings protested at the quick and sudden turn of events after my Mum's funeral. I said "let's not judge. We can't know what he's feeling or thinking and we won't unless we are in his position." I said "Dad what's going on? Don't you think it's a bit too soon? Surely my Mum deserves more respect." He replied

"What do you want me to do? Sit in and stare at four walls every night?" In Clacton, guess where I found him? He was leaning on a counter studying form in his local betting shop. I bought him a cold drink and left him some money. By the time I got home the phone rang, it was my Dad asking for some money. I said "I'll get back to you, I'll speak to Chris and Kay and we'll try and send you a few quid." I put the phone down and never spoke to him again. Fucking Embarrassing.

He tells me that they've been through the money from three houses, thirty grand cash equity from our family home and ten grand cash from a remortgage on the bungalow where they were living. Because of his lack of earning power, he had been talked into remortgaging, in my opinion scammed, for ten grand because it's all their earnings would cover. An eighty grand bungalow repossessed for ten grand! I said if you had signed the bungalow over to me, Chris and Kay I'd have given you the ten grand and let you live there rent free. At least I know some sort of inheritance would have come from Mum and Grandad even if I was giving ten grand for it.

A few years back in the run up to Christmas, a supposedly busy time for a cab driver, I went to my bedroom for a nap before everyone congregated for Sunday dinner. I was shattered after a sixty-hour week. I was woken by my wife who was emotional and she gently told me, "I've just had a call from my sister, your cousin Dawn has told her that your Dad's passed away." I had received the news third hand. I called my Uncle Brian who confirmed it and he said the funeral was on Monday 20th December. I called my sister and brother. We turned up to an address in Harwich. By now my Dad had a stepson and three children by his partner and added to a couple of his neighbours we attended his funeral. Me, my brother Chris and sister Kay never got a mention as reference was made at the service to his family and all his kids. Back to the football...

Season 1988-89 and it was all change. Pat Holland had done his best, in my eyes as good a job as possible. He experienced what I was to experience in my time as co-manager and first team coach. He had to walk the tightrope between first team coach and Frank Clark having the final say on any general overview. Ergo, credibility. Things fell nicely into place for Pat who immediately moved on to a job at Spurs. The new first team coach was Brian Eastick. On the first day he actually admitted that he'd asked Frank if I had caused any trouble. I was approaching twenty-eight and I told Brian I think I've grown up a bit since you knew me as a seventeen to twenty- year-old at Chelsea.

From day one Brian Eastick gave us something we had never had in all the time I had been at Orient and since I had left Chelsea and that was patterns of play, set pieces, and a defensive strategy copied and copied again. It was invented by Terry Venables, taught to George Graham when he was Venners' youth coach at

QPR, perfected and used by George and his players at Arsenal and now drilled into us relentlessly by Brian Eastick. It's the best defensive system there is in my opinion, especially if it's coached correctly. The relationship between me and Brian was eighty- twenty. I had repented and matured, he was less abrasive, but not to the extent that every now and again he'd give you a reminder of what was good for you. The main things he had going for him were his knowledge, coaching ability and character.

It was his willingness every single day to fight battles with players who would have preferred an eight a side instead of rehearsing patterns of play, free kicks, corners, throw ins or playing the back six against ten, or the back four against six, or retreating and marking in the box or crossing and finishing, I could go on and on. One or two actually looked to see my reaction or asked if I could have a word. I was non-committal to their face but inside I was thinking "no way" because it was helping us get results. Brian also had one or two rows and disagreements with Bill Songhurst and voiced his displeasure on more than one occasion as he saw and sensed the closed shop sycophancy. His best tantrums were reserved for Frank Woolf. Brian said "as a commercial manager you're a joke, I should have a sponsored car as assistant manager and first team coach." Something that over time I fully concurred with. In retaliation one day, "Woolfy" tried to ridicule Brian for putting his keys on the table at a pre-match meal. Eastick said "shut up Woolfy, don't tell me what to do, you're nothing more than Clarky's fag."

I assumed he meant the Tom Brown's Schooldays version not the American version. By now most of the messers, time wasters, bad professionals and shit players had been replaced. Behind the back four was the best goalkeeper outside the top division in my opinion Paul Heald. To me, the management and the back four he was like a breath of fresh air. A good lad, good pro, superb goalkeeper as well as a superb trainer, he looked the part, and absolutely played the part with his performances.

The back four was Kevin Dickenson, me, Keith Day and either Terry Howard or Steve Baker. Ironically one of the main complainants about Brian Eastick's sessions was Baker. He had played over one hundred times for Southampton and it was ironic in that when we looked to spring our offside trap from either open play or a dead ball after a signal was given by me, it was occasionally Howard, but mostly Steve Baker who had forgotten what he was supposed to do and played the opposition on side.

It wasn't a bad year for London, with the exception of West Ham who were relegated from the top division. The division that Arsenal won in the last few seconds away to Liverpool. George Graham called it "pure theatre." I couldn't agree more. I also found it inspirational for when little old Leyton Orient would be involved at long last in a promotion via the play offs. To round off the London scene Spurs were top six, QPR and Millwall were mid-table just above Charlton with West Ham Utd unfortunately second from bottom. The second division champions were my old club Chelsea promoted to the top division on ninety-nine points. In division three Fulham got in the play offs but missed out as Port Vale were promoted. At Leyton Orient, after ten months' hard work, forty-six league games, a play off semi-final then final, I had at last got a semblance of some sort of minor success as I skippered the team through it all.

That was the culmination of a lot of hard work over a football lifetime, not least the preceding ten months which has to be said didn't get off to the best of starts for me. I returned from the close season with a broken arm. The Sunday side that I coached were moving in the right direction and the committee rewarded us with a trip to Corfu that for me turned out to be a nightmare. A couple of us took our families, the majority of the squad didn't, so as you can imagine there wasn't a lot of sleep. The nasty owner of the apartments would randomly cut off the water so getting a shower was pot luck. One day my wife shocked him and everyone as she went ballistic in Greek at him. She had a baby to bathe. It was all a wind up and some of them are the masters at it. The club had a couple of friendlies arranged and I got itchy feet and joined in.

I collided with a centre forward... As I turned around I felt a searing pain in my left forearm. My mate Peter said "what's wrong Sitts? You've lost your colour." They got me a chair and it felt like a bone was cutting into the muscle. After a ride to hospital and the various x-rays it transpired I had broken my ulna, the smaller bone in your forearm. I was whacked in plaster and told the length of time I would be out which meant I couldn't hide it and would have to report for pre-season with my arm in plaster.

Either way you look at it I had to lie to Frank. I told him that I'd slipped on some wet marble steps after the boys I'd gone on holiday with had a water fight. "Yeah alright Sitts, don't give me that, it must have been something to do with drink." I couldn't say that I was supposed to be a professional footballer but I'd had itchy feet and five minutes of madness, so I joined in a game of football with my Sunday side. I by no means came off the worst with a broken arm. To celebrate the games and the holiday a few of the lads overindulged in tequila shots resulting in one of them falling into a fountain in the bar and taking out his front teeth on the granite. The other casualties were a couple of Greeks, I think known as Corfiotes (being Corfu,) who shouted up abuse at some of the lads in Greek not knowing most of our lot were fluent in the language.

Two of the lads picked up a table and dropped it on the boys with the offensive language from our second floor balcony. Out of three, two scattered and one spent the night unconscious, sleeping against the wall. Now it was the classic. I have to smile and repeat the warm feeling and smile I had when I'd sussed it all out when panic stations ensued. Frank had signed Keith Day, Mark Smalley and now, a ginger lump from the North East called David Corner, famous for gifting Norwich a goal in a League Cup final as he played centre half for Sunderland. It was a case of "take your time Sitts there's no rush, make sure the bone heals properly." All because Clark and Eastick now had four centre halves. A reasonable start turned into a diabolical run, with no leader, no steel and no real allies on the training field for Eastick as his training methods began to be questioned. From the stand you could see that Daygo and Smalley were too similar. Keith Day was a bit more solid and physically well-built than Smalley. They were both quick, adept with the ball, passed well, ran the ball in, but not particularly vocal. It needed someone to inform, implement and reinforce what had been rehearsed defensively on the training field.

In a dogged battle, a war of attrition, winning headers, clearing the ball, bossing, organising, meeting the physicality of the lower divisions over a season that's where I came in. It went from "take your time" to "Sitts you need to cram in a mini pre-season, we need to get you back." Eastick said, reminding himself to say, "competing for a shirt." What had gone on was obvious, Mark Smalley couldn't cope physically and almost every time I looked across at him on the coach, if he wasn't playing cards, he was asleep. The buy from Sunderland had also gone tits up. The management played him and he struggled, proving to be a bit of an embarrassment. Still, it wasn't the first time and wouldn't be the last, by a long chalk, that in Orient terms, massive money was wasted on players inferior to some of the players already there, including yours truly, on piss take wages. I was still on two hundred pounds a week and tens of thousands were wasted on players who ended up not playing or being in and out of the side. There were quite a few minuses that cancelled out the pluses in financial terms. Still, every manager makes mistakes, and nobody gets it right all the time. It's fair to say Frank Clark made his fare share. It's become more relevant to me over the years because I went without, when I should have been rewarded and in the future Orient fans got the hump over a signing I made for five grand. I have to laugh.

Alan Comfort who had arrived from Cambridge had hit the ground running. He started life at QPR and relayed stories of life under Terry Venables then getting England Youth recognition, then getting sent home from a tournament for a night out! He was a great lad and a great trainer. He provided width, trickery and a supply of crosses that had quality on almost every delivery. Mark Cooper turned up from Gillingham and added a bit of height and bulk.

The mobility and pace around him was provided by Lee Harvey. If "Harve" wasn't playing wide right sometimes Steve Baker played wide right with "Harve" played up front. Not all signings with fees, wages and signing on fees attached were endearing. Steve Ketteridge came from Crystal Palace reserves after serving Wimbledon before that. He could run all day and close people down but as he did he flattered to deceive when it came to the physicality of midfield in the lower divisions. His passing range was limited and unlike Steve Castle, didn't really contribute any goals.

I found myself asking "why sign him?" To compound it all he was full of negativity and never, ever, especially after a couple of defeats, passed up an opportunity to slag off Eastick, the training and in particular Frank Clark. This is where we get into it, when later on I talk about a captain choosing sides, leading, setting people straight, keeping things in check, watching the manager's back and promoting harmony, as well as sticking to the game plan rather than take the easy option that I've seen quite a few players do over the years, and run with a small pack of dissenters. Another name for it would be anarchy. Frank was lucky in that respect. He was still fairly well liked around the club and quite a few people, including me, watched his back. I had words on numerous occasions to the likes of "Ketts." He was always chipping away. He probably didn't like the fact that having come from Crystal Palace he wasn't an automatic choice.

He played a few times, but spent a lot of time as a substitute. It was one such time that we had words. It was a match day and I'd been out for a warm up. What I liked to do was come back in and go straight to the match day medical room to get my calf muscles massaged. "Eastick's a wanker, the training's shit. Wally Downes would've slaughtered him, the club's a fucking joke." Was Ketts's contribution to the pre-match build up and conversation. I started gently "Ketts, I thought you'd have got Eastick's pattern of play straight away, it's out of The Crazy Gang guide book, winger threatens the back, comes short, full back or centre half on that side with the ball stands the ball up to fade into the channel or at worse runs out for a throw to the opposition by their corner flag, push up, pin them in, surround the ball and try and win it back. I'd have thought that's right up your street." "It's bollocks Sitts.. we're no Wimbledon.. there's no Fash.. no Vinnie.. Wally would take the piss.. Clarky ain't got a clue, the goings on here... 'Harry' (Dave Bassett) wouldn't stand for it for two minutes..."

I replied after Ketts regaled us with tales of Wimbledon on tour in Majorca. "Maybe you should just knuckle down and concentrate on getting in the starting eleven." I knew he'd never get in front of Steve Castle but could maybe pinch the berth alongside Steve. Ketts kept on, now it was the turn of The Crazy Gang in Majorca and how a supposed "hard man," I just saw him as an irritation, a niggly and annoying little fuck, was left crying and cowering down behind a bar after upsetting the wrong firm who wanted to properly iron him out. Even his so called tough team mates didn't fancy it and apologised managing to calm the situation down with a sincere apology. The other story involved someone drunk who became quite high profile and a horse in a field with a semi-erection. Ketts loved a story. Which is ok as long as you keep the poison to a minimum. Again he goes off on one about Eastick, Frank Clark and Harry Bassett's way of doing things. I said "Ketts, Frank got you out of Crystal Palace reserves and I seem to remember when Dave Bassett first started, as he gave a team talk, players throwing sandwiches at him.

" Ketts laughed as he stretched his groin. I was getting a massage from "Big Dave" Bill Songhurst's mate. I said to Bill "I don't suppose you can call him by his proper name." Bill replied "what do you mean?" I said "well let's be truthful, Fat Dave doesn't have the same ring to it." "Anyway Harry would've.. Wally did this in the warm up, blah, blah, blah" Ketts is off again. I jumped up off the bench and screamed at him "can you see Dave Bassett here? Wally Downes? Fash? whoever the fuck?" "No Sitts" "Then shut the fuck up, fuck Wimbledon and fuck off back to Crystal Palace reserves, you're getting on my fucking nerves." I turned to Dave and said "Dave can you do the left one now?"

Little exchanges like that are ten a penny in football. I even know a story of a top ex-centre half now a respected broadcaster who took it a step further and layed out one of his own team mates as they walked up the tunnel at half time. The player left on his back also happened to be an annoying midfield player with a high opinion of himself. Julian Dicks told me the story at a cigar function and I've no reason to disbelieve it. Sometimes team mates can go too far, push you too far, but never have the wherewithal to recognise it and that you've given them the benefit of the doubt and not hurt them. Some of the shit I put up with so I wasn't seen as a bully amazes me even now.

Ketts knew I meant it and had it on his toes out of the medical room. He also knew I was serious about my football but it didn't stop him from fucking up what would have been one of the best goals ever scored at Brisbane Road. In one game that he started we were on top and I caught a centre forward on the half turn, pinched the ball, drove at the nearest midfielder and went past him, in a few strides I'd gone from the halfway line to the edge of the oppositions box, one of the lads made a run which distracted one of the centre halves. They were caught square and I went past the second centre half and by now I was to the right of the penalty spot with only the goalkeeper to beat. As I'm about to pass it into the net, Ketts pops up on my right shoulder and toe punts it along the floor.

The relieved goalkeeper stoops down to pick up the shot disguised as a back pass. I turned and said "you little cunt!" Shinners and Godfrey were pissing themselves for about ten minutes. Ketts says "sorry Sitts." Frank Clark screams "Sitts what are you fooking doing?" In his broad Geordie accent. The training under Brian Eastick was relentless. Patterns of play, throw ins, set pieces, defensive strategy and nearly every day he fought a battle with players to do what would suit the team and in the end paid us dividends. The other daily battle was to get up for training on a diabolical training ground with a diabolical surface. By now we were based at Douglas Eyre Sports Centre in Walthamstow. We now had somewhere to report every day. The downside was it was packed down mud, a bit of grass and covered in goose shit.

On a really bad day as we did patterns of play, crossing and finishing or defending in the last third, there was gale force wind blowing and if you weren't the victim of a wicked bobble and pinged the ball cleanly it would almost certainly blow off course as the wind came in off the adjacent reservoirs. The spirit though was amazing. There was a respect and togetherness that I'd only experienced a couple of times at clubs before. Everyone I feel, respected each other's contribution. It led to some good runs and amazing results. We came from hovering just above the relegation zone to a play off place. Shouts on the training field from Brian of "Bravo, Bravo," when he got what he wanted were met with "fuck me Juliet's on the firm again, we must be doing it right" from Kevin Dickenson.

He tickled me Dicko. It was now a good dressing room. Good players and good professionals who now had a bit of belief. This is where I have to recognise and say thank you to a thorough professional, strong willed, good coach and superb organiser Brian Eastick. We'd both mellowed slightly since our Chelsea days, I'd matured a bit and because I was in the throes of taking my own coaching qualifications, I started to see things from a different perspective. We all have to grow up in the end.

Although the latter part of the season went particularly well, it wasn't without its share of flare ups and dressing room tantrums. Bill Songhurst had to get between Frank Clark and Alan Hull after Frank went fierce and got right in "Hully's" face to castigate him for leaving his foot in on the opposition's goalkeeper. "This is not fucking non-league now son and I won't have a player of mine do things like that!" Hully went to get up and have it out with Frank and Bill pushed him back down. On another occasion Brian Eastick made a hasty exit after saying to Steve Castle "you fucking bottled it! You've got no bottle!" Steve went "Yeah?" And got up to go for him. Steve had been asked to play wide left due to Alan Comfort being injured. One thing I couldn't understand of any manager or coach was disturbing two positions. Steve had been magnificent at left centre midfield. If I was a poor man's Steve Bruce, Ian Bogie a poor man's Paul Gascoigne, then the least Steve would have been is a Big Issue seller version of Bryan Robson. Left footed, great competitor, contributor of goals, sometimes too brave for his own good and a good athlete that would lead to him getting the captaincy under Peter Eustace. A story I'll come to with I think a humorous twist in the tale. By now we'd had two long undefeated runs and a team meeting was called. Frank put the run down to what he thought was the main added ingredient, Kevin Campbell, a young centre forward from Arsenal. Me, Dicko and Daygo had a look and a mumble "what's that Sitts?" To a few chuckles from my brothers in the defence and Stevie Castle who screened the back four superbly I replied. "It's nothing to do with some of the clean sheets we've been keeping then" I got a curt. "Shut up you big baby!" The others thought I was spot on, added to the fact that I had contributed six to eight goals and assists well into double figures before "stats" were of any importance. Steve Castle was probably double mine. Still it served two purposes. Kevin or "K C" got the credit he fully deserved and at the same time I think it served to let him know that even though he was an Arsenal player and a Premier League star in waiting, a few of us didn't see him as above anyone else in the dressing room. Kev made himself at home, trained well, played magnificently and was a fully paid up member of the young nightclub goers in the group. I found him an all-round good lad.

The next foray into procuring a centre forward wasn't quite as successful. Justin Fashanu returned from America and did a deal with Frank. He was paid the equivalent of my year's wages to play for us for a couple of months. Frank also paid a lump sum on Fash's suggestion that he hold a press open day at a top London hotel to get the club more publicity. It took Fash at least a month to get anywhere near match fit. It's only my personal opinion but I thought it was a waste of money. At the time Fash was bringing out his autobiography and rumours were abound that he was about to come out as the first gay footballer. One day as we boarded the coach for an away game I actually asked him outright as I offered around to my team mates a sweet from two bags of my favourite confectionery. I had a bag of Marshmallows and Liquorice Allsorts. I said "Well Fash, what's the SP? Are you coming out as gay or what?" Fash took a pink

Marshmallow, winked at me, and said "Sitts you'll have to buy the book." Two more mini flare ups involved myself, Frank, Brian and David Corner. Big Dave who I christened "coconut head" used to fuck about a bit and try to throw his weight about in a humorous way but with a bit of an undercurrent.

He never missed an opportunity to tell of his wild ways at Sunderland, taking on blokes and bouncers in nightclubs. Apparently one night, so he said, he came unstuck and was battered by a couple of bouncers resulting in a small metal plate being permanently inserted in a part of his head. Until this book I've never bothered to tell of such escapades and scrapes that I got in. I said it must be a nightmare, particularly at airports, to some laughter from the lads who were present. One morning in the dressing room he thinks it's a good idea to do a Bruce Lee impression by kicking and punching, just missing lads he'd selected as we sat there changed and ready for training. He did the punch or kick, just missing someone's face, complete with a Bruce Lee scream. He threw a punch that just missed me and I said "be careful, because if you fucking catch me you'll have a problem." "Rrraaa!" He kicks out at me as I'm seated, I catch his foot, sweep the other one away and he's on his back. "Now fuck off back to your seat or you'll have a metal plate in the other side of your head you ginger coconut head cunt." The lads were pissing themselves. Coconut head went bright red and sat down. As he did he said "salubrious Sitts, salubrious." I didn't have a clue if it was an insult or not.

That season threw up some bizarre score lines and extraordinary performances. In the end, the final league table was to read true and fourth placed Scunthorpe met seventh placed Wrexham in one playoff semi-final, whilst having finished sixth we played fifth placed Scarborough in the other semi-final. The final was a two legged home and away affair rather than the big day out at Wembley in a one off game that was to come into force shortly after. Rotherham (champions), Tranmere and Crewe were already promoted. During the season we'd had three 4-0 victories, a 5-0 and a whopping 8-0 victory over local rivals Colchester.

We'd shared the spoils with the champions with a victory each and did the same with second placed Tranmere, however we'd only taken a point off Crewe. Out of the four semi-finalists we were probably the least fancied. Even a member of staff thought so, which I'll come to in due course and what happened could probably only happen at a club like Orient. Although by now the chairman Tony Wood had successfully changed the club's name back to Leyton Orient tying in nicely with the club's history, location and basically what the chairman wanted. The first leg of the semi-final was at home. We defended superbly. The midfield and up front Lee Harvey in particular were outstanding.

Craig Short who went on to have a good career at Premier League level and the divisions above our current status was torn apart by Lee. To add insult to injury, Lee was a winger converted to centre forward by Brian Eastick who recognised Lee's pace and our need to threaten the back of opposition defences. Up until then we never had that threat. Lee was a handful that day and we took a 2-0 lead to Scarborough for the second leg. We went up the day before. We trained, then after a visit to McDonald's for Steve Castle and Terry Howard and Percy Ingles for the rest of us, we got on the coach. After our evening meal I ordered an Irish coffee. Frank sent Bill over to protest as Alan Comfort joined me. I said to Bill "if Frank's worried about the cost. I'll pay for it myself, it helps me sleep.. the whisky. Let me know after you've had a sip from your thirty pounds bottle of wine." The next day after breakfast we went on Scarborough beach with bibs, cones and a bag of balls. Brian was determined to do patterns of play but with a force gale wind, complaints from the lads and an ally in a freezing cold Frank Clark, it was decided on a walk, a stretch, a jog and a paddle in the sea. The paddle was optional so I declined and said to Frank and Bill "I'd rather not have gangrene at this late stage." Afternoon kip, up for pre-match, then a team meeting where Brian briefs us leaving no stone unturned.

Then we're off to do battle and as a defender it was the type of game you live for. For long periods we were under siege, everyone expecting the southern softies to crumble. Scarborough scored then threw the kitchen sink at us. I remember being pinned in our box for the last few minutes and Dicko clearing a certain goal off the line. How he did it still defies belief. Healdy is beaten, Dicko scrambles across and clears off the line with an overhead scissor kick. It's like a pin ball machine, but as we cleared it again, the referee blows his final whistle and we're in the play off final. I clapped our away support and turned to hug Dicko and Keith Day.

I got a handshake from Brian and an arm around my shoulders from Frank. "Well done Sitts." Back to the hotel after ages in the dressing room. The chairman had to pull up some readies for us to have a meal. We got back so late the restaurant in the hotel was about to close. After a bite to eat, Brian and Frank had a disagreement over Brian wanting us to go to bed and Frank allowing the lads out to celebrate. Frank won. Well, he did have unanimous support.

Everyone went to a little enclave that looked like the set for Ray Say's last stand in the film "Little Voice." The staff stayed back at the hotel so we had a free rein, which was very nearly spoiled. I declined the offer of holding a player's whip round and gave the responsibility to Mark Cooper in the nightclub we had decided to stay in. Across the road was a pub, a restaurant and a casino. A few of the lads left, went to the casino, did their money, then came back to the nightclub. Craig Short came and had a drink with us, congratulated everyone and wished us good luck in the final. I thought that was big of him. He had his club tie and blazer on and so did all our lads which could have made us easily identifiable and an easy target, especially once "Coops" started performing. Coops started life at Cambridge, had a hundred grand spent on him by Spurs then went to Gillingham before coming to Leyton Orient. After his move to Spurs he treated himself to a new car, a mini, which according to Coops was vandalised by so called teammates as they saw he was out of his depth. I won't repeat the names he gave me, but nasty bastards who jumped up and down on the bonnet and the roof. If they'd done it to me, I'd have handed them the keys and told them they'd now bought the car.

Then again, in my time in football nasty bastards were ten a penny. We ordered our drinks and I had to tell Cooper to "shut the fuck up." He tormented the bar staff and the barman by waving two twenty pound notes declaring, "you've never seen a twenty pound note up here before have you?" He then blew his nose on one of them and handed it over. I was shocked and embarrassed. I also didn't want our victory and celebration spoiled. With my sensible head on I could see the situation playing straight into Eastick's hands, making Frank look out of control and piss poor headlines for the club. I told Coops to join the other lads who were having a sherbet on the edge of the dance floor. I then took the change and handed the barman a fiver back telling him "put that in your tips jar, sorry about him, I apologise. It's embarrassing, even more so because it's his first drink."

We drank, sang along to some tunes, took off our cheap blazers and had a little boogie. We left at closing time then went across to the casino. Because we had a flutter, drinks came up. To get on an even keel I ordered a plate of sandwiches. I then got called outside to try and calm down a few of the lads who'd stripped off and were having a streak on the beach and a late swim. Or early, depending on what way look at it. I remember calling out to Stevie Baker "Oi silly bollocks, you'll get hypothermia." After making sure they were wrapped up we headed back to the hotel to carry on drinking and we were met in the bar by Neil Warnock and chairman of his new club Notts County. Frank and the rest of the staff had retired to bed which is just as well because Frank and Warnock never ever saw eye to eye and on this particular occasion Warnock was more obnoxious than usual. In front of his new chairman as everyone drank and became more inebriated he remarked how Orient's back four had kept the tie in their favour. He congratulated me, Dicko and Daygo, then said slurring his words, "I might ring your manager and make on offer for you three." As I waited for the punch line I wasn't surprised or disappointed.

"Yeah, I'll make him an offer, thirty grand, for the three of ya!" Me, Daygo and Dicko looked at each other and took it for the back handed compliment followed by the insult it was. "You know, you know, don't ya, that if I'd still been manager of Scarborough you'd have been knocked out." I said "yeah, but you're not, and we weren't." "Ah big man, I'm just trying to wind you all up, but you've heard it all before eh?" "What? A coach or manager talking bollocks? Yeah loads of times." Warnock puts his arm around his boss "Chairman, I've changed my mind, I don't think I could have these three playing for me." Warnock had on a bright yellow shirt, short sleeved with epaulettes, white trousers and white shoes. Think nouveau riche northerner in Benidorm. A few of the lads had been standing on the periphery listening to Warnock's semi-pissed waffle and out of nowhere, Lee Harvey decides to put an end to it. He pushes past me and Dicko and shouts to Warnock at the top of his voice. "Quick, your shoes are on fire!" And throws a full pint of lager over Warnock's feet. Everyone cracks up. Warnock says "see chairman what did I tell you about these Southerners?" I stepped in between Warnock and the Notts County chairman as he was still chuntering on. "I've told you about these cockneys," he continued. I piped up, "look on the bright side Mr Warnock, you can get yourself a decent pair of shoes." Then I walked off, went to my room packed my bags, then joined the rest of the lads for breakfast. On the coach on the way home I'm almost certain it was only Frank Woolf, a director and maybe Bill Songhurst.

Frank had left early with Brian Eastick, no doubt to put the wheels in motion for training, travel arrangements and things like tickets for what was in Leyton Orient terms a big occasion. I'm almost sure I heard a story involving the toss of a coin or some sort of draw ceremony, with Frank Clark as Leyton Orient's managing director and Wrexham's manager Dixie McNeil in attendance to decide the order of home or away for the two legged final. We must have been looked upon favourably because the first leg was away. It has to be said, on a not particularly good pitch, after repetition, repetition, repetition of our patterns of play and particularly our defensive strategy, the first leg at Wrexham was a dour, turgid affair. During the game I'd had a good, hard, honest battle with Wrexham's centre forward Ollie Kearns. Me and Dicko also had a running battle of verbals with Eastick and Clark. They kept telling me and Keith Day to swap as Wrexham's nippy second centre forward might expose my perceived lack of pace and Ollie Kearns would get the better of Daygo in the air. I told Daygo "stay where you are, we'll pass them on, if we swap at the wrong time they'll be able to drive a fucking tank up the middle, just make sure whoever goes for the first ball, if it's not won, the other one's tucked round to tidy up." The reply to Eastick via Dicko was a bit more concise. "Dicko, tell em both they're paranoid, relax and shut the fuck up." Again.. "Sitts, here he comes, Daygo swap." Dicko says, "Brian, Sitts said shut the fuck up, you're paranoid, let us deal with it and concentrate." The game ended 0-0. In the dressing room after Brian says "well done everyone. Superior in every department." To a smile

from Brian I said "fuck me, that's a first, a bit of praise.

"The second leg at home was vastly different for a lot of reasons. One of the major differences was the weather. It was a hot, humid day compared to the cool, overcast first leg. From a player's perspective our safety was compromised because no formally qualified medical staff were in attendance on behalf of Leyton Orient FC. How it was allowed I don't know, but rather than disturb the regular trip made annually through France, Germany, Austria and ending in Rimini in Italy over the full six weeks of close season by Bill Songhurst and his wife at the time Sandra, in Bill's four wheel drive, Frank Clark allowed Bill to go. Prior to the semi-finals over the two legs, Bill openly stated to anyone who'd listen "I'm booking my holidays anyway, we won't win the semi-finals, we haven't got the bottle, my ferry ticket will be safe, we're not good enough anyway, you watch players will bottle it. " On the day our physio running on was Bill's mate, Big Dave. Or as I preferred to call him Fat Dave. I said to a few of the lads "if you get a knock, try not to get hurt on the far side, go down by the dugout, because by the time Dave gets to you, you could be dead."

I slept like a baby the night before, I felt calm, relaxed, confident and I had a strong feeling we'd get promotion. The lads seemed to have a good spirit, there was a togetherness. Although geographically and as a family man I always felt on the periphery of the younger drinkers and clubbers, there's no doubt every member of the squad respected each other's contribution. For ten months Eastick had been technically superb, his organisation second to none, his principles, appetite for work and resilience I think transmitted through to the players. He fought believe it or not, for the right to be able to show players how to win games and what was good for them as individuals, units within the team and the team as a whole. Credit to Brian where it's due, but we still had ninety minutes to impose ourselves and Wrexham to worry about.

On the day of the game I decided to err on the side of caution. After 0-0 in the first leg in a very tight game I was looking ahead and preparing for the fact that it might be another close game and may even go to extra time. So I decided to conserve some energy by insisting to my wife that we only make love for an hour. When we eventually got out of bed my wife asked me what I would like for a pre-match meal. On the advice of Bill Songhurst since I joined the club in 1985 I had already spent the previous seventy-two hours carb loading so I decided to treat myself. I said to my wife I'm going round the shop to get a paper but when I get back I want two eggs on toast, two sausages, bacon, tomatoes and black pudding with a pot of tea. There's only so much you can do and I honestly believe that a large part of football, apart from the obvious organisation and fitness, is down to your ability, will and determination, mental strength, fate and destiny. If I wasn't fit by now I was never going to be. I could give you several for instances of people I played under who couldn't have coached a team of under twelves never mind be allowed near a professional club environment. Then there's the medical side.

As I have mentioned a lovely man and a great GP was mentored by Bill Songhurst throughout his sport medicine diploma and went on to work for Watford, Arsenal and England. After continuous training with barely a day off and playing Saturday-Tuesday- Saturday for nearly two seasons since my ruptured achilles I remember going to the doctor and telling him I felt a little jaded and was there something that he could recommend or a prescription he could write in the form of a tonic or pick me up. His answer was "John when I feel a bit down what I normally do is eat loads of bags of crisps." So please don't tell me a large part of things are not down to being in the right place at the right time. Someone once told me "luck is where preparation meets opportunity" and quite honestly it could well be up there among the biggest load of bollocks I have ever heard. I'm still convinced to this day, without ever giving up personally, and always having had an appetite for work and knowledge since I made the mistake of walking out of my guaranteed O' Levels, that when you are born, without being at all defeatist, that God either kisses your forehead or kicks you in the bollocks and says "on you go."

I think what I'm trying to say is there are some things that are out of your control. What I did have control of now though was the way I prepared and as always the way I played. On this particular day I also had control over my wardrobe. I had about fifteen suits to choose from high street shops and I also had a nice little portfolio of designer gear from my contacts in the rag trade. I laid out on my bed, and bear in mind this is the mid-eighties, a Chester Barrie suit (eight hundred and eighty pounds) a Boss suit (one thousand pounds,) an Armani suit (one thousand eight hundred pounds,) a beautiful Valentino suit (also eighteen hundred pounds) and lastly one that I elected to wear which was a grey flannel Versace suit (two thousand two hundred pounds). It was single breasted with three silver buttons with the Versace lion's head on them and three buttons on each cuff with the same lion's head, with a crisp white shirt, a silk tie from Italy and a pair of black brogues that I had polished so much you could have seen your face in them. I thought I looked the bollocks. I thought back to when I was a kid and I had the piss taken out of what I was wearing and the people that did it. I couldn't help wondering what they were wearing today. Oh well, little victories.

During the run up to the game and from the word go it was as shambolic and chaotic as only it could have been at a club like Leyton Orient. I tried and succeeded in blocking it all out to concentrate on my own performance. Our physiotherapist Bill Songhurst had already elected not to cancel his holiday telling the manager Frank Clarke that we were not good enough and would bottle it in the semi- final. He was now well on the way to his mini tour of the vineyards of Europe that ended in Italy and him staying put for a few weeks on the coast of Rimini. So his mate Fat Dave was the sponge man, a lovely guy but with very limited medical experience and even more limited in football injuries. Our mercurial left winger and probably our most creative forward player also gave Frank a major scare. Alan Comfort must have also thought our chances were limited because he had elected to arrange his wedding to his sweetheart on the same day as the play off final second leg. I couldn't believe what I was fucking hearing.

Here I was, one of Orient's leaders, best players and best defenders on a poxy two hundred pounds a week and Alan Comfort had told Frank that unless other arrangements could be made he wouldn't be able to play in the second leg. There's more which I will come to and if it's happened to you my heart sincerely goes out to you, but if you reach a time in your life where you know you have been had over, been ripped off or had liberties taken with you, the realisation is not a nice feeling. From the off me and Ollie Kearns got bang at it straight away yet again. It was no problem to either of us because we were both up for it. I thought Ollie was grossly underrated, had good technique, was hard as nails and as honest as the day is long. Early on in the game we got a free kick. It was a free kick we had rehearsed countless times on the training ground. However, I over hit it. It wasn't the end of the world because it ran out for a throw in by Wrexham's corner flag. I took it as an opportunity to breathe deeply and remind myself to relax. Something I have always told players from kids to youth to seniors is good players should always talk to themselves, giving little reminders, assessments and reassessments because obviously the picture changes from second to second. "Relax.. control.. have a pass ready.. am I too tight? Should I space off? Am I marking on the right side? Is there pressure on the ball? I can win the ball here." We led 1-0 but not before a major shakeup to the side. My little mate at left back Dicko had to go off with a spasm in his back after what seemed like an eternity of treatment and diagnosis from Dave. It was early in the game so we didn't really need a breather but I thought at this rate we'd still be playing at the start of the following season and Alan Comfort wanted the ninety minutes over with because of what had been arranged for him.

All I remember of the rest of it is even though Wrexham scored, I still felt composed and quietly confident that we would win it. There was a half clearance played up to Ollie Kearns and because he never got his body in line with the ball I managed to get round him and with a sort of diving header I nudged the ball sideways. I think it was to Steve Baker. I'm almost certain the ball ended up wide to Lee Harvey who used his ability and pace to beat the full back and whip in a cross. It wasn't a particularly good cross it seemed to be behind everybody except Mark Cooper and as it sat up Mark swept it in on the volley. We were up. As we ran the clock down, what they now call game management, the ref blew the final whistle. I remember a pitch invasion, getting a smack round the head and as I turned round my brother-in-law and one of our friends Peter jumping on me and kissing me. Another sure sign that showed a lack optimism was no official presentation ceremony and the team, after calls from the crowd, being presented via the directors' box where we ended up standing above the entrance to the tunnel which was made of plastic and wood and which nearly collapsed. So we beat a hasty retreat to the dressing rooms and some bottles of champagne which was sent down by the chairman and one or two organisations in the club. Just as the champagne was uncorked I put my towel over my peg to cover my suit.

As all the players went from bar to bar to celebrate with the supporters I was summoned in the Vice- President's Lounge to attend the supporters club. It was to receive the away supporters' player of the year which is the only medal that I have to remember the day we got promoted. I lost out by one vote, although I should have won it easily, as players' player of the year. I didn't really have a problem with it as it went to my brother Keith Day. As far as I am concerned whether it was two, three, four or five awards that year they basically could have been shared out between Paul Heald, Keith Day, Me and Kevin Dickenson.

As I walked to the supporters' club I had just missed the helicopter that had been arranged and paid for by the chairman for Alan Comfort, to whisk him to his wedding, as it took off from the centre circle. I suppose in the end with what Alan contributed that year it was money well spent. I went back to the main part of the ground and upstairs to the Vice President's Lounge where the drink was in full flow and hasty arrangements for a celebration at a restaurant in Stratford called the Phoenix Apollo were made. My memories of that are basically the same as a lot of players' anecdotes who I have listened to over the years after winning promotions and cup finals. Basically I was too fucked to enjoy it. None of the first team squads' wives and girlfriends were there and Frank spent most of the night asking "what the fuck are they doing here? They're not getting pissed on my chairman's money" in reference to Peter Wells and Paul Shinners who had been let go the season before, turned up to watch the game, and tagged along for the free drink and celebration. The victory was short lived in my mind because I had a month left on my contract and having seen money, fortunes actually in my opinion, wasted on lesser players, I had already made a decision in my mind what figure I would be happy with to continue serving Orient as a player. That summer as I negotiated with Frank Clarke he remarked, "if anyone deserves a bigger slice of the cake, it's you Sitts." He was good at kidding me along was Frank. Especially after I found out what other players were earning. Most of them inferior to me as a player and professional. Obviously you don't expect football clubs to give money away and throw it at players. Particularly players who played in the positions perceived wrongly in my opinion as the easiest part of the game, which is defending. I had seen and experienced at various clubs where money was not only thrown away, but thrown away on the wrong players.

After my perceived poor conduct at Chelsea I don't think I ever came into that category. I was total value for money to the extent where not very long ago I reached the conclusion that it cost me money to stay in football. Which is totally wrong because I was a good player and a good professional. I could have quite easily called this chapter "When Will I Be Loved?" by the Everly Brothers but I wouldn't want anyone to think I was feeling sorry for myself. When I look at some of the defending now in all divisions, either the coaching or the player or players concerned are laughable. The more modern day defending I see I can only conclude the better the defender I was. Not to beat about the bush I told Frank I wanted my money doubled to four hundred pounds a week. He smiled and agreed almost immediately. Yet again I was a poor negotiator and I let him have his own way. It actually led to me thinking that I hadn't asked for enough as he turned what I said completely on its head. I asked for an additional loyalty bonus as a sort of signing on fee. He declared I'm willing to give you a two-year contract on three hundred and seventy-five pounds a week. The other twenty-five pounds a week over two years comes to two thousand six hundred. I'll give you two lump sums of one thousand three hundred pounds as a loyalty bonus.

After I signed I went with my wife and first born child to Cyprus and spent two weeks walking, relaxing, teaching my baby how to swim, and cycling. My wife had a cycle and I had one with a child seat on it and it was a fantastic two weeks. I finally felt I had achieved something and it definitely made for a better summer. As a footballer though your mind is never far away or at least mine wasn't, from the thought of returning for pre-season training and looking forward to a new season in a higher division. Especially after spending four years in the bottom division. I have to go on record and say that after all the hard work, all the training, all the preparation and the repetition of certain drills the euphoria in football is short lived. I don't know whether it's me, but as a player, coach and manager I tended to go over a defeat and be almost dismissive of a victory. Even the celebrations were marred and a bit of an anticlimax.

When we went back out to face the supporters the microphone was commandeered by Mr Charisma Terry Howard who spouted some bollocks asking "who's going to the dogs tonight?" Which got a roar followed by "who's going to Charlie Chan's?" Because no one could really think of anything to say.

My only suggestion to Terry was "give me the microphone so that I can thank the supporters" and just as he did the roof to the tunnel that we were standing on nearly collapsed so we had to beat a hasty retreat. After a few photos and some champagne in the dressing room I went off to collect my Player of the Season Award from the away supporters. I ended up in the Vice President's Lounge where the atmosphere could have easily been spoiled by a sleazy scumbag who in the not too distant future swindled people out of a lot of money and had to resign as Barry Hearn's vice chairman. He suggested to then chairman Tony Wood's niece that he would like to spray her breasts with champagne and drink it. This was our little bit of success, mine and my team mates and I've got to be honest I wanted to give him a slap. He was yet another rude and arrogant dickhead who didn't know how to conduct himself in front of strangers and ladies. Still it wasn't my place to police the situation.

The hastily arranged meal and drinks at the Phoenix Apollo restaurant was also somewhat of an anticlimax. Some of the lads even went home early. I thought something should have been done to involve the squad with their wives and girlfriends with good food, drink and music. Quite a few of the lads spent some of the time commiserating with the likes of Hakan Heyrettin who was deemed not good enough to sign professional and keeping away from Frank's tantrum because Paul Shinners and Peter Wells had shown up. I ended up having a quiet drink with Bernie Dixson and Paul Ward at one of the tables. The restaurant looked like it had been hit by a hurricane with empty bottles, glasses and remnants of food all over the place. Also laying around were the results of the what was a gag at the time performed by the owners as people walked into the restaurant and were shown to their table. One of them would walk over and cut your tie in half. I looked over and saw the chairman who often looked in the land of the bewildered sitting there with half a tie.

One of the lads nicknamed him "Compo" as he resembled the geezer in Last of the Summer Wine. To carry on the less than feelgood factor when we reported back for pre-season we were told that after a few days once we got our muscles working we would be training for a week at Lilleshall. I remember when we eventually got there we were called together and told to watch how we conduct ourselves by Frank. Brian Eastick added: "we have had to pull a lot of strings and call in a lot of favours to set you up here for a week. We've done you a favour so that we can help you focus on the new season and get ready for it." We were allocated our room numbers and keys and who we would room with before we were disbursed. As we went to break off as a group we were asked "has anyone got any questions?" Kevin Dickenson put his hand up and said "Brian can I just say don't do us any more favours for fuck's sake."

It was a very Spartan existence with rigid meal times, not a lot of rest and blazing hot sunshine. Brian and Bill Songhurst argued because Brian wouldn't stop half way through a session for the lads to replenish themselves with fluids. Bill had taken the time and trouble to sort each player out with their own Gatorade bottle with a name tag on it and because of the heat constantly said to the lads when you stop for a breather keep drinking. Brian was having none of it. It was a catch twenty-two because too many breaks make for a much longer session. Most of the time the bottles were left laying on the grass.

I could be forgiven for thinking the new season was pretty nondescript. Some of the things that happened only seemed to more or less directly affect me. I had to contend with the arrival of a new signing for what were in Orient terms a lot of money. Frank decided to pay just under two hundred grand for a centre half called Paul Beesley I think from Tranmere. He was six foot three, left footed and a superb athlete. He was a good centre back who could read the game very well. Obviously it was more direct competition for me than it was for Keith Day because I had been playing on the left and Keith on the right. I would hazard a guess it was at the request of Brian Eastick. I remember turning up at the training ground and getting a little talk from John Gorman. Looking back, it was a lovely gesture from John who I had a lot of time for.

I've always thought to this day that John would be the type of coach or manager you would want to play for and enjoy going to work for everyday. He said to me "I have been around the game a long time and you've just had one of the best, most consistent seasons I've ever seen a player have, don't get your head down, keep training the right way and you'll make them find a place for you." And so I did. While "Bees" was there I got a game as part of what on paper looked a very good back four. If Bees and Keith Day were centre backs I was normally played at right back with Dicko at left back. Bees had some very good games and was later sold to Eastick's mate at Sheffield United, Dave Bassett, for three hundred and fifty thousand pounds. The other thing that was to have medium and long term consequences for me and Leyton Orient Football Club was the arrival in the not too distant future of someone whose name kept cropping up in scouting reports. His name was Peter Eustace. After losing at home to Everton in the first leg of a League Cup tie, I think 2-0, it was a big ask to try and turn it around at Goodison Park.

In the scouting report Peter Eustace had submitted it was declared that the only way we could put some respectability on the result was to play the game at a fast tempo, defend to keep the pitch small and keep play condensed. We drew 2-2 I think. It was season 1989-1990 Leyton Orient finished below half way in fourteenth and Clarke and Eastick decided on the last game of the season away to Fulham that you shouldn't ask a boy to do a man's job so they stuck me at right back against my old Chelsea team mate Clive Walker. We won 2-1. Earlier in the season I had a blazing row with Eastick and Clarke at half time in the away League Cup victory over Gillingham. We won 4-1 but Gillingham's goal was due to a breakaway where me and Keith Day got caught two versus three. During phases of play in the middle and attacking thirds Eastick encouraged both full backs to join in. This was before any thoughts of the "Makalele role." It led to me and Daygo being exposed and outnumbered with Eastick laying the blame at my door. During the half time rant I just said "fair enough I will take the blame even though I don't agree." Frank said "shut up you big baby... What do you mean like?" I said "even Liverpool don't risk two v two with fucking Hansen and Lawrenson. When the right back attacks the left back tucks round and vice versa but you fucking have it your way." Again, "you big baby."

At the time, although I didn't know it yet, a new manager would come in, my mouth would get me in trouble yet again and I'd be retired from playing at the age of thirty-one. In the meantime, having completed all my preliminary courses and prep courses I was off to Lilleshall Hall to take my full coaching licence and then get home to see England in Italia '90. After the Fulham game we went on a long social that started on a boat on the Thames called Tattershall's Castle. Some of us then went on to a restaurant and we all ended up regrouping in a club that at the time was owned by George Best called Blonde's.

CHAPTER ELEVEN: LEYTON ORIENT 1990-1991

Hole in the Ground

Frank Clark said to me when I reported back for pre-season 1990-91 "you'll enjoy working with Peter, Sitts." With the benefits of hindsight and first-hand experience, enjoy might be too strong a word. I had just spent the whole summer dedicated to football. Since my ruptured achilles for better or worse I had played and trained continuously for five years with no real rest. The only time I ever had off was two weeks on holiday with my wife and daughter. The summer had flown and I had returned from two weeks at Lilleshall Hall where I had registered, paid for, and attended the Football Association Full Coaching Licence course with other candidates to form four groups of I think sixteen or eighteen. It was now a case of waiting for the results. Every candidate did four sessions and I was very happy with how mine had gone. I also took part in every other coach's session from eight forty-five a.m through to lunch at twelve thirty.

The afternoon sessions were from about 2pm to 5pm. After a shower and some food, most evenings were spent in a lecture theatre listening to theories from people who'd never laced a pair of boots on in any sort of competitive football. The group coaches as contradictory as it might sound were different class. I thought my head coach was exceptional and interspersed the sessions with the right amount of humour and encouragement. His name was Martin Hunter and his specimen sessions were spot on. Very organised and enjoyable. After a long day I often went back to my room to revise and I inevitably dozed off by about 10 o'clock. The group coaches were Les Reed, Martin Hunter, Mick Wadsworth and Colin Murphy. My group had a few faces in like Peter Reid who only four years earlier had played for England in the 1986 World Cup. Alan Irvine was another good coach, very forensic was Alan. A large Everton contingent turned up a few times to encourage Reidy. They stood under umbrellas geeing him on during the afternoon and went for a meal and a few Guinness's in the evening. Howard Kendall, Colin Harvey and Mick Heaney gave Reidy a big lift, especially in the second week when it starts to drag on and take its toll. Clive Walker was on the course who I had known at Chelsea, also Paul Goddard, Ray Hankin and Tony Currie so the demonstrations always had a touch of quality about them.

One day we were all invited to watch sessions put on by Dave Sexton who at the time was working with one of England's young sides and on one particular afternoon we got an invite to watch John Cartwright work with an England Youth squad. It was rumoured that along with Dario Gradi these coaches were the way forward with the F.A and England's teams below the seniors. On both occasions I was one of only five or six who bothered to attend. There was a disagreement one night in the lecture theatre between Charles Hughes and a candidate. The candidate was told in no uncertain terms that if he wanted any chance of success on the course he should comply rather than question. I would come to know how the candidate felt in the eight months that was to follow, back at Orient. Coaching and the game itself seems to have come a long way with coaches allowing players a certain amount of autonomy. Maybe it's veered too far that way, I don't really know other than what I see on the TV. My roommate was a Leyton Orient Centre of Excellence coach Colin Reid. He later parted company with the O's after I had pipped him in the short list for Youth Team Coach but that was in the future. For now we helped each other, checked each other's notes and importantly he got me up on time!

On my return home my wife and daughter greeted me and my wife confirmed that we had another child on the way which was due in December. I celebrated by being glued to the TV to watch England in Italia '90. A cliché if ever there was one but what a roller coaster! Struggling to beat Cameroon, nicking it against Belgium, going out in the semi-final to Germany just some of the highlights and lowlights of a great tournament. Only my opinion, but right from the opening ceremony through to the final, I feel it was one of the best ever. As I sat there filling up with Gazza and the rest of the country after Pearce hit the keeper's legs and Waddle blasted over the bar my wife looked at me like I was a silly bollocks. I snapped out of it because I had to lift my first born into her high chair for dinner. One of my favourite anecdotes from that World Cup involves Bobby Robson briefing Paul Gascoigne before the Germany game saying "to be careful, you're up against the best midfield player in the world." (Matheus.) Gazza replies: "no I'm not boss, he is." If you are going to have any chance in any game, from a World Cup semi- final down to any club in any division, that in my opinion is exactly what you need. A player with confidence in his ability, the balls to declare it and the character to deliver a performance that confirms it. Gascoigne is in my opinion the greatest midfield player born of these islands. He had absolutely everything.

After the third and fourth place play off and final I started to jog and stretch in readiness for pre-season. I'm glad I did. I went in one day to be told Brian Eastick had left, feeling he'd taken things as far as he could. With no massive transfer kitty on the horizon, I don't suppose he fancied mid-table mediocrity for another year. Funnily enough in the not too distant future, money, in Orient terms fortunes, would be made available and set two precedents both of which I suffered from as a consequence. On our first day we were introduced to our new manager Peter Eustace. He'd worked as number two to Howard Wilkinson at Sheffield Wednesday, did a stint as their manager and had various roles as a scout whilst out of the management loop. Frank introduced me, informing Peter I'd just got back from Lilleshall having taken my coaching badge. "What? the big one? Good lad." Alan Hull cracked some jokes as we all got weighed. Mr Eustace highlighted it saying "humour is good,

I like people who speak their mind and people who are funny." As captain I thought I might be ok with at least one out of two.

After having our weight taken, I automatically thought that pre-season had been planned and for the first day or two at least our bodies and muscle groups would be eased back into it. The best I had experienced in sixteen seasons as a pro had been Keith Peacock at Gillingham who was what you might call "player friendly." Peter took us out on the main pitch where Bill Songhurst and some equipment was waiting. We were in two groups, Bill took his group for a warm up, some terracing and a twenty minute run with lots of stretches. Peter had us doing body exercises, step ups on benches nearly four feet off the ground and some random plyometrics and aerobics. When I enquired where he had picked it up he replied "my wife saw it on TV this morning." We had a slurp of water from some filthy two-year-old plastic bottles that smelled of dry mud and got told to get on the minibus or in our cars. There was a race for the minibus that only held fifteen to sixteen passengers. We went in convoy to Epping Forest and stopped in a car park just down from the Royal Forest Hotel and Pub by a small lake. Without a stretch or warm up we embarked upon a seven mile run through the forest. Almost mind numbing but for the occasional wise crack. "Can anyone hear that? What? That screaming. What screaming? My calf muscles screaming for mercy!"

For the next few days we did exactly the same. Sometimes it was interspersed with team races or running in pairs on the small track walkways in the forest. It was also good for your change of direction, upper body movement and peripheral vision as you hurdled felled trees, ducked under overhanging branches so you didn't lose an eye, avoided logs and roots so you didn't cop for knee ligament damage and my particular favourite, running like a long jump or triple jump champion to avoid deep hoof prints in clay left by the horse riding brigade so you weren't out for a month with ankle ligaments. One or two questioned when we might see a ball. I said "what's a ball?" Frank as managing director sensing the unrest said "last year we were one of the fittest teams in the division, this year we'll be the fittest" totally in support of Peter. After all, he was Frank's appointment. During one recovery walk uphill past some bikers having a cup of tea by a shed in High Beach, Peter remarked that the team had to be fit, strong and powerful and with preferably no more than two players under six feet tall. I looked and saw the best left back I ever played with Kevin Dickenson and Steve Baker and thought their days might be numbered. In midfield two more of a similar height, Geoff Pike and Kevin Hales.

Later on as my mouth got me in trouble yet again this was to have a massive relevance to me personally. After the basic grounding of our "fitness" and running forwards and backwards uphill by the tea hut to the amusement of the aforesaid bikers we were told that a week's training and a couple of games had been arranged for us in Spain. Before we left Peter had started to crack down on certain cultural aspects at the club. Alan Hull a five feet six centre forward who had entertained the lads on the first day, was part of a group that I thought would be involved in a turnover of players, along with Bakes, Dicko, Pikey, Halesy and Andy Sayer in exchange for a more robust, physical approach to things. That's ok as long as there are strategies attached. After all a team needs as much going for it as possible.

I was among a group of players warned to stay away from congregating outside Harry Spinner's kitchen for a cup of tea and a chin wag about football, training, injuries, fixtures and current affairs. Harry and Jimmy, according to "H" were told to get on with their work and not get involved in chatting and distracting players. What a load of bollocks. To me that's how you build spirit... communication. Now everyone seems to be either staring down at their phone or walking around with headphones on.

The tour was cheap and cheerful and like an eighteen-thirties package with an early hours cheap flight and even cheaper accommodation. We landed and got through customs at about four in the morning to be met by a coach. At the airport the lads had a whip round to buy a ghetto blaster. I knew I wouldn't see it but I chipped in anyway. On the coach I noticed Peter Eustace's body language and told Greg Berry (who eventually went to Wimbledon for one hundred thousand pounds) to turn the music off. "No it's alright Sitts, what's the problem?" I just said "use your head" as I rolled my eyes towards Clark, Eustace, Bernie Dixson and Bill Songhurst. I'll never forget the record because I was proved right. Greg didn't get "the eyes" and a tune called "Dirty Cash" was turned up full blast. On arrival at our accommodation, think post second world war austere communist architecture, Eustace declared, "some of you seem to think we are here for a jolly up, not for work, collect your kit and meet me outside the main block ready to train at six o'clock."

I looked at my watch it was five thirty-five am. I roomed with Carl Hoddle and Chris Zoricich and the staff decided that we would have a room on the first floor and all the kit and medical skips would be left in our room. I knew it would be a pain in the arse and a massive piss take to our room and me personally. What chance have you got when you have got players coming and going, picking up kit and various medical supplies when you should be resting? Surely that should be the responsibility of the physio and other staff. I was captain and being treated like a fucking Joey if and when players wanted fresh kit or medical supplies. During the week I could be resting after training and there would be a knock at the door with a player requesting tape or socks, or boot polish or a jock strap. The staff stayed in a separate block so it was nice for me to stand on the balcony with "Zoro" and "Carlo," observing them as they returned three parts pissed in the evening. Chris and Carl bottled it when I bought some balloons and suggested water bombing them. You may have noticed there's a member of staff missing. Yet again Bill Songhurst did his own thing. He's divorced from his first wife Sandra for a long time now so I can divulge the fact that a young secretary who he'd employed in his sports clinic had gone on ahead on a separate flight and was staying in a hotel just down the road. He spent the entire week with her turning up only for games and the anointed time for training. At six am as clubbers came out of the various bars and discos in Fuengirola, like a bunch of twats we ran in the pissing of rain along the promenade to some piss taking from wannabes, tanked up on drink and doing the usual, which in my book normally consists of taking part in goings on and a level of bravery they seem to find easier to come by in a group and nowhere near how they'd conduct themselves while on their own and sober. After getting back to our rooms, Eustace told us we had the rest of the day off and we wouldn't train until the following afternoon at a pre-arranged facility.

I went to get some of the eight quid a day we had been allocated as expenses so I could have breakfast. After being awake for nearly twenty-four hours and arriving at an apartment block that looked exactly how I've described it, only with fewer facilities, I went with Carl and Chris to find some breakfast. There were no dining facilities on site, the rear of the building was a building site still being developed so it was a half mile trek to near the sea front. I got back and slept like a baby as Carl and Zoro joined the lads at a pool we had the use of in an adjacent hotel. I woke up, put my shades on, shorts, towel, flip flops and arrived at what looked like a beach party. Music blaring, girls chatting to one or two of the lads, drinks and a large bag of lemons that Chris Zoricich and Steve Castle had bought to squeeze on their hair as the sun came out and beat down to help them go bleach blonde. I said to myself some fucking pre-season this is going to be. In the evening the lads went for a meal together at a restaurant on the sea front. As we walked away from it Frank, Peter and Bernie were seated and beetroot red from a probable combination of sun bathing and drink. I was asked how we'd got on, what we'd eaten and if there were any problems. I said the main problem was no real opportunity to refuel properly. There was no breakfast unless you went to the sea front before training, nowhere to have a proper lunch for the money we had and the highlight was an evening meal.

Good food is important especially as a professional athlete, it's petrol for the body. I added at least no one will return to England overweight. Peter asked what I'd had that evening and I answered "a seafood paella, a salad, a glass of Sangria and a bottle of water." Bernie laughed and said "I thought that's the only kind of paella there was." I piped up, "you should get out of East Ham and Canning Town more Bern, there's seafood, meat or mixed." Frank said "fuckin 'ell Sitts, you sound like Fanny Craddock." We all had a chuckle and I was told to "keep an eye on the lads, no trouble and make sure they got their kit."

"Ok then." I walked on the sea front with my defender brethren. Dicko continued to crack me up. Keith Day was as funny as ever, then I became matchmaker after a girl approached me saying her mate wanted to be introduced to Andy Sayer. To a bit of laughter from I think Alan Hull she then said with my ears, I looked like Des out of neighbours. After a couple of glasses of Sangria, I left my roommates and some of the other lads, let's say "socialising," and went back to Stalag 17. Carl came back, then went back out. Then there was a knock, I thought "fuck me, what's he forgot?" I got up off the bed, opened the door and standing there with full cleavage on show and tits the size of Russia was the young lady who earlier said I resembled Des out of neighbours. "Hiya, can I come in? Can I join you?" "No darlin' not really, I'm watching TV, it's one of my favourites, I never miss it." "Can I watch it with you? I want to be with you. She added: What programme is it?"... no doubt trying to keep the conversation going.

I said "Neighbours" and shut the door. Then I was woken by Carl, Chris Zoro and Greg Berry who came back with the lads because he was locked out. Carl comes in my room and starts looking around "Sitts, you're unreal, look at this, kit, clothes, toiletries all laid out and immaculate." Then he starts giggling as he starts to re-arrange my soap, oils, aftershave, deodorant and shaving gear. We both started laughing because I could never, ever take offence from Carl. He was undoubtedly one of the loveliest human beings I've ever met in my life or football. Next up, Greg Berry is trying to sleep on the couch but he's keeping everyone up by complaining "it's too hot, the rooms have no air conditioning, blah, blah, blah," I said "come with me, this'll cool you off" and I picked up the cushions he was sleeping on, threw them on the balcony, then locked him out. Carl and Zoro are cracking up even though I'd shut my door and couldn't hear him. After a while Carl said "can we let him back in Sitts?" I said to Greg he could only come back in if he promised to go back to his own room because I wanted some peace and quiet or he can stay out there all night. After about five hours' kip, we boarded a coach with bibs and what looked like some footballs. After some sarcasm from one or two of the lads, Eustace said to the driver "stop the coach." As we got off he said "let's go, follow me." We ran up a mountain along a goat track, on rock hard ground, sun burnt and full of small boulders. When we came back down the other side the coach was waiting. Peter said "that's good for today, back to the accommodation."

The time to congregate next day for a match was given for our first pre-season friendly against a local side. That night before dinner, me, Carl and Zoro played a round robin of one-man baseball with a cricket bat and tins of octopus in its own ink. Zoro got Greg Berry to bowl and Greg got splattered with ink. We then got a few of the lads to sing the theme to Hawaii Five O as we raced down the hill on top of the skips as surfboards. I'll be honest, I was totally fucking fed up with my room being used as a medical room (with no physio in attendance) so we decided to make light of it. The Spaniards opposite looked at us like we were mental as Dicko led the chorus of Da da da da da da, da da da da da! That night I found us a pasta place and had a nice Bolognese, although the mincemeat could have been Shergar it was lovely, followed by salad and a coffee. Next day pre-match was on the sea front in a bar serving full English breakfasts. The owner was a Cockney cliché as he spoke out of the corner of his mouth. He half had the hump as we ordered tea, toast and fruit juice and jugs of water, instead of egg, bacon, sausage and beans. Out the corner of his mouth he said to me, Dicko, Daygo and Healdy "get a result for East London."

If my memory isn't betraying me, we only ended up playing one friendly instead of two. That in itself was a fiasco. All manner of nonsense like the Spanish leaving us to warm up in the sun as they delayed kick off to hopefully tire us out. Bernie was on the bench with Peter and Frank, no sign of Bill again, although being wrapped around a female less than half his age was preferable to niggly elbows, a boot left in as you passed, spitting, and in Andy Sayer's case a whack round the head every thirty seconds. Bernie told me after the game what he said to Eustace which was "he knew it was coming." He said "I'd give it anywhere between ten minutes and an hour - wait and see" and I didn't disappoint. Peter actually stepped on the pitch to have a word with the ref after Baker, Castle and Sayer again all just about avoided serious injury.

I got a fifty- fifty right in front of the bench and left the Spaniard properly ironed out. Bernie couldn't stop giggling. Well, you've got to give as good as you get, haven't you? Years later, in a physical encounter at home, I was youth coach and Glen Cockerill did the same to a particularly nasty opponent to stand up to what was going on and at half time Eustace said "at last! I've been waiting for that to happen since he stopped playing!" Pointing at me as he said it. Unfortunately, if you get an opponent who is being outplayed, it's not uncommon in football for them to turn to basics like getting overly physical and you have to show you can stand up to it. Believe me, down the years it hasn't always been TIKI TAKA. Our problem at every level is the same now as it was then, we're not streetwise enough. On the coach on the way home we sat around talking and Eustace approached saying. "Tomorrow we'll have a warm down then the rest of the day off and I want us all to go to a bullfight. Let me know who's up for it. Has anyone been to one before?" "Yes Boss." I answered. Eustace said "maybe you can convince the lads to go as a group. You're captain let me know." Most of them there and then said "it's not for me." Peter asked "what about you? What do you think? Would you recommend it?" I replied "not really, I went to one when I was over here with Chelsea, years ago, the Spanish insist on calling it a form of ballet. I think it's the torture and ritualistic slaughter of a beautiful animal, although I do love a steak."

Eustace had the right hump, he almost sulked like a child. "Eh, you're all soft" and walked off. Instead next day was a hastily arranged round of golf at a beautiful course with clubhouse, bar, restaurant and health club complete with pool. In any downtime, Eustace spoke constantly to the main golfers in the club, Geoff Pike, Steve Castle, Steve Ketteridge and one or two others. Eustace seemed to have a bond with Castle because of it and he was almost orgasmic in his admiration for Steve's athletic prowess in the forest. Although later on in the story Steve Castle's athleticism wasn't as great as he and Peter thought it was. I'll go on record and say that I thought Peter had a lot of personality and charisma. He was always very descriptive, effervescent and animated and he did a lot to interact with the lads. On the training field and before, during and after games he was a different animal. On one such occasion he spoke to a few of us as a group and asked "what do you enjoy?" Castle: "golf, gym, going out with friends," Pike: "I like a game of golf, being with my family." "Sitts, what do you do on your day off?" "Normally every year, I go in with a few mates and my brother to buy a shoot. Up at three thirty am, there in time for the crack of dawn, walk, shoot, a bit of decoy with the pigeon, barbeque, afternoon nap, then the night flight. We've got a cracking shoot near Essendon at the moment." "Mmm, what about you?" Pointing at Andy Sayer "on my day off, I like to relax and have a nice bubble bath." I knew it was going to be a long season, particularly for the back four.

The starting point for me with anybody, whether in or out of football is for me to show one hundred percent respect and professional courtesy. I then leave it for people, in this case coaches and managers to go out of their way to work their way back from that and start to erode that respect. With me and Peter it started at the golf day. Far more players were non-golfers than those who were. Eustace insisted everyone would stay together and be at the golf club on their day off. I remarked on behalf of the non-golfers that if the players had a day off, as long as we are responsible, we should be allowed to spend it how we want.

Peter was having none of it. So while he played a round of golf with the better players Castle and Pike, others followed on behind and the rest of us had use of a pool and adjacent bar and clubhouse.

A few of us lounged poolside and had a sunbathe. After about twenty minutes as me, Dicko, Healdy and Daygo were catching some rays, a Spanish geezer comes out and starts remonstrating that we must put our shirts on. Dicko said " it's a pool mate!" "No no, club rules, you must wear a shirt at all times." I piped up as Bernie came out of the bar "what if I want to dive in the pool? Does that mean I have to keep my shirt on?" "You must not remove your shirt at anytime within the grounds of the club." Frank and Bill were not there, so Bernie steps in and the guy says that unless we put on our shirts he'll throw us out. I remarked to Bernie that none of us wanted to be there in the first place, a day off is a day off. I don't play golf and I've got to sit here for half a day waiting for Peter and his sycophants to come down the final fairway. I then turned to the Spaniard and said to him that if he was going to eject us he might need to go and get help. Bernie invited the lads in for a drink and recommended to me a "LaMumba" it was a coffee with a liqueur in a separate glass on the side.

I must say I quite enjoyed it. I looked out and down over the last fairway to see Castle, Pike and Eustace on the last green. After they sunk their putt and shook hands, I sank my LaMumba and couldn't wait to get off to pack. We were off home next day after a week that for me was a waste of time. One game, one run along the sea front at six am, one run up a goat mountain, one day arguing with a geezer who wanted me to wear a shirt at the poolside of a golf course where I didn't want to be and one day playing baseball with cans of octopus and surfing on the kit skips. All this in surroundings where it was a mission to eat, drink, replenish and rest. It would have been more akin to an end of season jolly up. As we got off the coach, Eustace having obviously been briefed by Bernie called me over and said he'd heard I'd created a problem.

I explained it all exactly as it happened as he spoke of his love for golf and its standards of behaviour and etiquette and that's how it is and everyone must keep those standards. Now it wasn't what he said but how he said it. He felt he had to go nose to nose like a sergeant major with a new recruit when he said "do we understand each other?" (By the way Dicko and the others got off without a telling off, I was the only one singled out.) At this point I thought it was the first signs of "divide and conquer, divide and rule." The problems ended up being that in every single case, Peter picked the wrong side, backing idiots, made totally wrong decisions on certain players and people and in doing so ripped the heart and soul out of the club. He replaced too many players, replaced the wrong parts of the team and the consequences would have a ripple effect that in my opinion and the opinion of new owners, the auditors and accountants would have an effect for up to four years down the line. That was all in the future, for now I just responded by saying "Clear. I know all about standards and etiquette, I have been in and around the ancient equivalent of golf for years... Judo and Ju Jitsu, you are always trying to master something and playing against yourself as well as an opponent. Where your golf is concerned, I'm with Mark Twain." "Eh?" "Well he once said, golf is a good walk spoiled." At this point he was going just a teeny bit red and said "are you finished?" as he walked away.

At that time, not later on when I worked under him as a coach, I think he thought I couldn't read a comic. He's totally confused me with others in the group. As a little message, Peter loved a cryptic or a veiled message, as we waited at the luggage carousel he announced that he had a connecting flight back up north. He said he wanted to travel light and looking at Bernie said he wanted me to carry his golf clubs and other bag for him. Bernie asked me, I said "no, I'm a footballer not a fucking butler and I'm not carrying anything other than my own bag, ask Bill he's spent a week with his mistress instead of tending injuries and blisters."

Frank Clark had already left the airport. I think it's only relevant in the respect that everyone running this circus was appointed by him. After repairing a bit of the damage of two relegations with a promotion, he had been appointed for a while now, managing director. He was part hands on as opposed to being previously fully in charge and seemed to take more of a back seat and let Peter Eustace get on with it. We were back. Straight back to the forest.

This is where I had my next exchange with Peter. Some players were not being themselves, sycophantic and anxious to please. Steve Castle trying to look interested as Eustace pointed out two magpies shagging, Terry Howard laughed at Peter's northernisms and idiosyncrasies. Everyone bust a gut in the running and trained well. I think I surprised a few. So much so that Steve Baker complimented me on being among the front runners. He confessed to being surprised at how I was up the front.

I put it purely and simply down to having no time off and doing my full badge which was like a two-week pre-season anyway. It definitely helped me as I put distance between me and the usual suspects in the last third of the group. Always last or second from last was Terry Howard. Come to think of it Tel never had "a distance." Some players are quick over a few yards, some are powerful sprinters, some are power runners going box to box at just under a sprint, some are great at cross country, some players back then, although now at the highest level I'd suggest most players, can actually do the lot.

On a recovery walk Mr Eustace is marching alongside me and Steve Ketteridge who was still managing to get a wage out of football when he remarks "he wanted a team of very fit, intelligent dogs, let's say like Labradors." I piped up "Peter, Labradors are renowned for gaining weight, I've had every breed of dog going, don't matter how much you walk it, they put on weight." Peter replied "I want players who won't bite my hand as I feed them information, you know, turn on me." "Why class all players as dogs where in any club you only get one or two?" I ask. Peter responds: "tell me Ketts, what kind of dog is Sitts?" Ketteridge says: "Sitts (laugh) he's definitely a Rottweiler." "So he'd bite my hand?" I replied to both of them "firstly a Rottweiler is not the most vicious breed if provoked and fighting for his life, that's an American Pitbull Terrier, secondly a Labrador retriever is at this moment in time the most popular breed in the country, but they have many common ailments, normally hip problems and have the most visits to a vet. Consequently, a vet is more likely to be bitten by a Labrador than any other breed." Eustace, "you know dogs Sitts?" "Yeah I've had one all my life, including the breeds we are talking about. Ketteridge would be a Dachshund, a sausage dog" "What's its characteristics?" Asks Mr Eustace. Steve Ketteridge went red when I replied "Pointless completely fucking pointless. Not very aesthetically pleasing and does fuck all. In fact, a burglar would probably frighten it or volley it over the fucking back fence. At least a Rottweiler would guard the house." Eustace responded by saying "let's jog on."

Most managers, coaches and players will sometimes say, even confirm that pre-season can set a precedent. I am one of those who thinks that it does. Sometimes though, it doesn't matter how well you think you may have prepared it can all blow up in your face and the season can be a letdown, a massive anti-climax. In the third division of season 1990-1991 the likes of Swansea and Fulham finished below us and because over time they were shaken up, organised, restructured and brought in the right players would go on over the next few years to play in the Premier League. It's no good dreaming the dream unless you organise your club and put things in place to fulfil the dream. The others in our division who would go on to do the same were Reading, Stoke, Birmingham, Wigan, Bournemouth and Bolton. For me, ambition only has to be matched by foundation, organisation, fight, and will to win, which should go hand in hand with adding quality players and staff as you progress.

We finished thirteenth out of a possible twenty-four, so in effect, just below halfway. It's only my opinion but over the course of the next three years I thought the heart and soul of the club was ripped apart. What I mean by heart and soul is people were discarded who had a feeling and an affinity for the club and they were replaced with players and people who I bet couldn't believe their luck. Some of them were mercenaries getting a pay day in the twilight of their career. The fact that I spoke out against such things was to in the end, get me in trouble. Rather than see my comments for what they were, well meant with feeling for the club, born of quite a lot of frustration, professionalism and ahead of its time it was used against me by Eustace and Frank Clark.

The three main things to come out of pre-season for me were, thanks to Mr Eustace and training right through the summer, I was the fittest I'd ever been. I was thirty-one and I had, I thought, about three or four years left in me. Next up, chomping at the bit for the first game of the season at home to Swansea, I was kept on as captain by Peter Eustace who also openly complimented me about the way I led. He said, and I'll never forget the words, "you're my Mike Lyons." I asked "what do you mean by that?" "At Sheffield, Howard bought Mike Lyons from Everton. From day one, he was a leader, brave. You're like him a lot. When you go for a ball nothing's going to get in your way and stop you, you only see the ball. I like the way you speak up and give an opinion in team meetings and you're very vocal on the football field, you've got that "manliness" about you." I felt ten feet tall. I thought I was on the same page and I was appreciated by Peter.

Obviously Frank already knew my makeup. The third and last thing emanating from pre-season was a distinct lack of organisation compared to what we had under Brian Eastick. There was a semblance and any strategy we had was left over from Eastick's days. I picked up the thread defensively and with Daygo, Dicko and Baker or Howard we continued to shut the lines off and condense play. I was virtually hoarse at the end of every ninety minutes which I suppose as a leader you should be. The first game of the season was at home to Swansea and it was an emphatic 3-0 win. I felt like I could have played another ninety minutes. I felt strong, flexible and the running and physical training made me feel like I could compete all day.

The win was due compensation for giving up two tickets and backstage passes for a Rolling Stones concert the night before. My wife's bank were sponsoring a world tour and my Mrs even though she was disappointed, completely understood. She could see I was gutted, but that's just the way I was. She understood that football can be a selfish profession at times. We gave the tickets away so that I could concentrate on Swansea. This type of thing had happened many times over the years. I suppose I should now publicly apologise to all those hosts over the years who may well have thought I was a miserable sod because my wife and I were generally the first to leave a party, dinner party or just a few rounds of drinks. I always put football first. Even a rest day I didn't want ruined with a hangover so I could make the most of the time I had with my kids. I found out very early that drink followed by a hangover is a complete waste of a day and life.

I think its relevant that with hindsight I've always been more inclined to get home once I had a family, not a great one for networking. It's a shame because there are people with half the knowhow but twice the capacity for drink who sussed long before I did, that jobs back then were given out over half a lager or a game of golf. On top of relinquishing tickets for a once in a lifetime event, I got topped by Chris Zoricich in training on the Friday! All the fitness work, set pieces and a semblance of a pattern of play had been rehearsed, so it was a thirty-minute practice match and as I rolled a ball forward "Zoro" came in and upended me. My ankle came up like a balloon and I was taken off the field in Bill Songhurst's car and straight back to the main ground. It was the usual ice pack and anti-inflammatory tablets.

I had a fitness test at one thirty the next day and played with a heavy strapping rather than give up my place to either Zoro or a kid coming through, called Whitbread. I wasn't giving up my place, not after knocking my bollocks out for six weeks. Zoro was a Kiwi and I knew there was no malice in it. He was a bit of me. He trained how he played and was a typical New Zealander in his approach to his chosen sport. There were three good kids making progress, Kevin Nugent, Chris Bart-Williams and Adrian Whitbread. My next two disagreements with Eustace would be as a consequence of speaking up again, which I'd thought he'd given me licence to do anyway and both might I add were relevant points to our at times, piss poor performances and poor run of results. One was during a rare interlude at an indoor facility during a six aside competition.

I had the ball played to me and Chris Bart-Williams whacked me from behind and into the wall. I spun around and said "you whack me from behind? you little cunt, take it easy ..." Eustace stopped the game. He walked over and said "you fucking leave him alone, let him get on with it.. ." I replied that I was highly delighted that there was someone in midfield who was willing to put their foot in and compete, but one, if I wasn't such a nice guy I'd iron him out, so he'd quite possibly be without his best midfield player. Two, more importantly, I had my back to the game and was going nowhere, so all he had to do was stop me turning and force the ball back and he would have done a great job for the side. Instead, he'd given away an unnecessary free kick. Three, having invited pressure with the free kick, if he done it too many times he'd just be seen as a bad player who was always suspended.

I went on to add that he should be telling him that's unacceptable and coaching an alternative. Castle piped up with something to make himself busy but Eustace said "that'll do, in you go, get a shower." After a couple of games in the first team, Chris acquitted himself magnificently and to help and advise him and show him there were no hard feelings I took him out for a steak and a chat along with Kevin Nugent. He was a good lad "Bartman." His eventual transfer fee would help Eustace balance the books on transfers, paper over the financial cracks and keep the club running all of which came as a consequence of poor planning, foresight and an overpriced, poorly balanced, overpaid, ageing squad with no resale value. All this basically amounted to financial suicide.

The backbone of the club and the fulcrum of the side and squad was about to be ripped apart and replaced with all of the above. Over four years, youngsters like Bart-Williams, Whitbread and Nugent would be sold. Financial assets like Castle and Rob Taylor would be sold and the likes of myself and a backroom staff who loved the club, were let go. Harry Spinner, Jimmy Halleybone and Bill Songhurst all parted company. A turnover of staff and playing staff are all fine and dandy if it means progress. But over the four years or so that Peter was there, he confirmed what I have always felt was a myth and among the biggest load of claptrap in football.

I mean, it's no good balancing the transfer fees in and out if you're going overdrawn every week because of signing on fees and wages. Then compounding it by flirting with relegation even if in Peter's words in 1993-94 "it's an important year for me, these are all my players."

The old chestnut called "net spend." Except it wasn't and the medium term repercussions would bring Leyton Orient to the brink of bankruptcy. In Peter's defence someone above had to sanction it and the same has happened and continues to at numerous clubs. Let's look at the good business first. Chris Bart-Williams was a one off and with tack-ons his fee came to eight hundred thousand pounds, enough to underpin the club's losses for two years. The admission money from a predictable gate of between three and a half and four thousand and a non-performing, hardly contributory commercial department simply were not cutting it.

To stand in Bartman's way would have been criminal so he was off to Trevor Francis at Sheffield Wednesday. Ricky Otto cost four or five grand cash which was given to then manager Neville Watson at a club not far from where I lived, Haringey Borough. He went to a bigger club, Birmingham, for one hundred thousand pounds. The downside in case you and O's supporters haven't noticed is that you are taking away two creative players who could provide ammunition for the most priceless commodity in the game.. goals. Castle came through the ranks and only cost the club wages. A good athlete, box to box, fearless competitor and contributor of goals from midfield. He moved in my opinion sideways to Plymouth (at best), did ok out of the deal personally, brought in a few quid, but apart from weakening his own midfield, Eustace replaced him at greater expense with inferior player(s) who had absolutely no resale value.

Kevin Nugent followed Castle to Plymouth. A good lad, good pro, who came through the ranks so he had an affinity towards the club. In my opinion he was a decent technician but would have been good business. His goals to games ratio was in between one in four and one in five. Not that prolific. He was survived at the club by Cooper, a similar strike rate, but less mobile and less inclined to work hard and defend from the front, which I later highlighted and got kicked out of the club for. With signing on fee, relocation fee and wages, I was replaced by a Wolverhampton Wanderers reserve whose package came to nearly four times my contract. My other replacement was someone from non-league who was put on identical money to what I'd earned immediately. Not bad for someone with no pedigree. This after me being in and around a professional football club environment since I was twelve. Nugent's other replacement was a lad who walked with a limp and ran like a cripple after bravely recovering from several operations on a couple of serious knee injuries. Lee Harvey's pace and provision of goals was being pushed aside by another Eustace sycophant, although I don't know why, called Kenny Achampong. I'll concede that there comes a time when you should turn over your squad and freshen things up. Some transfers are even dictated by an offer (think Bart-Williams) for a player that you can't refuse, but supporters are bowled along just by the plain fact that their club has made a new signing and some managers don't consider anywhere near the medium and long term effects. That reminds me of one of Peter's sayings that he used frequently in his two-hour team meetings. "If you can't be affected, you can't be effective." He turned out neither effective and most certainly wasn't affected by spending money that Leyton Orient couldn't afford.

This was after going through match reports and talking up the opposition that made Bolton sound like Barcelona and Reading like Real Madrid. To be truthful I paid every opponent the same respect. I convinced myself to expect the unexpected, never underestimate a forward and always be alert and on tenterhooks until I was going up the tunnel at the end of ninety minutes. As a defender if you switch off you're dead. A defender has to get it right one hundred per cent of the time. A forward can fail ninety nine times out of a hundred then at last get it right and score the winner in the last minute. Where Kenny Achampong was concerned he rocked up from Charlton and an incident that involved him should have led to me going before I was pushed. During a practice match Eustace called him a nasty, ugly, heinous name as he coached Kenny and Steve Castle.

As captain I should have spoken up. If Peter wanted it to escalate I'd have had no problem laying him out and telling Frank Clark to cancel my registration. But shamefully, instead of highlighting and bringing verbal racist bullying into the public domain, all I could think of as I looked down at the goose shit was to protect my income and stay in football. I'd grown up in the sixties and seventies where such things were commonplace and it was always around. Through self-education, experience of racism, reading history, and awareness I should by now have taken a stand. I actually asked Kenny Achampong over our lunch of beans on toast why he'd let Peter talk to him like that. "That's just Peter Sitts man, he knows how to get me playing, he was the same with me at Charlton."

I just raised my eyebrows as it seemed a tad contradictory to his daily fashion statement. His outfits were always topped off with a baseball cap that was inscribed with "NWA" in large letters in reference to a rap group. Rap was en vogue and on the up and up as lyrical poetry was set to music about the social injustice of what had gone before, and what seems to be an omnipresent part of living in America for African Americans. I laughed as Kenny meted out his own piss take when on numerous occasions at Bill's clinic he'd ask to use the telephone and called his relatives in Africa. Game wise he was a talented boy, but the club as a whole had very few highlights that year. One was a cup tie against Ossie Ardiles' Swindon Town side. Another would be a cup game against Crystal Palace that went to two replays. At Selhurst Park it was 0-0. After a pre-match at a hotel Peter stopped the coach and he insisted we walked the rest of the way to the sound of Palace supporters asking if we'd run out of petrol.

I was the sweeper in a back five. Sweeper is all about gauging the depth and bossing people around you to keep any danger in front of you, not allowing the opposition to get in behind. I had a pop at I think, the lad Thorne who went on to manage Coventry after he came through the back of Lee Harvey. Andy Gray got involved and I called him out "in the gym if you've gone one, or if not, under the stand," so that someone would show we couldn't be bullied or intimidated. Ian Wright started and I just said "get in line son." Kenny Achampong knew these lads because of the previous ground sharing between Charlton and Crystal Palace. He came up to me afterwards saying they'd asked "who's that mouthy cunt at the back?" In the last minute Kevin Nugent lobbed Palace's goalkeeper, I think it was Nigel Martyn and hit the bar from the halfway line. At the final whistle after not having a shot, Ian Wright turned his back and jogged off as I went to shake hands. I called out. "See you back in the East End."

The first replay ended 0-0 again after extra time. Again our defending was exemplary and I think like most good defending it was overlooked and taken for granted. I think it's even more relevant now as I watch T.V and see laughable defending at all levels. It breaks my heart. My opinion is quite harsh, there's defenders particularly in the lower divisions who wouldn't have got in my Sunday side. Steve Castle held the midfield together and up front our only real threat was Lee Harvey who was getting kicked to pieces. This is where partnerships all over the field should have a blend, a balance and complement each other. Up front it was never the case with absolutely no bite or physical presence. At best it was soporific compared to Wright and Bright. One would be sharp, perpetual movement, always trying to threaten the back and get a shot off.

The other was a threat in the air and despite both of them having a nice, smiley disposition on TV they could both leave a foot in, give you an annoying nudge or body check, jump in, and one in particular made full use of his elbows. I looked sixty yards up the pitch and on too many occasions I'd see defenders have a very comfortable afternoon. My opinion as a player and coach has never changed, any team where good spirit is engendered is normally a team full of players who go above and beyond their remit to help their mate. Every player plays unselfishly. It's that willingness to be unselfish that makes a team harder to break down. With the exception of five or six, we never had that. Anyway, not one to bear a grudge, at the end of extra time, again I extended my hand and the pseudo hard cases at Palace jogged off.

We won the toss and it was a second replay at home. All to play for, although with Heald, Castle and a back five performing well, I still felt we needed more of a goal threat. Palace seemed to have it in abundance by contrast. Mark Bright was I always felt, a very good, if underrated centre forward. Ian Wright in my opinion was one of the best forwards in Premier League, even British football history. You couldn't take your eye off him for a minute. Good forwards, a threat from goal hungry midfielders and a fair share of honey monsters to deal with from set pieces. By comparison our rehearsals for set pieces had become like a Chinese fire drill. Cooper, not renowned for his bravery, movement and aggression when attacking the ball was put in my place and I was stuck on the near post where the minimum of movement to achieve a flick on would have suited Cooper far more.

Under Eastick I was identified as the one most likely to create space with some movement, attack the ball aggressively, put my head in and all this married to power and good spring got me a few goals and a shed load of assists before assists were at all fashionable. In either penalty area you have to have players prepared to scrap, battle, physically impose themselves, show aggression to earn the right to exercise the technique required to even get an attempt on goal. This is where Palace had the edge. Whitbread was ok, so was Castle. That left me, probably the best of all, almost in isolation at the near post trying to flick the ball on. As for Nugent, Cooper, Hull, Pike, Hales and Harvey, it either wasn't their game or the ball needed to land right on Cooper or Nugent's head, rather than either going after a ball and making it theirs. In the time I played and the people

I played with, the best at it was probably Steve Bruce. Anyway, in the last minute of extra time the ball was deep and on Palace's right, our left. Bright makes a run beyond the near post about twelve yards out, a long diagonal ball is hit, he gets across Daygo and Whitbread and does everything to win it, flick it on and deflect it goalwards. It sails in the top corner to Healdy's right. As we kick off and launch it forward into Palace's box the referee blows up. Palace nick it 1-0. After the game I went down looking resplendent in a very smart suit to socialise with the sponsors in the sponsors lounge by the main entrance of the football club.

As I sipped a drink I heard a load of shouting and hollering in the corridor and walked out to "where the fuck is he, where is he?" I saw Kenny Achampong and either side of him were a couple of players I'd had exchanges with on the football field during the game. I poked my head around the door and said "who are you looking for Ken?" The two Palace players looked at each other and one said to the other "fuck it, let's go." I either misinterpreted what they said, it was false bravado or the posse wasn't big enough. Or just maybe, I completely misread the situation but supporters don't realise stuff like that goes on all the time. I've seen many a fracas in the tunnel. I even saw Frank Clark chin an opposition player once, not too long after he'd told me to behave myself! Funny things happen in the heat of battle.

A couple of good solid performances, although there was no goal threat, were normally followed by a slump and poor run of results. As the results got worse, the behaviour around the place became more bizarre.

Just to confirm some of my opinions after I left as a player Chris Turner invited an old Manchester United team mate of his, Gordon Strachan, to a game up north and he (Chris) and Peter asked his opinion on a couple of forwards still at the club from my time there. "They look, run and play like a couple of Sunday Morning Pub players," was his assessment. Which in the end gave my opinion the credibility it deserved. Key word in football: credibility. It's assumed if you're a lower league player you don't know as much as your supposed superiors.

The bizarre behaviour was wide and varied. Most Friday nights as I walked back to my room I heard "crash, bang, thud," as I walked past Castle and Howard's room. I knocked on the door and Steve Castle opened it giggling. I walked in and said "what's going on?"

Terry was on a bedside cabinet laughing. They'd made up a game called "Sharks." The room floor was the sea, infested with sharks. They had a competition to see who could get around the room using beds, bedside cabinets, dressing table and doors without touching the floor or they would be eaten. I said "I take it TV and a book isn't good enough." I couldn't stop laughing as I watched Terry trying to get around the room. I had it on my toes before someone called reception.

Two long haul trips up north were next up. The club arranged to stay up there before and in between the games. I'm almost sure one of the games was Tranmere. Anyway after the first game, probably the other side of the Pennines we stayed at Hull University. So it was training, a defeat, student food, up again for training. It was pissing down with rain and Mr Eustace insisted on us leaving our all-weather waterproofs on the coach. "Yer all soft. Get wet, feel some good northern rain and wind it'll do you good." In my best cockney, thick as shit voice I said "Bill, can you tell me the point of rain proof tops if we can't wear them while it's raining?" "I don't know Sitts, jog on the spot." Next day was a six mile walk, (the day before a game) on the Yorkshire Moors where we had to line up and put a rock on a mound that served as a landmark for hikers. After the walk we went to a pub for lunch.

The pub was just about to close but Peter used his persuasive powers. So the squad, four staff, (Woolfy had made the trip) and Peter's wife and two daughters enjoyed wine, beer, fish and chips, a roast, or steak and kidney pie. I had a roast with lots of vegetables and some water to keep as close as I could to what I'd eat at home. Next day we were up for training again, a lunch and off to bed for the afternoon. Peter said there'll be no pre-match meal, just a pot of tea. I think we got beat 3-0. There were three games up and coming that showed up the inconsistencies and fickle nature of football and in my mind also showed up one or two people to whom I'd given everything, including when they needed it, profound friendship and support. Oh well.

Three games would ultimately determine my fate at Leyton Orient under Peter Eustace and Frank Clark. One was after spending Sunday to Thursday off with flu and returning to training on Friday to see a short, fat centre back from Sheffield Wednesday's reserves brought down on loan by Eustace. In training on the Friday I knocked my bollocks out to try and prove my fitness and in the tunnel after the practice match at the main ground I got very aggressive with Eustace and told him "I'm fit for tomorrow, he's not having my shirt." With experience and a change of attitude and being educated by bigger and better players than myself since then, I should have dropped out until I was absolutely one hundred per cent fit, allowing for the little niggles that most players carry with them throughout a season and waited.

Next day I was about as strong as a week old lettuce leaf and was out muscled by the lad Holdsworth. I remember being bundled off the ball and a player who shall remain nameless, but who I hand carried through his debut and sided with during games when he had a row with other senior players about pressing the ball and who I escorted off the training pitch when he started crying after splitting up with his girlfriend said within earshot, "that's fucking embarrassing." Believe me I didn't need to be told. I just thought what a treacherous little cunt! I carried on ever present having regained full fitness within a week and continued to hover around the holy grail for a centre back returning performances of seven to eight out of ten. Solid, reliable, dependable and consistent. For the record I think nine out of ten is someone who's particularly creative with the ball and maybe provides an assist. A ten out of ten is all of the above and a goal from a set piece. We went north again and I'm almost sure, but I can't be absolutely certain, that it was Bolton away that led to me speaking my mind and speaking out against players long before Roy Keane on MUTV.

If you're a good pro, a good player, you care, you're passionate and you want to win, there comes a time when you have to say enough is enough and stand up and be counted. As ludicrous as it sounds where certain players are concerned it's in their makeup and it doesn't matter whether its seventy-six thousand at Old Trafford or on a Sunday morning. You are what you are. Although it turned out not to be the career I wanted, a large part of my makeup after all, is what contributed to me having around five hundred games if you include substitute appearances in all four divisions. As we handed the team sheets in, unlike cockneys, it seemed to me that northerners are almost orgasmic in their admiration for each other when they cross paths. Frank Clark and Phil Brown, two Geordies were no exception. The only thing missing was a Geordie version of Doctor Livingstone I Presume.

We lost 1-0. No goal threat again. More relevant was the fact that Eustace and Clark gave little or no regard to the back four who were constantly under siege. By comparison I looked upfield and Bolton's back four against the likes of Cooper could have had a three course meal followed by cheese and biscuits, coffee, brandy and cigars. Our midfield even with the combative Castle were overran, out passed and the biggest crime of all, outfought. I looked across the back four and saw Dicko with a bruised instep after a forward left his foot in. I had a nice split over one eye courtesy of an elbow. I looked to my right and saw Keith Day with a split lip and blood trickling from his nose, although to be fair it was a fairly big target. I couldn't help thinking "fuck this, this ain't right." By this time we had had at least two or three if not four negative mini runs during the course of the season where we had lost four or five on the bounce or done something like won one and drawn one in seven.

After another alarming run of results and following a home defeat, one of six that season which is absolutely diabolical, I was interviewed on Clubcall by Chris Raistrick who asked what my thoughts were on how we would arrest the current slide and downturn in form. He asked what was wrong and what I thought needed to be addressed. I don't know if it was pride, ego or my mouth running away with me yet again or a combination of all three. I remarked that I had seen too many games where players had not shown a willingness to work and battle, compete and fight the opposition and come out the other side with that old chestnut of earning the right to play. Malcolm Allison once said "competing is everything in football. You can't have players who just say give me the ball. They've got to compete and go and get it themselves..." I said there are too many players who are pulling out of tackles when the ball is there to be won and there are players who are sending out the wrong message and showing borderline cowardice. In my opinion they shouldn't be in the team and they're not fit to wear the shirt. It was broadcast just before a home game versus Huddersfield Town and came to the attention of someone who is typical of football. By that I mean a mischievous fucker who will seize upon any semblance of a crack in an organisation and pray upon it and go out of his way to make the crack bigger when all they should be doing is worrying about their own football club. Maybe I shouldn't have broadcast to Leyton Orient's meagre following and spoken outside of my remit. Eoin Hand was Huddersfield's Town's manager and he seized upon it and breezed into Peter Eustace's office saying "Jesus have you heard your captain on Clubcall? I always ring the opposition's Clubcall to get news of any injuries to see if I can work out the team, I can't believe what he said." Eustace and Clark bit straight away. I was told by Eustace after, as he stripped me of the captaincy, that he sent Frank Woolf immediately to get a copy of the tape.

When I was summoned to the office there was a nonsensical exchange between me and Eustace, with Eustace actually saying, "you're accusing me of dishonestly selecting players." I gave him the excuse he was looking for to start to change things around and get rid of players who not only performed but had a feeling for the club and among those he got rid of were younger players than me with years ahead of them, who were replaced with old players on big signing on fees, big wages and no resale value. In reply I said to Peter "no that's bollocks I'm afraid, your interpretation is up to you, but I'm not accusing you of dishonest selection, I'm accusing your selection of a dishonest performance, there's a difference and you must be watching a fucking different game to the one I am playing in." I think it's pertinent at this stage that without naming the four players concerned, which is too big a burden for any side in any division to carry, out of those four, one of the players was just trying to avoid injury in the twilight of his career, and one of the players played only four games all season and was rewarded with a new two-year contract.

I played thirty-eight games and was given a free transfer. I'm hoping you as the reader will find it as strange, baffling and as nonsensical as I did at the time. Mind you it sums up perfectly that at times in football there's a reward for failure culture that seems to pass by supporters, directors and the media. I was called in by Eustace about three weeks before transfer deadline which was the third week in March. I was then left to stew as Eustace told me "Frank's not happy with you." When I passed Frank in the corridor he took his turn and remarked "fookin hell Sitts, Peter's not happy with you." I couldn't help thinking who's in charge and who's hiding behind who? I was up for everyone getting their balls out. After being stripped of the captaincy Peter addressed the squad and said Stevie Castle is the new captain. "The leader of our pack should be the leader of the pack in the running and because he is the best athlete he is now our captain." I couldn't help thinking and believe me I was tempted to say out loud "It's a fucking good job Sir Alf Ramsey didn't think like that..." One week after transfer deadline day Eustace called me into the office and said your contract will not be renewed at the end of the season. I said "if you decided that we weren't going to go forward together why did you encourage me as your 'Mike Lyons' and praise my contribution on the football field and in the dressing room. Why didn't you circulate other clubs to give me a chance of getting away? Why did you leave it until a week after deadline day to tell me this? I've been a good solid performer for six years at this club, so much for being a family you horrible cunt..." And I Walked Out.

My final humiliation was for the last couple of games to be named as a substitute.

The last game of the season was away to Fulham I think, and Eustace asked me to get up off the bench, jog round to the far side of the pitch and give Ricky Otto some instructions. Consummate professional until the end I did as I was told. But I'm pleased to say it wasn't before Peter suffered a couple of humiliations of his own. One was quite embarrassing and one was quite humorous even though I say so myself. God pays debts without money. The first one was away to Huddersfield and after an overnight stay we were told to report at nine am in full training kit. I thought it was absolutely bizarre, unprofessional and confirmed that only after a few months some methods were questionable and ideas were in short supply.

There was no time for breakfast unless you got up at seven am on the day of a game and as it turned out the pre-match meal had to be cancelled because of what happened. We embarked upon a forty- minute coach journey from the hotel to the middle of nowhere where there was a small schoolboy pitch with no grass and metal goalposts with no nets. On three sides of the pitch was a small council estate, facing us as we got off the coach was a massive, and I mean massive, as in small mountain, of slag. A combination of earth, coal, dust and landfill waste. Eustace then went into a ridiculous diatribe about northern grit, hard work and northern industry to create the wealth that you in the south get the pleasure of spending. He then went on to slag off Margaret Thatcher and his new captain sycophantically chipped in saying "the woman's a fucking nightmare." Eustace starting about the closing of the mines, the killing of communities, blah blah blah.

I was up the front because I was never one to stand at the back of the pack and I said "I didn't know you were interested in politics Peter or you Steve, I think it's what you call either lazy research or selected memory loss." Eustace said "what do you mean?" I replied "well for instance did you know that more mines were closed under Labour and the leaderships of Michael Foot and John Smith than under Thatcher?" He made us jog round the pitch back to him and he said "have one last look at them slag heaps before you get back on the coach." Eustace started to remind me of the school teacher in the film "Kes." The one played by Brian Hislop.. "I'll be Bobby Charlton.." There was no talk of Huddersfield's shape, pattern of play, dangerous individuals or set pieces. I just thought this is fucking ludicrous. We got back to the hotel, Frank said "what fucking time do you call this?" We had twenty minutes to eat our pre-match meal, clear out our rooms and get on the coach. I think we arrived at Huddersfield at a quarter past two.

Next match at home and it's a Friday, everyone is changed and is ready to train. Ten twenty, ten thirty, ten forty-five, eleven o'clock... the captain's missing. Steve Castle hasn't turned up. I just carried on doing my stretches while Eustace was running backwards and forwards to reception to make and take telephone calls. The story that was relayed to me and the lads went like this...

It had transpired that our leader and best athlete had gone up the West End with some mates on Thursday night, less than forty- eight hours before a game for a night out. After having too much to drink Steve Castle thought it would then be a good idea to go into a well-known pizza restaurant, have a meal with his mates and then exercise his athleticism by doing a runner and not pay for the meal. He was pursued and arrested by plain clothes police officers and had spent the night in a police cell, which is why he never made training on time on Friday morning. The team was picked, a practice match was played and Eustace tried to carry on as if nothing had happened. Now that's what you call embarrassing. At this stage I was still ever present in the side and I just kept my head down and got on with it. On Saturday before the game I kept to my usual routine and I was changed and left the dressing room just after two fifteen pm. I went out for my usual twenty minute warm up and came back in at two thirty-five to get a massage.

As I lay on the couch Frank came into the match day medical room and said "where have you been? the team sheets are late and we have got to hand them in." I said "what do you mean we?" Frank said "Peter wants you to wear the arm band today. Come on Sitts do it for me." All the physios looked down as I said "Frank am I right in saying that Eustace said the captain should be the best athlete?" He responded by saying, "well yes I suppose he did." I said "in that case give the fucking armband to the copper who gave Steve Castle a head start, chased him and caught him." Bill Songhurst, Tony Flynn and even Frank couldn't resist a little chuckle. I think it's absolutely relevant to point out that Eustace was nowhere to be seen. Like the whore with a heart of gold I got off the bench after Frank said : " come on Sitt's do it for me" and went with him to hand in the team sheets. Despite an everyday tirade from him calling us "Southern Softies" with a "soft underbelly" and "no passion" and "I bet you're all shit in bed" (I made the mistake in that particular team meeting by saying "ask your wife") he wasn't man enough to face me after the embarrassment of Castle making him look a cunt. Obviously Peter didn't disappoint. That's players for you, it doesn't matter who the manager is. At the end of that season I had three options.

One was to play under John Still at Dagenham and Redbridge. He offered me a poor basic wage and a very good signing on fee that seemed to me to defy logic unless there was an agenda that I wasn't aware of. I now had two young daughters so I wanted a bigger basic wage, telling John that I'd settle for a smaller signing on fee which we couldn't agree on. Next up was an offer from Ray Harford for me to join a club in Hong Kong which I declined saying I had two small children to consider. Lastly half way through pre-season, the first time that I hadn't done pre-season in sixteen years, I got a call from Kevin Locke at Southend. With hindsight maybe I should have taken the offer to play under him and David Webb where they had a great set of lads. Kevin said "come in and train and let Webby have a look at you." I felt that they thought I was dealing from weakness so I said to "Lockey" "Kev I have been playing against yours and Webby's teams for the last ten years, I've played five hundred games and I was educated at the club where Webby had the highlight of his career, I'm afraid I don't do auditions." He said "fair enough Sitts I'll tell him."

I was out on my arse and my self-esteem was lower than a snake's belly in a sunken submarine. After turning down an invite to train with David Webb and Kevin Locke at Southend and a possible contract I could quite easily write a chapter on how I spent from April when Eustace gave me a fuck off tablet through to September being totally depressed and not knowing what to do with my life.

I've given September as a reference point because for the first time in my working life I had to sign on the dole and when I cashed my giro I was almost made to feel ashamed by a self-righteous little prick who knew my mother and father-in-law. His great achievement in life was working for the Post Office for the most of it. I don't know whether it was shame or ego but I'd hazard a guess most certainly pride and defiance were involved when I said to myself "Fuck Him I've Been Paying Into The System For Fifteen Years." I'd gone from pulling on a training kit, or a kit on match day that transformed me, it was an immediate change of identity that made me feel like a superhero every time I laced my boots up. Now even though I had no debts, no vices, was surrounded by family, I felt something was missing. I had no sense of belonging, of worth, and no purpose. Everyone around me were getting on with their normal lives and it just seemed to make me even more depressed. Not for long. I refused to be beat so I got back in the gym and tried to turn towards getting some employment. The problem with the gym is it can never replace the banter in the dressing room or for me, better still, that smell of freshly cut grass as you walk onto the field of play and pinging that first ball of pre-season or as part of a pre-match warm up.

The only reason it had come to this was because I thought I had done a deal with ex Millwall chief scout Bob Pearson, on Frank Clark's recommendation to become player-coach and progress to player-manager at Slough Town F.C. Maybe deep down Frank thought that I had been hard done by. After all he had known me inside out and back to front for six seasons. One thing I have always admired about some people, and particularly Sir Alex Ferguson, is how they reward, endorse and support their former players who have served them well and pushed them towards coaching and managing careers. I would have been exactly the same. That particular appointment went tits up when David Kemp was sacked by Plymouth Argyle. I arrived for the first day of pre-season to find Kempy turning up in his ex-club car that he got as part of a settlement package and I was told that he had been appointed manager. I kept my cool and my dignity, shook hands with Bob and said no hard feelings, all the best, got in my car and drove off.

Along with the depression of being away from the only thing I knew and the bitterness of feeling ostracised, unwanted and unloved, I had to contend with not just the turbulent life I had after being a manager, but before that the turbulent ups and downs of life after playing. There were not only the very few fights and confrontations in the game, but quite a few fights and confrontations outside of the game which led to me being charged twice, times spent in a police cell, and one that led to me dissolving what I thought was a very good friendship. However I think it's fair to say I've continued to try and move away from what might be called stereotype.

This happened after I was sacked as manager of Leyton Orient and it only added to the difficult time that I was going through after I took a job at a local non-league club. My wife and I were very good friends with a couple, let's call them Neil and Carol because that's their names, and part of this particular story somehow had made its way to them.

I was on a wage and with the help of one of the committee I was given a small wage and eighty pounds to give to certain players as expenses. I gave one player forty pounds and spent the other forty pounds on a pre-match meal of tea, toast, bananas and jelly babies. We slowly but surely added to the poor facilities with things like balls, bibs and cones. The squad mainly consisted of Sunday morning players who were actually better than the ones who were already there. If memory serves me right, we were second or third from the bottom. Even that didn't escape the notice of a Leyton Orient Fanzine who never passed up the opportunity to have a pop at me asking "guess where they are in the league?" I'm all for a bit of banter but I'm not sure what anyone expects with a wage bill of forty quid. You can add this to the fact that they wouldn't have a club to support if it wasn't for me. Anyway, back to the job I was currently in and trying to do. One of many problems was a poorly run bar that was frequented by a family of scum who were now the third generation of wannabe tough guys and plastic gangsters. After keeping up their family tradition of drinking rather than working, at a home game as we kicked off, one of my players who was an ex-Arsenal youth trainee was the victim of vile, disgusting racist abuse and threats. I was asked by the referee to intercede, so I asked them to leave.

The four of them were sat in a car and one of them got out and tried to hit me. At the time I was training five, sometimes six times a week and I ridiculed him even though he was supposed to come from a boxing family. Isn't it funny how they always seem to. Anyway another one from the same family started the engine of the car and tried to crush me against the wall where I had just ridiculed his brother having blocked his three punches and thrown him. The chairman came out and told them to get out and as they pulled away in the car I thought that would be the last that I would see of them. They returned about ten minutes later and all the doors of the car flew open for me to see one armed with a wooden pole and a drill, one armed with an iron bar, one armed with an aluminium baseball bat, and one with a wooden baseball bat. All the committee and supporters ran into the club and locked the door behind them. All the players ran to the far side of the field including the full back, a Greek kid who I was paying appearance money to and never passed up an opportunity to claim he and his brother-in-law were Kung Fu experts with fighting prowess. I remember thinking afterwards "what's the point if you're a coward and you run away?"

With the exception of one of the opposition who was smashed across the knee caps with the wooden pole, the only person who tried to help me was a little midfield player who I had just signed from Waltham Abbey. He had his head split and his arm broken by the iron bar. I was occupied with the scum who I'd made look a mug earlier and was now holding the aluminium baseball bat. I blocked a few of his attempts to put it over my head and as I went in to finish him an even bigger cowardly scum sneaked up behind me and brought the wooden baseball bat diagonally down across my neck, back and head. I ended up with a big gash behind my right ear, three displaced vertebrae in my neck and a broken hand. Luckily for me the bat broke and I never went down. To their astonishment I just took a dab of the blood now coming down the side of my face and neck and I spun round and said "you dirty backstabbing little cunt." They turned and ran to their car as I ran after them. Less than forty- eight hours later I was contacted by a Detective Sergeant in the local area CID who wanted to nick them for GBH section eighteen. Aptly named because it can carry an eighteen year sentence.

After a brief conversation with him pleading for me to get them off the streets I said "I'm sorry I was bought up in a different era and not to be a grass" and put the phone down. When I relayed this story to the couple I thought of as friends to confirm what they had already heard, over dinner at their house, rather than show their empathy, sympathy and compatibility with my sense of honour, and dare I say it, moral victory over this cowardly attack from racist scum, Carol said "you've just got the hump cos you got bashed up." Like I said I don't mind a bit of banter and we were always teasing each other, especially when I highlighted the fact that her husband was hen pecked, but my wife nearly choked on her soup and made out she never heard it. I kept my cool and dignity and needless to say the friendship was dissolved. I haven't spoken to them since. She absolutely broke my heart, but no doubt there might have been quite a few who would have been glad to hear the news that I had taken a clump. Knowing what I know about physiology and anatomy through football and martial arts, I thought I was lucky not to have been killed or at the very least crippled but Carol just saw it as a chance to belittle me. Dear oh dear.

Now you know the truth and how it happened. I carried on in the job for about two to three weeks after but as I looked around at people who had left me to fend for myself and ran away after I had stuck up for one of us, I never felt the same. Even the kid who I stepped in for as he and his mother and sister were called all sorts of filthy, eighteenth and nineteenth century names never thanked me, so I left. The only consolation I had yet again was in knowing that I had done the right thing (supposedly) in standing by one of my own. I'm not so sure George, Terry, Jose, Alex and Arsene would have done the same. Then again I don't suppose they would have needed to look for work that far down. You know what they say "if you lay down with dogs, you get up with fleas."

Apart from doing a possible volume two on how to set up a football club from top to bottom and being able to put all my ideas down on paper I could probably do a chapter on economics, failed business ventures and how to react when a close relative leaves you holding the proverbial financial baby. It led to me being completely financially ruined, unemployed, desperate and yet again depressed, but not for long. My life savings were now decimated and the only thing that I did right was to have paid off my house. It was almost as if history was repeating itself. I now had to set about looking for some sort of income. I had heard through the grapevine that all was not well at Leyton Orient on both the senior side and youth set up. I had heard that the youth coach had lost control so changes might be afoot and with the first team struggling, particularly in defence, Bill Songhurst stuck his neck out and said to Eustace in front of all the staff "you could do a lot worse than bring Sitts back." I picked up the phone and called Bernie Dixson to ask about the possibility of coaching in Leyton Orient's Centre of Excellence which had the disparaging nickname of "Leyton Orient's centre of mediocrity." To make ends meet and pay the bills at different times I was staffing courses for the LFA, signing on the dole, coaching a Sunday side in the Greek League and now for the princely sum of ten pounds per night I coached at Leyton Orient's Centre of Excellence for two hours on a Monday and two hours on a Thursday in every kind of weather imaginable. The fee was a mega piss take but I wanted a foot on the ladder which I had to remind myself as I coached in a force gale wind with rain coming in at a forty five degree angle.

Never again. I've since learned I'm better than that and lesser men and lesser coaches have been better rewarded. Towards the end of the second year I'd got wind of the fact that there was going to be a change and I asked Chris Turner and Bernie Dixson to support my application to become Leyton Orient youth team manager. After two rounds of interviews I ended up on a short list of three alongside Kevin Hales and Chris Houghton. I was appointed and took the job for two hundred and eighty pounds a week, a petrol card and a red Lancia hatchback that looked like it had been in   a stock car race. The second year YTS that I had inherited were given an opportunity to stake their claim to earn a full professional contract. There were too many either not up to it or who had wasted a year. I decided to introduce all the new first year intake and what were previously poor results were turned into good positive results in the second half of the season. During that time highlights were turning a massive reverse against Spurs with a few internationals in their ranks into a respectable draw. We had a win and a draw against Arsenal and knocked Chelsea out of the F.A Youth Cup. I've got to say it was a very enjoyable ten months. The boys, who I saw as extended family, I treated like my sons. Sometimes humour, sometimes a kick up the arse, always encouragement, good advice and top coaching full of good information. I will never forget Sopp, Loomes, Shearer, the Bird brothers, Wilkie, Rufus, Cawte, Huckstepp, Perifimou, Weir and the second year boys who tried their socks off to make up lost ground. I've got to say looking back that I thought my routine for two hundred a forty quid net was a piss take. Maybe I should have stuck to renovating properties but I couldn't because my own brother decided to bail out and ask for his money back. I took over single handedly the problem of a bad tenant with, it transpired, six aliases. She came to me as a Scottish divorcee by the name of Mrs Ibbarrondo with her nineteen year old son and lived in one of our properties rent free for nearly a year. It took me ten months to get a court date. Looking back I should have thrown the cunt and her son out of a first floor window, done the time and come out to five houses. The equity alone within a couple of years was in excess of two million pounds. My brother went on to build his own property portfolio and I ended up skint.

Over the decades I wonder how many youth coaches can spot the similarity whereby they have been exploited for their love of the game and their coaching acumen and are among the lowest paid and poorly rewarded for what is one of the most important jobs in football, which is bringing through and improving young players. The life blood of the game. I took training on a Monday morning and afternoon, I coached at the Centre of Excellence on a Monday night, I took training on a Tuesday, I attended the first team game if at home on a Tuesday night making sure all the duties were done. I took training on a Wednesday. I was number two at reserve team games on a Wednesday night. I came in on Thursday morning to fill in all the progress reports on the youth team players. I coached at the Centre of Excellence on a Thursday night and Friday we had to train in the afternoon to accommodate a short practice match for the first team where we provided the opposition. So inevitably our organisation was done on Friday afternoon. Saturday morning was our normal South East Counties youth team fixture.

Saturday afternoon everyone had to attend the first team game if it was at home. On Sundays while Bernie, Peter, Chris and on his occasional return to London, Frank, congregated in a pub in Loughton, I had to report to the ground and put on a physical workout and some ball work for players returning from injury and those who had not played the day before. This led to a disagreement between me and Trevor Putney who laid on a bench in the medical room drinking a mug of tea. The pre-agreed time for everybody to congregate on the pitch to warm up was ten thirty. At ten fifteen I gave everyone a fifteen minute warning, at ten thirty Putney was the only one not on the pitch. I ran to the medical room to find him laying there drinking tea talking to the physio Andy Taylor and said "come on Trev everyone's waiting for you we are about to start." He said "yeah I'll be out in a minute." I ran back through the dressing room and up the tunnel and started immediately out of respect and courtesy to the lads who reported on time. Putney joined in twenty minutes later. Next day Eustace asked me how it went so I told him that everyone was on time and trained well except for Putney. He must have had a word with Putney because as I walked across the first team dressing room Trevor started singing the words of a record by the O'Jays "backstabbers." I said to him "you sarcastic little cunt. Don't get chippy with me.If you have a problem with me we go under the stand or we'll go and see the manager together." I remember Vaughan Ryan getting ready to step across me because he thought I was getting ready to chin him.

Eustace held the meeting between me, him and Putney. It was like an audience with the Pope and confirmed what I already knew. The club was run like a holiday camp by someone who had lost the dressing room to senior pro piss takers. Total anarchy and I was stuck in the middle. Eustace said pointing at me "you're to blame fifty percent" and pointing at Putney" you're to blame fifty percent." I just said "what part of fifty percent is a ten thirty start and a player's still laying there drinking tea until ten to eleven?" Putney just started giggling and said "no hard feelings Sitts." I just walked out.

Results that season were diabolical and resulted in behind the scenes disagreements one of which involved me having a row with kit man Pat Dellar who was a London cab driver and as far as I am concerned his main aim was to do as little work as possible. At thirty-three years of age I was too young to be insured to drive the club minibus. On the policy it said you had to be a minimum age of thirty-five. I'd already risked my driving licence by driving the minibus to take the players to youth team games. I'd already taken a chance by driving the Youth team to Portsmouth. What if there had been an accident? Now Dellar wanted me to drive the reserves and take care of the kit to a fixture at Cambridge. Can you believe it? Can you believe this actually went on at a professional football club? I flatly refused. Dellar wouldn't have it and kept winding me up and it led to an argument, me shouting at Dellar and being called into Eustace's office the next day. Once again Eustace sided against me and remonstrated that "with the club not winning enough games at every level how do you think it would look if one of the directors heard it?" I said "I have had enough, you're taking the fucking piss, can you do me a favour and sack me so that I can sign on the dole?" He said "I won't sack you but you can resign if you want." I said "if I resign I won't be able to feed my kids until I get a new job."

To me it was quite poignant when Peter said that Dellar was, "a typical football man with his stories." After another exchange I stood up and said "that's me done." I said to Eustace, "you don't know how to treat people, if you need an excuse I'll give you one" and I threw my chair at him. I aimed at his head, but It missed and hit his shoulder because I didn't realise how heavy the chair was. As I walked out of the outer office Turner and Dixson looked down and went beetroot red. By the time I got home Eustace rang me and asked if I had calmed down and he just said "forget it, draw a line under it and don't take it out on the people around you because to tell you the truth you bring a massive amount to this football club. I've seen more from you in the six months since you've been back than I've seen from others in the previous two years." I said " Just for the record there is no chance of me doing that, my family have nothing to do with my working life. See you in the morning."

It was a Thursday evening and I returned home from the Centre of Excellence about nine thirty pm. My wife said "where have you been?..the phone hasn't stopped ringing" I asked "why what's wrong?" She said Leyton Orient vice chairman Derek Weinrabe has called three times. I said "something must have gone on at the club." Slowly but surely I'd seen the club, the dressing room and the results deteriorate. The tension around the club was tangible and it culminated in Peter Eustace hitting Kevin Austin at half time in the dressing room at Cambridge. He probably picked on one of only three or four players who wouldn't have hit him back. As my wife and I were talking the phone rang again. It was Derek Weinrabe again and he said "Peter's gone, we need you to take the team on Saturday at Huddersfield." I asked what happened at the board meeting and Weinrabe said Peter had asked "have you got confidence in me to do the job yes or no?" The board apparently responded by saying unanimously "quite frankly Peter no." Peter then replied "in that case gentlemen the next time you hear from me will be through my solicitors and the LMA." He then shuffled his papers, picked them up and walked out.

It's worth noting that Peter continued to be paid for the next fifteen months, and his club car which was a Mercedes had the finance settled by his eldest daughter's boyfriend who was a car dealer in Yorkshire and took ownership of it. I said to Weinrabe, "let me phone Peter." I told Eustace what had been said and he told me, "go on son, get on with it, get stuck in." That season 1993-1994 the divisions were being restructured and four clubs would be relegated. Leyton Orient were fifth or sixth from bottom. In the five games until the end of the season we picked up the points we needed to stay up but I openly admit instead of alarm bells ringing I was blinded by arrogance and ambition. I thought my coaching would improve the club throughout when in reality one win and one draw from five games was quite clearly not good enough. On the Thursday evening before that first game Weinrabe rang me back and said "what do you want to do?" I said "I'm going to need someone by my side, the only link to the players left is Chris Turner, every player in that dressing room apart from Heald, Howard and Carter has been signed by Eustace and I've already upset a couple of them because I expected punctuality. Chris Turner might be able to help maintain a link, I'll do the rest with my coaching." We went to Huddersfield on the Saturday after me and Chris picking the team on Thursday evening at my home but not before more fireworks on Friday morning. Bernie Dixson turned up flaming angry and said to me that I was making a mistake. I should have listened to Uncle Bernie. His heart was always in the right place.

He said to Weinrabe, me and Chris should not be going with the first team, Sitts must stay with the youth team. Weinrabe said "what if I make you director of football and managing director?" Bernie said "I would accept it." Weinrabe said "alright it is done, but you have got to let Sitts organise the team so that we get the points to stay up." Bernie said "no, as managing director I want to give Sitts a new improved four-year contract to stay with the youth set up." He turned to me and asked (Bernie) "would you be happy with that Sitts?" I said "yes I would, I just want to do a good job for the club." Weinrabe turned to Turner and asked, "can you take the first team on Saturday?" Chris said "I'm not doing it without Sitts." Bernie then said "in that case I resign." He cleared his desk and walked out.

I went to an end of season function that was attended by all the players and the three staff that were left. At that function all the players, but in particular the senior ones, were canvassed by the directors as to whether I was suitable for the job. What a farce. At the function I was approached by Derek Weinrabe and Harry Linney who said that every single player had spoken in my favour and that my sessions and organisation were a breath of fresh air. They signed off by saying to the directors "we think he can do a good job." I find it funny how quickly things change in the fickle world of football, in my case over the course of only a few months as soon as you begin to place demands on people. I thanked them and said "I'll see you in the office in the morning." Next day I came straight to the point and said "what about my contractual situation, I've got a year left on my youth team contract and if my remit is now the first team I want first team money." Weinrabe said "we can't afford it, we can offer you four hundred and twenty pounds a week and a petrol card and one or two other bits of expenses that previous managers were getting." I replied "with respect to the petrol card, what car is the petrol going in?" Weinrabe told me "it won't be Peter's old car his future son-in-law has settled the finance and stuck it on his car front. You can have Bernie's old car."

This turned out to be a clapped out navy blue Vauxhall Cavalier. Weinrabe said "if I was you I'd take it, it might be the only chance you get." I said "alright I'll give it a go." I spent a week going through the books, transfer fees paid, contracts, wages and I was informed not by any directors, but by Maureen Hanshaw, the state of the club's finances. I should have said I'd changed my mind. Whether it was pride, ego, arrogance or being perceived as a coward I never did. It was too late there was no turning back. Chris Turner said he wasn't having a holiday but told me that if I wanted to get away he would stay and hold the fort and keep me informed of anything going on at the club during the summer. I then went away for a week to Cyprus with my wife and children, my brother-in-law and his wife and children, and while out there we met up with some friends. I was excited and I couldn't wait to get stuck in to the new pre-season.

However, when I got back I was told that out of the twenty-eight professionals, eleven players whose contracts were up for renewal had to be let go on a free transfer to get them off the wage bill. Courtesy of information from Maureen, wages for July and August were being paid by the only profitable organisation in the club, Football in the Community, headed by Neil Watson and Grant Cornwall. From then on it was constant fire fighting to pay the bills and put off creditors. The only relief came from the sale of Dominic Ludden to Watford for sixty thousand pounds. The down side was it now left me with sixteen players, three of which were goalkeepers. One of the goalkeepers Paul Newell was let go almost immediately but the number was back up to sixteen when we took Andy Gray on loan from Reading. It basically set the tone for the rest of the season and I suppose you could say the rest is history.

Players should have been sent out circulars in preparation for pre-season. Among other problems Chris and I encountered was the lack of co-operation in the office and the poor work ethic. This ran throughout the club and was not exclusive to some of the admin staff. The only exception was the most successful department which was Football in the Community. I think it's significant that as I've said already this was the only profitable part of the football club. As we prepared our manager's report for a scheduled board meeting on 6th July 1994, we put in writing our concerns regarding all aspects of the club. We'd inherited a professional playing squad and at least six had no chance of playing, they were too light and not good enough. The total wage bill, totally biased towards new signings and a squad poorly balanced, came in at five hundred and seventeen thousand one hundred and forty pounds per annum, added to staff who were still being paid, it gave a total of six hundred and thirty thousand per annum. Of the eleven players' contracts who were up, me and Chris were told that no offers could be made for renewal.

Back to the circulars. The players were given a time and date to report back, a training programme and a target weight. We asked one of the secretaries to take down some notes/dictation and send them out to the players. One letter, twenty-four copies, how hard is that? At least four players never received these and consequently arrived late on Monday and also having been left to their own devices, not as physically fit as we wanted. The secretary concerned was questioned on this in the nicest possible way and displayed a complete disregard for both the administering and consequences of these letters. Because of this, no action could be taken against the players concerned. Also, more importantly, was a sloppy approach to rules and regulations of the football league.

The club needed to be on the ball and ready with regards to things like a player's refusal of an offer, the preservation of the club's compensation rights and the legal rights of serving notice. Because the administration was sloppy, very poor and very unprofessional, this could have proved very costly to Leyton Orient. Particularly in terms of players having the upper hand in negotiations and ultimately transfers. This would render the club's aforesaid compensation rights null and void. The state of disregard and apathy, something the supporters, the supporters club and even the directors didn't see, and didn't want to know about, in my opinion was disgraceful. Nevertheless, the administration staff remained popular in those circles despite all of this. The players reported for pre-season on Monday 4th of July.

I naively thought that I should get stuck into the massive task in front of me and contractually things would take care of themselves, if it was perceived by those with the power to make these decisions, that I was seen to be able to do a good job and really sort the club out from top to bottom, which is what was needed. Not to put too fine a point on things, years of sticking plaster, short termism were highlighted by the most recent signings, something prevalent right across football, not exclusive to Orient.

Pre-season was something I sat down and planned with Chris and Andy Taylor the physio, determined not to replicate long, laborious, mind numbing runs through the forest, reducing the risk of injury as we only had a handful of players. Over the six weeks, it was built around two weeks' stamina building, two weeks building endurance, two weeks scaled down to everything being short and sharp. I incorporated lots of ball work, grids, keep balls, SSGs and the organisational phases of play required, bedded in just as we came into playing friendlies. I thought the friendlies were an ideal opportunity to rehearse all the above at match pace and with a competitive edge. We rehearsed patterns of play to suit the players we had, the main problem as I've mentioned being left with no pace up front to threaten the back of the opposition. The defensive strategy was also rehearsed and rehearsed, because unless I was allowed to get the players I wanted, I thought the best we could hope for was 1-0.

Every team needs goals and the threat of goals from as many areas as possible. We had virtually none. The training ground was a concern I'd had since being a player. I wanted this changed to UCL sports ground at Walthamstow's Crooked Billet. The pitches were like bowling greens and the facilities superb. The directors didn't show their whole hand just yet, saying the rent was a problem. We'd spent years at Douglas Eyre for nothing and you couldn't get cheaper than that, but the other price to pay was poor surface, force gale winds, goose shit, and the by-products of injuries and infection. The UCL was used by Arsenal for their under 11's, under 12's and under 13's. Yet Leyton Orient's 1st team couldn't afford it!! We moved from ground to ground. We had Wadham Lodge and Peter May Sports Centre. We had to change at the ground as Peter May was being redeveloped. I ensured I got there about twenty minutes before the players to set up the equipment so we could go straight into the warm up and on to the sessions I'd prepared.

Chris came over saying "Sitts, we might have a problem." I turned to see he'd been talking to four players and I walked briskly downhill towards them. It transpired that the four of them, had checked their bank accounts and monies they were due to receive as portions of their respective signing on fees, had not been paid. Gary Bellamy a good lad, good pro and very approachable and intelligent guy was the group's spokesman. He was PFA representative who'd been ridiculed by Eustace and called a "barrack room lawyer" who only spoke up when it suited him. Eustace had been used to me as a player and I'd have thought "Bellers" would have been a welcome respite, giving him some peace and quiet. Bellers said that the club were in breach of contract and the four players could not only withdraw their labour, but because the club had been in breach of contract, they automatically became free transfers.

As the colour drained from my face, I quickly calculated that things were not only more desperate than I'd thought but with Carter and Howard acting the goat on seven-day contracts, losing these four would mean (as Hague had not yet been signed,) if Carter and Howard continued to refuse new terms, eight outfield players.

Chris was at his best here, appeasing the players and ensuring them we'd get straight to it after training. Tony Wood had in the meantime returned to London looking shell shocked, staring into space like he was on medication. Of course as far as I know, he wasn't and when I cornered him to catch up, he told me what he'd been through and the business he'd spent his life building was decimated. He told me because of the civil war and all it entailed in Rwanda it had led to him being smuggled out via Tigali by a combination of United Nations and Belgian special forces. He'd gone home to his coffee plantation to see soldiers armed to the teeth making themselves comfortable in his house, on his bed, drinking straight from bottles of spirit and generally ransacking the place.

The people he'd employed, some he'd known for the thirty-eight years he'd been there even employing their sons and daughters, were scattered around the grounds shot and with various body parts missing, where armed to the teeth (its disrespectful to call them animals, particularly to animals) "soldiers" had gone to work with machetes. In his pool were floating some of his household staff, minus their heads and arms. I stared at him in disbelief, as he stared into space. The genocide in Rwanda that has since been reported obviously puts in perspective anything I was going through. Whether it's Leyton Orient or any other football club perceived hardships pale into insignificance. I've since read over nine hundred and eighty thousand lives were lost in the Rwandan civil war.

Meanwhile Tony had been taking on board what Chris had said to him and said he'll personally guarantee the money owed to the four players out of his own pocket. Something he was used to, as I couldn't see any other directors putting any readies in. I wanted the same carte blanche given to me by Tony Wood, who I always referred to as Mr Chairman that had been granted to Peter Eustace and Frank Clark before him, to make all his sacrifice worthwhile and that would show in the type of club we were running. In football doing what you have to do is very much a long way from what you want to do. The only jobs in football as far as I can see that has allowed the manager to do what he wants to do for the good of the club, short, medium and long term for thirty years has been at Crewe with Dario Gradi and at the top level Sir Alex Ferguson and Arsene Wenger. In my book pressure is pressure, whether that of expectancy or trying to salvage a club from the abyss of administration and, or bankruptcy. The way I saw it the pressure I had was the latter, but the reality, the whole truth, was yet to surface. When it did at least I would know where I stood. The problems came when certain groups of supporters were massively in denial. By and large pre-season went well. I enjoyed it immensely as I was in my element, coaching, organising and structuring youth teams, reserves and first team. I set about every day to stimulate the players with a theme relevant to how we hoped to play and not only going forward but, just as importantly, if not more so, defensively.

Obviously it didn't take the brains of Lloyd George to realise the squad was well short. Between me and Chris we weren't. Other critical areas of the club, if like me you were privy to the goings on, came up not just short but reminiscent of a Marx brothers film. Chris and myself attended a "meet the manager" in this case "managers" at the supporters' club. After a soft drink in my case, half a lager in Chris's, we got on stage with each being handed a microphone. The questions we fielded were none too taxing. The main protestations being asked in question form were why certain players were released.

At that moment it would have betrayed counsel and etiquette to tell the supporters that their tenner every other week wasn't going far enough in covering the club's outgoings and at that time it might have been the truth, but unfair to state Tony Wood was the only director contributing financially. This was credit to Hearn further down the line who said to me personally "it won't happen on my watch, I want to see what they bring to the party. If it's nothing, there's no place on the board for them." If only Tony Wood had been more demanding of the same people. Rather than go into my own personal demanding criteria for each player released and who never came up to scratch, I relayed that the wage bill had to be cut and restructured. Not that a centre forward who couldn't run, head the ball, scored approximately one in four, didn't contribute defensively and was at best soporific, languid and sanguine, wasn't my cup of tea. For the record this player was the one deemed a pub player by Gordon Strachan. In a nutshell he was neither a reliable target man for others to play off or a taker of goals in the penalty area. So what was he? Having been judged harshly all my playing career I would be no less demanding on forwards, midfield and defenders under me and the criteria for each position on a football field.

The game was going forward with players who not only did things well within the set criteria for their position, but they did them at pace. The centre half released was a failed full back. Not physically imposing, didn't win the majority of aerial duels, not feared in the tackle, wasn't vocal and organising and bossing team mates and when he or a team mate mishit a pass, in his case the majority of the time, took to shouting in ridicule at the top of his voice "shank" which although I don't play, I think is a golf term for a mishit drive. This spread, so warm ups and keep balls and small sided games became comedic and more of a piss taking exercise at his or a team mate's inability to pass accurately. As an ex-centre half I thought his reading of the game was poor and his marking in the box and sense of danger also left a lot to be desired. Centre half is up there in terms of how difficult a position it is and the criteria you have to fulfil to have the prerequisite all-round game.

In the meantime, at training in the week leading up to the first game of the season at home to Birmingham, Chris and I were approached at the training ground totally random by Trevor Putney, questioning why he wasn't involved anymore. I took the lead, telling Putney he was doing himself and the team a disservice by conducting himself the way he did. Poor in any fitness work, playing in training in a micky taking five a side mode, wise cracking and talking whilst I was setting the group up to do a session, with bibs, positions etc. and trying to joke around whilst organisational work was being done. Putney said "I know how it works, Sitts, good cop, bad cop." Which was which had already been allocated according to Putney as he looked at Chris. I said "I take it you've got Chris as the good cop, I don't want to be bad cop, just fair cop, you play fair with me, I'll be fair with you." With hindsight I think it's a fair bet that players saw how small the squad was and quite possibly concluded they had me, Turner and the club by the bollocks.

Pre-season was a good workout with some very promising performances beating Barnet, Charlton and Watford and narrowly losing to Premier League sides Wimbledon, Southampton and Nottingham Forest going down to the last two by the odd goal. We had been approached by Glen Roeder at Watford for Dominic Ludden. He was sold for sixty thousand pounds after I asked for one hundred thousand. Ludden had a couple of games for Watford. I thought he was no loss, small, lightweight and lacking in pedigree and football intelligence and without going into detail I wasn't over the moon with some of his off field habits, so I couldn't believe the deal we got even though Roeder thought he had got the best deal. Friday before the Birmingham game we ran through set pieces and patterns and did a defending session versus reserves and kids. We picked the team and as we walked off, Howard and Carter said "good luck trying to win with that team tomorrow." It was also heard by Barry Lakin and Darren Purse who shook their heads and looked up to see what my reaction would be. I blanked it, waiting for Lakin and Purse to indulge in a bit of self-policing. Lakin said "fucking nice to see we're all in it together." I smiled and walked on.

A footnote to the sale of Dominic Ludden was the conflicting opinions on whether the money received was absolutely necessary.

After being told by acting chairman Derek Weinrabe to reduce costs and the wage bill he actually went out of his way in the directors, sponsors and oddfellows lounges to say "we don't have to sell him, if Sitts wants to keep him, he doesn't have to let him go." Maureen came into mine and Chris's office and asked, "what's happening with Dominic Ludden?" I said "Maur, can you and Carol or Sue prepare the paperwork, we've done a deal to let him go to Watford for sixty thousand pounds." Maureen said "thank God, the club has no money. I've got to settle some accounts and there's no money for wages, at least now we'll all get paid for another couple of weeks."

Anyway, at the end of the "meet the managers" I like to think, although the feedback was at best non-committal, at worst indifferent and apathetic, the punters who attended were left in no doubt as to the club's predicament and they were underwhelmed when I told them with Chris's endorsement, that the players I'd earmarked for arrival at the club I'd sign with my own money, it would just cost the club their wages. My condition further down the line to Weinrabe and Hearn's sidekick Bernard Goodall would be I'd negotiate any outgoing transfer for them and take what I knew would be a profit. So much for my declaration of professional and financial commitment to the club. The board were not only underwhelmed but probably felt undermined, especially as there was still plenty of time to turn things around.

We'd followed up our impressive team performance in the first game at home to Birmingham winning 2-1 with a dire performance away to Barnet in the League Cup losing 4-0. I'd failed to attend going down with flu and thought best to stay away from our squad of at that time fifteen. Sitting behind Howard and Carter were two members of staff who relayed they'd taken the micky out of their team mates and sarcastically suggested to each other they should polish their boots as a recall was imminent. So as not to disappoint them and freshen things up they both played away to Bradford where we lost 2-0. At home to Barnet in the second leg we tried to get after them and force the pace but at 4-0 it was almost a thankless task. After drawing 1-1 and an early exit at the end of ninety minutes Barnet celebrated like they'd won the European Cup, with Mark Cooper jogging off to cheers from Orient fans who were sympathetic to his cause at being released. He gave a half-hearted wanker sign to me and Turner as he jogged down the tunnel. That was about as passionate as I ever I saw him with O's fans living six years in the past for his goal in the play off final that got us promoted. I thought that's ok as I started the move that led to it! Perhaps they'd be as understanding of my plight. No such luck as I've never been very good at playing the victim. We drew 1-1 at home in the next league game vs Hull. We took the lead away to Huddersfield only to go down 2-1, showing that "soft underbelly" Eustace spoke of to the players he'd signed. I thought our best contributors included Purse, a kid at centre half who'd already contributed more goals than any forward with two. We followed that up losing 1-0 at Brighton managed by Liam Brady. Mark Warren left his man unmarked in the box and they slotted.

Brady sighed with relief at the end of ninety minutes. He'd seen Lakin and Cockerill run the game taking it as far as no cutting edge around the penalty area. Obviously the same old problem, there long before mine and Chris's tenure. We'd managed to get in a couple of players and one was a fantastic talent, Jae Martin on loan from Southend, managed by Peter Taylor. I thought at £225 per week he was a steal. He was left footed which as I've said is value added premium he was strong and wiry, he had pace, trickery and was able to hold the ball up just as competently.

His speciality was if a defender got too tight, he was single minded and ruthless in his punishment. He rolled the defender skilfully and exploded shots with barely any back lift. I remember looking at Chris and smiling in training. There had to be something wrong surely? Alarmed at the fact he'd only had two sub appearances for us I took a call from Peter Taylor who said the idea of loaning him was for him to play. I said I want to play him, very much so, but I can't compromise the discipline in the dressing room and take the piss out of the players who can be bothered to turn up on time. I maybe should have tolerated him turning up late for two home games but I got bold when Colin West scored three in two games. I told Taylor what I couldn't forgive was him turning up for training after we'd completed our warm up and were well into our first part of our session. Approximately thirty minutes late I suppose. Taylor said "you'd better send him back, I'm not happy." I said "how do you think I feel?" So we lost him within a fortnight. I took a call from ex-colleague Kevin Hales who asked if I'd take Sean Brooks another ex-colleague into the fold to train and maybe play a couple of reserve games. He was staying at Kevin's during a separation and knowing his pedigree, ability and that we could work in shorthand, I agreed. Off the field things started to get a bit testy. People think that Christmas is a threshold for a team's fortunes. I've never ever agreed, I think things take shape, should be monitored and tweaked accordingly at the end of October. By then you've had fifteen or so games and an idea of your capabilities and the division.

We had three consecutive defeats at the end of September and no chance of resting anyone or freshening up certain areas of the team which it needed. Although our managers' report for September was short and concise it mainly consisted of our requests for players to no avail. One plus was getting rid of a problem in the squad, who I think and still do had taken the piss out of the club and everyone he came into contact with. In the manager's report we told of an enquiry for Steve Jones on loan from West Ham. Ironically unknown to O's fans, both I and Steve Shorey scouted him when he played non-league for I think, Billericay.

We could have got him for virtually nothing, the board wouldn't sanction it so he ended up at West Ham. I cited enough was enough, saying thus far, courtesy of yours truly on staff wages alone and even though the club were still paying

Eustace, we chugged along with a replenished staff doing more than one job each saving over £30,000 in staff wages. This was alongside a weekly saving of £3000 with players released and in Putney's case allowing him to go and play for his ex-team mate at Colchester who paid fifty percent of his salary. On an annual basis with further cuts at youth level I got the snake eye from everyone in attendance at a South East Counties League meeting when I'd proclaimed that having saved £38,000 on our previous budget, we'd managed to attach better qualified coaches to the club into the bargain.

Over coffee and biscuits, I got the look of a serial killer when Jimmy Armfield asked "where's the sugar?" I handed it to him from next to his cup and saucer saying "good vision Jim." He looked at me I thought with a degree of disdain, contempt and pomposity. Another one lucky enough to get a living when it was GBH with a ball and one up from park football at pedestrian pace. That's just my opinion. So called legends then, wouldn't get a game in division two now. Since then it would seem he also had a sense of humour bypass.

Losing five on the bounce didn't look good for anyone. In October we played away to Wycombe. The O's fans seated behind the dugout, clapped and cheered me as I took my seat saying "we're with you Sitts, keep 'em going." They drank vodka and tonic in glasses so big they looked like they were drinking from a fish tank. After three they were merry and well on the way. I found their support touching and it geed me up just when I needed it. At Wycombe Andy Gray, Lakin, Cockrill and Bogie were outstanding. I had Lakin and Cockrill taking turns with their runs off the front man with the other one screening the back four. We played 4-1-2-3 and Wycombe couldn't cope. When we lost the ball we retreated into a 4-1 - 4-1. We passed them all over the place, so much so Martin O'Neil invited me in for a drink. We both drank tea and he grilled me on what we did in training our conversation only cut short by a shout from Flynny that we had to board the coach. For the record we lost 2-1, Wycombe scored from two set pieces, one of them a free kick from the halfway line launched into our box.

It was a bit basic and disappointing to me that we never dealt with it. Before that was a five goal thriller at Oxford, the odd goal in their favour. We went 1-0 down, equalised, took the lead and two mistakes by Hague and Howard gave them two goals in the ninety and ninety-first minute. We were gutted, I'd thought we'd momentarily stopped the rot. Paul Hague and I have to agree with O's fans who were disappointed with him, came for £5k from Gillingham. I'd watched him in their first team squad and reserves and thought he'd cope better than he did and at the same time giving the seventeen-year-old Darren Purse a rest. Eighteen months previously he was on the fringes of England's youth squad and had since gone backwards. I thought I could reignite him. It turned out I couldn't and I didn't. I'd got one wrong, still some way short of my predecessors and others in the game who had wasted millions but not a habit I wanted to continue. We had a period of mixed fortunes, coinciding with Tony Wood's return to Rwanda and back to see what he had left. The directors fed up of mine and Chris's questioning either never met in October or met and didn't invite us. After Wycombe, we beat Chester 2-0 at home and Fulham 5-2 at home in the

Auto Windscreen trophy. Memorable for a number of reasons.

We lost to Rotherham away 2-0, Stockport at home 1-0 and beat Cardiff 2-0 also at home. After going down 2-1 away to Blackpool next up was the first round to the F.A Cup away to Tiverton Town. I'd created a bit of adverse publicity courtesy of Jimmy Hill and the Evening Standard after the Fulham game. In Hill's case his TV presenting and playing of politics within football had given him a profile that compared to mine was like comparing the prime minister to a fruit and veg stall holder. Your knowledge, intelligence and integrity is immediately dismissed. The cause of it was a player who I had previously come up against during his Brentford days and who'd get in any team of mine... Terry Hurlock. He was built like a pocket battleship, was vocal, a leader, had a great engine, great energy, had unbelievable enthusiasm and appetite for the game and above all, superb ability. His passing and movement were superb. He could also if he needed to, look after himself and be aggressive in winning the ball. I was protective of all my players and trying to preserve the small squad's fitness. One player in particular, a lovely human being and a credit to his family, Kevin Austin, I felt protective towards.

After coming from non-league Braintree he wasn't very well versed in looking after himself and was confidence wise always on the margins. He'd been constantly criticised and then chinned by Eustace at Cambridge. I'd worked with him 1 v 1 and 1 v 2 in grids, drilling the back four, then on his personal play with things like one touch clearances and distribution. We progressed to his movement and combination play with left winger Mark Dempsey and overlaps, under laps and runs outside to in with the left sided midfield payer, filling in for normally Cockerill, who was our best at running off the front man. This kept us compact if the ball was rebounded on us. It has to be said Kevin was a gentleman and a gentle giant. He was built like a light heavyweight boxer with a perfect physique. But he could never be accused of throwing his weight about. Hurlock decided to close him down and make an example of him. As Kevin clipped a lovely ball forward into Westy, Hurlock got there late and tackled him thigh high.

I felt the injury from where I stood, I screamed at the ref who gave a free kick and I can't remember, either a lecture or yellow card to Terry Hurlock. He (Terry) turned to me and we smiled at each other. I turned to their manager, Ian Brantfoot and said "you're one of Eustace's mates ain't ya, is that how you coach as well, you horrible northern cunt?" He stood behind me in the tunnel, not the dugout. He never said a word and just went red, his broken nose and hair the only things white and not embarrassed. Turner said "calm down Sitts," I said "the after match drink will be interesting" Brantfoot just looked down. Anyway, I just said to the small press conference, not realising my quotes could be used for some shit stirring, that some of Fulham's tackles would embarrass a pub team and I wasn't impressed. How to win friends and influence people again. Then a half page spread in the Standard by Hill criticised me for slagging off opponents. That's how I was when it came to my players. If your face fits it's ok, if not it's taboo. Anyway, rightly or wrongly that's just me, you're brought up to stick by your own.

People in football love it when you're no threat and they can pat you on the head, patronise you and turn up for an easy win. Over the years something I thought Leyton Orient had become used to.

It changes when even if they've caused it, you show your teeth and dare to bite back. All of a sudden, they play the victim and you're the lunatic. After all it was only little old Leyton Orient. I thought as a player, coach and if you want to call me it a manager, that Orient and its teams needed to change. A seismic shift from being a nice place to turn up and pick up a win bonus. For a long time, I've thought the history of a club stems from its custodians and the playing brand and any success are what follows. Whether one, two, five, ten, twenty, fifty or seventy years ago, the decisions made are what can determine a club's future standing in the game. That's my opinion. Off the field, Chris wanted us addressed as boss or gaffer. I didn't agree, as I'd played with two or three and I've always thought a reciprocal respect comes from how we work together not a name. I was content to be addressed as John or Sitts, as I was known in the game, right from my Chelsea days. I wanted any respect due to me from players to come from the help I was willing to give them on and off the field. Whether I could coach, organise a team and improve them individually. My respect for them came from how they treated each other, punctuality, courtesy, and training hard then playing to win. Too much to ask? Off the field I helped Mark Warren, who started off addressing me as "yeah mate, yeah mate" until I pulled him on it, as he'd said it in front of Lee Shearer a YTS who I had high hopes for, but needed a firm hand to guide him.

Mark called me Sitts when I had him in our office and helped him avert a domestic crisis. He'd had a run in with his former girlfriend and mother of his young child and her father wouldn't allow him access to either. He was on the brink of weeping, not the street cred tough guy he tried being around the lads as he tried to hold back the tears. We went after a centre forward after seeing him at Oxford v Arsenal in the combination league. It wasn't to be. I suppose some players would prefer playing in football combination for Oxford rather than be up for relegation fight in someone's first team. At Tiverton, after a nightmare journey we arrived to find we couldn't train because of the weather, the game was in doubt and the food we'd ordered on our arrival wasn't paid for in advance. I took the money out of the float given to us for fish and chips on the way home. Since the end of August, after one lot of wages being paid by funds from Football in the Community, courtesy of Neil Watson and Gran Cornwall, the PFA had stepped in and word had got round that they were footing our wage bill. The vultures had started circling. Chris and I spoke to Weinrabe who said "don't worry about it, we'll sort it out when Tony gets back." We spoke to Harry Linney who'd had a drink and boasted of buying a fleet of lorries and a

£6million tanker. I made the mistake of saying and answering back "Harry can't you sell it and buy a four million tanker and give me the other two million to keep the team up and the club afloat?" He just glared at me. We spoke to a recent approximately one-year addition to the board, John Goldsmith, an architect. The story relayed by Weinrabe was he'd got on the board as he was involved in the design of a proposed new stadium. Also there was another director Vince Marsh, a wholesale mushroom salesman based locally in Spitafields market. When Chris or I tried to get inside knowledge on the club or our futures he said "I'll know more when I get back from seeing my growers in Ireland. I'm going over and I'm taking Woolfy with me." I said "I hope it's not as a negotiator." Even Vince laughed. It was just a boys jolly up.

I remember thinking "how can this be right?" But Woolfy was to get his just desserts after years of blagging it. Vince went to Ireland and our illustrious money getting Commercial Director Frank Woolf went with him for a lads weekend to Dublin. I thought to just get on with putting things in place for if and when I got the green light to do it properly. No point in turning back now. Managers have done it many times since but I've just seen it as an act of cowardice. Tony Wood returned just before Tiverton and took a call from Chris Hollins and referred him to me. Chris wanted to come in on trial, as a wide midfield or midfield player.

I invited him in at his own expense. Yes, it's the Chris Hollins, BBC presenter, ballroom dancer and son of John Hollins the ex Chelsea midfielder. I let him down lightly with the age old get out of a dodgy situation excuse, that he was no better than what we already had and unfortunately our wage bill had no room for "maybes." Let's just say, he's a better presenter and dancer of the quick step than he was a footballer. A week or so later Tony Wood took a call from his father John Hollins. Tony Wood told me he'd offered to be Orient's manager. Tony told me he said to him we've already got two managers. Hollins left him the dubious luxury of letting Tony Wood know, if things change "give me a call."

I have a few regrets about my tenure. One of the biggest is not showing appreciation of certain players' efforts as they tried to help stem the tide. I'd started with praise and plenty of "well dones" when due, but taken to using an important victory in a cup game as an opportunity to highlight faults and criticise. We'd taken on Sean Brooks and I admit I thought it would help us both. It would help replenish midfield, release Carter or Bogie as a player off the front man and knowing him we could work in a form of shorthand. He knew me from my playing days with him. If I didn't go out of my way to massage any egos or overstate things to make anyone feel important he knew not to take it personally.

But that's the game now. For a long while it seems to be just as much about feel good factor and sending players texts as it is about improving, structuring and organising. In a word kidology. He was separated and had nowhere to live so I signed a good player, good athlete, well-educated under Venables and Cartwright at Palace and he knew the club. He immediately got somewhere to live. The only thing was the couple upstairs kept him up all night with their rows and sexual encounters. I got on the phone to my wife's cousin who had his own estate agents and letting agents and found him a new place. He was well pleased with his new place and said thank you. I replied I was happy to help and make sure players were happy, adding, thank me on the field. It didn't take us long, to have a minor disagreement which happened as we rehearsed a pattern of play doing a phase in the final third.

Off the field I was turning into a zombie at weekends. My kids were six, four and two and I'd gone from going to the park with them and a picnic, making camps in the garden, big family dinners with the in-laws and holding them all as we danced to the music we'd put on bouncing around the front room, to on a Sunday, staring into space.

Not to put too fine a point on it, the results over the holiday fixtures were dire. More alarmingly were some of the performances. I'd always told players, from schoolboy to youth team and now first team, I'd forgive mistakes, they could be rectified on the training field, but I could never warm to any player who didn't love football, want to train, want to play, want to improve and want to get results. At all levels this can come as much out of will, determination, pride, passion and hard work. An award picked up by Sir Alex Ferguson at the BBC Sports Personality Of The Year (2013) was acknowledged by him in saying he'd recognised in certain players he was fortunate to work with, having tantamount to an inner strength, a determination not to get beat and a self-motivation. It filtered back to me that when I'd said the same thing in Orient's dressing room now over twenty years ago I was ridiculed behind my back.

That hurt. Especially as a coach or manager when you want to do well and I'll say it myself, have a marrow bone deep knowledge of football. Even though I'll concede that your education is a continuum. No one knows it all and no one gets it right all the time. But long before me, at all levels, and since me, at all levels, you're as good as the players and staff at your disposal. This is probably best highlighted by the fact that I thought I'd dispensed with the services of players not on the same page. Using football as a means of conveyance socially and financially and putting that before anything else. I'd taken a personal inventory as well and having made a meagre living as a player, more or less based on the qualities I've listed, along with ability, the previous impact and freshness I'd introduced the previous year to stave off relegation which in the end turned out to be an inevitability, had worn thin. That's at best. At worst it'd completely worn off. The next stage which I never ever got to is to bring in your own players. Building your own squad. Players with technical ability, football intelligence and all the other attributes I've just mentioned. With hindsight I've looked inward and came to the conclusion I was blinded by arrogance and ambition, added to wanting a chance and a fair bit of naiveté I'd continued trying to do the job with a squad hastily put together and without much thought by inept predecessors. The only difference was it was now sixteen or seventeen of the same players previously not good enough instead of twenty-eight to twenty-nine. This group had been given virtual carte blanche by the previous incumbents to play and train with little or no organisation and it was coming home to roost as I tried to implement a cultural change beginning with two training sessions a day. Ironically these days it seems more commonplace even though the game is more physically demanding. Back then, for a lot of players it was more or less regarded as an inconvenience. A suicide mindset at that level.

Even Premier League players need structure. Apart from being guided on a route through Epping Forest there was no structure, not to the level I'm talking about anyway. I've always thought even to this day your job as a coach or manager is to improve individuals and bring organisation, structure and strategy to the team(s) at the football club that employs you. As I've said drills for technical skills, drills from other sports, fitness with the balls, stretching programmes, plyometrics, defensive team strategy, patterns of play, attacking phases of play, finishing practices and set pieces were now wearing thin. It probably explains my outburst at Brentford and the remark "fuck the technical shit, it's about this" (pointing at my heart and club badge). Pure frustration, which I didn't handle at all well. So what? My professional contribution and the conscience that should go with it is absolutely clear and so it should be. I've no qualms about believing or stating that in fact, I wouldn't be embarrassed to face anyone who was there at that time. It was football, football, football and what I wanted and at the time it seemed like nothing else mattered. Obviously if the result the day before had gone against us I replayed the game and goals conceded and diarised it to work on it in training. At the same time, I'd organise training around how we wanted to play and allow for some intense work on one or two individuals like Darren Purse and Kevin Austin, all the while making it a variation of a theme to provide some sort of mental stimulus to hopefully brighten things up and help the players push our most recent disappointment behind us. One thing's for sure, the people who suffered the most were the ones closest to me. Me and Loiza, childhood sweethearts, a devoted couple, happy to share memories in company but just as happy when it was just the two of us. We had come through a tremendous amount together and we'd always looked after each other, in both love and support. We were as happy going out with friends and family as curling up on the sofa in front of the telly. Well that's how it started anyway and probably explains three kids in four years!! Now I short changed my wife and kids putting my job, club, reputation and ambition first. First team scouting, I don't know why, we had no money to spend but I had one eye on the medium and long term, which probably explains the madness of turning up to watch Wimbledon reserves in the cold and pissing of rain at Plough Lane. Sessions with the youth team as they also now had to fulfil the majority of reserve fixtures and I had high hopes for two or three, perhaps more, Centre of Excellence still attended every Monday and Thursday evening and with Woolfy on the Guinness in Ireland with Vince Marsh I became part time commercial manager. In short, I'd become a shit husband and shit father, not paying enough attention to either.

The only story I've left out of this book is a story that should never have happened. The reason for leaving it out is simple. The people that suffered most, don't deserve to suffer again.

It was now Autumn and before we knew it, about to become another winter of discontent. But I didn't want my youth team to get cold. They had no warm up tops or tracksuits for the substitutes so me and Tom approached George Kilikita who owned Holloway Sports. Out of friendship he gave us the gear and in return, with no chance of it generating custom, because as the name suggests he was a long way north and we were east, we put his name in our match day programme. I couldn't see our three thousand supporters leaving the East End or Essex and out of gratitude for his support, buying their trainers off him. As I said he did it out of friendship, but I couldn't help thinking I was working outside and over and above my remit and shouldn't the illustrious commercial director be sealing off done deals to take care of all this? You live, you learn. On the training field we continued to work hard to pick things up results wise. Strategy wise, I think it's important for the few thousand supporters back then and the readers in general, to know that I wasn't a mug when it came to setting up a team. With no obvious pace in the team, particularly up front, it basically dictated how we would play. Already an inherited nightmare, but I'd made my bed. You can only concede possession and defend deeper if you have the pace to break quickly and hit the opposition on the rebound. Therefore, our defensive strategy was to defend immediately from the front, pressing high which seems to be quite fashionable these days and try and pinch the ball back in our attacking third. Worst case scenario we had to alleviate any pressure on the back four by winning the ball back in the middle third.

This is where you need players at any club, at any level, to be well-educated and receptive to playing any system. What had gone before, for years, was a basic 4-4-2. At the same time I didn't want to penalise the ever present players who'd not missed a training session all year and hardly a game, I thought and think now, a debt of thanks and gratitude was owed by me and the club for their magnificent input. The likes of Heald, Austin, Purse, Bellamy, Hendon, Bogie, Dempsey, West, Cockrill and Lakin hung in with Chris and me. But really and truly, I wanted my praise to be earned, even hard to come by. But although I was more lenient on 18 year olds like Wilkie and Purse, I still should have been more rewarding with my praise to the others. Some performances I'd taken too much for granted. I suppose I repeated history as I wasn't showered with "well dones" even when I thought I'd deserved it.

The problem was still goals. A priceless commodity at all levels at any time in the history of football. It wasn't for lack of work on the training field. The same went for clean sheets. Distinctly lacking, despite constant drilling of our defensive strategy and work on pairs and individuals. Alex Welsh, an intelligent former teacher and capable coach, could have the knack of saying the wrong thing at the wrong time. My turn came when he told me to look within. I thought if only you fucking knew the half of it but took my perceived criticism conscientiously. If we lacked magic and there was an accusation later of blandness, it came from straight up and down, hardworking though they were, players signed before my time. My eyes were on a mixture of physicality provided by Leo Fortune-West and the inventive, devil may care, selfish goal scoring, shoot at every opportunity, Sean Devine. Still available but no nearer signing as there was still an embargo and the wages were still paid by the PFA. My own thoughts continued to be on a productive and necessary youth policy, players wanting a chance or even a second chance, non-league and utilising the loan system bringing in players from a bigger club with one supposes higher standards. This in turn should raise the existing playing standards of your own well coached youngsters. The common denominator would have been my own insisted upon age threshold of no one over twenty-five years of age. The playing squad of previously twenty-nine, now seventeen, had too many thirty plus, with a few twenty-eight, twenty-nine, thirty year olds set in their ways, none of them with any resale value.

BONUS CHAPTER
Let Your Yeah Be Yeah

To you the reader I must say please forgive what looks like very basic and unsophisticated manager's reports but maybe it serves as a true insight into how little was going on at the club as a response to the progress Chris and I wanted to make happen. We covered basically what we needed to and that temporarily at least, what we felt we had influence over. Every single board meeting we went to me and Chris listened to and put up with a constant stream of false promises and delaying tactics. In December there was either no board meeting or me and Chris were not invited. A couple of meetings in the new year were cancelled whilst firstly Phil Wallace then Barry Hearn as prospective new owners of the club went through the club's accounts. These are copies of what me and Chris put down in black and white to the board with transfer targets, positions that needed to be strengthened and a way forward for the club. As you can see there wasn't a terrific amount to talk about but the warnings were there from day one. A big thank you to Mrs Turner for typing everything out all those years ago because me and Chris couldn't find anyone else who would. Before you read on I want you to take into consideration that a dead fish always starts to rot from the head...

MANAGER'S REPORT 6TH JULY 1994

The first team squad returned for pre-season training on Monday 4th July and although we are happy with the fitness level of the majority of the squad, as usual one or two were overweight. We have felt it necessary to suspend Nathan Beckett as he failed to reach his target weight of 14st 2lbs. He in fact weighed in at 14st 9 and a half lbs and his suspension has been dealt with in conjunction with the PFA rep, Gary Bellamy and Brendan Batson of the PFA. We will re-assess the situation when he returns on 18th July. At the moment we have Gus Caesar and Andy Gray of Reading on trial with us. Gray is 20 years of age and a forward. He has limited first team experience due to the success of Jimmy Quinn. He did however score three goals in as many appearances last season and we have arranged with Mark McGee that if we like the look of him, he will allow us to take him on a free transfer subject to Reading receiving 30% of any sell on fee. Whether Andy joins us or not it does not hide the fact that we do not possess any up and coming forwards at the football club. Last season the reserves did not have a natural centre forward and Darren Purse filled in as a stop gap. With this year's intake of YTS not having a natural goal scorer either, this very important position lacks strength and quality for the forthcoming years. This is a situation which naturally concerns us both. Gus Caesar is a centre half aged 28 who has playing experience with Arsenal, Cambridge, Bristol City and

Airdrie. Both these players will play in the matches that have been arranged behind closed doors in order that we can assess them.

With regards to the out of contract players all three i.e., Danny Carter, Paul Newell and Terry Howard, signed week to week contracts this week and we have to advise that we have received no strong enquiries. We have been contacted by David Pleat in respect of Danny Carter, but he then seemed rather cool on the transfer. We have noted that Pleat requires a number two goalkeeper and we have suggested to him that he could take both Newell and Carter as a package. As yet there has been no feedback or concrete offers for any player.

Chris Turner and John Sitton

BOARD MEETING 11TH AUGUST 1994 MANAGER'S REPORT

Dominic Ludden has been sold to Watford for a fee of £60,000. Watford paid the 5% due to Dominic.

Terry Howard has had talks with Port Vale, but his demands of a

£50,000 signing on fee and a wage of £900 per week put paid to that deal and it was called off.

Talking point

We would like to bring to the board's attention the frailty of our current squad. At this moment in time, we have a squad of twenty players, this includes both Beckett and Sweetman (two players who are not good enough for the first team,) Howard and Carter who could leave at any time they wished, that could leave us with sixteen players, which includes two goalkeepers. As you can see, if any injuries should occur we could be in big trouble with only fourteen outfield players.

Two areas that need strengthening are centre half and centre forward. Ideally one centre half and two centre forwards would be helpful and two forwards might help increase our overall goal threat. With regards to the centre forwards position, we are limited due to money as no club lets a quick, goal scoring forward go for nothing. However, there are possibilities around even if we have to consider a forward or two on loan. Our problems will begin if Colin West gets injured. We all saw how little presence we have if we play with two small players up front. That was exposed when we played Reading and Southampton. In order to make room for the players on a financial footing, we suggest making Beckett and Sweetman an offer on the remainder of their contracts.

Pre-season summary

We are pleased with the way that training and warm up games have gone. In recent years injuries have been picked up on the training ground, but we can report that no such injuries have occurred this year. We did have a problem with the air quality around the training ground, during the hot weather period, which resulted in a number of players having chest problems. In the warm up games a few players did pick up injuries but nothing serious and the squad is expected to be fully fit for the opening match against Birmingham City.

In the matches themselves, we believe that progress has been made since the opening match behind closed doors against Barnet. We have had wins against Charlton and Watford followed by defeat against Premier League sides, Wimbledon, Southampton and Nottingham Forest, losing the latter two only going down by the odd goal.

We believe that the class of opposition will have been beneficial to all of the players, but it was especially pleasing to see the younger players do so well against so called million pound superstars.

The new players, Mark Dempsey and Andy Gray, have settled in very well. Dempsey as we thought, has brought something we certainly lacked last year. Someone who can play wide and put in quality crosses into the opponent's penalty box and is a natural left footer giving us balance.

Andy Gray has started to form a good understanding with Colin West until he went over on his ankle during the match versus Reading, thus causing him to miss the Southampton and Nottingham Forest games. However he has been passed fit to resume training with us from today.

Chris Turner and John Sitton

BOARD MEETING 8TH SEPTEMBER 1994 MANAGER'S REPORT

Firstly, we would like to advise you that Ian Hendon is due the sum of £10,000 and requires £2000 immediately for insurance policies. Ian Bogie is also in need of further monies. Four players have reported unpaid monies. The consequences could be catastrophic because Leyton Orient are now in breach of contract with the players concerned. They could withdraw their labour and automatically become free transfers allowing them to leave and join a club of their choice.

Out of contract players

We have received no enquiries for Terry Howard. We are getting enquiries for Danny Carter from Cambridge and Doncaster but no firm offers.

We are making enquiries to bring in players on loan i.e. Steve Jones of West Ham and John Hendrie of Spurs but both were unavailable at this moment in time. One player we have had an eye on for a while is Jai Martin of Southend Utd. He is a talented forward with pace. We have spoken with their manager, Peter Taylor, who will allow Jai to come on loan if the player himself is willing. He currently earns £175.00 per week with £50 appearance.

Trevor Putney has joined Colchester United on loan for a month. We are going 50/50 on his wages but there is no question of a permanent deal at the moment.

Mark Warren has been fined one-week's wage for his sending off at Huddersfield Town. The referee's report clearly states that he struck an opponent.

Youth

The Centre of Excellence started on Monday 5th September. We now have five new coaches at the centre who are all qualified and hold a full coaching licence. This is a vast improvement on previous years. The feedback we have received so far from the parents is that Bernie Dixson's departure will have no adverse effect on the boys. Luke Weaver, last year's under fifteen goalkeeper has been selected for the under 16's. We have written to Luke's parents stating that we will offer him a YT contract on leaving school with a pro contract on his 17th birthday should he continue to progress as he is currently. Luke has made it very clear that he is very happy at the football club and although one or two Premier League clubs have been keeping an eye on him, Leyton Orient is his club.

Chris Turner & John Sitton

BOARD MEETING THURSDAY 24TH NOVEMBER 1994 MANAGERS REPORT

Transfers

Unfortunately following permission by the chairman and the board to do the swap deal involving Danny Carter and Mark Druce we regret to inform you that for a number of reasons the deal fell through.

Following the fall down of the Oxford deal preliminary enquiries from Peter Taylor of Southend to take Danny Carter on loan has also fallen through.

We have also reached the financial compromise with Colchester Utd whereby if we give Trevor Putney £2000 they will pay him £8000 and sign him. From December to June his wages are approx. £19000 which sees an obvious saving of £17,000 in the long run. If this suggestion is utilised we anticipate saving of £2000 a week on three players which we would like to use to replenish the forward line area at the football club as previously requested in our manager's report dated 11.8.94.

Injuries

Vaughan Ryan had a hernia operation and has come out of hospital and is 6 weeks away from training.

Paul Hague is recovering from a stress fracture and will be available in 4 weeks.

As you will be aware we are not satisfied with our current training facilities at Douglas Eyre. We are currently with the help of John Goldsmith and the Borough Council, seeking alternative facilities. We feel that if we continue to train at Douglas Eyre a training injury due to the conditions under foot is waiting to happen.

Contracts

We feel that in the coming weeks ahead that the following players' contract situation should be monitored. The players concerned are as follows:-

Paul Heald, Ian Hendon, Kevin Austin, Mark Dempsey, Colin West

The season so far, most of which you have witnessed, we feel there has been a big improvement in the structuring of not only the team but things inside the football club.

We anticipate further progress in all areas. The level of expectation could be heightened with one or two new faces and we feel that a freshening up of our small squad and a reinforcement of numbers can only be beneficial to our consolidation during this difficult time.

Youth Team

As you are aware that Tom Loizou and Steve Shorey have been working as Youth Team Coach and Youth Team Development Officer respectively. Tom Loizou has done a magnificent job in preparing and organising youth team matters. What disappoints us is that Tom is doing a full time job but unfortunately on part time money and is currently owed 3 weeks' wages, which as you will realise is unacceptable considering that Tom has devoted his own working day to Leyton Orient Football Club. As for Steve Shorey, for a number of reasons we feel it would not be right to offer him a full timeposition at this time.

Centre of Excellence

The Centre of Excellence has received rave reviews from our regional FA monitor following two totally unbiased assessments. Facilities, coaching, monitoring of paper work and general conduct have all been given recognition of an A1 calibre.

However, John Sitton having confided in Chris was forced to sack Lloyd Scott having found out he was working for Plymouth Argyle in a scouting capacity.

BOARD MEETING THURSDAY 5TH JANUARY 1995 MANAGERS REPORT

1. Transfer news

A circular went out last week as instructed by the board. These are the clubs that have shown an interest in our players:-

Ian Hendon - Port Vale, Carlisle, Dundee Utd. Danny Carter - Peterborough, Chester.

Ian Bogie - Shrewsbury, Rotherham, Port Vale. Colin West - Stockport (loan) Chester.

Terry Howard - Bury

We haven't received any firm bids as yet.

Vaughan Ryan, Gary Bellamy, Gary Barnett - No interest to date.

2. Nicky Sweetman and Nathan Beckett have both been released.

Sweetman has joined Hendon on a free transfer and Beckett has left with the co-operation of the PFA with four weeks' money.

3. Injuries and suspensions.

Injuries and suspensions have seriously depleted our squad, last Monday's game against Bristol Rovers we were down to thirteen fit and able professionals (that's including two goalkeepers.) If the game had gone ahead we would have had to use two YTS players as substitutes.

We are currently operating with a squad that is unbalanced, lightweight and undermanned should injuries arise.

4. Summary

We both feel disappointed that we have had to put on the transfer list our so called better players. We understand the club's financial position and as we have already been doing we will try and recoup some money for the football club.

We are sure you will all know the consequences if players like Hendon, Cockerill, West and Heald were to leave the club. We have said before at past board meetings that the forward position needs strengthening. We have approached you at previous meetings to make room for forward/forwards to come into the squad. We are now paying the price for not bringing in forwards and Colin West's injury and more importantly the lack of goals is reflected in our past seven league games.

To you the reader, I think all of the above is a sad insight and indictment of it all. No response to requests for players, either on loan or a permanent transfer, facilities, training grounds, finances, forward planning, retention of players and new contracts, all of which would have contributed to moving forward, and in my opinion not only saved the club from relegation, but from continuing mediocrity at best. Of course it goes without saying that I would have included, and should have had a long term contract for myself to run the club from top to bottom.

CHAPTER TWELVE
Own Kind Of Music

I think it's only fair to address the gossip and accusations by certain people that there was a disparity between me and the staff and the diabolical accusation of not speaking appropriately. The only disparity was my wages. My wife has a saying "everyone has their own truth." What I've described and my take on it is its not only "my truth" it's THE truth! There were plenty of people around at that time who spoke and acted like a pig. I wasn't one of them. If it's one thing I've got going for me it's the ability to hold my hands up when I'm wrong. I'll own it. It has to be said to Neil, Grant, Maureen, Carol, Sue, Flynny, Shoro, Chris and Andy Taylor, I was always polite, courteous and respectful. I've never forgot that I came from nothing and I like to think I know how to talk to people. The only thing that can change it is if I don't like how they have spoken to me. Along with trying to be professional I tried to intersperse it with humour. Something that I thought previously was lacking the majority of the time.

Frank Woolf I held in contempt. But only as my multiple roles unfolded and he got away with doing very little. You could walk into his office at any given time and he'd be peering through a cloud of smoke as he celebrated with numerous Benson and Hedges after clinching a sponsor for a match ball. May I suggest one of the busiest departments in a football club should be the commercial department. Especially at a club as low down as Orient considering the amount of choice people have on who to support and where to spend their disposable income on their own choice of entertainment. As people like Barry Hearn know only too well, it's about getting customers to part with their money, and once in and around the ground, a second, even a third time.

I don't even think we had more than one tea bar. Woolf got his comeuppance when Hearn parted company with him. Woolf told me he asked Hearn to just "give me a chance." I said "Woolfy, you've had a fifteen-year chance. How much longer did you want to get something going? I had ten months. The difference between you and me was I gave everything, juggling six jobs within a job one of those was the job you should have been doing so that we could afford a coach and you say give me a chance. I wish I'd had fifteen years." I'd be very interested to see what the commercial department's net income was for those fifteen years. But he was part of that mindset "don't place demands on me and I won't place demands on you."

Up until me, it had worked very well for all concerned. Suffice to say the fairest way I knew how to work was I gave people back what they gave me, and most of the time I'd hazard a guess I gave more. Unfortunately there's a down side to it all that leads to what really goes on in football. That is you can approach it like it's a job for life but in reality you could be sacked on any given day. So what happens? I suppose instead of suffering like me from an ideology you look after number one placing the accent on short termism, hoping to curry favour with the people around you including fans, directors and players. The sack was in the not too distant future. In the meantime I was still fire fighting. I think I put out more fires that year, some lit out of mischief than the whole of London's fire brigade.

In the end I think it comes down to a few things going on at the time that could well have been major contributory factors in the perceived fractious, fragmented feeling around the club. One was my personal precarious contractual situation that was ongoing. I now realise I took on board massive responsibility with no power. Thinking back it was a nightmare equation. I can assure you I've seen and witnessed the exact opposite in football since my time. And I even feel some of the people concerned should have been nowhere near any seat of power. To them it matters not with the ample reward for failure culture that exists in football. Too many times people get duly compensated for failing to build a team which is very difficult but easier than what I was trying to do which was rebuild a club. Over several generations at my many different clubs I'd seen and heard of stories where the oversight on fees, salaries and compensation packages for the permanently revolving door of staff had nearly brought a club to its knees. Something I was now in the epicentre of at Orient. In the volatile mix of what I was experiencing was also a culture, the antithesis of what I wanted. The only place I experienced what I wanted was at the Centre of Excellence. That is hard work, honesty, application and a thirst for knowledge.

To me, as an ex-player it was non-negotiable. It seemed as I've said certain parts of the club were antique and the departments where certain people worked contained institutionalised individuals determined not to change, work hard for the manager, in this case managers, and maybe the greater good of the club. Over a desperate December, after winning 1-0 at Fulham in the Auto Windscreen Trophy, we lost four out of five games. We drew 0-0 at home to Bradford and we needed to win as on our travels, it needed more than we had to get a result, this was an obvious recipe for relegation. Malcolm Alison used to say "good teams win at home, VERY GOOD TEAMS WIN AWAY". It seems we were neither. The higher you go, the more you should be able to take for granted. Some of the players couldn't even perform the basics and I must admit I struggled at times to deal with that. I took another call from Bill Songhurst he told me to duck, say less, do less and gave up the absurd idea, totally unethical and unmoral, of giving myself either a four-year youth team manager's contract or so as not to arouse too much suspicion a two-year playing contract. Laughable but that was typical Bill. No wonder Londoners get a reputation for being lairy barrow boys. I quite easily resisted the temptation to appear even more absurd than I ended up doing and committing fraud into the bargain.

One of the games was a F.A Cup Home tie vs Bristol Rovers. We lost 2-0 with fifteen players available that included three youth team players. We fielded what was our most experienced and strongest team available. On top of it all, what didn't help was one of the lads getting sent off. Our confidence was low, resistance low, scoring capabilities low and teams knew to contain an opening fast tempo onslaught, normally consisting of three or four attacks and on recognising apart from Bogie and maybe Carter (still on a seven-day contract) there was no pace, no trickery and no invention. So once those two were kept quiet the opposition gradually strangled the game and brought pressure to bear on an already under siege back four. You can't win a game without forwards. Up to now, December 27th, we'd had I think twenty-nine games and kept two clean sheets. We'd been clumped three or four times, but we'd dished out a couple ourselves. Notably Peterborough and Fulham. But in the main, the most disappointing thing was getting beat by either the odd goal, or capitulating to the tune of conceding two or three. So it seemed one extreme or the other. Playing some good football as far as the opposition's eighteen-yard box, then having no real cutting edge to lose by the odd goal or if we conceded a goal, becoming affected and capitulating.

There's times when perhaps through frustration and spinning so many plates, not throwing them, I'd not praised players enough. But stopping just short of performing acts of man love, I'd spent from March the previous season, pre-season and a good lengths of time into the new season, delivering the "well dones," "well played," "good boy," "good stuff" at the appropriate time. But one thing I couldn't forgive was any player feeling sorry for themselves and in the course of ninety minutes capitulating. It's fair to say, I agree with the summation that one or two started to play for themselves. Spirit? I've got my own take on that. It wasn't in abundance I'll readily admit. But how do you get it? That's where my opinion as a former player, coach and co-manager comes in.

At Chelsea the situation had been very similar. Club skint, players like me given a debut long before it was due and I was ready, because the best of the generation in front of me were sold to underpin losses. At Millwall and this is where we start to get into it, any spirit was from the nucleus of players who'd won the youth cup. I don't care what anyone says spirit comes from the feel good factor of winning. It was nurtured by the likes of George Petchey and good pros who cared like John Mitchell, John Lyons, John Jackson and Barry Kitchener in particular. Because of the inconsistency in results that usually comes with a young side the spirit was held together by a good nucleus of players and staff. I like to think that I could include myself in that and let's not forget what it's like to play for Millwall supporters who appreciated not only my bit of ability but my work ethic and never say die attitude. After a good run of form I was touted by one little firm, who joined us in the Jubilee Lounge as a cross between being the new Barry Kitchener and the new Harry Cripps. I thought it was an honour to know and play with Kitch and I thought I must have been doing alright to be mentioned in the same breath. Truly an accolade. Even if I didn't agree, I wouldn't necessarily argue with them. They enjoyed taking on opposing supporters, police, and even police dogs. So it was beers all round and I made sure I ran through brick walls for them. Then along came Peter Anderson. If you couldn't play for Millwall supporters, you shouldn't be playing. After Kitch retired I should have been at the back with Sam Allardyce with Dave Martin screening the front of us. You could have had Bill and Ben the flowerpot men as full backs and we'd have still kept clean sheets for fun but Anderson didn't know what he was looking at, so big John made way for bigger Sam and Paul Roberts stayed on as one of the full backs, the two positions that I could play. I've got a sneaky feeling that Anderson was undoubtedly influenced by someone else at the club who had a vested interest in self promotion and self preservation. I've got to say it meant a lot to me when I left Millwall, to finish above them in the league with Gillingham.

At Gillingham it was relaxed and a little more sedate. But the lads every last one were different class... all men. We trained hard, we had good league form, good little cup runs but the spirit although helped by results was in my opinion engendered by men who trained, played and conducted themselves like men. Decent, polite, courteous and respectful men. Everyone respected each other's contribution and it manifested itself in the way we treated each other. Ron Hillyard, Micky Adams, Steve Bruce, John Sharpe, Colin Duncan, Mark Weatherly, Richie Bowman, Dick Tydeman, Dean White, Colin Powell, Trevor Lee, Kenny Price, all top boys. Then I thought some odd loans and buys by Peacock upset the status quo and the spirit in the camp. I must also add that when a manager brings in a player or players, those brought in should be good people who are good players and improve on what you already have at your disposal. At Gillingham I don't think that was the case, the side got broken up and it never felt the same. I would have gladly left if Peacock had accepted the bid from Fred Callaghan at Brentford after my first two years. The third and fourth year were never the same. All this went through my mind, the ingredients, most of which come from the players and their personalities, as I continued to fire fight and paper over the cracks. The best I knew it at Orient was the promotion winning side in 1988-1989, a team I captained.

The players and personalities involved were close where it mattered in my opinion, on the training pitch and in games. In fact, as one of the older ones at twenty-eight, I took it upon myself just to keep an eye on, police, and offer the odd word of guidance to the younger, social set inside the dressing room. So spirit and where does it come from? Let's start from the beginning, say the squad of 88-89. I got on with everyone whilst keeping true to myself and my own identity. I preferred to train, rest, play and intersperse that by using any spare time I had, by being with my wife and child and extended family. At the time, a large extended family. I enjoyed nature and animals particularly dogs and horses as pets and to admire. I think they are the most noble of God's animals. I enjoyed shooting and got up with not much happening for seventy-two hours (or I wouldn't have done it) at 3am to walk and shoot, cook on a barbie with the lads, kip and wait for the night time duck flight and rabbit. So what would I have in common with Healdy, Castle, Howard, Harvey, the young ones in the team? They preferred a nightclub to a field full of pheasant. Keith Day, Dicko, Baker, I'm sure did as I did and went for a meal with their missus. Campbell came on loan from AFC and joined up with the clubbers.

Alan Comfort was all about relaxing with his studies and I shared his love of concerts and the theatre, so we had that in common. One or two others loved golf. Most of us lived on opposite sides of London and its suburbs. What pulled us together to achieve something? I'm convinced it was the only things that can. When we had to work, we worked. When you train as you play, in most cases the whole squad were fiercely competitive, determined not to be mugged off in training, you earn respect. I still think to this day another ingredient where spirit is concerned comes from the respect you have for each other as team mates. As a defender you'd look across and fancy Campbell to score, or say to yourself I wouldn't fancy marking Harvey or Comfort and this is reciprocated when they can't get any joy in training. In a football club you need to be able to look around the dressing room and say to yourself "I'm glad he is on my side..." You constantly, inadvertently, raise each other's standards. And I'm sure the forwards were happy not to have me, Keith Day, Kevin Dickenson and Steve Castle battering them into submission. So you take the field looking at team mates you are glad are on your side. You win. You get on a run. And you know the reasons, the ingredients that everyone brings to the table and it earns respect. The spirit, or as I prefer, belief and feeling for each other, comes from what you've put in on the training field and taken into games. In my opinion it doesn't matter what the sport is, each individual if they do a bit of self analysis will know that in the end when you enter the competition or take the field, apart from the obvious which is ability, it's about focus, one hundred per cent commitment or desire and never giving in.

Of course all these are big umbrellas that cover things like pre agreed strategy. The spirit people misguidedly talk of coming from a golfing weekend or a two-day bender on the drink, is in the first place, a false, shallow, spirit, when it should be at the end, the icing on the cake, once all the other boxes are ticked. Starting under Frank Clark and Peter Eustace I saw plenty of players who put the cart before the horse. Initiating things like The Tuesday Club that I inherited and disbanded, where junk food and drinking oneself into oblivion off the back of a substandard performance and defeat, were deemed acceptable. That kind of thing is ok but the timing has to be right. I know football inside and outside the games confines is a social event. But surely, even the most stubborn, anti-Sitton pockets of O's punters, should at least question their misplaced loyalty towards certain players. I'm also hoping any football supporter who reads this will now perhaps understand that I wasn't a walking cliché and a fair way from stereotype.

Players spoke of loyalty and respect for the club and its supporters. Supporters who are the club and pay the wages who I supposedly never took into account. Any player not at his optimum physically, playing poorly, overweight, taking wages from those same supporters with whom they supposedly had a reciprocal respect and loyalty out gambling and drinking anywhere from three to six times a week was never going to be my cup of tea. Is that the type of player who respects and is grateful for your admission money? I'm not a complete moron, I could maybe find a way of overlooking the odd thing for George Best or diplomatically sidestepping a problem with Peter Osgood. But they didn't play for us. All I did came from a good place, and based on my own brand of common sense. In the end I'll leave you to decipher it all and make up your own mind.

December 1994, the season of goodwill. Except at Orient there wasn't any. I can't remember if the players got a turkey or a bottle of something as is the usual custom, courtesy of the club. I approached Ian Hendon who was the captain to tell him if the lads fancied it to arrange their own thing, so I could allow for it in any training schedule. Dave Burton went to the Rising Sun near Whipps Cross Hospital with his mates. Maureen, Sue and Carol went for a Chinese. I said to Shoro, Andy Taylor, Chris, Tom and Flynny we'll go and have a nice meal and drink somewhere. In the end, me, Chris and Tom went with our wives to a restaurant in Wanstead. The bill came to £60 a head so £360 or just under. You wouldn't believe the row and fuss it caused when I told the restaurant to send it to the club. Frank dined there in his time so they knew the club and trusted us. Just to set the scene or in this case the table, at Orient for previous regimes there was for away games a £150 float for fish and chips on the way home and Friday night drinks for the staff. Me and Chris got £50 each for both so inevitably our Friday drinks came out of our own pocket. Probably unheard of. Also previous incumbents of the managerial position according to Maureen, had a monthly entertainment allowance.

The sum £100-£200. It was more annoying for me because as youth coach when the staff had a social, Eustace insisted the bill was split four ways. So out of my £230 net I paid my share but he kept the bill and got all the money back. So I assume, the "entertainment allowance" was to either take agents to lunch, wine and dine any prospective signings (forgive the heavy sarcasm) or the most likely, take the missus for some posh nosh. Like the gaff in Wanstead. Chris and myself, because of the club's plight and our own misguided honour, relinquished the monthly allowance. We committed the blood curdling crime of a Christmas meal with the wives that we thought the club should pay for out of gratitude. Chris said "there'll be hell to pay." I said " let's wait and see if anyone has got the audacity to question it after the work we've put in." I didn't legislate for a hopping mad Carol Stokes.

Knowing what I know with regards to any abuse of "hospitality" in football I'll leave it to others to decide if I was out of order, although my conscience is clear. Because I had signed the bill f.a.o Carol Stokes, Leyton Orient FC she stormed into mine and Chris's shared office ready to throttle me. I'd always preferred to talk and act believe it or not, with humility. Not this time. I decided to take a leaf out of history and act with unjustified arrogance just like my predecessors. I said "give the bill to Maureen and tell her to send a cheque, we haven't even had a glass of wine for nine months down to the club, no overnight float, no entertainment expenses, so the club can pay for our Christmas dinner with the wives." She saw the look on my face that told her I meant it and I added "shut the door on your way out we were in the middle of a meeting. Funny that Carol, you wouldn't have done it to Frank or Eustace unless the main stand was on fire." She went red and walked out.

This I suppose is what was perceived as talking down to staff by the likes of Terry Howard in his book, but I felt engulfed, consumed in the realisation that Chris's predictions were beginning to ring true. Meantime, football wise, as I attempted to sign three forwards Phil Wallace put a common sense approach to helping his team go through the accounts, part of which involved another temporary self-enforced embargo with no incomings, outgoings or outlay of monies. I just wish even more information could have been passed out to show that every time I found a way out of this mess, this maze, this inherited disaster, I was re-routed. Phil told me and Chris, spot on as it happens, what he thought our individual strengths were, what he saw us doing and who was good at what. I warned him of the mess, he said "I know it's getting worse as we go through the figures." His press conference, not really shown on the C4 doc was chalk and cheese to Hearn's. The reason it wasn't shown was because on deciding he (Phil Wallace) wouldn't be leaving Borehamwood for Orient, he took out a court injunction not allowing the production company to air his proposed takeover. He said and thought I was a good organiser, "on the ball" as he put it and he remarked being an Eastender, I was a good communicator.

I must say, I felt far more at ease in his company than I ever did in Hearn's. You do, it's fair to say, get a feel for people. The bombshell came not long after. Chris asked outright, "well? how's it looking?" Phil Wallace said very forensically, just like his accountants I suppose, "administration chaps, that's what it's looking like. Administration." I said "can you explain Phil?" He replied "it's the first step towards ultimately, liquidation. But we'll see, we're trying to make it work." Anyway, it now seemed like everything was on the edge of the abyss. Would there be any respite on the horizon? I think the manager's report for December, delivered to the attending board members, was self-explanatory. For the record Phil went on to take charge of Stevenage. Since he has, it's been a solid club ran on a firm financial footing.

Meanwhile the busy holiday period was approaching and I wanted to treat the players fairly but remain professional. I asked Hendo and Westy to canvass the players and see whether they wanted to train on Christmas morning and spend the day with their families or spend all day at home and have a light session early evening. I still maintain you can be professional without being dictatorial. We had a break of nine days between games, then two games in two days on the 26th and 27th. I gave the players plenty of rest in readiness, building up gradually after the 2-0 defeat at promotion favourites Birmingham on 17th December in the hope anyone with a knock had recovered. The players could have a social, do their shopping and we'd still have bags of time for our drills, organisation, patterns, defensive work and set pieces. I thought nine days was plenty.

They say no good deed goes unpunished. With a nine-day window, I still had belief in myself, the players and proposed new signings to be organised enough and to pick up the amount of points needed to stay up. So, even though we'd done it once or twice already with the help and support of an organisation inside the club "The Oddfellows," we procured some tickets for the David Lloyd Centre in Chigwell. It was a chance, at the expense of the Orient Oddfellows for a little light training and light relief. So, we set off from the ground in the minibus and it resulted in unrest on the bus because it transpired that after a five a side competition in a gym the day before with the kids, Terry Howard couldn't run. He had sore feet. The soles of his feet were giving him pain and he couldn't even put his feet down to walk. I spoke to Terry and Andy Taylor the physio. I deferred to Andy and Terry. TH thought I didn't believe him or trust his word. That came from his own mindset and possible paranoia. There was plenty around at that time. I had absolutely no reason to disbelieve him and trusted everyone to tell the truth until it turned out otherwise. I'm not sure, I think he stayed behind for treatment. Anyway, a few groans went up when we stopped the bus for the lads to have a slow jog and some stretches, a loosener really, to the reception at the Lloyd. On arrival it was water aerobics followed by Sauna and Jacuzzi and a round of refreshment at my expense. Some of the lads even put in a gym session before their aerobics. One or two who'd been dedicated trainers more or less ever present now started to resent the boys often injured or taking days off for minor knocks. I again deferred to Andy Taylor, but sensed the guys who had a clean bill of health felt penalised for staying fit. Quite a few had lunch or a drink with me and Chris, a few shot off as I was flexible, not insisting they stay to engender the false spirit I've spoken of.

During that period, Carol intentionally or unintentionally got her own back for the arrival of the bill from the restaurant. I'm sure at every club in every organisation there's a vetting process shall we say, that any visitors to the aforesaid place of business has to go through, to get to see the manager or in mine and Chris's case, managers. Unless it's Orient where you ring the chairman directly and ask for the manager's job, or to put in a derisory offer for one of the players. Just two of the things that wound me right up. Now a third wind up appeared. Carol buzzed through to me and Chris, saying there's someone to see you. I said "Who?" The phone at the other end went down and a couple of minutes later a knock, the door opens. It's Carol with a guy, dark, Mediterranean looking about 6'2." "There you go" she says. Afterwards I'd worked out, without asking, that he obviously wouldn't take no for an answer or Carol couldn't handle it, or both. I said "Hello I'm John, this is Chris, nice to meet you, how can we help? Would you like a seat?" "Nah, I'll stand. D'ya need a goalkeeper? I'm a goalkeeper, I see you've only got one goalkeeper." I asked what his background was and who he had played for. " Guvnors 11" he said. "What?" "Well" he said shuffling, but fixing me with a stare, "I've just got out of prison." He looked like a cross between Marty Feldman, eyes out on stalks, mop of dark curly hair, but the facial expression of an extra from one flew over the cuckoo's nest. "Is this a wind up?" I said. "Nah I'm serious, I wanna be a goalkeeper, I'm fit." "I can see," I interjected, this bloke had muscles like Popeye. "But I don't think I can help unless you give me your background, a verbal CV will do. Where have you been? Who have you played for? Any representative honours?"

Anyway, while I was speaking to him Turner, sinks down in his chair pretending to read a match report, from Ivan one of our scouts. He's pissing himself, I can see his shoulders going up and down. I said out loud to this guy "this is very unusual, I wonder if the previous two managers experienced anything like this?" Chris laughed even more. I said to our friend, I'm almost sure his name was Chris as well, "How long were you inside?" He said "I got fourteen years, but I did eight years." "Ok... well, we had a player before who got his life back on track, a winger. Maybe I can help you, but we are going to have to watch you first (a quick exit strategy I thought) do you play for anyone? Sunday side? Non-League?" "Nah, just in the gym. Got a merit, Guvnor's 11." I tried to show genuine concern, but I never knew the guy and whether he was serious or a lunatic off the street. Like I said no vetting. I said out of interest "I'd like to know why did you end up inside?" "I killed me Dad." Turner nearly exploded, the guy looked over, Chris shut up immediately. Like a fucking orderly trying to humour a lunatic I said "oh yeah" all matter of fact. "What caused you to do that?" Thinking all the time, how the fuck am I going to get him out of here? "He used to hit my Mum, he did it one day, I said you touch her again I'll kill ya. Anyway they had a row, he clumped her, I thought I had to do it, so I plunged him." Anyway, after looking him up and down, I noticed he had hands like a shovels, like Lenny out of Mice and Men and from what I could tell he was just as simple. This wasn't Steinbeck, this was real life. I tried to think of something positive to say on which to part company. "You've definitely got goalkeeper's hands" I said. "Thanks" he said. "You could probably catch the ball one handed. I'll tell you what, let me write down your details and if Healdy or Chris here get injured we'll call you in, have a look and if you're as good as you say you are, we'll sign you non-contract at first and see how it goes." So I write down his name and the address that he admitted was a halfway house and I walked him out calling out to Carol "it's alright Carol I'll see him out." I went to the dressing room toilet to make sure I didn't need a change of kit and came back to find Chris still laughing shaking his head, beetroot red from the laughter and probably, blood pressure. I said "only at Orient Chris, only at Orient."

At a football club, everyone from top to bottom has to be pulling in the same direction, on the same page and sharing the load. The club was at crisis point and we were having our wages paid by the PFA from the end of August. Along with trying to recruit new players and needlessly scouting as there was a transfer embargo, contrary to popular or perceived opinion, Chris and I did all in our power to try and nurture or improve relationships throughout the club. We spoke to Neil Watson and Grant Cornwell, who as I've said ran FITC and we all agreed it would be a good idea to have all the staff together once a month to air any grievances anyone might have, chat, share our problems and any ideas or advice on how we could take the club forward. Unfortunately Frank Woolf was proved right. When we approached him he said "it won't work, we never did it under Eust or Frank." "Besides, people won't say if there's anything on their mind, they'll clam up" and after three months and three meetings, with Chris pouring wine and me making tea, that's basically what happened. Everyone sat there in silence. There was Carol Stokes, who had been there since leaving school. There was also Sue Tilling, Charlie Hasler, Frank Woolf, Dave Burton, Grant Cornwell, Neil Watson and physios Andy Taylor and Tony Flynn.

Along with me and Chris, the biggest contributor, was Maureen Hanshaw who tried to help me and Chris and keep us informed. Charlie (groundsman of the year since the Flintstones) Hasler asked why I occasionally liked to use the main pitch. All the other clubs I'd been at the Friday ritual was to report to the main ground, have a warm up, run through your set pieces, patterns, and defending the opposition then small sided game, few sprints, shower, lunch and either get off home to rest or board the coach for an overnight stay. Charlie said all his and his lads' work was done, and he didn't want to be going over the pitch after us using it. To explain, for Terry's sake and the supporters' sake, because Hasler was well received in the supporters club, I just remonstrated that the be all and end all is obtaining three points for the first team, and the surface at the training ground was piss poor (as I've said), so to rehearse, we need the ball to run true. He shrugged and said "I'm not happy." I said "no one is but the training ground is shit and the greater good of the club and first team must be the priority." I used it four times and each time I sent Tom who was good enough to help with the youth team to my office with the key to the bar that was stocked by Dave Dodds, courtesy of the supporters' club.

The supporters who listened to Charlie complain about me and my occasional insistence we use the pitch paid for Charlie to clear out mine and Chris's bar of wine and spirits. We had a case of beer delivered every Friday, before home games by a guy called Mike Childs for our staff and visiting manager and his staff. But Charlie had taken the brandy, whisky, gin, vodka and wine in exchange for letting us use the pitch. I don't drink that much so I didn't give a toss, but any opposing manager, when offered a drink and wanting a nip of whisky would have struggled to believe my explanation for its absence. That's how badly I treated Charlie Hasler. Terry Howard couldn't handle the stress of a run in the forest under Eustace but calls into question my relationships with others around the club. I wonder how he'd have coped with people who are meant to have the club's best interests at heart and tell anyone who'd listen that they do, meanwhile sabotaging the prospect of rehearsing set pieces because it meant more work. I can't quite believe I have to explain this and that me and Chris had to waste precious time justifying something so petty. I'd be shocked if any other manager had to put up with such petty bullshit. It's funny, I've heard stories of at least one very high profile manager who having evaluated all the staff when he took over, made a point of sacking an uncooperative groundsman. That's in comparison to how I treated Hasler. It's as if rolling the pitch was a hardship or not in a groundsman's remit. I've no qualms in saying, apart from a friendly good morning, I had as little to do with him as possible. If I'd got the three years Hearn initially promised me, part of my portfolio on the reorganisation of the club and its staff would have seen a lot of changes believe me. I can't quite believe myself sometimes, that I'd waste so much time on explaining these things, thank God it's ancient history, but I feel supporters should know and Howard, because of the accusations in his book, should know what went on. They should know that me and Chris and the first team not only had the opposition to beat on a Tuesday and Saturday. There was plenty of opposition inside the club, each one with their own agenda. Normally the agenda was to have as much free time as possible, not the greater good of the club. The junior secretary Dave Burton was different class. Affable, funny, polite, helpful, hardworking and despite his age, always showed concern and offered help.

Me and Chris couldn't have asked for more and a couple or so years later I was choked that he left. He seemed suited to it all, the hustle and bustle. It's worth noting that Barry Hearn parted with Hasler. Maureen was like a Mother Hen to everyone and took all the calls and all the flak and bounced a few cheques on behalf of the club, keeping administration and possible liquidation at arm's length. The stress on her was a piss take, as it was on all of us. I lost count the number of times Chris said to me "why are you bothering? I'm fucking telling you now, we're babysitting this club for someone else." I said "Chris, we keep being told you're holding the fort, doing a good job under difficult circumstances, you're both part of something longer term. What are we meant to do?" Chris said "you believe that?" I said "we've been told all this at various board meetings and individually by different board members as well as the chairman. If someone comes to my house and I know they are thieves, I'll lock everything away but you don't know if someone is lying to you until they've lied. So take them at their word." Chris's theory was proved right. In the meantime, I thought I was right and set about outlining to Tony Wood and Derek Weinrabe how the club should be restructured and run. Something I was to repeat with Barry Hearn. All to no avail. I had earmarked four forwards to lift the playing staff, which should answer those perplexed and who commented on getting in a defender. I'd earmarked, having cultivated relationships, managers for every age group from under 9's to under 16's, a new youth manager, a new youth development officer, a non-league scout, a Centre of Excellence director and assistant director and all the financial implications and who'd do what was put down on paper, and about eight pieces of A4 were pinned to the blackboard. I even had a specialist goalkeeper coach for the kids, who I would have had working with the senior goalkeepers. His name was Mick Payne and I loved watching him work.

Thorough, knowledgeable, great coach and a very approachable and funny guy. As much as anything about him, I loved his humour. I thought then, and still do, that everyone on a staff at a football club must pull in the same direction, with no dissenters. Have discussions and disagreements, but no dissenters. Players need to see that whatever the aim, staff are together, united, impermeable, unbreakable and the manager has chosen wisely. I think even down to a coach's personality. When times are hard, results poor and morale low you need a coach with humour as well as coaching ability. Every single coach in the football club was now fully qualified. Before my time it wasn't always the case.

That shitty, nasty, ancient blackboard. So old it couldn't take chalk anymore. A true story... I'd been refused a flip chart because of the initial expense and having to renew the paper and pens. Anyway, back to the staff. It was well known that the club secretary who'd worked her way up and had been there since she left school was Carol Stokes. When I was a player, Carol had always helped me and I thought I got on quite well with her. It seemed strange crossing over from player to coach to joint manager for both of us. I like to think we kept it civil. Between her and Maureen, I was informed of what had gone before and was then left to make my own decision based on the information I'd been given. On the whole we just both got on with what we had to do with very little time for pleasantries.

The monthly meetings? Unfortunately, Frank Woolf was proved right to the dismay of me, Chris, Neil and Grant. At times despite Chris's attempts with myself and the FITC guys at humour and the initiation of a discussion it was like sitting in a dentist's waiting room. Awkward silence broken by Chris suggesting "that's that then! anyone for another drink?" And bursting into a giggle as he looked at me. His face said "what the fuck are we doing?" We'd go back to our joint office, giggling and shaking our heads. Twenty one years on, places like the bank where my wife works, and I'm sure other banks and corporate environments, call our monthly attempt at the coming together of staff involved in the structure of the place "brainstorming." Unfortunately for me, Chris, Neil and Grant our attempts to involve and include everyone in forming ideas, discussion and decision making so the club could move forward, was a flop. At best we sat there in silence, at worst, it became more fragmented.

Who knows? Maybe the rest knew more than me and Chris and that our days were numbered. Hopefully people like TH and his comments in his book are now addressed. We extended our hand and it was slapped away. Not by some major mover and shaker high up in the corporate world, but by one or two who in my opinion were bang in the comfort zone and had become institutionalised, sheltering behind a steady income. Maybe in the past, they'd suggested things to other regimes and had them dismissed so they gave up.

Years later, Carol who I felt gutted for because she'd worked tremendously hard for years for all the regimes at the club, long before and during my time there under Frank Clark and Peter Eustace was released by Barry Hearn as a new broom swept clean. I saw her and she came over as I was mentoring Paul Roberts an old Millwall team mate to do a job for the Press Association gathering statistics. As I sat at the back of the old stand at Orient we said hello, asked how each other was getting on. The usual stuff. We now had more in common than she'd first thought. Any chagrin was now a thing of the past. Determined not to be seen as down and out, which I virtually was, I just remarked in reply "surviving Carol, I'm surviving." I didn't go into detail as I had to concentrate on the game. After a few outings at Orient, Millwall and West Ham, I'd been praised and rewarded with nine seasons at every Arsenal home game. But that was in the future on behalf of the PA gathering stats and data. It was to become one of three part time jobs I juggled while I did the Knowledge as I had vowed not to be beaten and to get my wife and children to new pastures. I didn't know or think at the time that I'd be ostracised and kicked out of football and I'd have a normal job.

Our three bed, end of terrace with front, side and rear garden was now in an area that went from being "villagy" where all the neighbours knew each other, spoke, shared barbecues, Christmas drinks, New Year's Eve parties, kids' birthdays, to something resembling a cross between Beirut, the Gaza Strip and Belfast on a bad night. I find it amazing that social engineering still exists in the twenty first century.

So I swore to get my kids out whilst they were still young enough and more importantly still in one piece.

Anyway, back to football. It wasn't all doom and gloom. Not yet anyway. Chris spoke to David Pleat who made us aware of a behind closed doors game at London Colney between his Luton and Arsenal, at that time under George Graham. It has to be said George, one of the biggest names in the game, an illustrious playing and management career, put himself out to say hello and enquire what we were doing there. For me, it was to look, learn and carry on the football tradition of plagiarism. Chris talked to David Pleat and I listened to him reply with an abundance of advice and common sense. At the same time I continued to run the rule over two forwards, Paul Read and Paul Shaw. George offered some animated advice to centre half Pal Lydersen, who when I looked at him I thought I should have still been playing. Those three inches in height and yard of pace nagged away at me again as I listened to George try to help him. I'd spent weeks ringing round, so had Chris, asking for help. Ray Wilkins manager at QPR, gave what was for him, a curt, "hello pal, what can I do for you?" when I called him. I asked him about a couple of players and was told by Ray he had no one to let go. Ironically, two of the bigger names in football were the only ones to show any concern or interest in mine and Chris's plight. George Graham and Harry Rednapp. I regret not taking up Harry's offer of taking on loan a very young midfielder, Matty Holland. It would have given more options, bought much needed appetite, bite and enthusiasm and it would have kept one or two players on their toes. One in particular, who had carried on his lifelong commitment to underachieving.

I always thought Sean Brooks' biggest battles were with himself and I tried to place trust in him and his ability. In my playing days he was head and shoulders above anyone at Orient in terms of football intelligence and technical ability. As a kid at Palace he'd worked with two of the best in Cartwright and Venables. The problem was, towards the end of the 70's and throughout the 80's coaches and managers went with 6'3 honey monsters as midfielders who could run all day and tackle a dumper truck and probably leave the dumper truck injured. That was in all divisions, but particularly prevalent in the two divisions we played in. I'd trained, played with and watched Sean become more disheartened with the game. But I told him you've got to overcome that and rise above the clumsy challenges and then get on and do your stuff. He acquitted himself superbly in the 2-0 defeat of Spurs in the League Cup at our place. Although the London cab driver, who had by now become Spurs manager, remarked how well Kevin Hales had played, for me Brooksy was on a different level. At Palace, he went Charlie big time with his clothes and social, and spunked his dough. At the O's for reasons best known to himself, he played second fiddle to a short, fat, midfielder with plenty of spiel who flattered to deceive and made no impact on any game I watched or played against them in. It's just my opinion but I didn't get it, with regards to the player concerned I'll go on record and say I thought he was nondescript and not a very good player as I struggled to see what he brought to the party.

Talking of Brooksy he actually scored the best goal I have ever seen, even though it was in a pre-season friendly against West Ham. Every defender tried to take the ball off him and when they couldn't they tried to kick him. He got the ball just inside their half to the right of the centre circle. He opened his body as if to pass it wide and as someone tried to block it he cut back on to his left foot, a second West Ham player came rushing in and he nutmegged them, he was now running at West Ham's back four. He shaped up to shoot on the edge of the "D" and as the block came in, dummied the shot and went round the centre half, the left back came flying across and as he slid in Sean went around him, he was now on the penalty spot with the goalkeeper rushing at him to narrow the angle. He feinted to shoot again and put the goalkeeper on his arse and as he jogged the ball towards an empty net a West Ham defender came flying across and Sean dragged the ball back, then rolled it into an empty net as the West Ham defender carried on sliding and got caught in the netting. I just stood on the half way line and clapped him. It was a travesty that goal never got the exposure it deserved.

Sean had a few off field struggles that I tried to help with. Namely financial, out of work and nowhere to live. But for some reason, I trusted him to perform. Sean turned out to be the reason, or one of them that I was banned by Hearn's mouthpiece, Bernard Goodall, from Brisbane Road. I called him when I heard he'd made some disparaging remarks about me and he said "I don't need this..." and put the phone down. He then went to Bernard Goodall and played the victim and I was banned from the ground. Did he have me over? I'll leave you to decide. Anyway, Harry couldn't spare any forwards, but I told him when he asked if I knew anything, the liking I had for a kid at Billericay, Steve Jones and told him I wanted to sign him but the board wouldn't sanction it. I told him it went up as the weeks went by because they hadn't acted quickly enough and Tony Wood said he was thinking of selling the club. It went from £1000 to £2000 to £5000 to £15000. I told Harry that with West Ham's profile and with them adding to his education, if he didn't cut the mustard, worst case scenario was he'd get the money back if they sold him. We thanked each other and I'll never forget his attempt at the offer of help with Matt Holland. George agreed a loan deal provisionally with Paul Read and said his nickname was "Goals" but that he lacked that yard of pace. We spoke of his reserve partner Paul Shaw and George said he wanted to make it a clean break and would want money. Oh well you can't win 'em all. I suppose two in one day was too much to ask. He (Paul Shaw) I think, went to Millwall for about £100k in the not too distant future. All I knew is, things needed to happen and happen quickly. I'd monitored reports on a raw kid at Bishop's Stortford under the stewardship of one of my three favourite Arsenal players when as a kid my Dad took me and we stood on the North Bank, John Radford. For the record, the other two were George Armstrong and Charlie George. I went and watched him incognito paying to get in and forty eight hours later rang John Radford to ask if we could get the player. His name? Leo Fortune-West. I've never subscribed to when managers don't trust their scouts and start asking other managers if they will release a player for a week, two weeks or a month's training so they can look at him.

In my opinion you either know what you are looking at or you don't. We agreed a fee of £5000 in cash. He told me what Leo was getting and that he was ambitious. I could barely contain myself and went to see Tony Wood. He sat in the main office having been filmed answering the phone saying "hello, Leyton Orient, yours for a fiver." I went into one. At the time I felt sorry for him. But now, no way. In the end who felt sorry for me? Certainly not Tony Wood who said "even though I think you are full of Bombast, you know your stuff and your heart is in the right place." I feel the same way now as I felt then, he could have sold the club but still rewarded me with the contract I deserved. But then with the effects of Rwanda, his business and the planned youth policy and dynasty firmly in the rear view mirror, (although the dynasty bit seems laughable, it was very much in my opinion achievable) things had obviously taken their toll on him. He sat there dishevelled, unkempt, like a forlorn Big Issue seller. I laid out all the paperwork for him, talking of instalments due on players like Otto, Bart-Williams and Whitbread as well as sell-on percentages. With money saved it was already well on the way to cancelling out that season's deficit. I also had short, medium and long term plans up my sleeve and three non-league players who would stop us going down with goals and when their time came would turn a profit.

He just sat there looking gormless and remarked that Weinrabe's contacts in the rag trade who were thinking of buying the club, the Kumars, hadn't panned out, but a guy in non-league called Phil Wallace, chairman of Borehamwood, was interested in buying the club. He said he'd also taken another call from John Hollins who he said had enquired about the manager's job. I said my main concern is being made to look a messer with no credibility in front of George Graham, John Radford and a personal friend, Chris Georgiou chairman at Fisher Athletic. I had started with a successful wide man Mark Dempsey, a not so successful centre half Paul Hague, who at least gave Purse a rest and released Ian Hendon and Kevin Austin to play in their correct positions, and now, most importantly, arranged deals for four forwards to get us the goals to stay up and get out of the relegation zone. I said you've already naused the Steve Jones deal making me and Shorey look idiots and now a loanee from Arsenal costing only his wages and two players costing the grand total of £5000. Leo from Stortford, the other one, Sean Devine playing at Fisher, could also get flushed down the toilet and make me look ridiculous. It doesn't matter who the manager is and at what club, if you let people down with deals your credibility is blown to smithereens. You end up getting a bad name. That's how I was brought up. As a kid I saw my Grandad spit into his hand and shake hands to clinch a deal. If he got let down he'd never deal with that person again.

I told Fisher's Chairman I couldn't meet the £15,000 he wanted but agreed a free transfer with Fisher getting 30% of any future sale. I rang him back and gave them some spiel saying the chairman insists on only 25% to get more money for Orient in the long run. He agreed.

Historically, everyone will now know only one out of the four deals I'd lined up came off. Supporters need to know it wasn't a case of not moving on to the next one if my preferred one didn't come off. Basically every effort made was sabotaged and I look back and see Chris Turner was proved right and we served as scapegoats and sacrificial lambs. O's supporters need to know that with two or three out of the four players I wanted we would have pulled off the minor miracle of avoiding relegation even amidst the chaos and mayhem that was happening around us. That's my belief and it will never change. That's on top of getting the football club back on an even keel and a firm financial footing. In the end me and Chris were only able to perform one out of the two.

CHAPTER THIRTEEN
Young At Heart

After the run of results and the not very nice run up to Christmas I thought the gradual incline in training during the nine-day gap was the right and more importantly, professional thing to do. Towards the approaching fixtures on 26th and 27th of December I also tapered off at the end making sure that players at least the few we had, were well rested. I also started to add one or two more of the kids to training. We might well have needed them and as it turned out we did, so training with so called pros would only benefit them. I took on a young trainee released by Charlton Marvin Rufus, brother of Charlton centre half Richard Rufus. He needed more time to physically fill out as he still had a boyish frame. But as a midfielder he could control and pass, had good movement, a good little engine and had courage. Both types. The courage to put his foot in and the courage to want the ball. He had the asset of being very neat and tidy and had been nicely educated by John Cartwright and had the football intelligence to be coached and apply what we'd worked on in training. He was like a breath of fresh air. Not only a good player but he had the other most important ingredient you should look for, he was a good human being. He always put in a shift to use a now well-worn cliché, in training and games. I conversed with him a lot about his lifestyle and he seemed to me a credit to his family, a son any man would be proud of. He had unswerving principles and stuck to them. The other bonus was it gave me another midfielder who I had high hopes for, and a chink of light that he could progress, whilst also providing competition for places.

At professional level competition for places should raise everyone's game if the players involved have any pride. Probably one of the main ingredients in a football club is competition for places. That year as far as I'm concerned it was the main ingredient missing. This was obviously down to the enforced cuts and the precarious financial situation the football club was in. Where we finished in the league and my future career were concerned, the consequences were to prove dire.

There was another young midfielder by the name of Mathew Bird. I'd worked with him since he was a small kid, now, four years on, he was almost overnight a young man. He shot up to six feet in no time. I heard the complaint he was a bit one paced but he rarely got caught in possession. What I loved about him was he never gave the ball away, passed and moved well, did his defensive duties, bossed people and always looked to break forward off the front player. If you fast forward and wanted to nitpick on being one paced, so was Cesc Fabregas."Birdy" always did right by the team and there's a lot to be said for that. Too many coaches and managers look at what a player can't do rather than what he can do. Purse was already making headway and we had another competent young defender Glen Wilkie who due to his hard work and intelligence could be utilised anywhere across the back four and as a screening midfield player. Right from schoolboy level Glen had the work ethic and appetite to make the most of his ability and to make himself a player.

There were another young centre half Lee Shearer, two good goalkeepers Luke Weaver and Daryl Sopp, Bird and Rufus in midfield but still no strikers coming through. This I had tried to address. Under these guys in a couple of age groups down due as the next intake of YTS was an excellent left footed centre back who was also a nice size. Scott Honeyball. Scott would have and should have been a professional footballer for years to come, but was mismanaged after I left. He picked up a serious injury after being sent on loan to I think a team in Scandinavia and played continuously for over two years. At eighteen years of age this was lethal. Just as much thought should go into strengthening, conditioning and the correct amount of rest as any coaching at the development stage of a young player. Especially one with a bright future. Someone did well out of it but it wasn't Scott. Scott's brother Danny should also have been signed YTS in my opinion but Bernie Dixson preferred a kid called Jody Loomes. My instincts on Danny were confirmed when he dropped down to non-league and won numerous player of the year awards. In centre midfield on the left another natural left footer Jeff Brazier (now in T.V and broadcasting) and a cracking little right winger Anthony Jones. A year behind them, I'd signed a little left back called Nicky Shorey on Centre of Excellence forms. A two-star nap to be YTS. He absolutely worked his socks off every time I saw him train or play and had a nice left foot.

He seemed determined to make himself a player. These are the type you want at any level. I thought we had a nice little nucleus ongoing, and the makings of a community club. It's only my opinion, past and present, but I feel there should always be a nucleus of home grown in your first team. I wanted to lay the appropriate foundations and build from the bottom up. Since then I've heard time and again about it being a "Community Club" but it seems to me the polar opposite. Chris looked at me like I was mad and let me get on with it. I still attended the Centre of Excellence every Monday and Thursday as well as all youth team games. Chris and I shared the load with the reserves, because mainly it was a good opportunity to look at the youth team lads who doubled up, representing the club at youth and reserve level. One of the best prospects Lee Shearer suffered as I did at Chelsea and started to act out after I left and my services were dispensed with by Barry Hearn. The staff obviously had to concentrate on the first team and he (Shearer) slipped back on all fronts.

Although players are perceived as commodities I like to think I had taken a great deal of interest in the welfare of my players, particularly home grown players. Shearer and Honeyball should have had good careers for years to come as Leyton Orient centre halves. Where the loan of Scott Honeyball was concerned I'm not even sure it served Scott as a player or whether he at least gained from it financially. What's the good of a loan fee if it stunts, or in Scott's case ends a promising career? I learned from bitter experience that as a young player there is as much to be gained from rest, replenishment and strengthening as there is from training and playing. It's always a regret to see good players become the victim of circumstances beyond their control. Where Leyton Orient are concerned, things like bringing through their own players through a quality assured proactive youth policy seem to have played second fiddle to once again, costs spiralling out of control if rumours are correct. Something like eight to ten players have come through in twenty-one years. Scandalous at a club whose average gate, if figures are deemed correct, barely cover two or three player's annual wages. It seems the current owner has brought it full cycle, underpinning the club's losses like Tony Wood did when I was there. Unless there's an agenda I'm not aware of.

It's ironic that at the time, Chris Turner showed no interest whatsoever in younger players coming up behind. Full marks to him and his correct assumption that for him, it was all about his short term survival and ultimately the longer term protection of his future in the game. Ironic in the respect that his first job after Leyton Orient was in youth football under Mark McGhee at Reading. Good luck to him. I don't think I hardly had a crossed word with Chris and as far as I could tell we got on pretty well in our brief time together. He made the most of whatever his assets were and I didn't it would seem.

In the meantime the main concern was trying to get a performance out of what we had. Whether self-induced or the victim of piss poor, prejudiced editing, my reputation was about to be cast with a half time rant in the fixture away to Brentford. It's not until you have the benefit of hindsight, that I looked back to see I was blinded by arrogance, ambition and unwavering self-belief. I must also add to that an embarrassing naiveté on at least three occasions. One of them was not realising that any form of journalism is based on sensationalism. I'd in the future, mistakenly trust the documentary makers to edit what they had in a fair and balanced way, reflecting my contribution to Leyton Orient and its management and survival at every level of the club. Then again, working as coach and manager and relentlessly drilling the first team defensively and in patterns of play, taking training and fitness work, coaching the reserves prior to a fixture, putting on afternoon sessions for the youth team I'd left behind, organising and restructuring the Centre of Excellence, raising money as unpaid commercial manager, scouting and turning up twice weekly to the Centre of Excellence I don't suppose makes for good TV.

The existing squad with three or four signings, three or four loans and kids coming through, I thought could progress, get better and most importantly, be positively influenced and shifted towards a coaching culture and a feeling for the club and its environment that we'd all contribute towards. Healdy was one of the best goalkeepers below the top division and a cracking pro as well as good human being. Was it Robson? "Don't just sign good players, sign good people." I couldn't have a better base to build from than Healdy. Hendon was our right back and Chris and I agreed in pre- season that due to his vocal contribution and the way he trained and tried to play, he be made captain. No doubt he was a competitor and streetwise. As a player I set the standard myself for the type of footballer and human being I wanted around me. Reliability is massive in football. As a player consistency and reliability are what seperates the contenders from the pretenders. That's just my opinion. Under Frank Clark, if I'd gone down the road of certain players, who at the time formed the majority of the squad, Frank might have had three relegations on his C.V instead of two and may not have gone on to achieve what he did in his managerial career, no matter how many times Brian Clough endorsed his capabilities. But for Bill Songhurst looking out for Frank and good pros like me, Dicko, Keith Day, Alan Comfort and Chris Jones it would have been like a holiday camp, a beano, a glorified sixth form piss-up. I looked at Frank, I was twenty-five nearly twenty-six when I joined and after my indiscretions at Chelsea and the let downs and bad luck I'd endured at Millwall and Gillingham, I wanted to do right by him. After all, Frank was the closest I ever got to meeting, apart from George Petchey, a coach or manager who was 100% straight with me.

Even that was spoiled, when after numerous man of the match awards and player of the month awards he'd bollock me to use reverse psychology on players not performing, but couldn't be bollocked because in his words "they couldn't take it, they'd crumble." This highlighted for me the fears and cowardice in managers not convinced by the bravery of their own players. He called it after inviting me in the office ("put a towel round you Sitts and come in the office.") "Man management." I said it's dishonest and I don't agree with you using me as a fucking verbal punch bag. Still he saw fit to play me week in week out and make me captain which got him a few brownie points upstairs taking the place of a player and his captaincy on three times my money. So the point being, your captain can interject in the dressing room, contribute in meetings, and extinguish any unrest, just like I did. Or you can be one of the boys. I had run ins with Hendo undermining myself actually in a sarcastic way because I always believed and still do, in any information I was imparting and coaching ability I had. I openly accused him of patronising me and condescending to me and Leyton Orient having worked at Spurs under supposedly good coaches. Some of his performances were inspiring, some contradicted his street wise persona.

Even if you think you have a good relationship and the person you are dealing with is a solid professional, it doesn't hurt to throw out a little challenge every now and again. Every player needs to know you're watching their every move. I was chomping at the bit and looking forward to getting my own players in. It would have been nice to be in a position where players couldn't play games with my career. At centre half I'd already agreed with Gary Bellamy on an extension to his deal counterbalanced with a cut in money. It seemed after he and Terry Howard thought I used "I" and "Me" in an address to the first team too often for their liking, he came round to my way of thinking. He could see the work I'd put in and where I wanted to take it. Despite Eustace's previous accusations of Bellamy being no more than a barrack room lawyer, even though he was Eustace's signing I thought he was a good guy and good pro. An intelligent centre half who would help Purse, Shearer, Honeyball, Austin and Hague make progress. He always spoke well and gave good advice. So I knew he was on board and could be trusted. I think Bellamy actually recognised that I was a bit more cerebral than I've ever been given credit for. Purse was coming on leaps and bounds and not long for this level, going higher, for in the end, not enough money. I'd already turned down a £50,000 piss take bid from Chelsea. I wish I'd let him go when I was eventually sacked. He went to Bernard Goodall's "friend" Maurice Evans at Oxford for 75k. In my opinion not enough money and lower down, obviously, than Chelsea. Make of that what you will. I thought so much for the acumen and wheeling and dealing of Hearn and Goodall. If you sell, knowing it'll weaken your playing staff, it's got to be for the money you want. If not, you sit tight, keeping both the player and the club, contractually strong. I think when they let him go it was for the sake of cash flow and the small amount of publicity it got.

I can never understand a player being allowed to go for seventy-five thousand pounds even with a large sell on percentage. That's not how I would negotiate. If as a club you have developed the player, why accept a twenty-five per cent to thirty per cent sell on for a one-million-pound player? You end up with two hundred and fifty, plus the original seventy-five, whilst the club who masquerade as "taking a chance" pocket six hundred and seventy-five grand! Me? I'd have been ok as long as I had that conveyor belt turning and I knew it was. I'd have had no problem trusting and playing the youngsters because apart from their ability they were all good people and I'd coached them since they were 13 or 14. The only reason for young players not to be given a chance is because the manager at whatever club doesn't trust them or their education that they've had at that club. If the correct habits are taught, they're good enough athletes and they've been moulded correctly with regards to their mentality, I say throw them in. Coaches and managers, by and large because of the paranoia surrounding their job, are normally pragmatists always erring on the side of caution. But I wasn't at all reluctant to throw in the kids, I got to the stage where I thought could they do or be any worse than the players I'd already inherited? You have to remind yourself nothing grows in the shade.

Kevin Austin was on my retained list. A big, good looking, polite, man mountain. If Hendo's legs were like tree trunks, Kevin's would have been Californian Redwoods. He had the upper body of a light heavyweight boxer. He enjoyed being coached and helped, a good pro. And up there with my old roommate Carl Hoddle as one of the finest human beings I'd ever met in not only football, but life in general. An absolute credit to his family. Terry Howard should have taken my advice, let me protect him and signed for two years for the same money. I'd have worked on him as an individual and taken a personal interest in him. He needed concentrated fitness work and he needed to get back to basics. I'd have influenced his mentality. He needed to cut all the negative shit out of his life. I wouldn't have fucked about with sticking plaster initiatives like seeing a psychologist. I'd have insisted just between me and him that he kept a diary so that feeling good, feeling fit and sharp were the norm rather than the exception. I tried to warn him that a major financial change in the way the club was run was imminent.

Something under Tony Wood, Phil Wallace or Barry Hearn I fully concurred with. The club before me was on the verge of extinction, bankruptcy, and with no sign of any Arab Sheiks on the horizon it's what I meant in the documentary when I said` "it's been done too wrong, for too long." It had veered away from producing home grown talent, towards transfer fees, signing on fees and high wages on players past their prime with absolutely no resale value. Suicide for a club of Orient's standing and the gates they had been historically used to. Along the way me and Tel had a few ups and downs and the conclusion caught on camera, broke my heart for years afterwards. That's my fault. But I was fed up being the meat in a spit roast between him and his unreasonable demands and directors who smiled and shook his hand, then told me at board meetings. "Can't we get rid of him?" If he'd trusted me he'd have got his testimonial. In the meantime he was a player who I'd have liked on board. He could play anywhere in the back four as well as centre midfield. He was also a popular boy in and around the dressing room. Everyone liked Tel including me. But very poignantly as they say from the mouths of babes, Marvin Rufus made a comment after I parted company with him. Marvin said "a good footballer who lets you down is like an unfaithful girlfriend. Imagine you've got this girlfriend, beautiful, intelligent, funny, good conversationalist, dresses nice, smells nice, she's even a good cook, you have great sex. You realise after a while, you've fallen in love." I said "yeah and" "Then you find out she's been unfaithful, she's betrayed you." "So Marv, what's your point?" "Well it's no good having everything going for you if she lets you down is it! It's the same with footballers," he said. This kid was coming up for eighteen. As I walked away I said "Marvin, let's hope after that, you don't let me down." Marvin would have got at least eighteen months off me. Paul Hague, I confess was a disappointment on the fringes of the England Youth squad and fading fast when I took him. I'd have helped him recover and earn a new deal, or he'd have been given a free transfer. As a manager, very few people get it right 100% of the time. I paid five grand for Hague and he'd come up short. But let's put it into perspective. It was nowhere near the money wasted on bad players and bad professionals that I'd seen come and go during my time at the club. And it pales into insignificance when compared to millions, sometimes tens of millions, that has been wasted on signings by so called top class managers at the highest levels of the game. Still this didn't stop Orient supporters from complaining about Hague and using it as another reason to question me. Glen Cockerill I could speak to easily. He was like Bellamy, he had a go for me. He knew when to party and when to get a sweat on. Most of the time anyway. He'd always been a tremendous help and a good pro as well as a good player as far as I could tell. I'd have looked forward to having him around. Ian Bogie was always called and destined to be a poor man's Paul Gascoigne. I loved "Boges." Good footballer, good pro, a good, funny, intelligent guy. He used to get bollocked for not shooting enough. He'd have made a good latter-day Arsenal player, trying to walk the ball into the net!!

Wide left was Mark Dempsey, a fantastic crosser of the ball. He only needed half a yard and boom! He'd deliver. He had the odd trick, would contribute defensively, although not having blistering pace he was a good athlete with a good engine. I'll leave it to supporters to draw their own conclusions, but my eventual dressing room would have had more energy, youth, good people, ability and togetherness instead of a cluster of mercenaries. Good older players who I'd vetted and younger players I'd nurtured for a few years now. They knew me, my humour, when to listen, when to ask and most importantly of all, the difference between when it was time to work and when it was time to be a little more light hearted. I looked upon them as sons. So as I collected defenders and moved forward, it left only Danny Carter wide right or someone else being the more likely outcome as he insisted on taking the other extreme when addressing me. This was on top of his insistence on still signing a seven-day contract. Just a quick observation for you to mull over, it seemed certain people couldn't get their head around me trying to build a team from the back. Although historically, that's what every successful club has always done. There's even books that have been written about it. One in particular compares a football team and the business world. A good football team and a successful company both start from a position of giving nothing away.

Chris wanted us as I've said called "Boss." I said no, I'm ok with Sitts or John, if you call me anything else, just make sure I don't hear it. The YTS lads called me Boss but I'd wink at them and we'd both burst out laughing. But Danny took it to the other extreme as he passed me in the corridor saying "Morning Johnboy" which is what he called me when we were team mates. I suppose it would have been like me saying to Frank Clark when I passed him in the corridor " Alright Frankie baby?" or at Millwall saying to George Petchey " Morning Georgy Porgy." Dear oh dear. I don't know where he ended up when I left, but his insistence on a seven-day contract and the delusional figures he came out with sealed his fate with me. Short term up front, a fit Colin West. A good straight honest pro who'd been around the top and I felt I got on with him and I always found him easy to talk to. He was a guaranteed twenty plus goals a season for that level. But he was shot. After a career that spanned Sunderland, Watford, Sheff Wed and Glasgow Rangers, his body, legs and particularly his ankles were in bits.

I look down and the last time I saw ankles like that they belonged to Peter Osgood. A sturdy, reliable trainer, good listener, good application to strategy, but his career had taken its toll on him. But yet again he tried to have a go for us. If we nicked a goal, it was usually Westy. Off the field he was a top character, good bloke, good pro and family man. Barry Lakin a good pro and solid performer in midfield, but if I parted with Hendon, could be another option at right back. Mark Warren's assets were pace and power. I could utilise him at centre forward. So, along with Rufus, Shearer, Wilkie, Bird and the signings hopefully of Fortune-West, Read on loan from Arsenal and Sean Devine from Fisher, the squad would have taken shape and leaned more heavily towards the youngsters that I wanted. Obviously Leo F. West and Devine were, I hoped, going to be long term signings to bolster the attack. If it all came together we could survive, consolidate and push on. Apart from a sprinkling of experience, I wanted no one over the age of twenty five. To me it didn't take any working out especially at a club like Leyton Orient.

The only real reason for this chapter is because contrary to one or two opinions that mine and Chris' management style was "crazy" I like to think I've given you a brief insight into not only my forward planning, but the forward planning involved in managing a football club. Earmarking players should, and probably does, happen on a weekly if not daily basis. You should always be looking to improve things, including yourself. But I hope you also begin to appreciate the daily, weekly and monthly fire fighting that Chris and I were having to perform. This was to enable the club to survive on a weekly basis, pay the bills and staff wages.

A vital period was now approaching. Yet again. As I sat through Christmas Eve watching my kids get excited I was happy that players had asked for a Christmas morning and Christmas Day with their families electing to have a short session on Christmas Night under the floodlights at the main ground. It's only relevant because of what I was accused of, namely the sixty-five min session was too long, before our 11.30am KO to Brentford the following day, Boxing Day. I'll talk you through my day, then the session and you can make your own mind up if the 3-0 capitulation inside twenty-five mins at Brentford was as a consequence of a sixty-five minute training session.

At Christmas I did the normal tradition that I'd always done. It started with Midnight Mass Christmas Eve, joining my ma- in-law at the local Greek Orthodox Church out of respect really. I think I'm spiritual without being religious. I'm C of E but was blessed in a Greek Orthodox Church to fill a criteria required for us being married in my wife's religion. Then, when my father-in- law got home from his work as a chef we'd have a night cap, then home to bed to be awoken by three very excited kids opening their presents at silly o'clock Xmas morning. Me and my wife like toast and smoked salmon on Christmas morning with a pot of the best coffee. Then we go off to pay our respects to the graves of my Mum and Grandad. That's before we get to the Greek version of the food part of Christmas Day!!! Normally about six courses, followed by continuous grazing for the rest of the day. Why explain this?

Well I think it's totally relevant to the evening session we had and the fact I'd had a full day as well as trying to generate a bit of enthusiasm for the task at hand. Sadly lacking in quite a few of the players. Rather than dictate I gave the choice of a full day with their families and kids. I let the lads choose. And so an early evening session it was. I actually thought the timing lent itself to the lads maybe having their supper, a bath, a nightcap and a good rest at home. The main thing being a good night's sleep. After a prelim stretch and a very light jog, ten to fifteen minutes max, we walked through Brentford's set pieces and their shape. We'd already rehearsed our patterns, set pieces and defending the day before. I picked up the thread and continued the warm up with the balls. We then had a SSG for fifteen minutes. All of this was on a clock and done moving efficiently through each part of the session. How it should be for every session in my opinion. We parted company with I thought no problem. The next day I sensed nothing different on boarding the coach, changing, warming up and then as the game kicked off. I think with the exception of Bellamy, Bogie and ironically a poorly protected and livid Paul Heald in goal, no one performed. Every other player let down every Orient supporter who got out of bed, left their Christmas celebrations and their families to come and support us. On camera unfortunately, I went ballistic. When I remarked "forget the technical shit" obviously it's slightly contradictory, because it's vitally important. Anyone with half a brain will know full well what I meant.

I was questioning the player's pride. The pre-agreed verbal contract that the players had agreed with me and Chris, concerning patterns of play, defensive strategies, set pieces and retention of the shape of the side had been poorly applied, verging on discarded. It's as if the players brains were like the scrambled eggs I had that morning. So coupled with a few players whose pulse and having a heartbeat could be called into question, it was now about heart, pride and respectability. But it was fast lurching towards, and I don't know why, players having no respect for themselves, for each other, for me and Chris, for the club and despite what they say, or had said, the supporters. It was a nightmare as all the quality coaching and hard work I'd put in around the club blew up in my face. On the Channel 4 documentary edited and condensed for just 50 minutes to accommodate adverts it looks like I was permanently angry. I should have used Tiverton and the 3-1 win as a gee, but opted to look for perfection, needlessly criticising and nit picking, so I admit I was wrong. Sometimes you should just settle for the victory and I have come to realise that management and coaching is sometimes just as much about what you don't say, as it is about what you do say. Barring a few terse comments after the Barnet cup defeat and throwing away a 2-1 lead at Oxford to lose two goals in a couple of minutes and lose the game 3-2 it was a long way forward to now and me flipping my lid. I said there's no players any more, probably a strong, harsh, generalisation. But echoed to a degree in Harry Rednapp's book. He talks of the few weeks he was out of a job after Spurs. He spoke to George Graham and Joe Royle in particular, who remarked when he made their acquaintance that maybe it was meant to be, it was right that they couldn't get back in, because to quote Joe Royle "there are too many players who don't give a fuck anymore Harry." So I'd said the same thing eighteen years earlier and was in one paper who reviewed the C4 doc, perceived as a "pitiable ogre." If that's the case, then the journalist concerned was in my book a lazy ignoramus. He only had to call me for me to justify what I'd said. Or maybe he was lazily endorsing Hearn's ultimate decision to part company. Which was still very much in the future as we were still awaiting the decision of Phil Wallace whether to take over or not. In the meantime I felt ready to burst, the frustration was almost unbelievable. I'd always been decisive and knew what I was doing and where I was going.

So with the best case scenario in mind, I'd been trying to get things done and get them done now and that my services would be retained. I'd started to have an eye on things to come as well as the day to day fire fighting. I'd earmarked players and their assets and their compatibility to the club, the new culture I wanted to put in place and just as importantly, whether they could help in the seismic shift needed in moving away from turning up for wages, ticking over and underachieving to some semblance of success, relative to the club's standing. But I think as much as anything, giving supporters hope and a belief in knowing that their team would never give up. I'd made a living as a player with that as one of my assets.

It's been said that over the years a team generally reflects some of the traits and composites that make the manager, or as we have since headed there, the head coach. I have to say definitely not in my case. I will admit though I should have handled certain situations a bit better. If however there are two major mistakes I made it was expecting players to approach training and games the way I did and on the odd occasion being unforgiving.

I think we can take that as read the work ethic inside parts of the club, the football intelligence of some of the players, their effort, application, will and determination to win, or at least not get beat, was at this juncture, poles apart from me and how I felt about football and what I was hoping to achieve in the game. The worst thing right up there as a player, coach, or manager, is to be lacking in my opinion, ambition. After ambition comes the task of trying to turn that ambition into reality. The realisation of a dream. I've gone on record, that I'd have been disappointed in myself and fallen on my sword, if in the future, I hadn't been a steward of some sort of success relative to the club's standing, including producing mostly our own players, as well as cup runs and promotions. After all, I know players and managers are well rewarded, but they all start out just like supporters... chasing a dream.

At around the same time as earmarking players for my retained list and recruitment I thought I was putting together a nice little hard working, tight knit staff. We now had two physios, having given Tony Flynn his first full time job in football as the club's kit man, it was credit to Flynny that he was a grafter, who continuously upgraded his qualifications and was a thorough and competent physio also. A big plus for me and the club. Tony always came across well and was humorous and approachable, always looking to help and went, like all of us, except a few of the players, above and beyond the call of duty. Steve Shorey approached me and Chris for Bernie Dixson's job. For the time being, I let him get on with it. He fulfilled all of his professional obligations and because of his poor pay, kept up his other part time job outside the game. Apart from the fact he was coping well how could I say no? Like everyone, he had bills to pay. I could sympathise. A few years later I bumped into "Flynny" who was still physio at Orient under Martin Ling. I turned up with Enfield to play the O's in a friendly. We had a mixture of triallists and players returning from injury and Orient played a team consisting of first team players coming back from injury and youngsters. I think we lost 3-1 and it seems Tony Flynn went down the same road as Steve Shorey some years later. As I smiled and extended my hand to shake his, despite giving him his first full time job in football, "Flynny " said "Alright Son."

It wasn't the Tony Flynn I had known and I felt insulted. I was trying with every ounce of knowledge, hard work and belief I had, to build some sort of future. My choice for future Youth Development Officer and Centre of Excellence Director was a good coach, good administrator, good with people and knew a player; Les Reed, who I'd met as a staff coach for the F.A. He wasn't renegotiating with the

F.A. and at the time wasn't happy there and I saw an opportunity to procure a good all rounder. He was approachable, knowledgeable and had a work ethic. Further down the line, for the record, when I was sacked and I obviously couldn't appoint Les who'd agreed a drop in his wages and working conditions to get a foothold in the pro game, Les was retained by the F.A. I think he ended up getting a settlement when they parted company. He was then employed in a couple of roles, one of which was a disastrous spell as manager of Charlton. His credibility, (remember what I said?) shot to pieces in the press, saying "who's Les Reed?" My head youth coach, was going to be Neil Banfield. Previously employed by Charlton, but anxious to exercise his coaching ability back in the pro game. He'd worked with Cartwright, after a brief playing career at Crystal Palace, Orient and in Australia, with Charlton's age groups. From ten year olds, through to the youth team. I arranged a meeting with him in a wine bar, called "Whipps" in Leytonstone somewhere.

He talked straight, knew the game and we'd come through our badges together. He met my other criteria of wanting a chance and being ambitious. He was determined to do well. You need hunger on board in my opinion in any organisation and in football I think it's helpful if it's transferred through the club and through to the players. I probably didn't explain myself too well on a YouTube interview, when without naming Neil, I implied that it was wrong of me to be out of the game and roughly at the last count, he'd been at Arsenal, holding down various coaching positions for nearly two decades. With all that Neil at Arsenal and Les Reed has achieved at Southampton I have to credit myself and my judgement on those two in particular. In no way have I ever been envious or would I ever be, of anyone's success. It was aimed more at football clubs who failed to forgive me and help educate and rehabilitate me and turned their backs completely on any coaching and organisational ability I had. Maybe it was the documentary, maybe it wasn't enough networking, maybe it was my supposed prickly disposition or maybe it was a combination of all three, who knows? In the end I had to reluctantly pick up the phone to Mick Maguire at the PFA for their help in financing courses so I could reinvent myself and get a living.

Not to put too fine a point on it, because of my anger and frustrations, that manifested themselves in my language and temper tantrums I was an outcast, a leper, at least those were my future prospects. No bung scandal, no cocaine, no alcoholism, no gambling addiction, no kerb crawling, no underage sex, just a few of the crimes forgiven over and above my crime of wanting to save a club from administration and wanting to win football matches. My crime was allowing my frustration to boil over when neither seemed likely. But for now Les and Neil were on board and ready as soon as my longer term future was in place to commit. My GK coach through the C of E age groups was Micky Payne.

Different class, great GK sessions, brimming with good coaching, enthusiasm, and humour. He was ably assisted by Lloyd Scott. I also asked Alex Welsh but he was already at Arsenal helping their young GK's.

Down the line I let Lloyd Scott go when he was at a minimum duplicitous. I asked him to watch a reserve game at West Ham and do a report on a player. He said he couldn't as a fireman he was on shift. I went to the game myself and who was sitting in the directors' box? Lloyd Scott. I asked him what he was doing there and he told me he was doing a report for Peter Shilton, then manager of Plymouth. I said "why?" He said "because he pays more expenses."

I said "I pay your coaching fees at the Centre of Excellence and expenses for scouting, what more do you want? With us, you'd have two important jobs." I kept my cool and dismissed him the next day.I let him go, giving him an undeserved explanation that you can't serve two guvnors or run with deer and hunt with the hounds. We shook hands and that was that.

I then called all the coaches together and told them I expect 100% loyalty to me and the club. They said fair enough Sitts, at least we all know where we stand. From the following Centre of Excellence season, I'd agreed for Neil to take the youth team and the U/16's so he could monitor the next intake of YTS and give it some continuity. The other age groups could be staggered so that they had the same coach in charge, staying with the players for two years. At U/15 and U/14 I had Tom Loizou earmarked for the job. He could work in tandem with Neil, promoting players who shone and had made good progress. He had a patience, calmness and approachability. The kids would relax and play under him, and be taught well. Tom actually did his full badge under Les Reed.

It was important to me that they relaxed and produced their best. Or at least be given the chance to do so. My other main coaches included a guy called Steve Embleton. From U/10 to U/13's would have been Steve's remit. He was superb to watch especially with the real young players. He coached good information and had a lovely, gentle manner with them. It also helped that he was roughly the same height, I think it helped the kids relate to him. Coaching wise Steve was my pocket dynamo. But on a serious note, I had it all ready and waiting. The common denominators are running right through the group of men I wanted on board. Knowledgeable, able coaches, good work ethic and humour, all proper people. I knew all the age groups would have been in good hands. Where did that leave Steve Shorey? Well, I wanted him retained as a scout and I thought his speciality was non-league. He would have been salaried doubling as Centre of Excellence assistant director to Les. But his main remit would have been recruiting scouts and building a scouting network, doing match reports on future opponents and players we were monitoring. So, I thought going forward, a good tight knit group of staff. Phil Wallace even asked my plans and opinions on how to take it forward if he took over. It wasn't to be. After the Boxing Day debacle at Brentford I thought along with Chris, maybe the players should be given a chance to redeem themselves and because of lack of players there was only one change we could make anyway.

I've always thought a player should have enough respect for himself to be the best professional he can be and be given a chance to turn his form around along with the results. I can only look with the benefit of hindsight and in a few cases there were some genuine boys who I should have praised more but they got cancelled out by the players not sharing the load. To work very hard at your organisation, fitness and team strategies as I've said should be a minimum prerequisite, especially if you find yourself in the lower divisions. Sometimes the dividing line, the margins, call them what you want, are wafer thin, but for everyone involved, there's normally a couple of valid reasons why you're not at Liverpool, Arsenal or Man Utd and you're at a lower division club. So it's imperative that a team ethic, the greater good of the club, and listening to your leader is what everyone buys into.

CHAPTER FOURTEEN
White Rabbit

Just to re-iterate I tried to steer Terry Howard in the right direction. The minimum benefit to Terry if he had listened or taken on board what I advised him and tried to do for him would have been fewer visits to the bookies or the dog track. I even know of one story at the very top of the game where a manager gave everyone a day off except for his assistant and a player who was brought in to keep him away from the bookmakers and off cocaine and drink. They ran the bollocks off him instead. Think about what I have just said, the absolute top echelon of the game. As I approached the time at the turn of the year that is of paramount importance to where the team might eventually finish it also coincided with the main incident that was to cost me a friendship or acquaintance, the dressing room, and ultimately any chance of continuing to be employed at Leyton Orient or in football in general.

It had been festering for a while and as I've remarked I was sick of the directors and players and their blatant duplicity and disregard for me and the club. I could be forgiven for thinking that some of the players and directors would have struggled with pandiculation. Although I'd only "lost it" three or four times during the season one of them not particularly badly after the cup victory at Tiverton it had all been caught on camera. I didn't know until a long time after that Chris had sought advice and elected to say little and stay out of camera shot. So yours truly carried the can and as I've said the day to day nature of the six jobs I was juggling and informative, bright and effervescent though it was, the coaching wasn't sensationalist enough for TV. On top of that despite what he thought I tried to protect Terry Howard. I thought it's part of the duty of a manager and coach to protect players from themselves sometimes. Although most people and the players involved rarely see past themselves. Contrary to popular belief I am patient, giving and helpful. But like everyone else I have a cut off point. As a coach or manager you have to give players time but you can't let that privilege be abused. The game waits for nobody.

I still don't see the problem though. If you the supporter had a business that you'd put me in charge of and although over simplistic I caught someone who failed to commit to our project, our business, kept his options for employment elsewhere open and in the meantime was taking £750 a week, whilst cheekily he was insisting he was worth 30% more plus a gratuity for working there (my analogy for a rise plus a testimonial) you'd probably wonder why it was I hadn't sacked him or at least taken the relevant industrial action. I couldn't then and I still can't now fathom why it is so many supported him and felt sorry for him. Don't get me wrong, not for one minute do I want to be seen as weak or having a problem with making unpopular decisions. This was all done on a purely professional basis and if it made me disliked, I could to live with it. Although all I actually did was utilise the club's option of serving two weeks' notice after Terry Howard insisted on signing a seven-day contract. I never ever said "sacked." That term "sacked" was down to the sensationalist editing of the C4 documentary maker and people's own conclusions. With hindsight my mistake was not doing it behind closed doors within the confines of my office. My mind wondered back subconsciously probably, to when Frank Clark bollocked one of his best players (me) to try and get a reaction out of others who sometimes could have been questioned on whether they had a pulse or not. A little adrenaline rush to inject some urgency should never hurt anyone. Least of all supposed men in a professional football environment.

In Terry Howard's book full of contradictions, he opens himself up completely to my thoughts, impressions of him and accusations that I levelled at him based on his lifestyle alone. He was over years, not just the ten months I was in charge, although looking back I was never really in charge but you know what I mean, taking the supporters, the club and his privileged profession for granted. In blunt terms I thought he had rarely been the best he could be. As a coach or manager it was no good to me. I had seen both sides of the fence and after indiscretions as a younger player I knew I had given everything for the managers I'd played for.

Before the incident he'd already asked, yes asked, to be substituted on New Year's Eve's away to Crewe. I held my tongue as I had for months until that incident that was to banish me from football forever. Even on YouTube to give you an idea of the treachery and duplicity that surrounded me the arty, pseudo intellectual, who'd lied her way through the door saying that she had been commissioned by Channel 4 is consoling Terry Howard, asking "you okay? Are you alright?" While slagging off most people's conduct around the club to Chris Turner and myself. On the positive side it gave a young defender Glen Wilkie a chance to be promoted from the youth team and travel with the first team squad and make his debut. If ever there was a polar opposite. Wilkie had earned a YTS and a one year pro contract through sheer hard work, application, determination, ability and football intelligence that he was happy to keep adding to because he enjoyed being coached. Still, he only had to come on for Terry against Danny Murphy.

"Ooh" (the title of Terry Howard's book) a chapter was dedicated to me and Chris Turner I should reciprocate and with the facts help redress the balance. It's merely a reckoning not more time wasted on an individual. I'm bigger than that, but it's important to me that you have the facts.

He (Terry Howard) openly admits that he had a growing problem, in my opinion having read his book for the first time in 2013 I thought it was a massive problem not a growing one, with gambling, among other things which I'll come to. I can honestly say that as a teammate, a coach, or manager, I never knew. He says he was ever present at Romford dogs, Monday, Wednesday and Friday (of all days). Walthamstow Tuesday, Thursday, Saturday interspersed with Hackney on a couple of afternoons.

I'll come to my point of view quickly, when you add Hollywood's night club and Charlie Chan's as well I have to ask Terry and O's supporters if it's the life an athlete, although you'd never accuse Terry of being an athlete, should be leading? Training, rest, preparation, games, recovery and correct refuelling and replenishment are what should be on your mind during the football season. Is it too much to ask a player to live seriously for a while? What you do, if you live your life right to give you the best chance of success in the little down time you have left is up to you. May I suggest in the brief window of your life when you are supposed to be a professional sports person if you do things correctly with regards to the above there's very little time left for anything that would have a negative effect. That kind of lifestyle can only ever be destructive to you, your career, your friends and family. I'd always conveyed the message and lived a life where when your football or any athletic career is over, you can eat, drink, gamble and do whatever you want in the thirty to fifty year "afterlife." I've always called it the "afterlife" because having lived it, once you come out of professional sport, for me it's been a massive downer and almost a countdown to death. Nothing can ever replace the few highs I experienced. Weaker men than me who can't handle it go off the rails, although we've all got or had weaknesses. I don't think it's too much to ask for a privileged footballers lifestyle to be compensated by someone just being asked to be professional and the best that you can be in what is after all a short career and a brief time in your life. Live it seriously, take it seriously and you never know what you might achieve. I'll be perfectly honest, I've got very little time for human weakness and the numerous temptations. I've discussed it at length with my wife and children. You know you're at home when you've found someone who you can trust with your innermost thoughts and feelings. Anyway we are all agreed that whatever the addiction, it starts with temptation. Over simplistic I know but you actually have to push yourself through a barrier. As far as I'm concerned you actually have to climb a mountain of self destruction to reach the summit. Then what? People who started out as sensible people look down from the peak and say "I shouldn't have climbed all this way... can you help me?" Life is already too short, and too few people are priveleged so why make life harder for yourself by spunking money on drink, drugs, gambling and anything else you can think of that ensures you become a statistic? I think the higher you go, the better the player, the better the person, the less motivating they need.

Oh well I suppose it takes all sorts. The modern game now is ruthless in its efficiency when finding out players who have not lived right, trained right, prepared right and consistently played well. The flip side is even on the side of modern day players. Especially at the highest level. They seem well paid for seventy minutes' football and are then subbed, then rested in squad rotation. I'd hazard a guess some play the equivalent of half a season. Back then I needed all hands performing at a competent level on deck. At Leyton Orient that season, I knew, everyone knew unless it was someone either totally selfish or totally out of touch with reality, that we needed all hands to the pump, no passengers, everyone on the same page, up for the fight and up for the challenge of a full season. That is what basically constituted my pre-season address to the players when they reported back for training.

I'll leave supporters, particularly Leyton Orient supporters, to read the facts and draw their own conclusions. Hopefully your intelligence won't feel insulted like mine was as you wade through the nonsensical micro management and problems that presented themselves. Although to be fair to Terry he wasn't the only problem or even dare I say it the biggest problem. Let me give you another for instance of the type of charmless animal I inherited who was signed without any form of due diligence regarding his character. The people involved think I don't know, but a regular occurrence by a couple of regular liberty takers, one of whom was a so called member of staff, was a long drink after a home game. This was followed by the staff member driving the club's minicoach to Mile End Road or Brick Lane for a curry with players on board, all two thirds pissed. Can you imagine the headline if there had been a fatality? Anyway a player so drunk he was barely coherent thought it would be a good idea to urinate over the seats.

Seats occupied by the youth team and their parents on a Saturday morning. I felt sorry for that minibus, it had been used to deliver post, brochures and parcels by the same member of staff who drove them to Brick Lane and was moonlighting on the side and also been used to cart building materials (at the club's expense) for a previous staff member to build his conservatory. It was me and my youth team who swept the spilled sand and cement after it was used and left under the stand by the groundsman but I'm not sure we'd have fancied shampooing the seats to rid them of the smell of a particular player's ablutions. See what I mean? It's pointless and futile to name the player who urinated on the seats and totally disrespected the club, staff and club facilities, but suffice to say I got very little help and very few performances from a player almost permanently injured, and lucky to be on the contract he was on in professional football. I wanted and expected more from such a player who was one more who came from a supposed higher level, bigger club and in my opinion patronised and condescended to Leyton Orient and the club's supporters. I promise you this, don't think for one minute I wouldn't have dealt with it. I'm not knee jerk, again contrary to popular opinion, I couldn't see the sense in decimating an already small staff and small playing squad. I was hoping to work through it all and get my ducks in a row.

But, let's stick to the topic at hand and a long overdue reply to TH and his disciples. My honest opinion is, it's not only the wrong way to live as a footballer, to me, as someone who has seen the downside of gambling with my own father and father-in-law, it seems to me a waste of valuable time, life and leisure time. Time that could be used more constructively. Anyway for this he turned to a sports psychologist. Reading between the lines he had limited success acting as a guinea pig for Peter Eustace. At the time I had left the club as a player and was coaching at the Centre of Excellence.

I thought Terry's explanation of the guy's methods (his name was Jack Lamport Mitchell and when I was reintroduced into the fold as youth coach I met him) are in my opinion laughable. "If you could imagine yourself as any animal what would it be and why?" (Question from Jack) Terry Howard picked a Tiger. He was about to cite the fact it was beautiful but stopped at and settled for "because they're big and strong." Jack then gave to Terry's self-confessed amusement an imaginary commentary on an imaginary match. "Terry Howard's running up the tunnel onto the pitch he looks good, looks the part, looks ready" and two players Terry Howard and ironically Danny Carter tore the opposition apart. 2 v 11 and their passes, crosses and goals won the make believe game 3-0.

Terry said he couldn't confide in anyone. No girlfriend and he didn't want to burden his family. As a team mate I always thought Terry and his family were loving and close. So why not? Especially as further down the line his sister was supposedly wanting to slap me after I told her little brother a few home truths and fucked him off. Which would have been a shame as I had always got on with Terry's sister and brother-in-law. Maybe that was the problem, a 28-year-old man hiding behind his sister. Anyway at the time when Eustace asked my opinion as his youth coach I didn't subscribe to it or the methods. I was, and still am open minded but when I asked Lamport-Mitchell for a specimen session in front of Eustace, Turner and Bernie Dixson sitting on the running track at Brisbane Road it went totally against how you'd coach a forward young or old, in his finishing. I thought the whole thing was a nonsense. With Terry the proof of the pudding is in the eating. He recommended to Eustace it was no good to the lads "they'd probably take the piss" and for one session, they absolutely did. So no more group sessions then! Even after the initial impact, help, or in my opinion, novelty value success with Terry Howard, even he says it wore thin.

I just think Eustace had run out of ideas, options and alternatives for Terry Howard and the group and became exasperated. For the record his specimen session for forwards to me, then youth coach, consisted of visualising an area behind the goal you're aiming for and focusing on power, strike the ball to burst the net, to hit a target beyond the goal and because of the pace of the ball it would go past the goalkeeper. Totally against things like "hit the target," "force a minimum of a save from the goalkeeper," "make him work," "accuracy before power," "try and find the corners," " pass the ball into the net," depending on your session, etc. etc. He spoke total bollocks. Total fucking garbage. And I said so. I told Eustace it was an emotional crutch. Another reason or excuse for players to fail. "How?" I was asked. I said "well for one, what if the session itself doesn't go well? It puts doubts in the mind of someone already full of doubts. Anyway I can give more relevant, truthful, factual reasons not to have it on board." Chris and Peter asked "what are they?" Almost in unison. "By the way you prepare, the way you train, the way you play, you give yourself belief." For me personally as a player it was about repetition, good habits and doing extras on the training field. I went on to say "No psychologist controls the ball, passes, heads, tackles, crosses, shoots, bosses teammates, reads the game. You do. It's the repetition in training, concentration, application..." and to their laughs I said "I've never heard of a fucking psychologist who'll do pre-season for you either." As far as I'm concerned it wouldn't be right for someone else to tell me as a man, a professional footballer what I can do. Particularly what

I've been able to do since I was a kid. This is where my take on coaching comes in. If a player is having problems I've always thought my duty as a coach and a friend is to strip the game down to simplify it. Any psychological barrier can be overcome with the correct coaching on the training field. In a game where there are more variables than any other sport I think it's ludicrous to increase or add to the variables. The only time you want imagination is from your coach, manager or midfield and forward players.

But each to their own. I've tried to live and let live although for me you rely on yourself not someone else. I would never need a psychologist to get me to believe I can or might be able to do something although on occasions my wife has said I might need a psychiatrist. Next up he admits to being a regular contract rebel. Funny that. Apparently it wasn't new when I was in charge. Things that occur to me are if you're that good and I humbly say it as a lower division player myself involved in three transfers, why no posse of clubs banging your door down when you're out of contact? During their time Clark and Eustace said the players who hadn't re-signed wouldn't be considered for selection. With injuries and a softening stance on both sides, Terry Howard signed and played. Why didn't they sell him and replace him? Maybe there were no takers. Anyway with Terry Howard on a seven-day contract I never had that luxury. All I could manage, after he had an appalling pre-season was to leave him out of the opening game of the season vs Birmingham. We won. That was short lived as he sat there laughing at the 4-0 first leg defeat in the League Cup vs Barnet saying to his fellow contract rebel Carter "better shine our boots Dan." Whilst taking the piss out of team mates. He added that he was glad we "had the arse ripped out of us..." Nice eh? Or maybe that's what O's supporters deserved. In my opinion it's not the action of someone who supposedly loves the club and has a respectful relationship with his team mates, the club and its supporters. You know, the ones who paid his wages. For a long time now since I've had a chance to reflect on being out of the game I'm in no doubt that for some players their loud, brash and supposed effervescent larger than life personality went a long way to earning them new contracts at clubs. It's the same with managers, coaches and pundits. As I have got older and matured I replay a lot of things that happened in my life and the people involved. I've drawn the conclusion that a tremendous amount of people got by on sheer "front." You'd be surprised how sheer bravado, especially the amount I have come across in football, can mask a lack of ability and professionalism. I can tell you it wasn't their ability and athleticism. I didn't and still don't get it. Maybe I was wrong at Chelsea, Millwall, Gillingham and Leyton Orient. I should have been louder and strutted around thinking I was the dog's bollocks or Jack the biscuit. With hindsight there are plenty of people I have come across, and after meeting them walked away wishing that I also had a diploma from the university of bravado and sheer front that they went to.

It's important to me to redress the balance to answer some diabolical accusations. It's not about justifying any decisions. Far from it. a. we're years on, but b and more importantly, you can only try and educate and I'm sorry if that sounds at all patronising, supporters, players and anyone interested enough in football to care. Refusing to jump fences has cost me work. As a manager you can't explain and justify every single decision whether minor or major. Which ironically is what I am actually doing now. I got to the stage where the fences I refused to jump and this was in non-league not pro level, were justifying myself to a chairman that you were taking his club in the right direction. To highlight this I resigned from my last job when the chairman approached me after four games and said "I'm not 100% happy with the way we are playing." At the time we had played four, won three, drawn one, scored twelve, conceded two and were second in the league. I drew the conclusion and told the chairman that if this is what you are like now it begs the question what kind of support can I expect if we lost three on the spin? It's probably the only time in my life I have been unprofessional. In training on the Thursday I let the lads have an eight a side instead of coaching and organising. I then fulfilled the fixture on Saturday and resigned immediately afterwards. Ever since I can remember and at one stage in my playing career I include myself, sometimes supporters, players and even chairmen just don't know what is good for them.

Call it naivety on my part but I won't lay down to someone else's idea of a football utopia because very few players are open minded enough to look past themselves and consider anything that might be for the greater good. In the modern day game with so many people to please, too much time is spent on shallow kidology rather than profound information. With experience and hindsight I'll concede maybe it should be both. I know one thing you can't waste time on a little boy inside a man's body. Ontopof thatatall levels, andthe highest level in particular, you can't please everyone. I sometimes shake my head in disbelief as I listen to phone-ins. Directors, supporters, agents, players... what next? Groundsman? Laundry man? the list is endless. Normally it's about whether a player is fit and do they play? If the answer to both is yes, any observations they make are normally cocooned in with does it benefit them and their daily ideal world. There's not enough hours in the day to be justifying all your methods and decisions to staff, directors, supporters, players and least of all Terry Howard. I suppose dedicating a whole chapter to it all is slightly contradictory but I have to set things right it's just the way I am.

This is about a reckoning. Putting my side. Hopefully you'll see every point as a tangible, common sense counter to the almost acidic accusations made by Terry Howard in his book directed at me and Turner. Consider all sides and decide for yourself how wide of the mark, if any of it was, the split second decisions I was constantly making whilst working above and beyond my remit to stave off liquidation and ensure people got paid, trained properly and competed in games. But having said that, you do what you can and constantly justifying every little or sometimes larger decision could have been sniffed out as a weakness by certain players. You must use the facts at your disposal, think it through then be assured and decisive.

In his own book Howard makes comments about "Some old Orient" after throwing a lead away and eventually losing to Stoke. He rightly protests about two players being hit by Eustace (Sam Kitchen and Simon Livett). He remarks that after a defeat in a midweek game vs Port Vale when players were fit, the squad were brought in and Eustace ran the bollocks off of them saying unless you go over the technical stuff to eradicate mistakes just running solves nothing. So, we agree on three things already. I never hit anyone, punished players with running, and I actually echoed Terry's own thoughts in the footage of C4 doc, saying actually "Typical Leyton Orient" after winning two then failing to keep run going with a below par, substandard performance. In my defence I was a consistently good coach who wanted to work with consistently good players. That's the frustration.

He levels criticism at Eustace for chopping and changing. Failing to study it and find an interpretation of why. My only variety was in training. Eustace actually was very sparing with his praise. Another Terry Howard accusation. I was usually full of praise for anyone who actually just played with a bit of energy and passion. TH complains that there was no consistency in selection and systems were not persevered with, players shifted around etc., etc. under Eustace. Makes you wonder what excuse players will look for next doesn't it? When I played I didn't give a fuck what the system was or where I played as long as I was in the starting eleven. My education at Chelsea ensured I could play within any system that was coached. Just as importantly I understood it. Under me, with fourteen then eventually sixteen outfield players, the team practically picked itself. Which I'd suggest is a different kind of problem. I can't stress strongly enough you must have competition for places, or worst case scenario at least some cover, which we never had.

I'm shocked that Terry least of all would want to accuse me and Chris of being or feeling threatened by Trevor Putney, something to do with him "being a giggle" doing things like training, inevitably, (quote) "in his own sweet way." It seems on this occasion, looking after your own best interests in terms of contract, fitness and playing regularly escaped TH, who said Putney's larger than life character was too much for me and Chris to handle. Along with a lot of other stuff it's contradictory. TH cites the gambles (numerous) on signings and good contracts for players made by Eustace that in the end blew up in his face and cost him his job. Of which TH might like to know, Putney was one. Putney was thirty four, no resale value, twenty games plus over nearly three years for a deal costing O's £165000. If you shave off the odd game and odd £5000, I'd worked it out that Trevor Putney cost £8000 a game. Don't forget at this stage Orient were losing £10000 a week. Complete madness in my opinion.

I actually said at the time to a Director " this is crazy, for eight grand a game you probably could have got Maradona on loan." But you decide. This is because Trevor was rarely fit. At the same time I find it strange that the impact it had on TH and one or two others who were already at the club for years, was to them palatable as it left the cupboard bare for them to get any rise when negotiating. And for the record, I absolutely don't mind any sort of so called big character. I've seen and known enough. As long as they are a good big character. Back to Bobby Robson's "sign good people" again. Trevor in my opinion, treated Orient, the supporters and team mates as a joke for his own personal amusement. Not get the result, get the job done, then we'll party. Aside from the fact that the club and his contract was of no value to Orient short, medium or long term, I think for him it was a latter-day social, accompanied by an Atm in the twilight of his career. As a coach and manager I recognise the fact that you need big characters in training and in the dressing room to buy into the organisation and passion you bring as a coach. You need big characters around you as a coach who you can trust to lead and be a mouthpiece in training and games on your behalf. You need big characters to be a leader in matches, to show they'll compete, and stand up and be counted and never give in.

Big characters get a grip on a game. Sometimes almost single handedly. The history of football is littered down the decades with them at every club at every level. For me TP was no more than disruptive, an irritation, a comedy act. So what did I have to fear? TH's definition of a character, is I'd suggest, different from mine, and I'd say most other coaches and managers.

Quite recently I had a very surprising and touching phone call from Vinnie Jones in Los Angeles. Towards the end of the conversation he said something that absolutely blew me away: "I'll tell you what John, I'd have played for you... they just didn't get it..." There's a saying, I may have read it or heard it, but being me I stored it mentally. "It's better to have character than be a character." I think it's fair to say that if you go deep enough and take a long hard look at Vinnie Jones, he is typical of that saying. He has the type of character whereby he has demanded of himself that he get the absolute maximum out of his life and his ability.

I will go on record now and debate until Armageddon one thing Putney wasn't and that was treated badly. If a player is not selected it can normally be traced back to the way he conducts himself, the way he trains and the way he plays. In the end TP was signed too old, he had a bad hamstring injury in his first year, couldn't run, didn't train well and fucked about. What did they expect me to do? Let it become Butlin's with Putney chief Redcoat or Bluecoat, whatever they wear? There's no way you can have that in a football club. I was one who took my profession seriously.

We had a couple of civilised chats that culminated in him going to Colchester on loan and play for his ex-team mate at Ipswich George Burley. To me it was like getting rid of a nasty smell in your lounge. A better environment to train in, with no nonsensical comedy routine going on while you're trying to work. Ships that pass in the night. I'm sure Trevor was happier too, because he could use the same material on a new audience.

For me there's plenty of time before training and after training and in hotels before games and over pre-match meals to be conversant, a wise cracking village idiot. But when warming up to get your body ready for training or in preparation for a game, is it too much to ask for any player to knuckle down and concentrate on his work and that of his team mates and reproduce what the coach has shown or told him? For some, it seems even 10-12 hours a week is too much. But that's always been the case and still is, including up to two games per week, even though quite a few players play the equivalent of half a season.

TH gets all dewy eyed and romantic when breaching the subject of Peter Eustace sacking with Chris Raistrick on Clubcall. Out of work, wife and kids, no joke etc. Apart from the fact Eustace continued to be paid his full salary for another fifteen months, I'd submit the suggestion that any manager who selects you, in my case inc. sub appearances 505 times, you should feel romantically inclined to run, compete and try your bollocks off for him for the belief he's shown in you. This I'm sure would leave two things: fewer managers being sacked and your conscience being clear.

I'd be interested, deep down to know how many players were genuinely sorry that they'd let Peter down. Especially as he'd signed them all and put them on very good contracts. When it happens it's too late, so paying some crème caramel lip service to the situation doesn't wash with me. But that's football and that's footballers. Don't think TH is any different. Why? because life goes on and it becomes yesterday's news as far as players are concerned. Any grief or pity is either short lived or nonexistent. Yet again I have to defer to Bill Songhurst's saying from 1985: "Football Is A Microcosm Of Society..." Suffice to say we have a short term, immediate gratification, throwaway culture and it's now even worse.

I've a couple more things to sign off and put to rest the laughable take by TH on Trevor Putney being significant enough to be perceived as a threat by me or Chris Turner. I think it's right that the flippant, blasé approach by both of these players away from the eyes and inevitable opinions ably formed by supporters should be held to account.

Things like TH and TP doing things in "their own time" and in "their own sweet way" is alarming to say the least and perfectly sums up their lack of professionalism and the predicament I was in, better than I ever could. After all the opposition during the week and on a Saturday don't really wait for you to do things in your own time and in your own sweet way. So as I'd suggested to all players, youth, reserves and first team, train and play with tempo, energy, passion and set yourselves and your team mates the highest of standards. You have to ensure as a player that within the framework of a team you as an individual are absolutely ready for anything and able to deal with, or at least compete with, your opposite number on a match day. Plain simple fact is TH and TP were among those who weren't and couldn't.

TH should have known better. He like me came from Chelsea, where for years, there was as much bad as good. They were always finely balanced with a fifty-fifty split. I remembered the good people, good coaches, good pros, good men, who tried to help me. I also remember as it's part of your growing up and unfortunately inescapable, the bad that countered it and sometimes cancelled it out. There were many older pros who fucked about, were cynical, negative and just plainly didn't give a fuck about the coaches, about training, about improving and about helping anyone around them. Least of all a seventeen or eighteen-year-old John Sitton. After I left I vowed never to be like that. I swore that if at all possible, I'd help any young player I could, on any part of his game and in any part of his life. And by the time I'd got to Gillingham, I started. It was by now my third club and I'd had a good few games so if anything was asked of me I'd tap into what limited experience I had to help.

The likes of Putney contributed the exact opposite. We no doubt had very different ideas on harmony and mutual respect in the dressing room, with the accent on porn in the dressing room (as pubescent boys will do), disrespectful filth about team mate's wives and girlfriends, treating any approach to treatment, rehabilitation, training or games as a joke, and the perversion and corruption of younger players by initiating and forming The Tuesday Club. Pizza and Booze until you puke basically. No good to me is it? Especially as I was a thirty four year old manager trying to make my way in the game. That's why me and my influence or that of any coach or manager who knows his stuff, is the most important one in a football club. Particularly over and above the likes of these two. The only thing unpalatable to some, particularly the two players concerned and their sycophants was the way I dealt with it.

Here's my general overview. I feel Putney should have been got hold of as a youngster and steered in the right direction. In my opinion that direction should have been as a custodian of the game. His assets made him perfect coach or management material. He knew the game, he could play good football, he was magnetic, charismatic and articulate. He also had a good sense of humour. He could have used it as a coach to help permeate sessions and lighten tense situations. Maybe he took a wrong turn, maybe he just didn't love the game of football enough. All I know is, at one time inside him was a good footballer. He'd been at Ipswich, Norwich, Middlesbrough and Watford. So he knew his stuff football wise. It's a shame he never used his vast experience to better effect. I could have done with his help, not his opposition. Sometimes it's just a case of two people who have different ideas on things and how they should be done. One thing life has taught me is, it's all about timing and fate.

Despite what TH says re being "torn off a strip" when we beat Tiverton in FA Cup I've always thought it better to accept we were not only lucky, and even though we scored three good goals from work on the training field and made our own luck, we needed to impact that on the players, and make them aware that there was still a lot to be ironed out. A footnote of truth is the fact that we all struggled to keep a straight face, even me at the height of my anger, when as supporters filed past our dressing room and through the window which was open we heard a supporter shout "Kev, show us your knob" in reference to Kevin Austin's Shergar like appendage. Also for the record it was Orient's first away win since 1993, nearly a full calendar year.

After a 0-0 at Peterborough, a priceless away point and clean sheet, Bristol Rovers beat us in the next round, when Glenn Cockerill was sent off. My personal criticism from TH on signing Paul Hague wasn't welcome. He should have concentrated on his own job and left me to mine. I knew we needed forwards, I had three in the pipeline, but I still felt we not only needed to build from the back, but the defence also needed reinforcing, as you have perhaps seen done at higher levels than these. TH could leave at seven days' notice, Purse's departure was an inevitability, I just didn't know when. I didn't know how long we'd be able to rely on Gary Bellamy. So to buy the upcoming Lee Shearer some time, I signed Haguey. We gave the captain's armband to TH on an upturn in form, when Glenn was sent off. I still felt there was a way back for Terry but his take on it was quite different. TH calls the management style "crazy." Not at all. You just do what you can at the time. I was now in the epicentre of a previous lack of planning and foresight. In the end both Hague and Howard let me down, not just Haguey. If I ran a club for any length of time, the planning and foresight was something I feel I'd have been more than capable of. I'd leave the organisation I worked for in a stable condition with foundations laid. Unfortunately, the supporters didn't get to see or appreciate the debt me and Chris had worked to eradicate. Turning a half million deficit into a club in excess of two hundred thousand in the black, a proportion of which was given to Pat Holland, my successor, to speculate with.

The criticism of the Christmas Day workout which for TH was too long (65 mins) and the half time rant at 3-0 down is there for all to see on YouTube. TH confesses to feeling like he weighed half a ton that day. The way he played, I'd guess he wasn't too far off it. Then the substitution of TH at Crewe. Again he's economical with the truth. He asked to come off with a migraine about fifteen minutes into the second half. After playing cards on the coach all the way there, and again in the hotel, some of the players including TH fitted in the game at Crewe. (We lost 3-0) and TH's migraine cleared sufficiently for him to carry on in the card school all the way home.

"Why not ban cards?" I hear you ask. Well, I agree with TH it can help alleviate boredom. More to the point, believe it or not, I thought rather than be petty it might be best to trust them as men and you hope it doesn't impair their preparation. There's pluses and minuses to everything in the end and I tried not to be as tyrannical as I was perceived. The truth is, I was only ever all about the business when it came to training and playing. The only way a player could get on the wrong side of me was to not be properly replenished, rested and ready. The rest of the time even though I was perceived differently, as long as players gave their all, were punctual and serious about winning and battling their socks off for the supporters, I let them spend their down time how they saw fit. They're meant to be grown men.

Eustace insisted on videos of nature programmes or trivial pursuit. I wasn't like that and even that in the TH book was criticised. If you want an excuse to fail, you find one, as players tend to do rather than spend any time looking at themselves.

TH then admits to being a "little unprofessional" but at the same time, says his respect for me and Chris being at an all-time low. When I looked at things from a player's perspective a manager with me only had to be fair and honest. It's not about me being right, the players being right, it's about what is or should be right for the team, the club, the supporters. I suppose this was where our interpretations of what a footballer should be are different. For me, contrary to TH's belief, it was never personal. I was even accused of trying to kick a player in training. Me and Chris only joined in once, that was a six a side competition at an indoor facility. Chris and I felt that we needed a bit of light relief and knowing that players loved six-a-sides we felt it was an ideal opportunity to allow them to express themselves while getting a sweat on.

I hadn't played for three and a half years. So after closing a couple of people down, I was blowing hard to say the least. I don't think I got close enough to anyone to make a tackle, never mind make contact with someone. Quite ludicrous lies. I've been stupid, said stupid things, but to risk injuring a player with a fit squad of 15-16 players would even by my standards take stupidity to another level. It's important to me that people know that. I've heard some bollocks spoken in my time but that deserves a winner's medal. The accusations levelled at me by TH in trying to kick Mark Warren are shameful. Mark played forty-eight hours later and scored a hat trick vs Peterborough in a 4-1 win. Maybe me joining in and the thought of me kicking him injected some urgency into "Wazza". TH's observations on his release contain some very insightful points of view. The main ones being it was for his and the club's benefit. On that we agreed. Also that it was, or had been something that was waiting to happen. I think TH as much as anyone, apart from two-faced directors who wanted him out, preferably for some money, must take a large slice of the responsibility for that. Things like lifestyle, weight, poor form, training, I can't go over it again. Next up, I refute the fact that I spent ninety minutes talking about myself in a crisis meeting of all the players, including youth and reserves. If I interjected with "I" or "Me" it was in a suggestive manner rather than a dictatorial one. Sometimes the powers of suggestion have more impact if you're dealing with intelligent footballers. I always preferred that method rather than "you will do this or you will do that at such and such a time..." I implied that I would prepare for games in such and such a way etc. etc. Surely the point of experience (the name we give to our mistakes) is to pass it on, particularly to younger players to help steer them away from making the same ones. Although Gary Bellamy agreed with TH that I used "I" and "Me" too often trying to lay some ghost from my playing days. What a clutching at straws, load of bollocks.

All I did, ever, was compare my no nonsense lifestyle and approach to training and games, even at this lowly level, and relay my thoughts, preparations and how I would go about trying to win a football match. I did it in an almost brotherly attempt, truthfully and honourably in the hope some would take something from it. In the end, it seems it became another reason to try and undermined me and make me an object of ridicule. It's a shame, but there you go. I'm obviously disappointed in myself that I came across that way. But in the end what's relevant to me now, more so than at the time, the cards were overwhelmingly stacked against me. The contradictory factors in TH's book roll off the tongue. He talks laughably of loyalty and it counts for nothing in football. I couldn't agree more, although it depends on the people and personalities involved, there tends to be very few codes and morals. I was on Terry's side. As a coach I was on every player's side but as I remember saying to Bernard Goodall, Hearn's number two "loyalty is a two-way street." You don't have to love one another, but knowing how I was as a player should have given TH insight into how I would be as a coach or caretaker manager.

I'm not one of those who needs to keep giving high fives and getting in a huddle as an outwardly show of my togetherness. If I say I'm your friend, your team mate, your coach or your manager it means I'm shoulder to shoulder with you and we'll take on what's in front of us together. I won't be the one to turn and run away from it and leave you on your own. But forget me, any coach or manager will tell you that sometimes, unfortunately, you have to jump a lot of fences and tolerate a few morons along the way just to get your message across. Even as a player myself I sometimes failed to recognise what was good for me. Maybe me remembering Terry's love for life but not for training and maybe even football clouded my judgement and poisoned my relationship with him.

You sometimes have to protect players from what they are inadvertently not aware of or don't see for themselves. Terry himself was all over the place and I now know it was for a number of reasons. I think his shallow existence and the perceived fun he thought it entailed if he'd stopped for a minute and thought, was wearing thin. The laughs were getting old and it was now catching up with him. A couple of common threads ran through his book. One is his observation on the lack of goals in Eustace's team. Going "X" amount games without scoring. He mentions Frank Clark and how it surprised everyone having the success he did at Forest. But there were no surprises when Clarky had a couple of upsets when it looked like players never had their heart in it, or gave less than 100% or showed a bad attitude.

There was a story that filtered down that he was less than impressed at times with Stan Collymore's attitude. Then TH praises Clarky and the relationship they had. And how Clarky wasn't a coach but a good man manager. Which in my book basically means being able to handle, coax, coerce and suck up to an errant child in a man's body. I've said before good players and good men are easy to manage, because they manage themselves. So it was good enough for Clarky not to suffer fools, or messers as I call them, but not for me. More recently at the highest level, managers have come in and released so called club legends because they quite simply don't fit the criteria.

TH and I also agree on the money spent, supposedly on "ready made" experienced players by Eustace. Which unfortunately not only cost him his job but cost me mine as well. I just had fewer to choose from. As Terry says, there were still lots of pieces of the jigsaw missing when they came in they were all older, they were all on good signing on fees and wages and some cost money on top, leaving the cupboard bare. Not just for TH but for me as well. I thought at his age TH should have studied himself more. Sooner or later you have to take responsibility for yourself as a man, not laugh and skip your way down the street like a seven-year-old. By that I mean the number of times he mentions his fitness or lack of it.

Just to remind you, I saw it all before with him (TH) when we were team mates.

He (Howard) talks of feeling weak, unfit, lethargic, lacking sharpness, being sluggish, overweight and susceptible to illness almost on a constant basis. Then having a purple patch of form and fitness. Surely you diarise or analyse what you did in the run up to a game with regards your training, lifestyle, nutrition and replenishment and repeat it so it comes the norm, a continuum. That's what I suggested to him. I'll never be as confused, puzzled, perplexed as when I read this selfish, almost juvenile nonsense. Still that's what it comes down to I suppose. I'm convinced that's another good reason why I failed as a manager or first team coach. I made the mistake and committed the cardinal sin of assuming that everyone would be as serious about football as I was at the time. Assuming they'd take the same approach to training and games as I did. Apart from Paul Heald or unless I'd set up an afternoon session or some concentrated practice for a couple of individuals for after training, I can't ever recall anyone saying to me as I cleared away the balls, bibs and cones with Chris or one of my Youth Team "Sitts can I take a bag of balls to do some ..." That confirmed to me what I'd inherited and that my two sessions a day was to inevitably be a culture shock. My youth team in comparison with their thirst for knowledge and appetite for work were chalk and cheese. All I ever asked of any player was honesty and appetite.

Honesty in training and games and appetite for work and gaining knowledge and football intelligence which I feel is where my coaching acumen at the time would help form a relationship with a player. As long as you recover appropriately and are not risking injury, you should take every opportunity to polish some part of your game every day. At least that's what I did anyway. I suppose for me it was about pride and feel good factor, the little physical and mental things that are part of a footballer's or any sportsperson's make up. I didn't want to lose headers, miscontrol the ball, misplace a pass, not feel strong or flexible, so I did extras at least two or three times a week as a player. Looking back, I suppose I shouldn't have been surprised that none of those players did who Eustace put together. Being paid to play football in my opinion is the best time of your life. Coaching football is the second best time of your life. TH is shall we say economical with the truth in referring to the contract he wanted. But at the same time openly admitting that any move to places like Bradford under Lennie Lawrence and Bournemouth where he somehow deduced a revolving door of management and boardroom upheaval was supposedly evident wasn't an option for him, opting for the existing madness at Orient instead, not leaving his, one assumes, comfort zone.

The truth is he never asked for a £50 rise. He asked for a £200 rise and appearance monies bringing him up to £1000. If the money had been there I'd have sympathised with Terry on that. I've always thought that good, loyal, consistent servants like myself and maybe Terry, should be better rewarded or at least on par with incoming players and new signings as due recognition and a thank you for your level of performance and loyalty. I've come to realise what it's like to be exploited as a player. Believe me the realisation is not a nice feeling. That can only be put down to either the poor judgement or exploitative nature of the people in charge at the time. I believed then and I believe now that any funds you have available to you should be spent as carefully and as wisely as if it were your own, but I would always reward a player who was consistent and loyal.

The game throughout its history is littered with managers who have bought recklessly. Wasting millions and lining the pockets of their agent mates. Why? Normally it's because of a number of reasons. They've bought poorly in the first place, someone they bought has got injured, they constantly feel the need to refresh or replenish the squad, which at times you should, but things go stale quickly in football particularly with certain players. Rather than provide a stimulus and or a winning run with the training, the coach or manager stays the same and just turns over the playing staff. Sometimes of course, it's just down to incompetence and every now and again a manager tries to buy his way out of trouble rather than inch their way to safety or success with coaching or organisation. Now it's worse and becomes a vicious cycle. Because chairman, directors, supporters and in the age of the PLC, shareholders want overnight success. That's why for top tier teams I'd keep the transfer window in place. It helps to put any perceived coaching or managerial ability to the test because you can't on a weekly, fortnightly or monthly basis buy your way out of trouble. Although I would allow the priceless transfer market to be utilised all year round if a premier club was buying from a lower division club. This used to be part of the lifeblood of a lower division club's finances.

Anyway the stalemate involving TH's contract could have been avoided. But the figures in TH's book are not the same ones he came out with in front of me and Chris. He conveniently glosses over the fact that he not only wanted a testimonial but that the directors should kickstart his fund with putting in £2000 each. A ludicrous suggestion I thought. For a few reasons. Two reasons would be no money for tea bags and an unpaid milk bill. Anyway he words it that "the club put a few quid towards it and I'd have been happy." I told TH without betraying any confidence or professional etiquette this was unlikely, not that it was highly unlikely because they couldn't have a whip round to pay the milk bill.

Pre-season had changed over the years. Players for years had turned up in a diabolical state, then realised the impact of training in pre-season on their bodies was at best negative and counterproductive and at worst, dangerous and could lead to an unfit, weakened body having a long term injury. So players, not TH though, changed with the times. Players for a while now did a mini programme of jogging and stretching to get their body and muscles ready for the 5-6 weeks ahead that usually comprised pre-season. In his book he (TH) remarks that shares in KFC and Carlsberg must have rocketed in the summer almost solely down to him. After experiencing about an hour of various step ups, body exercises and circuit training under Eustace myself on the first day then loaded onto a minibus to be driven to a seven mile run in Epping Forest, TH shouldn't have been surprised at Eustace taking the squad, after I'd left as a player, to an army camp. In his book he readily admits to being so sore he struggled to get up in the morning and being able to put his kit on and lace up his boots or trainers. Fast forward to his pre-season with me. My regime was a lot more gentle, planned, and player friendly, believe me.

After a long warm up with stops for fluids and a long and varied range of stretching, TH complains that a twelve-minute run was too much. I'll leave you to compare and work out if this should have been beyond a supposedly professional sportsperson. Yet again TH complained. His escape could have been to go to John Rudge at Port Vale. If Tel had seen what I'd seen when Rudge was a guest of Eustace, while I was youth coach in our offices he wouldn't even had answered the phone. I sat and listened to this guy and couldn't help thinking and if I'm being ignorant, I apologise "what's your playing record?" As he continuously criticised and slagged off his players, saying he'd resorted to five at the back not because it was a good system but to paper over the cracks of a not very good team or group of players. I made the mistake of piping up and asking who signed them. I got the look from a red faced John Rudge of someone who'd just been diagnosed with crabs.

Anyway, taking into account what Port Vale were offering and having to uproot and relocate, TH without saying it to me or Chris personally must have concluded how generous Leyton Orient and some of their previous managers had been to him. TH then has bollocks the size of grapefruits and words his displeasure at being left out of a friendly against Nottingham Forest on the Monday after being given Friday and Saturday off to try and negotiate a move away from Orient to Port Vale. See what I mean about players and supporters' perception of them? I call it having your cake and eating it. Despite it all he still got a call from John Rudge and despite a

£150 a week rise TH still said no and didn't want to go to Port Vale. Let's not forget that at seven days' notice Terry could have left at any time, but he still wouldn't sign the two-year deal I'd offered him. To say in his book that he rescinded on his demands were a blatant lie. Firstly he actually never asked for a £25k signing on fee. He wanted a 30% rise, appearance money, loyalty bonus and as I've said a testimonial with the fund started at 2k each by the five so called directors. Ergo £10k. To say in his book he rescinded and all he now wanted was a testimonial and a fifty pounds a week rise is a downright lie.

I want O's supporters to know that. And because he wouldn't compromise, neither would me and Chris. A tactic which was honest, but not one he was too happy with. Where I come from, you made your bed, now lie on it.

Next up and even Andy Taylor pulled a face and raised his eyebrows Roger Moore fashion when on the first day of the season TH called in saying he'd be late as he was nursing a migraine. He also said to a third party he wanted Orient to lose at home to Birmingham as he felt betrayed. I think it's important for Orient supporters to know the true feelings of one of their players.

TH then remarks that we (me and Chris) were unhappy with his mate Putney, turning up half hour before the start instead of the 1.45 we insisted upon for home games. As a player I'd always reported at the latest 1.30 anyway allowing time for unforeseen circumstances. If Putney wanted to play he should have shown he wanted to play. I mean being punctual is just common courtesy. I'd advise any coach or manager it's up to you how lenient you are, but don't be surprised if you are lenient when a player continues to take the piss and they expect you to carry on with your generosity of spirit, overlooking their tardiness. I preferred to exercise my right to the other option which is to expect punctuality and respect or you penalise the lads that are good pros by allowing bad people who are bad professionals to fucking run the show. I'm all for being understanding, believe me, but you do have to draw a line.

Howard's version of a run in between me and Putney is also 100% wrong when I was youth coach. I think I've explained what happened in a previous chapter, suffice to say TH only knows what he thinks is the correct version, which is Putney's. Again a truckload of complete lies. It was down to their speculation, born of paranoia that stemmed from their conduct that there was any perceived grudge held by me against Putney. It's only now, putting it down in print, that I've had an opportunity to not only redress the balance, but in its purest, most truthful and as it happened factual form.

Next bone of contention for TH is his omission from the squad away to Barnet in the League Cup. He openly states he was happy that we, "had the arse ripped out of us" at Barnet and lost 4-0. It's nice to know they also took the piss (Carter and Howard) as each goal was scored and on reflection how stupid was I to think that everyone cared, everyone would stick together, everyone wanted Leyton Orient to do well. Certainly not Howard and Carter. Again I want supporters to recognise and appreciate the climate around at that time. There were times when at my four clubs I was out of the first team picture. This is where people, and people's standards are different. I didn't knock on the manager's door, ever. I didn't sulk. I didn't wish a team mate injured and I certainly didn't take the piss if the first team got beat. I redoubled my efforts and became a force of nature in training and if required, in reserve team games. My belief will never change. By sheer will, determination and optimum performance you have to make it impossible or embarrassing for the manager to leave you out.

The remarks from TH about me favouring Darren Purse and Darren Purse being my boy and I never criticised DP and if DP did well, I'd do well... I never, ever saw it that way, that might be how someone like TH would think as a youth coach, but not me. I'd known and coached DP from under fourteen and as I've said unless you don't know what you're looking at or what you're talking about certain players jump out obviously at you and barring poor coaching, poor decisions on the players' part, poor decisions made by management and injuries you know they'll be a player. And depending on the player, able to get a career out of football. But as anyone knows, I left the club before DP. Also if they know me, they'll know I'm not an idiot and I try, unless I'm pushed away like I was with a few to take a personal interest in a player and his development. Now, the "I'm not an idiot" part comes in recognising at an early age in DP's case he had a bit of my make up in him. Which I thought was a plus. He was very self-critical and got upset with himself, sometimes getting down. So for TH's benefit, who accuses me of praising DP with the ulterior motive of self-promotion when he never deserved praise, it was to help DP get past it. Don't forget, he debuted at seventeen and he was now eighteen. Any disappointment in yourself over a mistake must be over with quickly. Something I never had as an eighteen-year-old. I was not helped by the majority at Chelsea and my age and inexperience not taken into account when any mistake in Chelsea's first team was hammered by a crowd, rightly pissed off with results.

People like TH should have looked at their age twenty eight or so and seen that and looking to get my approval rather than whether another player was. DP was a kid. And he needed and got my help. Did I profit from it? You decide. All I know is initially DP was sold ridiculously cheap and as he went on to other clubs his true valuation which was closer to mine revealed itself and he had a good career. After I left I spoke to his (Darren's) Dad Tony once. I was walking to Arsenal's ticket office for my ticket to do my job for the Press Association and I sent my best wishes to DP via his Dad. I actually think the team Darren played for beat Arsenal at Highbury that day. Then I saw Darren play for Birmingham at Spurs who they beat in the League Cup. Darren came into the press section and gave me a hug as they celebrated. He offered me his shirt.

A refusal would have been offensive and I gave it to my youth coach Tom. He said (DP) in my ear, as the crowd was a mixture of City celebrations and Spurs boos, "thanks for everything Sitts, I've played under a few coaches now and all you needed was a bit of luck, a break." I just said "thanks Darren." I got a bit choked but on the way home, I lived not far from the Spurs ground at the time, I smiled, I felt re-energised, I felt ten feet tall, I felt like I'd contributed something. It's nice sometimes when a coach or manager is appreciated by one of his players . After all, who motivates the motivator? At the time I was on the Knowledge juggling three part time jobs and on jobseekers' allowance. So much for benefitting from DP making his way in the game. For a bright boy TH could be a fucking idiot. Never mind, we've all been one at one time or another. As a footnote DP's wife, years on, was holding a surprise 30th for Darren. His ex-team mate and another one of my youth team Glen Wilkie, was the one who called to invite me. At the time I think we had an away fixture whilst I was coaching for Enfield or Leyton so I declined, putting work first. At the time I was on the dole and DP, so Wilks told me, was learning to fly a helicopter.

Next up I was criticised for sending beers in after the League Cup debacle vs Barnet, courtesy of me and Chris. It was called "propaganda" by TH who says we tried to deflect things while thanking the players for their effort on the night. The second leg was 1-1. When it suits them, the likes of TH all of a sudden realise what a disaster the 5-1 defeat against a team a division lower was. He's right. But firstly, you reward the good performance vs Birmingham on the opening day where we won 2-1 and keep the same side. No one could foresee a lacklustre, apathetic performance delivered in the first leg. I definitely couldn't as I sat the game out, at home with the flu. As a consequence of the Birmingham result Howard never played in either fixture but returned for the 1-1 versus Barnet at home. So he is half right. It was a thank you and a bit of reverse psychology to help the lads look forward to our league encounter on the Saturday. And for twenty-four hours at least, take a relaxed, philosophical view of the defeat. Next issue we agree on. There were too many times that we conceded late goals. Not just the part of the season TH talks about but right throughout a roller coaster tempestuous season. That's down to a number of things. Individual or group errors, bad decisions, a blatant poor technical mistake, lack of professionalism, not upholding momentum, concentration, discipline, game management. You name it, at one time or another it applied to us. Once a player crosses the white line a coach or manager can only have limited influence. That's when you need leaders to run the game. You would not believe the overwhelming delight I got from reading exactly the same thing in Ray Parlour's autobiography, a player who was at the highest levels of the game. The other thing I enjoyed reading was his outright honesty about Arsenal being able to "mix it" if they needed to. It endorsed what I have already said in an earlier chapter. I thought it was a good book. That's why some of my managers were lucky to have me because

I needed little help and was very consistent, although my pay never reflected it. I'm not happy that TH says I "basically said something and Chris agreed with it." Quote, unquote. That's disrespectful to Chris, his knowledge and playing pedigree. If Chris had a different slant on anything he was professional enough not to confront me on camera and show the players we were together and couldn't be divided. Some players who I've named would have smelled that particular weakness, and they'd have your eyes out and used it to divide, conquer and go back to the anarchy under Eustace. Forget me and my tantrums, Eustace gave the impression he was in control, but of all the coaches and managers I met or played under, particularly with that group of players he always had the least control of all. The price as always was paid by the supporters. TH remarks about playing with a sweeper at Oxford to accommodate people. TH was one of three possible central defenders.

In answer, it's a system I liked, we had an abundance of defenders, some of whom could play in more than one position. We had very few players to provide competition in other areas, so it made sense to put in the only players we had, in their correct positions and try and get a result. That changed a couple of times further down the line which I'll come to. But for a bad mistake in defence by the three centre halves Hague, Howard and Purse who got caught square, we'd have got a result. After going behind we pulled it back, then (I agree again with TH) symptomatic of our luck that season, we conceded in the last minute to lose 3-2. By the way, at the time Oxford had won five and drawn two of their first seven games. Our performance deserved far better but that's football. Yet again we came away with a well done Orient, well played, what a great game. Point wise though the most important statistic, we got fuck all. Oxford's staff, Denis Smith and Malcolm Crosby were very complimentary afterwards. And not only genuine, but seemed straight friendly guys.

Next up, persecuting Putney after bringing him back from Colchester on loan. Nonsense, absolute nonsense. Any extra work me and Chris gave him, overseen by both of us should have signalled to Putney we needed and wanted him competing for a place in the team. The squad was down to the bare bones but you can't let players dictate and hold a gun to your head. Maybe that's why I'm not still in football because I won't have it. I'd rather put the youth team in. It was nothing to do with any inconsistencies TH has accused us of in his memoirs. Trevor Putney went to Colchester for a month, and although he played, he came back heavier. To show him we cared, that we could have done with him having a positive influence instead of a negative one we worked on him. It doesn't take any working out. If we didn't give a monkey's about Putney or the team, or the atmosphere he created, more poignantly, we'd have left him to his own devices. Believe me, that's the time to worry for any player, when the staff ignore you.

Not too far down the line TH uses shock language like me being fickle and his take that I was the most fickle he'd ever known. A word to the wise, my inner thoughts are easy to fathom if you can be bothered to look and Tel obviously couldn't be bothered. TH says one minute John Sitton loved you, the next he hated you. It's simple really. I'd always said I'd forgive any player anything. There's only one or two issues I wouldn't forgive. They are lack of application to our verbal contract, written and agreed in the week during training, on pre-agreed set pieces, throw ins, patterns of play and defensive strategy. You go out and express yourselves and use that framework we've worked on to make your own decisions and try and use your ability to play well. Use your initiative and play according to what you see is the type of thing I'd say. I gave players freedom, especially in the attacking third, to use their invention and imagination. I think it's important to give players liberty of thought. I could never forgive lack of energy, passion or players capitulating. And I think you'll find, that's the only time I blew my top when I thought those ingredients were missing. To answer TH directly, I'd say my relationship with a player and the consistency of that relationship depended on the consistency shown by the player. I'd only go to war with people I could depend on.

I suppose one of the major things TH is right about is the fact that I wouldn't have served him his two weeks' notice on camera if I'd known the trouble it'd cause. Obviously the trouble as it turned out was all mine. And I've now for the umpteenth time admitted it. Contrary to Tel thinking I wouldn't be big enough to admit it. People like me with big ideas, big characters, sometimes make big mistakes. I never got the chance to learn or recover from mine and that has taken a long time to come to terms with.

Football has bigger problems than me supposedly losing control and dignity. Even though I spoke very lucidly, which is overlooked. The gambling, drugs, alcohol, corruption, bungs, unsavoury goings on in hotels, racist remarks, kerb crawling and under age sex and manslaughter actually helped relieve myself of some of the guilt of what I'd done to myself, my future, and gave me a low down the pecking order of smugness. It's not as if I hit anyone is it? Or kicked a boot and hit a player in the eye, or threw a pot of tea and some sandwiches, or even head butted an opposition player on the touchline.

You the supporter, you the reader, must decide on where in the grand scheme of things my perceived crime is placed. Who I wanted to sign from the youth ranks was none of TH's concern. Not really, so his speculation of making room on the wage bill by serving him the two weeks' notice, the conditions by the way that he elected to work under, instead of the two years I offered him, is beyond me. After all is said and done, he stayed in the game for a while at Wycombe and he admits that he was relieved to be away from Brisbane Road. If the tags of someone who lacked pride, passion and professionalism hurt Terry he should have done something about it at Leyton Orient as far as I'm concerned, not Wycombe. But a player who moves, right through football history at every level, is temporarily reinvigorated and is a better person for the club he arrives at than he is for the club who let him go. Momentarily at least.

I bumped into a director, the same one as Tel, Vince Marsh. I saw him at a health club in Chigwell. Tel saw him at West Ham vs Liverpool. TH asked why nothing was done about me and Chris parting with him and that I'd got away with murder. Vince was fine with me always and I've no doubt he was fine and dandy and sympathetic towards Terry as well. Perfectly summing up the directors at that time. Quite duplicitous. Actually I'd be surprised if Vince was around when it happened. Maybe as Tel said, he could have said "No! That's not right." Instead of which I was charged with protecting the Castle and its grounds. Then Vince agreed with Tel that I'd got away with committing murder in doing so. Bernie Dixson's name crops up. I never had a fall out with Bernie. Ever. This might surprise TH and his observations, again, couldn't be further from the truth.

Bernie resigned the day before the first game that me and Chris were in charge versus Huddersfield Town away. He protested at being overlooked to Weinrabe. I was there, a yard away. Weinrabe said "I'll make you director of football and managing director" (Clarky's old job). Bernie accepted on the spot. Bernie said "my first decision is to give John Sitton a new longer contract, but he stays with the youth team." Turner said "I'm not doing the job or taking the team to Huddersfield Town without John." Bernie asked me "what do I want?" I said, not trying to be at all evasive, "I just want to be a coach and do a good, thorough, professional, conscientious job for whatever club I work for at whatever level I work at Bern." Weinrabe said "I'm overruling you as vice chairman and acting chairman Bernie. Sitts goes with the first team tomorrow." Bernie said "in that case, I resign as director of football and managing director." So within the space of five minutes he'd agreed to and resigned from the same job. He was seething, went beetroot red and as he cleared his desk and packed his briefcase he warned me I was making a mistake. He walked out and was never seen at the club again. TH's speculation at what he thought happened or a story relayed to him, not truthful in any way is wrong in that I'm accused of falling out with Bernie and how I supposedly spoke to people led to him walking out.

At Wycombe it's nice to read that TH realised Martin O'Neil couldn't be taken lightly or messed with. That O'Neil had another side to him after a 2-0 defeat to Cardiff. See what I mean? It must be more a case of credibility rather than what's said or the way it's said as O'Neil lost his temper and TH accepted it. Any coaching ability, profound knowledge and information I had and was able to give to players seems to fade into obscurity when someone supposedly higher profile comes into the equation. I'm still perplexed because everyone starts somewhere and you need the fundamentals that I have highlighted, a good group of players, a winning run to get the recognition that earns credibility. I became part of a frightening statistic, especially in the lower divisions where you get one chance (if you can call it that) don't do very well on the face of it and sink into obscurity without a second chance. Howard speaks highly of the fact that after the next game he went to a pre-arranged short break in Spain with his new Wycombe team mates. He remarks on missing transport back to the hotel. That it was like being on an 18- 30's holiday and spending the four days completely pissed. So that's where I went wrong! Maybe the way forward for me was to take a leaf out of Mr O'Neil's book and after two consecutive defeats let the lads recover from it in the disco, at the bar and on the golf course.

That must have been my inexperience kicking in. As a thirty- four-year-old I was anxious to do well. Anxious to impress. Too anxious to show I could coach. I allowed my frustrations to surface instead of having a piss up. Still that's the beauty of the game everyone has different approaches and different opinions on how things should be approached and should be done. That explains one hundred percent the goings on and the relationship between myself and Terry Howard. I'll let you decide on what's right or wrong. Me? I am reconciled and my conscience is clear. In the end it's about putting out there the type of man I am and where I was coming from. Unfortunately in doing so I've had to put the spotlight yet again on the type of people I had around me at the time and give them more unjustified publicity. The only regret I have is being out of professional football for twenty one years and my coaching ability being wasted driving a Licensed London Taxi. It's a shame I never gained employment somewhere in some sort of capacity but that's the way it goes. Again, if football is a microcosm of society I was outcast for brutal honesty, being unPC, not hiding and staying to the end of the fight and not giving in instead of playing the victim. Now having told my side, the truth, I'm still at the stage where I don't give a fuck what nondescript amoebas think. Like hundreds before, they can have it, I'll leave them to their ignorance.

CHAPTER FIFTEEN
Mr Know It All

Phil Wallace who at one time was a potential chairman was completely different to what I was used to. Whilst he went through the club's accounts I found Phil understanding, communicative, aware and as a consequence dare I say it, a little sympathetic towards all that was contributing to mine, the team's and the club's plight. I found him engaging, easy to talk to and very switched on to understanding the football side of things as well as the financial side. He said to me I knew my stuff and being an East End boy was a good communicator. At the time it was a nice gee up.

He seemed like a man you could work for as well as a capable and ruthless decision maker. Nothing wrong with that I thought, it's nice to know you have common ground and also where you stand. I don't think you can ask any more than that. It's fair to say I liked Phil Wallace although I was to only see him twice more and speak once on the phone.

Even as I remember it all I can't help thinking "what was I doing?" Why assume responsibility for such a debacle, such nonsense? Even today people are paid tens, no, hundreds of thousands of pounds to troubleshoot and sort out such a mess. The game or as it is now "the industry" of football is about opinions. There will be players, coaches, managers and directors who can relate to the fact that the opinions of previous regimes can set a precedent and set a football club back years. So I suppose why should I have escaped?

No one in football, or very rarely, walks into an ideal ready made club, full of good players, with good staff, good youth policy and a productive commercial department. If they did there would probably be no need for change.

The contrast in Barry Hearn taking over compared to when Phil Wallace gave a realistic, truthful press conference was massive. Phil had about five journalists present and no cameras apart from the ever present fly on the wall documentary camera. Barry had all of the upstairs hospitality lounge packed with cameras and journalists. There was standing room only. He said three things that I remember like it was yesterday. One was "we're gonna have some fun" which in my opinion you can't have unless you're winning. That took him a while to fulfil. Two was, with a twinkle in his eye "I don't know why I didn't think of it before." (Owning a football club.) After all one bought for nothing, even though it was running at a loss, on a big site, with a blank canvas, that could be completely restructured and had always had potential even if it had been unfulfilled was I assume very appealing.

Third was his insistence that Chris Turner and I had tried to manage the club under difficult circumstances, probably the most difficult in its history. But having said that he also said he wouldn't give us a vote of confidence as he'd been made aware of what that meant in football. That only served to make me uneasy, a little paranoid and believe it or not, under even more pressure than I already had been. A big bank balance does wonders for your self confidence and self-esteem. One assumes anyway. But I wouldn't know. My youth team contract that I'd mistakenly taken the job on with a petrol card ran out on June 30th. But realistically I had eight weeks to show I knew what I was doing and what I was talking about.

After the dour 1-1 at home to Oxford we carried on in a not very good vein of form. To Brighton and Hull we lost both scoring none and conceding five. I'd said to Barry the forward line still needed replenishing at all costs. Next up was the second leg at home to Birmingham in the area final of the Auto Windshield Trophy. Next stop would have been Wembley. There's an old saying "It's not the dog in the fight, it's the fight in the dog." For most of the season we'd resembled a Pekinese pocket dog. Not scoring apart from Westy, and if we conceded, ultimately capitulating. I knew then and I still maintain now, the coaching and information I'd given the players was top drawer. I'd happily put on a session and be graded by any top coach in the game. I left no stone unturned which led to my self-deprecating pop at Ian Hendon saying "if Don Howe or Terry Venables were giving you the same information maybe you'd listen and act on it." In doing so I was trying to highlight there's nothing wrong with the information but it's either me or you the collective of players. Call it suicide but I threw the gauntlet down to try and get players to look at themselves. Surely it can only be laziness, lack of application, lack of football intelligence or lack of pride and passion.

The second time we met when he eventually took over, I remember being impressed by Barry Hearn's enthusiasm. The first time we met he addressed me (I'm sure being friendly) as son and I asked if we were on the set of Eastenders. Now he sat with about three or four people going over and over the accounts. Me and Chris were no longer at board meetings, that's if any were held and I couldn't help thinking the existing board of Wood, Weinrabe, Marsh, Linney and Goldsmith were even more conspicuous by their absence than normal. Tony Wood and Weinrabe in particular stopped coming in daily to the office to see me and Chris and discuss the latest story, going round in circles, busy doing nothing. At a football club, fatal. Then one day it happened, Barry came in and as owner I don't suppose you need to, without knocking the door flew open and he said "that's it, the other bloke's gone, the club's mine. The other bloke's done his dough, now I'm taking over, I'm chairman of the club, the legal side's been done, the papers are signed. A word of warning I'm a businessman, not a philanthropist so it'll be run on a cost effective basis."

I stood up with Chris and we both shook his hand, I said I don't know whether to congratulate or commiserate, there's a mountain of work to do. He said "I know, but when me and my people are finished you won't recognise the place." We had a walk in the changing rooms he pointed and said "I can't see that staying" pointing at the massive communal bath. He said on more than one occasion "I don't know enough about you two, we'll work as we go and I'll be as quick as possible on whether I think we can work together." I just said that would be appreciated. I think we can do a job, either individually or together but the sooner the better for everyone's sake at the football club. It's time to move forward the situation's been allowed to fester for too long. He then declared "I want something in writing giving me an idea on how you want to take the club forward." I said "Barry it's done, I've just got to tweak a few bits." I'd already shown some of it a while ago to Tony Wood and Derek Weinrabe. It had included a retained list, recruitment, contracts, commercial ideas and probably the most important of all at a club like Leyton Orient, a productive youth policy. I had to move on, my previous pleas to Tony Wood not to sell had obviously fallen on deaf ears. He'd had enough. He was battered, some of it down to the goings on at Orient. I'd suggest most of it was the fallout from Rwanda which was understandable. He was absolutely crestfallen. I'd given him reasons for not selling. I said trust me, it doesn't matter how hard the fight, how hard the times, I've got plans to rebuild the club from the ground up. I gave him all the figures on money owed for transfers some were instalments, some as a consequence of sell on percentages. I'd given him figures on money saved on players' wages, staff wages and the youth policy.

The Centre Of Excellence was now more cost effective than ever and staffed by some great coaches who were great people. The scouting network was being put together as we spoke and adding good quality people to our numbers. I said "Purse, Shearer, Heald, Austin, Jones, Brazier and eventually Luke Weaver, Scott Honeyball, down to Shorey at under fourteen level, would all be financial assets. But ideally I want the club to be built around them." Something I was to repeat to Barry Hearn saying "I want the nucleus of the first team to be home grown who don't just turn up, but turn up and care." I'd told him short term I'd try and generate money by parting with some of the big earners some of whom would maybe have fees attached. If we take a step or two back and get stick from disappointed supporters I'd cope, I'd take it on the chin. "In the meantime we should sit down with John Goldsmith about the redevelopment of the ground, find a new training ground (I had two in mind) and get Frank Wolfe in and renegotiate with him with the accent placed on demanding more from him and having his contract being heavily incentivised.

He just looked bewildered as I went from first team down to the under nine's and said "I don't think I can go on any longer." So I had to try and sell myself all over again to Barry Hearn.

At first I thought I was doing OK. At least Hearn's feedback indicated that. He seemed to get my humour, saw I was organised and seemed curious to know more. Particularly the recruitment side of things. I must admit I wasn't sure out of courtesy and respect for the fact that he was now chairman whether to speak out and show mine and Chris's displeasure at how he started to go about finding out more and whether we could work together. You can probably add he wanted to know if I knew what I was doing and what I was talking about. I knew I did, but Barry Hearn needed to know it. If the truth be told, like a lot of regimes, Barry Hearn had no football background. I believed then and I believe now all the way up to National level you need football people making football decisions. Hearn's own private investigator came in the form of a man introduced to me and Chris as Bernard Goodall.

With his short black hair (I thought he perhaps dyed it) parted at the side and greased down, I thought he looked like 60's gangster Mad Frankie Fraser which made Chris laugh. He was introduced to us and with the three of us left in the room stated he'd accompany us everywhere. Training, match day, pre-training briefings, pre- match talks, half time and post-match summaries and in hotels at away games, both when we ate, and at team meetings as we ran over our own strategies and those of the opposition. I looked forward to away games because on request, the hotels we stayed in could provide a flip chart and some coloured felt tipped pens, something Leyton Orient couldn't.

Given my time again, it's crazy now to think that at thirty-four I was mad to put up with this as part of the working conditions attached to my one and only chance at first team level. Now it's inconceivable. I think yet again it was at best undermining making Chris and me devoid of any semblance of credibility. The players must have thought what's happening here? At worst it ridiculed us and showed a lack of trust in our abilities and knowledge of the subject matter. Totally demeaning, it had a control feel to it.

There are no team shapes, tactical systems, defensive strategies or set pieces that haven't been tried. As a coach I was on top of all of them, aware of them and as good coaching is a continuum, had a razor sharp eye on when and where to come in and coach. I also personally never stopped applying myself to picking up and learning new ideas. I never passed up the opportunity to listen to or watch another coach work. Often attending coaching sessions or seminars with different associations and coaching clinics. But it has to be said when it comes down to the nitty gritty you need a few basic ingredients to win a football match. Good players with good habits who are honest, a solid defensive strategy with everyone contributing towards you being hard to break down and hard to beat, and as many players as possible providing a goal threat. Even at this lowly level a big factor in our 88-89 promotion was a goal threat spread throughout the team. The squad I inherited was the polar opposite. Even as I took over and helped stave off relegation towards the end of the 1993-94 season the only goals in the team seemed to come from Colin West.

In the end it's 11 v 11, and to win the 11 v 11 each player has to win his personal 1 v 1. It can sometimes come down to who wants it the most, but the basics still need to be put in place.That's where my opinion counted on sweeping changes needing to be made. I wanted players who cared, not just players. From the off me, Chris and Goodall viewed each other with a certain suspicion. I'll come immediately to the point, the guy asked a million questions some of them nonsensical and he tried his best to drive me and Chris mad. Although we'd already been accused since of crazy, insane management style, particularly in Howards' book, I still maintain that the patience of even the most pious would have been tested. I'm not one, and never have been one, to tolerate fools for too long and having a normally decent disposition grated on daily can certainly put your patience to the test. As you read, and if you flick back through the pages, most of what happened didn't just happen once and let's move on and forget it, sometimes things happened a few times or in the worst cases continuously. It made the incompetence and negligence a form of daily torture.

Bernard Goodall insisted at the club on attending training. Barry Hearn's arrival which I suggest was opportunist, coincided with the Auto Windscreen area final vs Birmingham. Birmingham were big spenders in our division and we were up against it. What didn't help as we trained and prepared was the constant barrage of questions from Goodall. He adopted an arrogant presumptuous stance, hoping I feel to bluff me and Chris into thinking he knew football. He'd already said to us his main employment was a kind of trouble-shooter sent in to reorganise and restructure ailing companies. Our recent average form of two wins, two draws and two losses, meant we had to organise ourselves to defend well at Birmingham and give us a formation that would give something different and create some problems for them.

After losing 1-0 at Plymouth to a goal from a corner in the last few minutes due to Mark Warren's poor marking allowing a free header, we told the players we'd spend our time not only preparing for Plymouth beforehand but intersperse it with work in preparation for Birmingham game (as we assumed they'd get a scouting report) in training. Goodall insisted his friend in management did lots of 11 v 11 and SSG's. He spoke in glowing terms, like he was the West Country's answer to Bill Shankly. I knew Maurice Evans was Reading manager when my old Gills teammate Richie Bowman played there under him but other than that I had heard nothing of his playing career or coaching and management credentials. I did patterns of play with the team, combination play in the middle and attacking thirds, defending as a team from the front, set pieces, finishing practices and phases of play. I drilled the back eight relentlessly for the Birmingham game deciding on three centre backs, two wing backs, obviously the goalkeeper and two screening midfield players. In Leyton Orient terms, and even more important from a financial point of view, the area final against Birmingham was massive. We decided to play Ian Bogie off the front two in rotation with Danny Carter. Goodall asked why we had such a thing as a phase of play and why play eleven vs eight to drill the defence? I replied that in a game there will come a time when the front two have been played round and bypassed and the furthest midfield player forward will be making a recovery run, so eight behind the ball at times, might be required to defend when outnumbered. Sometimes defending is not always about winning the ball immediately , it's about delaying an attack or making it benign and predictable, then you win the ball back.

He just said Maurice Evans wouldn't do it like that. I remember the session going well and the players looking as up for it as I'd seen. The summary after training finished on a high until Goodall walked up behind me and Chris. Westy shifted his eyes to warn us. Not put off I did my address and Goodall said "I'll see you two at the car." Chris said "he can fucking walk through walls that boy." It got a giggle. I then said someone should hang a fucking bell around his neck so we can hear him coming which increased the laughter. Goodall just looked over his shoulder as he walked through the mud. I called out "Bernard, can you help us get the balls, bibs and cones in?" Chris looked down and pissed himself with laughter. I risked the impertinence.

The next battle on behalf of the players was to prepare right on match day. Me and Chris approached Weinrabe saying we wanted to travel in the morning, have lunch, get the boys to bed, three hours' kip, up for pre-match meal, team meeting, then off to do battle. He said he'd run it past Barry. It was done which was a nice change. Everything nearly went to plan. We defended superbly. We made the most of our overload in midfield, Hendo and Dempsey played cat and mouse superbly at wing back and although Birmingham nicked a goal we should have gone on to win it. The information coming from amongst Birmingham's players and their bench was mostly confusion on how to deal with our overload, second forward and not being able to get behind our back five.

We had a not very inspirational bench of Turner, Hague and Mark Warren. I was absolutely delighted with the side particularly the back five and particularly Hendo, who was excellent against ex Orient player Ricky Otto, one of Birmingham's many game changing options. He (Hendon) finally performed at the level I thought he should. We brought on Mark Warren in place of Gary Barnett who along with Glen Cockerill, Danny Carter and Ian Bogie ran themselves into the ground. There were lots of games like that and I allowed my own frustrations and search for perfection to impede and inhibit what I should have done, which looking back is get back to praising the players more. If you're going to create a siege mentally the mistake I made probably through inexperience, was not creating a siege mentality of me, Chris and the players against the world, including those who in my opinion had been at best negligent in their running of the club.

Mark Warren came on and as Birmingham got tired the mood of the game and the tide changed. The lads like Bogie, Carter, Dempsey and Cockerill who could provide ammo absolutely did, Warren had three one on ones with Birmingham's keeper. He hit one wide, the goalkeeper's legs with another and acting on the information I gave him if he got another, commit the goalkeeper and lift it. He did and he hit the top of the bar. At the final whistle Barry Fry, Birmingham and their supporters were relieved to say the least. Chris said and I agreed we fancied our chances at home, a day at Wembley and some much needed readies. In the hospitality lounge afterwards Barry Fry tried to talk business, no doubt a mischievous tactic designed to unsettle the players concerned and surrounded by her entourage Karren Brady held court as she sipped either white wine or champagne.

I said to Chris see you on the coach, got up off my seat and left my drink on the bar. We didn't even eat. For the next few days training was busy. By now the wages were back in the hands of the club and the embargo was lifted. We played Birmingham on February 28th. The embargo had run from August so for seven full months no players could be added. Now we had managed to get Paul Read in from Arsenal to help share the load with Colin West who like a few of us had been magnificent and gone way above and beyond the call of duty. He fitted in straight away, he grasped our defensive strategy having done it under Pat Rice and George Graham, and was a breath of fresh air. He helped press from the front and refreshingly for me when coaching him, he only needed telling something once, which helps, because it means you can move on and only revise things when it's appropriate to do so.

Although we had lost to Plymouth we still had to play Cardiff, Bournemouth, Cambridge and Shrewsbury who were just above us and Chester the only club below us. The next four days were as important as any and making a change, Read for Barnett, we drew 1-1 at home to Oxford. Two more points dropped. Who duly obliged? It was big Westy again. His body must have been creaking but a decent pro and as honourable a man as I've met in football. A very straight, honest guy I thought. I think he had a conscience and tried to help me and Chris. He had immense pride and cared. At least that's what I thought. What I also liked was he'd try and help guide the youngsters.

Just before the second leg of the Auto Windscreen Area Final at home to Birmingham a woman asked at reception if she could see me. It was Maureen Hagerman the mother of a guy I knew from school and the old Craig Park Youth Club. She came in and said she'd watched my career and now she wished me luck as it seemed I'd been devoid of any. She said I really hope you turn the corner starting tonight. Why? Well two reasons. That was how the old neighbourhood used to be. Wanting each other to do well and wishing them all the best. I used to be one of them. Secondly, while I was at Millwall, her son Stephen had died of cancer. I was approached by the boys who wanted to raise some money for his young widow. I approached George Petchey who was different class. He insisted on a team with me in it be sent to the Henry Barras Stadium in Edmonton on the borders of Ponders End to play the boys. And Mrs Hagerman had never forgotten it. She said she hoped I'd be repaid with goodwill and results. A lovely gesture. I thought she spoke from the heart as her own son had gone.

As soon as the second leg kicked off we got going straight away. Hendo started it with a marauding run and strike from right back and hit the bar with a great strike, putting Birmingham on the back foot. Then an offside trap we had to immediately regain possession was not rewarded, the three-yard margin not enough for the linesman who never raised his flag. Birmingham scored. When the second Birmingham goal went in the lads could have been forgiven for thinking, especially after the season we'd had, that was it. All over, 3-0 down on aggregate. We battled on and scored two. Birmingham killed us off with one more. We lost 3-2 on the night, 4-2 on aggregate. It was a cracking two legged cup tie. I wanted to taste more. Even though we'd lost I loved it, I felt in my element. Where I should be, contesting games, preferably big games.

Which for Orient this was. Not the Champions League, I know, but it's all relative. My ambition had no ceiling at the time and I wanted to stay in football to manage or coach at as high a level as I possibly could. I enjoyed competing.

I loved organising a team. Especially against a big club, the biggest in our division. One who had money and wasn't afraid to invest it. I shook Barry Fry's hand and said good luck in the final and he ran towards Birmingham supporters, arms aloft. I knew he'd had tough times at Barnet and he'd grafted, probably different to how I'd done to make his way to a club like Birmingham. I looked over and couldn't help thinking you lucky so and so.

We ran Birmingham and their expensively assembled squad very close. Afterwards with the packed house and Birmingham's supporters singing well after the final whistle all I remember was seeing my old Chelsea team mate Jimmy Clare and his Dad Terry, this was because we were signing Jimmy's son on schoolboy forms.

As my wife commiserated with me, Maureen Hanshaw cut in seeing the devastation on my face and not really picking her moment much to my wife's annoyance. I was clinging on by my fingernails. The press who'd been speaking to me and Chris deserted us as Barry Hearn walked in. It was like some people may have experienced at a party or social gathering. You find out you've been talking to someone particularly shallow because they say excuse me and go over to someone more high profile, more important or higher up the food chain. Barry insisted that good times were ahead "if we get support like that for an area final of a small cup, we must look to have more times like it." And to be fair since then he's tasted it a couple of times with a couple of promotions under Tommy Taylor and Martin Ling.

It might be worth mentioning they both had four to five seasons each as manager which proves that a bit of patience from the chairman and the supporters and a bit of continuity can pay dividends. I've got to be honest I'd have been disappointed in myself and probably fallen on my sword if I hadn't been able to match two promotions and a couple of decent cup runs in the twenty one years since. With that in mind there was everything in my opinion to fight for. A minor miracle in staving off relegation against all the odds and along with it my future. From my point of view in light of the circumstances the financial mess the club had been in, the five or six jobs I'd been doing, the day in day out micro management, for my money it would have been the equivalent of a promotion. As Tommy Docherty pointed out "football management is like nuclear war there are no winners, only survivors." And survival of O's in the division mine and Chris's were now the focus. I maintained at the end of it all and it's still my opinion now Orient could have had Wenger and Ferguson as joint managers, George Graham as defensive coach, Terry Venables playing "Diamonds" and "Christmas Trees" and Jesus with holy water as the physio and I don't think they'd have done a much better job than me Chris and the small staff we had. They probably wouldn't have made the mistake of allowing cameras in but that was too late now. Or parted company at half time with a poorly prepared, poorly focused and poorly committed player. I had, and I couldn't turn the clock back even if I wanted to. I accept it was dealt with poorly but I've never been one to suffer fools. It's a shame supporters couldn't see past the over reacting and that I wanted value for their money with a change in culture and mentality. The evidence that they wasn't getting it for me was overwhelming. I felt we could still stay in the division and pull off a minor miracle of avoiding relegation, while at the same time having cut costs. Added to money coming in from instalments on transfers, and the big money generated from the area final against Birmingham, the club was also now firmly back in the black. It was now decision time. Allow the current managers to get the players on board that had been required all season to help the cause or allow relegation? I suppose the upside of relegation would be, although there are no guarantees, if the club is then promoted the supporters would have a hero or heroes who had contributed to glory, thus cancelling out any perceived previous failure. All that remained was the question of who the hero or heroes would be. History says that it wasn't to be me and Chris.

On a rare occasion in pinning Mr Hearn down I amped up the drama by saying, "Barry the house is on fire, you have the power to put it out (as in save relegation) and we only have one or two burnt out windows or you let it burn to the ground and start again meaning guaranteed relegation." I said the same to Bernard Goodall on another journey in his Lexus to the training ground. They asked what I wanted, I said three forwards, it was four but we now had Paul Read to share the load with Colin West who barring injury had been magnificent. Along with Purse, Hendon, Bellamy, Heald, Austin, Cockerill, Bogie and Dempsey he'd done all he could. But nine wasn't enough. I allowed myself to be distracted by the form and inadequacies of the rest of the squad. Besides there would have been times when those players should have been rested. They were more or less ever present in training and games. And it's with hindsight and experience I have to show due gratitude for their professionalism and endurance in all things. Not least of all lumping them all in when it came to criticism of our meagre squad and my frustrations.

A call from Keith Peacock on behalf of Charlton led to the loan of Scott Mcgleish. He was young, a bit light and not yet mature. But he wasn't a bad player. He went on to have two successful periods at Orient further down the line. But when he came in he was the polar opposite of Paul Read. Ready was a good pro, good trainer, easily adaptable and coachable. He fitted in immediately as one of a team. Clean cut and immaculate in conduct. That's always been the thing about Arsenal, they don't just turn out good players they turn out good human beings. Most of the time anyway. Me and Scott didn't really see eye to eye. I was in no mood to hear him complain in his comparisons of Orient and Charlton. Everything from kit to training, to training ground, to rest, days off, team travel and accommodation. On it went. I just said "we need goals and you need a career." Not very diplomatic I admit, but I said it's a step up from Charlton's reserves and youth to Orient's first team and was a step in the right direction for his career and he needed to acquit himself and start building a reputation. Not think he was doing us a favour by being there. I'd lost out on Leo Fortune-West but due to our personal relationship, I still had a chance of Sean Devine. I knew the Fisher chairman well and he wouldn't renege on our deal. I had him in training and he was an immediate handful. A selfish goal scorer, with pace, power and an unerring left foot. As it turned out he'd score goals for fun at that level but unfortunately it was to never be for Orient.

He ended up at Barnet after a stint abroad, and it's worth noting I got him both moves. I said to Barry Hearn and Goodall I'd buy him, it would only cost Orient his wages but any future prospective transfer, I'd negotiate and want the fee. They deferred, leading me to think they either had no money, didn't trust my judgement or I had no long term future at the club and wanted as few players as possible to be inherited by any future management. I could relate to and appreciate the last point in particular. So yet again I put Fisher off and kept my money in my pocket. Barry Hearn said if you're that convinced sign him. I said "no if I'm gone, I wouldn't want someone else to get the benefit." I continued to make the O's bland by playing Purse (18) Wilkie (18) Perifimou (18) Rufus (18) and Shearer (17). Chris had a very rare outing as we lost 2-0 at Hull. We started Mcgleish and Read up front with Westy. Mcgleish was sulking because we asked him to fill in wide right for the now injured Danny Carter who along with Sean Brooks was in the treatment room.

We lost at home to Huddersfield 2-0 then stopped the deep rot with an away point at Cambridge drawing 0-0. Ironically the corresponding fixture where a year earlier the rot had well and truly set in for Peter Eustace, with the half time rant and ending in him hitting Kevin Austin. We beat Shrewsbury 2-1 at home and lost 2-0 away at Bournemouth, Mark Warren going through three times one on one with the goalkeeper again and hitting the target once. He actually hit the bar again if my memory serves me right. This was a game with added significance because after the game as me and Chris spoke to the press about refusing to give in and trying to stay positive a member of the press, I don't know where from asked what Barry Hearn had brought to the club. Was he a plant? Was he a contact? Who knows? All I know is the fall out was like the Nuremberg Trials. Me and Chris were questioned over and over again by Bernard Goodall about who said what and "what did you mean?" The crime, just in case you're curious, was Chris's reply to that question about what Hearn had brought to the club. Chris said "at the moment all he's brought to Orient is some publicity." It was like a scene from Perry Mason or Crown Court as Goodall demanded to know who said it. I wasn't about to grass Chris up and said "I don't remember either of us saying it, maybe it was the reporter's own assumption." Goodall said "let's get one thing clear, Barry expects total loyalty in his organisation." I said "fair enough, but tell Barry, loyalty is a two-way street."

I got on with doing what I was doing and thought to myself "what's this all about?" And my pride begged the question "who the fuck does he think he is?" I had to smile to myself it was like amateur dramatics with Goodall trying to put on a sinister stare and take the tone of his voice down to demand loyalty, like a scene from "Goodfellas" being done in the local church hall with a drama group. Still, money talks or at least getting the figures straight did, so I had to go along with it until I either got the players I wanted or was told otherwise. When I actually spoke to Barry next he said as he and his organisation was coming up he spoke to as many people as possible to draw on their experience. One of his interests was obviously in boxing and he spoke to someone who had seen it all, Micky Duff. Apparently Micky Duff had advised him: "Barry, if you want loyalty, buy a dog."

Then next up another hard luck story away to Cardiff City. Goodall asked what more I could have done and why I hadn't gone through the 2-1 reverse at Cardiff straight after the game. Why after taking a 1-0 lead I'd been so gentle, telling the players to spend a couple of days with their families, rest, reflect and try and be fresh and ready for training and the run in, beginning with a hard game at home to Crewe on the Saturday. We had a couple of days to retune things. Why? Because everyone on the staff and I include some good conscientious players in that, were brow beaten, battered and beat up from a season of little respite. The respite being what you look for most which are victories. Wins put a spring in everyone's step and believe it or not Chris and me made a pact that regardless of any result we'd turn up Monday or next day if it was midweek, chipper, smiling and enthusiastic. Ready to crack on again.

As a coach you have to. As a manager you have to. You've got to leave what's said in the dressing room and hide your bitter disappointment. Goodall persisted with his senile mind fuck. I just said it was the right thing to do. I can't rip into kids like Purse and Perifimou and at the same time bollock seniors like Heald, Hendon, Cockerill and West. Westy had already had a running battle of verbals with Eddie May on account of the fact Westy had played for Swansea. Two things I'd never bothered with were verbals with opposition players or officials. Someone like May who made me sound like Shakespeare, I thought had ran out of things to say to his own players so turned his attention to Westy. I've always thought its bollocks and a waste of time, energy, and in certain cases like May's, limited vocabulary. I said to Goodall "I thought you suggested a cooling off period. And any inquest should be held 24-48 hours after. Make your mind up." This didn't go down too well particularly in the guide book of interpersonal skills and diplomacy. He gave me a disapproving look and sarcastically said "really, you should manage how you see fit." I knew I was on thin ice. It comes down to very simple reasons. Firstly results. Results would only come courtesy of a miracle and the antithesis of what had gone before. Good, young, ambitious, hungry players. Salaries that should have been incentivised and a club that had a work ethic and were organised. I said as much in an interview trying to redress the balance with Hearn after the "he's only brought publicity " faux pas. I said Barry seems very organised and seems to put thirty-six hours into a twenty-four-hour day. I had to try and patronise, then hopefully build some sort of relationship with Goodall and then in turn, Hearn. Even though Goodall knew nothing of what he was looking at apart from the pounds, shillings and pence side of it. I tried to look interested in what he had to say and look interested enough to take it on board. Even though he had very limited knowledge and used a lot of guess work. As he scrutinised me I was lacking in all but two of my self-imposed criteria for a coach/ manager. I knew the subject matter, I could coach, so far two out of two. Then there's credibility. Why I had to be questioned on that I don't know. I'd known the club inside out for ten years by now. Then lastly I felt and always have, if you win enough games you pick up a professional reputation. Your professional track record is usually accompanied by admiration (for winning) and how you set up your club, added to either being liked or being feared. Although for me it would be preferable to be somewhere between the two. No club wants a mug as their manager.

The fear at big clubs is easy, it comes from being surplus to requirements. I was struggling to achieve two. I don't know that credibility should immediately stem from winning but it does.

This has been proven since and convincingly by people who have successfully managed without really playing the game. My own opinion ably formed through experience and watching what goes on at clubs at every level and football in general is that "results" can also be misinterpreted and paper over the cracks or in Orient's case crumbling foundations. May I suggest that results that were just as relevant were results like five youth team players making a first team debut. Then the results of an area final of a small trophy raking in over one hundred and fifty thousand pounds and helping to eradicate an annual loss of half a million. The biggest result of all was helping Orient avoid administration and ultimately liquidation. Even if me and Chris never got the credit.

After a meeting with Goodall which was the morning after the Cardiff game (away) it turned out to be fifteen minutes of fuck all. Or maybe it was Goodall starting a competition to see who could go the longest with the least amount of sleep. We went over old ground with me wanting more players, what my retained list would be, who I wanted to move on and what other plans I had on reorganising the club. Then Chris came in asking me if I knew what was coming I should tell him as he'd been summoned to a meeting with Barry Hearn. I said I had no idea but it was obvious Chris feared the worst. We were both kept in the dark right up until we were individually culled.

Chris wasn't in there long and he came into our office, his face bright red with I think a mixture of shock, rage and embarrassment. He was angry and upset to say the least.

I'm pleased for Chris and always have been that he'd started to wisely make his own arrangements looking for work while he was in work. Chris came straight to the point. He'd been told that his contract wouldn't be renewed. Come June 30th he was a free agent. Barry inserted a big, quite shocking addendum, telling Chris he was free to leave immediately if he'd accept a proportion of money on the remainder of his contract. I asked him what he intended. He said I'm still under contract as a player so I'm going to sit tight. I assumed the offer of a lump sum wasn't what he wanted so he elected to see it through on a weekly basis. He asked me again. I said I'd been given no idea whatsoever. Which I honestly hadn't. Like everything else it was all about timing. And the timing had to suit Barry. What struck me almost immediately about Barry is that he seems like the type to get all his ducks in a row. Which when you run any business is absolutely fair enough. It's fair to say I wish I'd done the same ten months earlier. If experience is the name we give to our mistakes I'd made mine through trial and error. No help, no mentor, no experience and a huge financial mess.

A Little Knowledge is a Dangerous Thing. A Life in Football - John Sitton

The biggest fact when asked and I answer with hindsight is that I was foolhardy, arrogant and too ambitious in taking the job. I actually bit on something Eustace said to me about my future while he was still manager and repeated by the LMA Secretary or chairman Jim Smith. They both intimated that Don Howe can afford to be choosy about the job he accepts so can Terry Venables but you have to consider if you get a chance will it be the only chance you get? Which seemed in the end yet another self-fulfilling prophecy. The debacle at Orient was to be my one and only chance.

I suppose now for Chris it was about planning for his immediate future which initially turned out to be Youth Football under Mark McGhee at Reading. In the meantime he performed a minor miracle in keeping it quiet from the lads. He may have confided in Westy who he ended up working with but that's just a guess, past telling his wife. The results by anyone's standards were not good enough, unacceptable and an appalling win rate and it was the biggest thing to have to take on a personal level. Although they compare favourably with some modern day stats where managers and head coaches have survived after an appalling win rate and definitely under better working conditions than Chris and I had. I'm sure every coach and manager has racked his brains going over games, training, rest periods, travel, etc. etc. but I would have defied anyone else to do better with an over aged, over paid, small squad of initially fifteen players and one goalkeeper and a seven month transfer embargo with no money for wages.

People and supporters doubt your knowledge before questioning anything else, and where players are concerned, especially themselves, when you don't win enough. Then it's your coaching (or information and organisation if you like) that's the next target. As a player for years, I'd been a good player, good pro, socialised and been a recognised family man. So although not crazy socially, it seems I wasn't liked. Men can get over the four temper tantrums on camera and move on like I did as a player but some chose not to and used it against me. Feared? Definitely not. The main reasons being no player can fear a manager if the manager can't leave him out, sell him or buy someone to provide competition. All the players (my fault entirely for working under those conditions) were on longer, more lucrative contracts than me. So although at the time I thought I could work through it and win over players and directors with a freshness, enthusiasm and good coaching and knowledge, which at first I did, I look back and I'm annoyed at myself for being so blinded by the arrogance and ambition I've spoken of. Not to put too fine a point on it, I was fucked. And certain people revelled in the chance of treating me as a minion. Some people have said since it all happened that I lacked dignity. At the time I never even considered my dignity, for me it was all about getting a job done.

Not that I had an ego because in the business of a football club I'm of the opinion there is no room for egos. It's about getting the job done and for things to run smoothly. But I do have a lot of pride. Pride got me a living as a player. It was as a player I received a green folder from Barry Hearn's Matchroom inviting enquiries from players if they needed an agent or representative. On his own admission, Barry said during a documentary on the famous Benn v Eubank fights that in the late 80's early 90's Matchroom was on its knees and in need of a break, it came in the form of Chris Eubank. As Barry said in that particular documentary, the rest is history.

He now owned his own football club and Matchroom had gone ballistic in terms of accumulating sports related businesses. I had been shown the door in 1991 as a player. I'd reinvented myself staffing coaching courses, coaching kids, Sunday teams, O's youth team and for 11 months now, fire fighting inside the club and coaching the first team. I thought I could push on and go again. Sadly for the first time, or the first time I'd heard it anyway, "Sitton Out" reverberated around the ground as we were outpassed and outclassed losing heavily at home to Crewe 4-1. Dario had built his career coaching, improving and producing players he had at Crewe for years and it showed. Creating space, clearing space, passing, rotating, movement to create overloads, we were carved open. It was an education on believe it or not, where we had to get to and where I wanted to take us. Particularly for Kevin Austin who came off with his head spinning. It was well known he'd come up from non-league and a true eye opener for him and everyone else on how good football could be played at the lower division level. Sometime later l learned and it's only second hand information, interviews were being conducted to decide on who would come in as Orient's next manager behind my back and while I was still in situ. I've no doubt that Barry had very limited, at the time anyway, knowledge on football and its players, coaches, and managers. So I assume he was given a nudge in certain directions by people inside the club at board level and by one or two who'd left the club in recent years. One story that filtered back was an interview conducted at the Waldorf in London's Strand, Aldwych. How true it is I don't know, but the out of work manager, by the way an established Premier League manager for now nearly two decades, got up and shook Barry's hand saying, "you don't really need a manager Barry, YOU ARE THE MANAGER." It's a story I heard second hand so I can't really confirm that particular sequence of events.

After defeats to Bristol Rovers at home 2-1 and Swansea away 2-0 my last game as it turned out was at home to Brentford. It was eerie to say the least. My only two gripes with Barry Hearn arose from a long meeting in the old boardroom and at first following my dismissal, some unpaid money. Firstly the meeting in the boardroom led me to believe I'd survived one of the worst periods in Orient's history and I might add one of the most embarrassing. Apart from the C4 doc and all it entailed what kind of business is run so poorly over time that the milk is stopped? Pause and reflect for a minute. Never mind the PFA paying wages for nearly eight months, a transfer embargo so strict loan players weren't allowed, there were instalments of signing on fees not paid to players which begs the question who sanctioned such signing on fees in the first place? Then there's the wages which on average were 30% more than the players already at the club and even the club account with a certain coach company was frozen. It's terribly sad but as you would have been able to see on the C4 documentary without my intervention and initiative we wouldn't have even been able to travel to some of the away games.

Believe it or not at the time I was where I wanted to be, in professional football. It's important to me that supporters know the circumstances. A manager at any club in trying to achieve his aims and ambitions and fulfil the club's ambitions should consider the club's turnover and cut their cloth accordingly. I think prior to me little regard had been shown and resulted in massive losses incurred as a consequence of a poor recruitment policy. For a club like Orient I thought it was suicidal to try and bring in supposedly readymade players particularly with no resale value. Historically Orient in no way had been able to remain solvent on gate receipts. It was a club and remains a club that would only thrive on the turnover of good young players. This is where I thought I would be a big asset to the club with foresight, planning and nurturing young talent. A lot of good, young talent that came through the ranks were sold, and in my opinion like any good football club, the money should have been reinvested more wisely. But that's the crazy world of football.

Different managers have different agendas and do the job differently. When I was sacked it was done quite humanely by Barry. He looked a little embarrassed but it was swift. Personally as strange as it might seem I was shocked. The door burst open Barry walked in and said "there's no easy way to say this Sitts, we've got to part company." He then went on to remark there was no place for me in the club in any capacity. He said he needed someone more experienced and high profile to satisfy sponsors and people who were putting money in. He replaced me with a Spurs coach who had worked with their youth team and reserves Pat Holland. It seems even our definition of "high profile" differed.

CHAPTER SIXTEEN
Here I Go Again

My honest thoughts on choosing a manager and this is where I thought I would have been good for Orient or any club like it, is first of all you have to decide what kind of club you are and what kind of club you want to be. Orient had always been one that produced home grown players and success relative to its standing, even if you are dealing with players who are Arsenal, Spurs, West Ham "left overs." That's if you call two promotions in twenty one years success. However I suppose in a "result driven business" you shouldn't be at all surprised when you're sacked. But as you may have seen as I held court which Chris allowed me to do with the local press you can see the shock, anger and embarrassment on my face in the C4 doc. I was gobsmacked. I'd been told on numerous occasions by vice chairman Weinrabe to keep my head down, not say as much and try to keep not only a lower profile but desist from making public, locally at least, the state of the club, it's infrastructure and playing staff. But I was carrying the can. It wasn't a case of not keeping my own counsel. I couldn't believe Barry had given me such a significant amount of false hope. I'd have preferred to have been told almost immediately like Chris was that I wasn't in his plans. As I've said, things like contracts for me, staff and players to be retained were only the start. Barry Hearn and I spoke of players, transfer targets, plans for the youth, stadium, commercial and scouting departments. Which only served to make me think I was on board. He even got as far as mentioning salaries saying "the job's worth fifty grand a year, but you'll be getting thirty-five with the rest incentivised." And to just confirm after several interviews so I'm led to believe, and a few prospective managers discounted, I nailed the lid down on my departure by requesting Pat Holland as my number two with Barry Hearn smiling and staring off into space as I said I'd like him approached. After clearing out all my paperwork, diaries, copies of transactions under previous management and training schedules, I left.

The second problem I had with Barry Hearn a little while later was as a result of him not fulfilling a contractual requirement. That's if you have a contract! I was still under contract as youth coach on two hundred and eighty pounds a week, but as I stated previously my salary based on a handshake was actually four hundred and twenty pounds a week gross. Where the appointment of Pat Holland was concerned I couldn't help thinking that there were at least four people involved in putting Pat's name forward. Four people who knew me very well and who I also considered to be on friendlier side of just being acquaintances. Out of the four, two of them were involved in insisting I took the job in the first place. One of which I'm sure thought I'd just be a mouthpiece, and de facto he'd run the club. That's until Barry Hearn arrived. One of my last memories of Barry Hearn was him turning up in a hired stretch limo, supporters being easily impressed as he took the director concerned on a ride round the block.

As they got back they both got out of the limo, for an unnecessary long walk to the entrance. I couldn't quite make out who was supposed to be Michael and who was Fredo. Total showmanship of course. Anyway mind racing I decided "I'll show 'em." Barry Hearn said keep the car (a Vauxhall Cavalier) and the petrol card and use both to put yourself about and try and find some more work for yourself. The only job in football for years, where the sale of young players to balance the books, leading to the never ending conflict between either relegation or promotion, was at Crewe under Dario Gradi. Although latter day many clubs have to go through the same painful process of breaking up a promising young side to keep the banks happy. Even more so because of the unfair and unbalanced distribution of money in the game. I've always thought average gate wise, attendances at Orient needed to be supplemented by a conveyor belt of young players sought by other clubs. Now, with legislation favouring bigger clubs that's much harder. But at the time which I told Barry, married to the loan system, free transfers and pilfering non-league it was a must. Now it wasn't my concern so I cancelled Sean Devine's transfer.

Meanwhile word had got round that I was out of work and refreshingly people who I never expected to hear from got in touch. I was offered a chance by someone who I thought at the time was a friend. It was a rich Greek businessman who had ties in Cyprus to politics, football clubs and was even highly thought of in the Church. This was probably as a consequence of his personal and financial commitment to all three. He said that a job was about to become available. After the shit I had just waded through I didn't need asking twice. At the time it seemed like I might have two bites of the cherry. I thought it might lead to at least one out of two offers materialising.

It tied in with a possible post at the non-league club where my so called friend was chairman. I think the invitation came out of him knowing I was fully competent and led at the time to him offering me first the manager's job then the first team coach's job, then the general manager's job, then director of football. All within the space of a week! The manager's and first team coach's job never materialised because the guy at the helm said he wanted his own staff around him. I'm not sure about his football background or coaching qualifications but despite my friend being chairman, it seemed everyone else's loyalties lay with the guy in the job.

The other main contributor to the club was Barry Albin of Albin and Sons funeral directors based at Culling Circus atop the Rotherhithe Tunnel. They're still there to this day although the club concerned Fisher Athletic is not. I felt like it wasn't meant to be especially after the job description I was given covering the general manager's job and director of football. Despite having plied my trade a few years earlier only down the road at Millwall I've got to be honest, the vibe didn't feel right. Sitting with my mate and chairman of Fisher, Chris Georgiou, Barry Albin, two other committee members, and having met briefly with the manager, it seemed there was an internal tug of war with regards to what direction the club and people within the club wanted to go. With all this in mind I sat with Chris at his office in Crouch End an affluent part of London as he confirmed tickets for us to Cyprus. For a stone rich boy moving in certain circles it never ceased to amaze me the way Chris spoke to people at times including myself. Despite my warm friendship, winning doubles and trebles for his Sunday side, professional conduct and courtesy he never passed up an opportunity to greet me with "Hello Malaka" or "Yiasou Epoushti." Thinking it was funny, he did it to everyone. For the record in English it's "Hello Wanker" and "hello, good day, cheers or goodbye poof." Maybe it explains why there aren't many Greek comedians. So along with so far four broken promises, going back on his word, he added insult to injury. A few years later he passed away, losing a fight to an almost lifelong illness.

In all our time together I never ever took a penny from him or was paid by him to coach his Sunday side. Lots of people in the Greek community think I was paid, and questioned, some sarcastically, why I never attended his funeral. Well all I can say in answer is respect should be a two-way street. For reasons I can't even fathom, for years I'd acted like a gentleman and it seems good manners even as far back as my Chelsea days were seen as weakness. For the record Chris added injury to his insults and broke his word after making me a couple of promises. Something with me you should never do. That's just how I am.

Cyprus apart from the climate turned out to be another waste of time. The events and offer to take the place of a manager lying second in the league were laughable, the people there overly deluded and symptomatic of everyone being any expert manager at the end of ninety minutes. I couldn't help thinking why were they looking to change manager while second in the league? I remember a fat Bulgarian taking training with a cigarette and a cup of coffee whilst watching an eight vs eight. Asked if I had pro experience I handed my CV to a committee member. I spent the next five days, swimming, eating, sunbathing and learning backgammon at the poolside of the Palm Beach Hotel in Larnaca. I sat there thinking I was the last one this club needed to worry about being professional. A manager smoking as he watched training? I had never seen that before.

I returned to England and went to Orient v Wycombe (0-1) and the return of Terry Howard and the threat of a slap from his sister, so he says in his book. I couldn't help thinking a twenty-eight-year- old should protect his sister not the other way round.

Me? I had no one to turn to least of all a big sister. Apart from Loiza and my three kids I had no one and it was my duty to man up and be strong for my wife and kids and provide and help keep 'em fed.

At the time it probably wasn't what I'd anticipated doing. But I dived into trying to get a living coupled with living out the youth I'd never really had. At approaching thirty-six it was the boys I had coached in the Greek League that I turned to but that didn't last long. The casinos and all-night card schools didn't appeal to me. Apart from the fact I had no money I don't gamble anyway. My mates were businessmen from the Greek community and in a couple of cases getting a living anyway they could. With land, cafes, houses, flats, coffee bars, car lots, clothes shops, they all had a few quid. I distanced myself after doing the weekly rounds of Charlie Chan's, Epping Forest Country Club and Faces. It was at those venues they showed their disdain for me as they must have thought I had money and I was just tight. They ordered scotch, tequila and champagne by the bottle and they started to call my life into question and where I'd gone wrong. I called for a round and got some eye treatment when I said I'll lay out for beers but I can't afford champagne.

They must have thought in their defence that I'd made a few quid from playing, coaching and a year as manager. They wasn't to know. But feedback told me I was being slagged off for not going large and other conduct unbecoming. If the football world is small and word gets round the Greek community is even smaller. I wouldn't name names but I just thought of them as hypocrites who followed Arsenal round Europe leaving wifey at home, in some cases with kids, unaware of the goings on during the course of their seventy- two-hour pass. She had the trade off latest BMW or Mercedes, a Luis Vuitton bag and either a Cartier or Rolex, while her husband cheered on Arsenal then indulged in the nightlife of the city where their opponents were from. The stories were astounding but I didn't judge, unlike them. Woman on one arm and a bottle of scotch or tequila in the other, ready for an all nighter swapping rooms and girls as the night wore on. I detached myself completely and stopped going out. Partly ashamed that I couldn't pull up £100 for a couple of bottles of champagne and that I was being judged for it. I thought with friends like these I didn't need enemies. Again.

In the meantime Tom had been let go by Pat Holland to be replaced by Paul Brush. To Tom it was water off a duck's back because that's what he's like. If anything it raised his coinage in his own community and has led to him having jobs ever since, four in non-league and two as part owner of the club. He still coaches now. He always loved his football and he's very tolerant and even tempered even under the most demanding circumstances either on a personal or professional level. My second gripe with Barry Hearn materialised when I got my last or second last pay cheque. I never got the bonus I should have, the same as everyone else for the Birmingham two legged area final of the Auto Windshield trophy. I telephoned immediately. At first he was out, then I called back very angry and told whoever was on the line, I think it was Dave Burton to stop fucking around and covering for him, put him on NOW, 'cos he owes me money.

I said to Dave if he tries to fob you off and gives you an excuse to fob me off, tell him there's two things he doesn't want me doing. One is me turning up, and if I have to I'll wait for him, and two, going to the press. Why? because apart from my mortgage I've never owed anyone money in my life and I expect that to be reciprocated. This was after him saying that I had a few rough edges but he'd help me polish 'em up during my proposed contract under him. Now, someone supposedly from a Dagenham council estate owed me money. The amount owed was £2700 gross. Barry Hearn came to the phone immediately and said "turn up this afternoon, bring the car, club phone and petrol card and we'll do a deal."

That's Barry all over I thought. I said "why did you do it? Why did you withhold my money? I've got a family to feed and I'm out of work thanks to the shambles you now own. You've taken a liberty." He said "you've taken the liberty" I said "yeah, what's that?" He said "overuse of the petrol card (he gave me a date and said I'd filled up twice on the same day,) but here's what I'll do..." (Like he was doing me a favour paying me what he owed me.)You're owed £2700. After tax and N.I it should leave £2300 and change. I'll give you a cheque this afternoon for £2000 or the only winner is the taxman." I said "Barry if you're that hard up for £300 take it, I just can't be arguing over £300." But Barry obviously could. "I've worked for it so have it there at two o'clock."

When I arrived, along with my cheque was an ex gratia agreement along with other legal documents saying I was not entitled to anything else and severing all ties and contractual arrangements to do with Leyton Orient Football Club. Barry Hearn was nowhere to be seen. He left all the paperwork to Dave Burton who took my mobile phone, car keys and petrol card. After working my bollocks off for Leyton Orient for ten years, six as a player, four as a coach, this is what it had come to and how I was rewarded. Literally having to go cap in hand for money they owed me in bonuses that I had worked my socks off for. Perhaps now I know why certain people have a mercenary attitude to life and football. I wouldn't have sued anyway. Pride wouldn't have allowed it. I didn't want them to give me a fucking thing and that's the truth, only what I'd earned. I've got to give Barry Hearn credit where it's due though. He's great with figures and people and making money from other people's talent as a promoter. With the money that was owed to me I took my wife and kids to Majorca.

Pre-season I got an unexpected and much appreciated call from ex-team mate Kevin Hales, manager of Welling. Les Reed was an ex F.A colleague now at Charlton with Alan Curbishley and Keith Peacock. He told Halesy I knew my stuff and needed another chance. Although Les stopped short of giving me a chance as Charlton youth coach when I applied for the job saying "we'd lose kids as a consequence of the fallout from the Channel Four documentary." They gave it to a guy called Terry Westley. I agreed to meet Halesy and help prepare the side for a pre-season friendly against Charlton where I spoke to Les who told me a few home truths. The main one being, I had to start again, reinvent myself, rehabilitate, renew a now tarnished reputation. He said Halesy knew me, would give me my head, but step in as a more or less career long colleague and give me a nudge away from overstepping the mark. Les knew I could be better perceived if I concentrated on being constructive and carry on giving good information and not giving way to my frustrations which is what I was all about really not the temper tantrums you saw on a C4 doc. I was more about the years I'd spent coaching kids and youth teams to improve them.

At the time, I was on a mega downer thinking I'd miss the full time day to day involvement of a pro club. I'd tasted for years, the excitement of playing, then coaching, and barely containing myself as well as the buzz you get from players, when you put on a good session and they see something that works, to improve them and help organise and improve a team. O's supporters could be forgiven for thinking it didn't, considering results, but truth be told, you have lots of obstacles to overcome and enemies if you like in football, the main one is time. Initially I just wanted to protect Orient and its supporters from wasting their money on cheats, non-triers and fraudsters. They can't hide in football for long, although it's not found out as easily or highlighted as much in the lower leagues because mistakes that are avoidable are not punished as quickly or readily as they are at the top level. But that was Pat Holland's headache now and his number two Tommy Cunningham who had been an ex-player at Orient.

I'd put Tommy in the same bracket as Glenn Cockerill at the time. That's to say Barry wanted value for money out of Glenn's contract and Barry approached me with the idea of having him as my number two. Both good pros, both knew the game, but at that time as far as I know, both Glen and then Tommy under Pat, had no formal coaching qualifications. I wasn't sure what Glenn and later Tommy Cunningham would bring to the table if asked to teach the game, improve an individual, put on a session, or organise a team.

I'd said the same to Bill Songhurst a year earlier when he rang and asked on Tommy's behalf if there was a role for him coaching at the club.

At Welling Kevin Hales introduced me around, I met the chairman and board and got on ok with the players. Then it was time to talk money with Halesy who bless him had his hands tied and by the sounds of it his feet! He offered me £80 a week. I said, training twice a week, travelling from home to Welling, two games a week, it's a commitment that would mean I'd either be out of pocket or I'd owe Welling money! I said thank you very much for picking the phone up but no thanks. I refused rightly or wrongly to deal from weakness ever again and in the end, I had to be practical and look to bring home money for the household as well as try and repair a tarnished reputation. Although I wasn't the first manager to be relegated, it was a fair bet I'd been the first under those circumstances.

After constant reassurance by the independent film company based in White Lion Street, Islington, that I'd be ok and portrayed fairly and despite an injunction by Phil Wallace to cut out his part in the C4 doc. (Channel 4 is who they sold it to.) The documentary came out around October 1995. I was on the dole, no chance of work, especially now, and ostracised from football. My wife took a job in a sandwich bar to help make ends meet and pay the bills. I was at a complete loss. I've heard Brendan Rodgers recently talking of management styles and coaching blueprints and virtually dismissing as archaic the tantrums I'd brought to the table on the C4 doc. I was desperate to ring in and ask him how he'd handled his own frustrations, like when players don't or can't try what you've rehearsed in training. How did he deal with the players, who couldn't or wouldn't perform, sometimes the simplest of techniques, patterns of play or basic defending? I mean it cost him the league at Liverpool. That classic line : "they snatched defeat from the jaws of victory."

Did he look to replace them or work and improve them? And lastly what if he couldn't replace them? You see at Reading and Watford, he was dealing with inferior players to ones at Liverpool. So in my book, it's easier to come across learned, studious, calm and erudite at a club where you win more than you lose. At Watford and Reading he never had the same success, so I'd be interested in how he dealt with it. Was it luck or did he do what football (some) people do and look for a porthole, an escape and get your agent to move you out and up, or stay and try solve the problem in front of you? It goes against the grain for me not appearing strong, not being decisive, devoid of strategy, not showing mental toughness and inner strength but for the first time in my life I had no idea what direction to take. Against the grain insofar as it suggests I couldn't have coped with a job in football, least of all, the total rebuilding job that it needed at Orient. Now I had to concentrate on rebuilding my home life and my esteem as a man by finding work or re-training to get work outside of football. The problem I faced was knowing nothing else other than being in and around the environment of a professional football club from the age of twelve. I was now approaching thirty-six years of age and still dreamed of staying in football. I set about applying for every job that I'd heard had become available to try and stay in the game. After fourteen months if became obvious to me, after not even receiving the courtesy of a reply, I was flogging a dead horse. Not enough networking, not enough high profile friends and the added negative impact of the documentary had ensured I was outcast, ostracised and paid the price in full for allowing my frustrations to come to the surface and boil over. I had no idea where to turn and what to do. I felt like a spare part. For a little while I felt worthless because I had made football my life and I was now no longer part of it. I looked around and saw people getting on with their lives and it just made me feel more depressed. Not for long. Not me. I got back in the gym and I went back to Martial Arts. I got a scholarship funded by the PFA and trained five, sometimes six times a week to get to a good level and become a teacher.

There was one more tangle with the O's hierarchy which came at a tribunal. Not for me I might add. That's not my style. Although me and Chris had in Chris's words "babysat the club," I'd believed the promises made to us and took the handshakes from three different regimes on trust and at face value. Naive? You betcha. I take people at their word. But towards the end of my tenure, I was called before the club's solicitor to give evidence in a case brought by ex-chief scout and YDO Bernie Dixson. Because I told the truth unwittingly reinforcing Bernie's claims, Weinrabe and the club were told I shouldn't take the stand. On the day, it was another unsavoury fiasco. Before a panel at a tribunal in Stratford Town Centre, under court like conditions Bernie's only other witness was ex kit man Pat Dellar and strictly speaking Dellar wasn't even in the room when it all blew up between Bernie and Weinrabe.

Bernie's case of unfair and constructive dismissal was blown apart. Dellar wasn't in the room when it was verbally agreed between Bernie and Weinrabe that Bernie would be director of football. Basically taking Frank Clark's old job. The four in the room were me, Chris, Bernie and Weinrabe. And as I've discussed before, Bernie accepted the post, then resigned within five minutes when Weinrabe insisted I stay with the first team and not go back to youth team level on a four-year deal. Bernie, who was now doing a bit for Chelsea, had been given Glenn Hoddle's blessing and also some financial assistance by his employers to pursue his claim. Which he lost. This is where it gets unsavoury and undignified and on Weinrabe's part, not lacking in fantasy. Bernie was beetroot red, barely able to contain his rage. As I commiserated with Bernie, Weinrabe came over to shake his hand and declare, "no hard feelings." Bernie was having none of it. Barry Hearn wasn't there.

Rightfully so, it wasn't his mess, so one assumes he was happy not to have to clear another one up. Anyway, I sarcastically remarked purposely within earshot of Weinrabe and Vince Marsh as they sang the praises of some liver and bacon, mash and peas they'd just eaten, "how many more fucking lives are they gonna ruin before they look at themselves." Bernie said "I'm glad it's over and I'm out of there, but Sitts, you're right, that little mob have a lot to answer for."

When you are inside, it's different to being on the outside and picking up the phone and taking a shot in the dark, almost cap   in hand and hoping someone will give you a chance. I remember seeing Teddy Sheringham and having a chat in the locker room at David Lloyd Centre in Chigwell. He said "Sitts, it's contacts, ain't you got someone you can ring to get you back in?" I said "Ted, I went from being out five nights a week to staying locked in with my wife and kids, you need to be pals with someone high profile who gets jobs and trust you as a friend and being professional enough to do a good job for them. I've never been busy now I'm paying for it." And I've been a lower division player nearly all my career. If me and you are going for the same job, who do you think would get it? He said "chip away, keep your head up what happened on that programme has happened thousands of times before and thousands of times since.

Don't give in." I thanked him, he's always been a down to earth good guy, right from when he was a youngster at Millwall. Mind you, when I went to Gillingham it didn't stop me trying to kick him. The realisation of how I was betrayed by the programme and its makers, and how nearly ten years of continuous coaching, a fourteen season playing career and twenty-five year association with pro football and being in a professional environment was washed away in a fifty minute documentary overwhelmed me. I was devastated. When it became apparent I wouldn't be good, tall or quick enough to have long career in Chelsea's first team I was grief stricken but had to hide it and come back from the disappointment. When my Mum died, I was trying to be strong for my Dad, brother and sister. Now this was my life, I'd made the gross mistake of placing too much stock in football. It had been allowed to dictate who I was and how I'd led my life and now it was gone. At pro level anyway. As a player, there's always hope if you work hard enough. So my career as a player was partly repaired and I managed to eke a living in lower league football at Millwall, Gillingham and Orient. You just get on with it, play your best, train your best, even though it was never the same, earn your next contract and put Chelsea a great club, who I had a deep feeling for, like a love of your life, in the rear view mirror. As disappointing as it is, you overcome the knocks and if you want to stay in league football you bounce back. At the time, I knew nor wanted anything else. Unfortunately, my coaching career had always been in the hands of players I had never signed, some I'd never rated, and some I had no feeling for or rapport with. I think all those ingredients are important to give yourself the best chance. Every manager or coach needs the opportunity to be able to get in his own players. Unfortunately for me it wasn't until well into pre-season that I found out the club not only never had money available for transfers but the debts incurred meant the club was sinking fast towards liquidation. The mistake had been made and I was chomping at the bit to rectify it. It was a case, even if as it turns out, an unrealistic one, of looking forward and trying to prove some people wrong and a few who rated my coaching capabilities right. On the plus side I think I showed a moral strength in taking the conscious decision to show that I was a person who doesn't give up when it would have been much easier to do so. To be a lesser person because the journey would have been less arduous and demanding.

This means at some point also having to deal with the fear of coming up short and facing rejection.

For a while Tom had been coaching at Cheshunt. Then he left and got the Enfield job. Work wise I was ok, I was staffing F.A courses via the L.F.A, working part time in a private school, labouring part time for £40 a day and signing on the dole when I had no work. Loiza went to work in a sandwich bar, so we made ends meet. So much for being a "Wag." Bit different from a multimillion pound pay off even though it's the same game. I had a meeting with Tom and the Enfield chairman at the time, Tony Lazarou. The upside was, it was work and it was work doing what I wanted and all I'd ever known, which was football. The downside was Lazarou had taken over Enfield, laid out massive budgets of up to, at one time

£350k plus a year and had a succession of managers who had no problem spending it. People like George Borg and ex Spurs player Graham Roberts. How did I know? And why was it relevant? Well, after a poor run of results with a mixed team of players from the previous manager (a porter in Smithfield meat market) and players we recruited from Sunday football, to hastily rid the club of troublemakers and its top earners, (sound familiar?) Lazarou took a passing interest and questioned what was going on. I piped up and said, "training on a ploughed field in Brimsdown with literally one floodlight, that was so poor it shone like a forty-watt bulb, didn't help. And we could use a sensible budget. Out of interest, what have you been used to spending?" He went red, shifted embarrassingly and said, more recently about £150k a year, before that, under one of his, on paper, high achieving managers about £330k, one year, nearly £400k I said, that's a long way from £1000 a week for staff and twenty-two players. He said "I suppose you've got a point." Enfield had gone from a traditional top non-league club from the south, achieving honours, with its own ground, a massive site, massive car park, bar, and its own nightclub, to under Lazarou, renting a pitch for home games at Borehamwood. Lazarou had sold the whole site in favour of the local council and to the demise of the local non- league club. The site was developed in favour of revenues for Enfield council, holding a multiplex cinema, a Pizza Hut, a steak house (Outback) and to probably satisfy any covenant, a sports centre and pool with its own car parking all round. Two things arose from the meeting. After getting my background, Lazarou said I sounded like I had "baggage" from my experiences at Orient and with Hearn.

I said, you asked, I told. I prefer to call it motivation. I predicted at the time, and it's turned out to be the case, that football clubs starting a long way behind Leyton Orient would overtake them. The other was my remarks to Tom, predicting that after a reasonable "search" for new premises for Enfield and a respectable period of mourning for a once great non-league club, Lazarou would let it fade organically and ride off into the sunset with the reputed few million from the sale of the club. I put him on the spot and said, if you want to do it properly and you want a proper job, I want a proper contract. Tom was caught in the middle and happy to work on a loose agreement, based on trust and a handshake. We went in as fire fighters and staved off relegation and we were given the reins a while longer. I got a letter of agreement from Lazarou, outlining details of a promised contract. Then we were told this would be our last year at Borehamwood. So Enfield had nowhere to play. I negotiated with Lazarou and out of the 10k promised in wages, I took an immediate settlement of less than half and walked.

Tom left a short while after and I gave him half of my settlement as a thank you for giving me the job in the first place. I was back to square one. I signed on the dole. I even had to put up with a look of total contempt from a close neighbour who worked in the local post office as he cashed my giro. It made me feel uneasy, uncomfortable and embarrassed. But I thought in the end, fuck him, he doesn't know the half of it. But my pride morphed into a form of paranoia. It's funny but I have never felt, or had any sort of sense of entitlement. Everything I've had in life I have worked hard for.

I have to say at Enfield most of the lads were different class, punctual, enthusiastic, thirsty for knowledge and organisation. Every now and again though, I'd flare up with the odd bad apple trying to infect the rest of the barrel. One player in particular totally betrayed me and Tom and broke my heart into the bargain. I remember the game like it was yesterday, Harrow Borough away. Their manager was one of the Stein brothers, Eddie. We bossed the game for eighty minutes. We led 2-0 and I reinforced all my previous coaching and organisation as I screamed at players on what to do to run the clock down, what they now call game management. We had signed a Greek lad from Purfleet who had been very unhappy there. He claimed that he was the victim of bullying and racism. He complained to me and Tom that he had been called "a lazy Greek bastard."

As a ball went into the corner deep in the opposition's defending third, I screamed at him to close it down to stop the ball from coming forward. He turned, looked at me and Tom, and walked. The ball was rebounded on us and they scored. From the restart we gave the ball away (the same player again) and Harrow Borough equalised. We were now holding on for a point after being 2-0 up. Once again we passed the ball into the channel and the same player failed to get his body in and keep it. Harrow Borough launched it forward and scored the winner. As we kicked off for the restart the ref blew the final whistle. As you can imagine I was livid, but contrary to popular myth I was very forensic and lucid in my analysis. I complained to the player about his diabolical, unprofessional and selfish attitude towards his team mates. I added "you've made Edwin Stein look like a cross between Bill Shankly and Bill Nicholson and you've made Harrow Borough look like the fucking Lions of Lisbon." I then asked "have you got anything to say?" Do you know what his reply was? Unbelievable but true: "I think you're a bully..." Just to underpin my frustrations I couldn't believe Tom had paid a small fee, given a good signing on fee and made this pathetic excuse for a man the highest paid player in the club. I can only concur with the people at Purfleet who dismissed him as a fraud and a cheat. I got straight on the coach in my tracksuit without a shower and our captain Nicky Geoury came and sat next to me to try and talk me out of what I had just done, which was resign on the spot. I got very emotional as I spoke to Nicky, and that I could even be perceived in the context of being a bully.

Since it all happened I've seen the person concerned in a supermarket with his wife and kids. He tried to exchange pleasantries but I just ignored him, called my little boy, and walked away shocked that he was able to even father children. After watching him train and play I was surprised that he ever managed an erection. I've seen him twice more at a wedding and a funeral where he extended his hand for me to shake it. I looked into his eyes and refused. I've since seen him at another funeral and he offered neither a handshake or a hello. Result. What a liberty to accuse me of something I have never been, always erring on the side of gentlemanly conduct and against all the odds and sometime my better instincts, not reacting to provocation even when I'd have been justified in doing so. But it has to be said, in the main, the good guys were in the majority.

There was another major idiot though. When he was a kid, someone had made the mistake of thinking, then telling him, he could play. He was invited in for evening coaching at Spurs. In small sided games, he would shout, scream and act out in make believe temper if a decision was given against him. He'd then take the ball and smash it goalkeeper style out of his hands and out of the ground. The previous manager saw fit to put him on a contract. To rest players, he was promised a run out. I wasn't at the game because of a prior engagement on a radio show and he completely fucked about in the warm up. Tom decided not to start him. I was cornered and questioned by his deluded father and the father's friend in the bar at the next home game. I just told him how it was and referred them both to Tom. Both totally delusional, I could see the apple hadn't fallen far from the tree. By and large, in non-league semi- professional football, I'd say we did alright with a team made up by a majority of Sunday League players who we had just taken the time and trouble to organise. After the disappointment of not even getting a reply, never mind an interview, one thing I know is how to behave in the company of strangers, women and kids. So the Les Reed theory that he had taken the time and trouble to explain to me that I'd have an adverse effect on Charlton's youth policy because of a C4 documentary, was blown to smithereens as I held down a part time job as a PE teacher in a fee paying private school in North Chingford. I got on famously with the kids and their parents. I ran after school clubs as well. Both oversubscribed with waiting lists. One was a self-defence/martial arts class and the other a soccer school, an hour's coaching for anyone who wanted to sign up. I have to say, it gave me a buzz, a big lift and a lot of satisfaction. We put on a couple of good little demos at the end of the school year, with a bit from me and a chance for the kids to show off what they'd learned. In the meantime, Tom had been recommended and interviewed for another job at ironically Leyton FC. Literally around the corner in Lea Bridge Road from Leyton Orient. He asked me if I fancied it, I said absolutely. I quickly made myself at home. At the time I'd been continuously coaching and was on blob again. Bang in the zone. Seeing and ironing out a problem almost as it arose. I was putting on set pieces, patterns of play, defensive drills, a team defensive strategy, little phases of play to improve combination play in the middle and attacking thirds and getting players to recognise and utilise overloads and the players loved it.

The players seemed receptive and buoyant. Happy that they were being improved individually and as a unit. We got some cracking results. But there was one underlying big problem. It was the chairman's money. The chairman seemed to want his cake and eat it and for us to feed off the crumbs. He wanted control over player recruitment, and a major say in who played and where they played. But the coaching was down to us, and more importantly, the results. Again, massive responsibilty without power. Always a less than ideal, and precarious situation. It goes without saying this caused friction. It seemed everyone who was sycophantically attached to the chairman had an opinion, an expert one, and they seemed to have no embarrassment in voicing it. As I have said before, everyone's an expert at a quarter to five. A corporation of London gardener, a HGV driver, now a driver-cum-dogsbody-cum- bodyguard for the chairman. The male secretary and two barmaids even had a say. I said fuck me, not again. They were blowing smoke up his arse, because he threw thousands at the club and the team. I had to wonder where all the readies came from. The chairman was a builder, with a property portfolio. But he spent dough like it was confetti. Some of it on players who he or his sidekicks deemed good enough, but quite plainly were not. To my trained eye anyway. Tom was pushed too far once too often, kept his dignity and calmness intact and parted company. I sat there gutted that a club that could have been a cracking little force in non-league, was once again in my opinion infested with a few wrong- uns. The final straw came after a cup defeat, caused by a couple of players who thought it was ok to get in at six am on the day of the game.

I just thought it was a shame that a good staff including a good medical and backroom set up and a good set of lads, good being in the majority, were let down by a couple of liberty takers. They played only because the chairman insisted they played, so for me and Tom to make an example of them would have been a futile exercise. We had our bums smacked 3-0. It could have been six. By and large, my respect, love, and admiration goes out to all the players and staff in non-league. When I say staff, it's all of them. Managers, coaches, physios, kit men, admin, the lot. You see in the main, you have people who get paid part time money for a full time commitment, which tickles me because of the irony attached to some of their professional counterparts, who get paid full time money, then some, for part time commitment. Or at least some of those that I came across. My opinion only, but, being a pro footballer, especially now, or attached in some capacity to a pro club, whether scout, kit man, physio, coach or manager, is about as good as it gets. I thought it was great to train and play. What must it be like now? Suffice to say, I said to the chairman (after Tom saying "I've now left, you can do what you want, stay on if you like,") "it's a shame it's come to this, thanks for the opportunity, here's your training kit, good luck for the future." I then shook his hand and walked out. The only person who stayed on, was a guy who came with us as kit man. A kit man who ultimately had aspirations of wanting to coach. Don't they all? Me? Yet again, work wise, I was more or less back to square one. Coaching wise at least.

The F.A had by now introduced area monitors for regional courses. I was overlooked. It paid in the high twenty thousand band of wages or maybe thirty-two thousand and mileage for expenses attached. I said I wouldn't staff anymore courses because I now had two gripes. One was, to upgrade my qualification meant having to go back to Lilleshall for two weeks and not only have two weeks of no pay or dole money, but also pay for the course to get the prerequisite teaching certificate that would enable me to staff courses to generate more money (in the tens of thousands per year now) for the F.A and that's just me, one coach!!! The second gripe was me being overlooked as a monitor, approximately five hundred league and cup games, in favour of two school teachers who'd never kicked a ball in anger at any level and a guy who played for Arsenal and spent most of his youth in their youth and reserve teams. I smiled and said it's amazing how far you can get on three games for Arsenal. At all the coaches' meetings, when there was a moan or groan about equipment, venue, wages, petrol money, they all sat there mute and gutless. Me, yours truly, I'm the one who spoke up and got them their exes, or new balls, or wage increase. Good luck to 'em. Maybe that's why the English game and some of the coaches are now comparable to third world. One of the coaches concerned even managed to get his son qualified who then went on to be involved for a while with the England women's football team.

The PFA helped when they informed me of a possible pay cheque for gathering stats at games. It meant a training day at PA HQ on Vauxhall Bridge Road. It was a doddle. As a coach, it was easy to get your eyes into a game and engage, throwing out the prerequisite information required. The ban at Orient had to be lifted when the PA requested tickets for me. It would have been restraint of trade. So the club never had a leg to stand on, plus, I thought enough water had gone under the bridge. Since being out of football after the C4 documentary, it's been difficult at times to come to terms with. Then I go a little deeper and stop beating myself up over it. I've been seen and dismissed sometimes even through non verbal communication as I've walked into a room as a foul tempered, foul mouthed thug. A parody, someone archaic, a controversialist, confrontational. It seems it's unPC what I did, even back then, although I could bore you yet again with the list of misdemeanours I have witnessed or read about since. The most recent one, a while ago was when I picked up a dishevelled figure, suitably inebriated, in my taxi. It was a manager who recognised me from our time together at Lilleshall in 1997 and as they say "en vino veritas." He confessed to not wanting me to sit next to him in the dining hall because of the C4 documentary and didn't want to be perceived as a friend or acquaintance in the bar. I suppose guilty by association. He added that with hindsight perhaps I'd been "hard done by." A while later in his career as the pressure mounted, he head butted an opposition player on the touchline as the ball ran out of play. I just said "would you like a receipt sir?"

All I wanted was for players to own their performances and have enough professional pride and football intelligence to raise their game when I challenged them on the training field or in the dressing room. I think it's your job as a coach to try and take players past what they expect of themselves, and better still, past what supporters expect of them. In football, like life in general, I think personal accountability has been lost as the onus seems to be on coaches and managers to please the world around them, a large part of that world being the players. I started ok, but the mental stimulation of new sessions and good information I now realise was only a part of it. There's no doubt that kidology is just as important. Some coaches and managers I played for were more blessed with stories, anecdotes and kidology than they were with bright, effervescent sessions laced with good technical information. But can you imagine spending your whole life lying?

I now know through harsh experience that I had too much of one and not enough of the other. I threw the gauntlet down, albeit after seven or eight months of laughable working conditions because I had decided that if I was going to leave the party, I'd leave on my feet, not on my knees. No doubt, if you examine some of the dialogue on the documentary, I turned out to be the biggest non-conformist of all. It seems looking back that there is what seemed and seems to be a "tick list" of acceptable answers and solutions. It's funny, ironic, or whatever appropriate word you can think of that some of those who pointed the finger at me and then preach a certain way of doing things as the only acceptable way, perpetrate misdemeanours like I've listed, and have the audacity to judge what I did as unacceptable! I was at a club that for too many years had people working there who were happy to go with it, instead of going after it.

As a coach or manager, maybe because of my precarious contractual situation, don't matter how polite I worded it, as soon as I placed demands on people, they knew they'd been sussed, became defensive, closed ranks, became a club within a club and painted me as the villain. I'm convinced that in football, but at Leyton Orient in particular, if supporters were to wake up from the dream they're in, there's a good chance they might ask for their money back. As Arsene Wenger once said which has led to me having a lot of time for him and what he has to say, "never judge a manager until you know the circumstances under which he has managed." Now you know. I could self-promote and tell how I would have set up the club from under tens through to under twenties with age groups overlapping.

A four to six-year plan for each age group and player. A scouting network that would have eyes everywhere and more importantly a coaching syllabus that could and should be copied at National level to streamline and place excellence on all aspects of coaching and coaching qualifications. But I'd never volunteer information again. Never again would I give out good information free of charge. With the ideas I have, the F.A would get my wages back inside two years from course fees alone. For a start if we take diet, nutrition, core strenghtening, stretching, physiology, plyometrics, blood test readings, rest periods, stats,charts etc etc etc as a given, with most clubs and national sides fairly even, with nobody having an advantage, then in my opinion over the course of the fifty years since we won the world cup it can only be down to coaching, coaches and players . I think the syllabus and the qualifications are wrong and not profound enough. The whole thing needs restructuring and radical changes need to be made. I'm convinced everything comes as a consequence of how the game is taught and by what coaches. It's incredible that all the ideas copied, even by our National manager, haven't copied some of the most obvious ones that would benefit our game. Incidentally there's a throwaway comment in his book by Mr Allardyce that, paraphrase: " playing a diamond can leave you open to conceding goals..." If I was sitting around a table with him, England manager or not, I'd challenge him and I'd say "not if it's 5-diamond-1 it wouldn't, especially with my defensive strategy.." You see, with that formation, it forms a double diamond. It reinforces the back line and the midfield, matches any opposition overload in midfield, provides width when we have the ball and would commit numbers at the appropriate time in the attacking third. It would deflect the ball wide, then you'd show inside and it would make play predictable, benign and allow you to hold a high line at the back. These are just a few ideas I have picked from a cacophony that I have had swimming around in my head for over twenty years. I could have quite easily called this chapter "Maggie's Farm" by Bob Dylan. What springs to mind are the lines, "he hands you a nickel, he hands you a dime, he asks you with a grin if you're having a good time?" Definitely applicable to my time as a player and a coach. Preparation is everything in football. In fact from Leyton Orient all the way up to the National side I'd say a lot of mistakes are made before a ball is kicked. Another line would be, "I've got a head full of ideas that are driving me insane, it's a shame the way she makes me scrub the floor." Never again, not without a water tight contract with loads of noughts on the end. Lesser men than me have been rewarded with fortunes. So why shouldn't I be? In the end, I'd like to think I've given quite a few answers and it has made you the reader more aware of what was going on. Then again, I've been told, only once mind, "they're excuses, no wonder you failed." So, when does an answer become an excuse? Who determines that? To paraphrase F.Scott Fitzgerald "One should never confuse a single defeat with a final defeat." Here's one final answer, or if it's a time wasting insular moron, like the one I spent nearly an hour with on social media, a final excuse. It's not what I did at Leyton Orient or on the Channel Four Documentary, it's what some of those around me didn't do.

Desiderata

Go placidly amid the noise and haste, and remember what peace there may be in silence. As far as possible without surrender be on good terms with all persons. Speak your truth quietly and clearly, and listen to others, even the dull and ignorant, they too have their story. Avoid loud and aggressive persons, they are vexations to the spirit. If you compare yourself with others, you may become vain and bitter, for always there will be a greater, and lesser persons than yourself. Enjoy your achievements as well as your plans. Keep interested in your own career, however humble, it is a real possession in the changing fortunes of time. Exercise caution in your business affairs, for the world is full of trickery. But let this not blind you to what virtue there is, many persons strive for high ideals and everywhere life is full of heroism. Be yourself. Especially, do not feign affection. Neither be cynical about love, for in the face of all aridity and disenchantment it is perennial as the grass. Take kindly to the counsel of the years, gracefully surrendering the things of youth. Nurture strength of spirit to shield you in sudden misfortune. But do not distress yourself with imaginings. Many fears are born of fatigue and loneliness. Beyond wholesome discipline, be gentle with yourself. You are a child of the universe, no less than the trees and the stars, you have a right to be here. And whether or not it is clear to you, no doubt the universe is unfolding as it should. Therefore be at peace with God, whatever you conceive Him to be, and whatever your labours and aspirations, in the noisy confusion of life keep peace with your soul. With all its sham, drudgery and broken dreams, it is still a beautiful world. Be careful. Strive to be happy.

Found in Old Saint Paul's church, Baltimore, dated 1692.

I found and read these words for the first time in 1986. I've tried to live by it.
I haven't always succeeded.
Fuck It. Maybe In Another life.

John Sitton

A Little Knowledge is a Dangerous Thing. A Life in Football - John Sitton

If ever anyone deserved to be a spolied WAG...

298

My Treasure

Printed in Great Britain
by Amazon